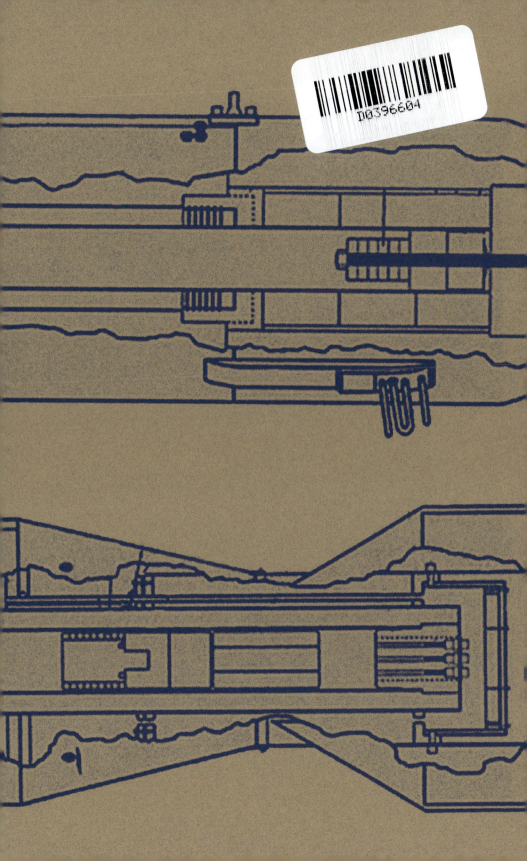

THE GENERAL AND THE GENIUS

THE
GENERAL
AND THE
GENIUS

GROVES AND OPPENHEIMER

THE UNLIKELY PARTNERSHIP THAT

BUILT THE ATOM BOMB

JAMES KUNETKA

Author of *Oppenheimer: The Years of Risk*

REGNERY
HISTORY

Regnery History™ is a trademark of Salem Communications Holding Corporation; Regnery® is a registered trademark of Salem Communications Holding Corporation

Diagrams reprinted with permission from John Coster-Mullen

Library of Congress Cataloging-in-Publication Data

Kunetka, James W., 1944-
  The general and the genius : Groves and Oppenheimer : the unlikely partnership that built the atom bomb / James Kunetka.
    pages cm
  ISBN 978-1-62157-338-8
  1. Atomic bomb--New Mexico--Los Alamos--History. 2. Manhattan Project (U.S.)--History. 3. Los Alamos National Laboratory--History--20th century. 4. Groves, Leslie R., 1896-1970. 5. Oppenheimer, J. Robert, 1904-1967. 6. Generals--United States--Biography. 7. Military engineers--United States--Biography. 8. Physicists--United States--Biography. I. Title. II. Title: Groves and Oppenheimer : the unlikely partnership that built the atom bomb.
  QC773.A1K87 2015
  355.8'25119092273--dc23
                              2015004467

Published in the United States by
Regnery History
An imprint of Regnery Publishing
A Division of Salem Media Group
300 New Jersey Ave NW
Washington, DC 20001
www.RegneryHistory.com

Manufactured in the United States of America

10 9 8 7 6 5 4 3 2 1

Books are available in quantity for promotional or premium use. For information on discounts and terms, please visit our website: www.Regnery.com.

Distributed to the trade by
Perseus Distribution
250 West 57th Street
New York, NY 10107

Books by James Kunetka

Non-fiction:

City of Fire
Oppenheimer: The Years of Risk

Fiction:

Warday

Nature's End

Shadow Man

Parting Shot

For Robert D. Krohn

Who was there and who opened the door for me

Contents

PREFACE AND ACKNOWLEDGMENTS

The partnership between General Leslie Richard Groves of the U.S. Army Corps of Engineers and the theoretical physicist J. Robert Oppenheimer is one of the great stories of the Second World War, and it was as unexpected as it was successful. There was little in either man's life before 1942 to suggest that the general and the physicist would ever meet, much less form a close working association to develop an atomic bomb. They came from very different cultural and economic backgrounds. Their careers alone would have kept them apart, had not the war thrown them together and changed their lives utterly. In Robert Oppenheimer, Leslie Groves found the man to help him achieve fame and success through the creation of a secret weapon that could end America's greatest war, if not all wars. Oppenheimer did that by recruiting scientists and engineers, inspiring them and, under Groves's supervision, leading them in creating the new bomb. In Groves, Robert Oppenheimer found the man who would reinvigorate his career and give direction to his life. Groves did that by giving him an unimaginably grand scientific and engineering task, along with virtually unlimited resources, and an opportunity to serve his country in an unprecedented way.

Equally compelling, however, and the parallel subject of this book, is the story of the building of the atomic bomb itself. The conception and development of a theoretically complex and technologically advanced weapon, made from materials heretofore unimagined, in two and a half years is an extraordinary tale in its own right. And while the Manhattan Engineer District managed by Groves was a vast and expensive network of large industrial plants and smaller research installations, the atomic bomb was designed and built at a secret laboratory high in the mountains of northern New Mexico. It was on the plateau called Los Alamos that General Groves permitted Oppenheimer to gather some of the most talented scientific minds of the time for the sole purpose of making a weapon of war. Los Alamos was the heart of the Manhattan Project, and the story of the laboratory is inseparable from that of the atomic bomb.

Thousands of people in research laboratories and plants across the United States helped to create the atomic bomb, but the successful development of this weapon in record time is in no small part due to the complex, sometimes tense, but always productive partnership between Groves and Oppenheimer.

This book is not a biography of either Leslie Groves or Robert Oppenheimer. Fine, recent biographies of both men are cited in the bibliography. Nor is this book the story of the larger Manhattan Engineer District, more popularly known as the Manhattan Project. That history has been elegantly told by others as well. It is the story of two men, their wartime partnership, and the atomic bombs they helped to create.

Undertaking and completing such a history would not have been possible except for the support and assistance of many persons over the course of several decades. Although many of those who generously spent time with me and shared their wartime stories have since passed away, their contributions and place in history remain as strong and vivid as ever. It is to them that this book belongs. Many others assisted in the acquisition and declassification of documents and other historical materials, arranged interviews, and opened their personal collections and archives.

I am deeply grateful to Harold Agnew, Norris Bradbury, Robert Bacher, Hans Bethe, John Manley, Emilio Segre, Arthur Schellberg, Berlyn Brixner, Hugh Paxton, Bill Stratton, Carson Mark, Ralph Carlisle Smith, Marge Dube, Del Sundberg, Bill Regan, Faith Stevens, Art Freed, Dave Heimbach, Gilbert Ortiz, Bill Richmond, Al Van Vessem, Bill Norwood, Dorothy McKibbin, Frank and Jackie Oppenheimer, Peter and Virginia Oppenheimer, Peggy Pond Church, Alice Bullock, Barbara Storms, Ray and Elizabeth Gray, Malcolm and Emma Knowles, Priscilla Green Duffield, Bill Cunliffe, Jill Ellman, Jack Kahn, Walt Bramlett, Bob Masterson, Jeannene Mattingly, Les Redman, Louis and Eleanor Hempelmann, Charles Poisall, Charles Marshall, Melvin Neff, Richard Hewlett, and Edwin Reese.

More recently, I am indebted to Christina Hamblin at the Department of Energy, National Nuclear Security Agency, Office of General Counsel, for her help in processing FOIA requests. At the Los Alamos National Laboratory, I am grateful to Steve Sandoval and to the talented historian and archivist Alan Carr. Glen McDuff generously read the manuscript for scientific and technical accuracy.

Others to whom I owe thanks for their assistance, editing advice, and encouragement are Jim Hornfischer, Dennis L. Boyles, Donna Pfefferle Sanders, Bruce Krohn, Frank Schubert, Norvell Northcutt, and especially Cyndi Hughes.

John Coster-Mullen generously shared research and photographs with me and permitted the use of several illustrations in this book.

My editor, Tom Spence, deserves considerable credit for his patient and skillful work in helping to make this a better book.

And last, I owe a particular debt of gratitude to my late friend and Los Alamos alumnus Bob Krohn. He generously shared with me story after story of his remarkable life and career in Los Alamos.

James W. Kunetka

Austin, Texas

Chapter One

JULY 16, 1945—EARLY MORNING

———————◦———————

The storm rolled in from the southwest around midnight like a dark wave and spread out over the bleak ninety-mile stretch of New Mexico desert. Without moonlight, the sheer emptiness of the landscape was cloaked except when lightning struck, revealing a vast, flat basin hemmed in by distant mountain chains. Two hundred years earlier, Spanish travellers had named the region the Jornada del Muerto, or Journey of Death.[1]

By 3:30 a.m., the worst part of the storm had passed, although there was still a cloud layer with wind and sporadic light rain. Standing safely inside a concrete bunker poorly lit by bare bulbs, Major General Leslie R. Groves of the U.S. Army talked quietly in a corner with his chain-smoking companion, the scientist J. Robert Oppenheimer. Groves was in his khaki uniform, his two stars glittering, Oppenheimer in a loose, dark jacket worn over a blue chambray shirt. A half-dozen other men, most in their twenties, worked in the confined room, monitoring electronic equipment and dials;

a few others drifted in and out. The structure was almost two stories high, with thick concrete walls on three sides and the roof. The rear wall was a combination of wood and tarpaper with a set of double doors. The exposed front of the bunker had been protected with a long, sloping mound of earth that reached to the edge of the concrete roof.

Oppenheimer stood at six feet and Groves just under, and both had blue eyes, although Oppenheimer's were deeper and more striking. The physical similarities stopped there. Groves was far heavier, around 250 pounds, though his weight varied with travel, diet, and the stress of his job. He had wavy brown hair and sported a neat moustache. His face was handsome despite the beginning of a set of jowls, and there was still a hint of the former West Point athlete. Oppenheimer was the opposite: thin, with narrow hips that made him look even thinner. As an adult he rarely weighed more than 125 pounds, and tonight his weight was below 110. His dark, closely cropped hair exaggerated a slender, attractive face with tightly drawn skin. Some thought it was the face of an aesthete.

Groves was composed, as always. Oppenheimer was not. The scientist was agitated, close to exhaustion, and deeply concerned that the bad weather would spoil or force the cancellation of a test of a new and powerful explosive device that both men had come to the desert to witness. Groves countered that the weather was improving, but Oppenheimer repeated a litany of problems, gesticulating with his cigarette as he spoke. Mostly he worried that the storm wasn't over yet, that it would last until dawn, or that rain had short-circuited electrical connections or damaged sensitive equipment. Groves had heard all this earlier in the evening, and not just from Oppenheimer but from younger scientists who had similar concerns and who had argued that the test should be postponed at least twenty-four hours or even several days. Oppenheimer was unable to make a decision. Groves finally had said no: there was too much at stake to accept a delay. Yet even with the decision made, Oppenheimer remained apprehensive and jittery. From across the congested room, Brigadier General

Thomas Farrell, Groves's deputy, watched as Oppenheimer seemed "about to explode," until Groves intervened and quietly but firmly suggested that he and Oppenheimer get some air.[2]

Outside, they studied the sky: the rain was little more than an occasional sprinkle, and a few stars were visible in the night sky. The weather was improving, if only slightly. Light spilling from the open door of the bunker lit the insignia on the general's collar and the special white security badges that both men wore clipped to their shirts. After a moment, Groves reaffirmed his earlier decision. It was now 4:00 a.m. The test would occur at 5:30, three and a half hours behind schedule. Everyone associated with the test had an hour and a half to make final preparations. It was cool and muggy after the rain, and the humidity neared 80 percent. Lingering in the air was a trace of the ephemeral desert perfume conjured up when rain saturates dry, baked earth.

Groves and Oppenheimer walked around the bunker and looked north. Barely visible in the distance was a slender column of light emanating from a ten-story metal tower five miles away. In the top of the tower, a large, dark metal ball five feet in diameter rested on a wooden floor. It was divided into three sections by two thick, vertical bands, and thick coaxial cables ran like tentacles from the sphere's surface to sophisticated electronic equipment. The object looked ominous, but few people could have guessed that it contained an extraordinary invention, deceptively simple in its components, but breathtakingly complex in the theoretical principles that governed its design. The metal ball contained more than five thousand pounds of high explosives, as well as aluminum, uranium, and a new man-made element named plutonium in layered spheres. At its core was a small ball, less than an inch in diameter, containing a mixture of polonium and beryllium. In less than two hours, in a risky test, the high explosives would be detonated. If everything worked and device's contents compressed, a flash of light briefly brighter than the sun would burst from what had been the object's center.

The men who built this device called it Fat Man,[3] the Gadget, the Device. It was the first atomic bomb, and the reason it needed to be tested was that no one was entirely sure it would work.

———————

The steel tower stood out conspicuously in the desert. At night, floodlights caused the metal cabin on top to shine like a jewel in the dark sky. In the daytime, when sunlight caught the ribs of the frame, its shimmering form could be seen more than five miles away. The designers of Fat Man and the tower called the epicenter under the tower Ground Zero. The test itself bore the code name "Trinity."

Groves and Oppenheimer stood at a large bunker to the south of Ground Zero. A second bunker was located to the north, and a third to the west. Each bunker was ten thousand yards from the tower. Five miles farther south was "Base Camp," a collection of one-story wooden barracks with green tarpaper roofs that housed scientists and GIs, laboratories, latrines, showers, storage areas, and a mess hall. There were also tents to accommodate tonight's overflow of special visitors. The atomic bomb, if it worked, was supposed to have the power to destroy an entire city. It was the weapon that could end the war.

Three men carried the heaviest burden at the Trinity test. Leslie Groves was the army general who for almost three years had managed America's most secret wartime effort, the Manhattan Project. Its purpose was to develop the atomic bomb. Not yet fifty, Groves was best known for leading the Army Corps of Engineers' construction of the Pentagon in record time and under budget. Robert Oppenheimer was the director of a secret scientific laboratory high on a mesa in northern New Mexico. At forty-one, he was perhaps the nation's preeminent theoretical physicist, a former professor at Berkeley, and the man who over the last two years had led thousands of scientists, engineers, and workers in designing and building the gadget that now sat on the tower. Kenneth Bainbridge, a forty-year-old

Harvard physicist, was one of Oppenheimer's key scientists and the man in charge of the Trinity test.

There was so much that could go wrong. The rain and wind might sever the electrical connections, throw off sensor calibrations, or even wreck the equipment. On the gadget itself, the coaxial cables could come undone, the electronic components could short-circuit, and any one of the thirty-two specially designed detonators could fail. If lightning hit the tower it might, despite precautions, detonate the high explosives prematurely, scattering some 13.5 pounds of an isotope* of plutonium physicists labeled Pu239, the real "secret" to the atomic bomb.

Shortly after four o'clock a.m., Groves left his deputy, Brigadier General Farrell, with Oppenheimer at the south bunker and drove to Base Camp, where he would watch the test with the assembled dignitaries. His decision to intervene earlier this evening, to make the call where his director could not, was not unprecedented. It was part of a pattern that his interactions with Oppenheimer followed from the very beginning of their relationship. Groves was accustomed to making difficult decisions—like going ahead with the test despite the weather—and living with them. He never relinquished his roles as general and chief executive officer. A subtle tension underlay the relationship between the two men, but overall it was cordial and respectful. Ultimately, however, Groves was in charge, making or approving all major decisions, something Oppenheimer learned to accept, if not welcome.

Still, it was Oppenheimer who directed the research at the Los Alamos laboratory high in the Jemez Mountains, 220 miles north of Trinity. Since early 1943 the laboratory had grown from a scattering of buildings and a

---

* An element such as plutonium or uranium can have several forms, each of which contains the same number of protons but a different number of neutrons.

few dozen men to a complex of more than 6,500 scientists, engineers, technicians, and their families. By mid-July 1945 it was a churning, seven-days-a-week enterprise. For most of its brief history, the driving force behind the laboratory's work was simple enough: since the late 1930s, the United States had received intelligence reports that German physicists were working on an atomic bomb. Fission—the process in which an atom is split and energy released—had been discovered in 1938 in Germany, the home of some of the world's best physicists. After the German occupation of Czechoslovakia over the course of 1938 and 1939, the Nazi regime gained access to a generous supply of uranium. The threat of a Nazi bomb had evaporated, however, with Germany's surrender in May 1945. Now Groves's and Oppenheimer's bomb was seen as the weapon to end the bloody war against Japan.

Oppenheimer's laboratory at Los Alamos was only one component of a much larger organization led with considerable skill by General Groves. What was officially called the Manhattan Engineer District, or MED, included a small reactor and a series of enormous production plants in Oak Ridge, Tennessee, for the processing of uranium; a complex of three giant nuclear reactors and support buildings in Hanford, Washington, for the generation of plutonium; another uranium separation plant in Berkeley, California; and a collection of smaller projects and laboratories scattered across the country. Almost 150,000 men and women were employed by the MED, and Groves's total wartime expenditures so far neared two billion dollars.

The huge investment was paying off. In a little over two years, the MED's industrial machinery had churned out enough fissionable uranium and plutonium for Los Alamos to design and build two types of atomic bombs. In both weapons, the uncontrolled fission of atoms caused an explosion, but they achieved that explosion through different means. The Fat Man design, which sat quietly on its cradle a hundred feet off the ground at Trinity, was a plutonium bomb in which all of the components were "compressed" through implosion.

The alternative was a uranium bomb, in which a mass of uranium was fired from one end of a gun barrel–like tube into another mass of uranium at the other end, causing an explosion. There was high confidence that this method would work, but also concern because the United States had access to much more plutonium than uranium, and if defeating Japan required more than two or three bombs, it would need Fat Man weapons. Trinity was a test of whether the Fat Man design would work.

Oppenheimer was tired and gaunt and had barely recovered from an attack of chicken pox. His face seemed tinged in gray. He showed more visibly the effects of stress than Groves did, though it was Groves who suffered from high blood pressure. Of course, his responsibilities were far greater than Oppenheimer's. He had a huge military-industrial complex to manage. In 1945, he had two overriding objectives: keeping his plants on schedule to deliver uranium and plutonium, and ensuring that Oppenheimer developed a weapon that would actually work. He stayed in constant contact with Oppenheimer, exchanging countless memos, letters, telexes, and telephone calls, often several times a day, as well as paying frequent visits to the Los Alamos laboratory and ordering his director to meetings in Washington or Chicago.

President Truman, who did not learn about the secret new weapon under development at Los Alamos until shortly after taking the oath of office, was hoping that success in the New Mexico desert would do more than bring a swift end to the war against Japan. The president was in Potsdam, Germany, preparing for his first meetings with British Prime Minister Winston Churchill and Soviet Marshal Josef Stalin. Truman hoped that the successful development of the bomb would not just end the war but give him political leverage to temper and contain Stalin's already evident aggressive postwar territorial ambitions. If the Trinity test succeeded, the good news would be sent immediately, in code, to Truman in Potsdam. The test was timed, in fact, so that Truman would know the results during the Potsdam Conference.[4]

The situation in the war against Japan was grave. Japan's defeat was inevitable, but there was no movement toward surrender. Decoded diplomatic messages from Japan suggested they would try to use the Russians in negotiating an end to the war. Other intelligence reports suggested that the Japanese were preparing for a fight to the death. Aerial reconnaissance revealed a massive stockpiling of weapons and materiel on mainland Japan, especially on the island of Kyushu. The cost of the battles of Iwo Jima (twenty-six thousand American casualties) and Okinawa (sixty-two thousand American casualties) had shocked Truman, the military, and, to the extent they knew the details, the American public. For the Japanese, who had been ordered to delay the American advance at all costs, the price was frightful: more than seventy-five thousand military and 158,000 civilians dead. Of the twenty-two thousand Japanese on Iwo Jima at the beginning of the battle, only 216 were taken alive as prisoners at the end. The impending Allied assaults on Japan portended casualties in the millions.

———————

At the south bunker, Oppenheimer hovered by the doorway and made nervous conversation. The interior walls were lined with banks of metal cabinets stuffed with electronic monitoring equipment. Voices and static from two-way radios clattered and echoed from conversations between the bunker and other locations. Cigarette smoke hovered in clouds near the ceiling. A small desk was crammed into an open space where the physicist Sam Allison would eventually sit, watch a clock, and give the countdown over Trinity's public address system. There was little that Oppenheimer could do to help. The test, with its elaborate network of experiments and cameras, was now in the hands of others, and soon even that control would shift to a mechanical computer. As the minutes ticked away and 5:30 approached, he clung to a post for support.

With the decision to go, Bainbridge threw a final bank of electrical switches at the base of the tower and locked them into place—the bomb was now armed. All over Trinity, men adjusted their equipment or readied their cameras. At bunkers, at Base Camp, on a nearby rise in the desert called Compañia Hill, and at dozens of small sites scattered all over Trinity, men made their final preparations. Glowing dots from the ends of countless cigarettes lit the desert night like fireflies.

Chapter Two

REVOLUTIONARY
DEVELOPMENTS

———————◆❂◆———————

T he summer of 1939 was mild in New York, and on the eastern edge
    of Long Island the white flowers of the sweetbay magnolias had
    turned to red seeds, and the sycamores continued to drop their
leaves. On Wednesday, August 2, three men in a dark sedan drove slowly
on Old Grove Road in the rural coastal community of Peconic. They were
looking for Albert Einstein's rented vacation cottage. They knew the street
name but not the house number. They stopped several times to ask directions, but no one had heard of Professor Einstein. Finally, one young girl
with braids said she "knew a nice old man with white hair" and pointed
to a house less than a block away.[1] Moments later, Edward Teller pulled up
in front of Einstein's summer retreat with his companions, Leo Szilard and
Eugene Wigner. Despite the warm weather, each man wore a wool suit.

They were an interesting trio. All three were Hungarian—born in
Budapest within a decade of each other—and in America as refugees from
the Nazis. Academic physicists and mathematicians, they had studied or

worked under some of Europe's greatest scientists: Niels Bohr, Enrico Fermi, Max Planck, Werner Heisenberg, Wolfgang Pauli, and even Einstein, among others. What brought them to Peconic was a portentous event in Germany less than nine months earlier.

In December 1938, the chemists Otto Hahn and Fritz Strassmann, working at the Kaiser Wilhelm Institute for Chemistry in Berlin, bombarded what they thought was ordinary uranium 238, known as U238, with neutrons. When they analyzed the uranium, they unexpectedly found that it contained a radioactive isotope of barium. The neutron absorbed by the uranium atom had caused the nucleus to divide into two approximately equal parts. It was soon learned that the form of uranium split by Hahn and Strassmann was the isotope uranium 235, or U235.

Scientists everywhere quickly realized that theoretically a chain, or self-sustaining, reaction was a possibility. If fission occurred, additional neutrons would suddenly be freed from the nucleus during the reaction and in turn release immense amounts of energy. The implications were monumental. If fission could be controlled, it could produce heat and power. If left uncontrolled, the process could result in a powerful explosion. U235 was the critical material that could do either. But it was the possibility of a bomb of immense, unprecedented power that led Teller and his companions to Old Grove Road in search of Einstein.

Further research on fission in the spring suggested that a bomb was not just theoretically possible but likely. This was of concern to many scientists in America but particularly to a handful of refugees from the Nazis, who knew that their former colleagues in Germany were similarly engaged in fission research. With war seemingly inevitable, a powerful new bomb would be of obvious interest to Hitler. These scientists believed that the United States had no choice but to undertake a rapid and serious examination of how such a weapon would work and how soon it could be developed. Szilard in particular took it upon himself to take the case to Franklin Roosevelt, and he decided to do that by asking Albert Einstein, perhaps the most famous scientist in the world, to write a letter to the president.

Leo Szilard was brilliant, imaginative, and a true eccentric. Short and stocky, he more often harangued his listeners than conversed, and as Teller affectionately said of him, "he could hardly talk without giving orders."[2] For much of his adult life, until he married in his early fifties, he chose to live out of hotel rooms and suitcases. As a young man, he took courses from Einstein and Max Planck and subsequently became a lecturer at the University of Berlin until forced to leave as the persecution of Jews intensified.

He was convinced that the situation in Europe was quickly deteriorating and persuaded his friends and fellow physicists Teller and Wigner to approach Einstein, whom they believed had the scientific authority and the international reputation to lead a campaign for support of fission research by the American government.

Teller, like Szilard, left Hungary to study in Germany, where he earned a degree in chemical engineering from the University of Karlsruhe and a Ph.D. in theoretical physics from the University of Leipzig under Werner Heisenberg, the first of several prestigious professors under whom he would study or work. While a student in Munich, Teller lost his right foot in a streetcar accident and was forced to wear a prosthetic foot for the rest of his life. In the early 1930s, he left Germany, going first to England, then to Copenhagen to work with Niels Bohr, and then in 1935 to the United States, where he had been offered a professorship in physics at Georgetown University.

Wigner, too, had moved from Hungary to study and work in Germany, where he met Szilard. He studied chemical engineering as well as mathematics and quantum physics, becoming an expert in nuclear reactions. In 1930 he was offered a job at Princeton, which led in time to an appointment at the University of Wisconsin.

Einstein welcomed his guests, served them tea, and after listening to Szilard make his case, agreed to read and sign the two-page letter

Szilard and his colleagues had prepared. It stressed the necessity of urgently investigating the possibility of producing an atomic bomb. With the signed letter in hand, the three Hungarian scientists returned to New York City.

Einstein was genuinely concerned, but not just with the dark possibilities of atomic fission. He worried far more about the human capacity for killing one another. Earlier in the year, he had contributed a message to the "peoples of the future" that was buried in a time capsule on the grounds of the New York World's Fair in nearby Queens, to be opened in the year 6939. His message had ended with a warning: "Peoples living in different countries kill each other at irregular time intervals, so that also for this reason any one who thinks about the future must live in fear and terror."[3]

In less than a month, Adolf Hitler invaded Poland and launched the Second World War.

―――――――――――――――

Szilard recruited Alexander Sachs, an economist with personal access to Roosevelt, to deliver the letter to the White House. On October 11, 1939, Sachs met with General Edwin M. Watson, an assistant to Roosevelt, and several other military advisors to the president, and was then taken to meet with the president. He repeated the implications of fission for a powerful bomb and emphasized the need for government support. The president listened carefully and joked that he "didn't want the Nazis to blow them all up." Roosevelt told General Watson that action was needed.[4] Within weeks Roosevelt established the Advisory Committee on Uranium and appointed Lyman J. Briggs, the director of the National Bureau of Standards and a long-time civil servant, as its director. Briggs was given a budget and instructed to fund whatever research projects would help answer the many questions surrounding an atomic bomb. It was assumed that most of this money would go to universities.

In June 1940, Roosevelt took a more significant step. He established the National Defense Research Committee (NDRC) to coordinate scientific research needed for national defense, and he transferred the Committee on Uranium to the new organization, where it became known simply as the "Uranium Committee." Vannevar Bush of the Carnegie Institute was asked to serve as chairman.

The son of a Universalist parson, Bush received doctorates in engineering simultaneously from the Massachusetts Institute of Technology and Harvard University. He developed an analog computer, helped found the Raytheon Corporation, and between his inventions and extensive corporate consulting became a wealthy man. In 1938 he was invited to become president of the Carnegie Institute in Washington, D.C., where he oversaw the funding of numerous scientific research projects throughout the United States. His increasing prominence led to appointments on the National Advisory Committee on Aeronautics and subsequently to the NDRC. Tall and boyish-looking but serious and bespectacled, he looked like a high school principal.

Two other members of the newly created NDRC would play important roles in the growing fission enterprise. The first was Richard C. Tolman, a professor of physical chemistry and mathematical physics at the California Institute of Technology. Bush appointed him to the NDRC, where he served as co-chairman of the Armor and Ordnance Division. The second was the president of Harvard University, James B. Conant. Unlike many of his scientist colleagues, Conant had served in the army in World War I, working on poison gases. He returned to Harvard as a member of the faculty, and in 1933 he became its president. Appointed to the NDRC in 1940, he later became its chairman when Bush moved to direct the new Office of Scientific Research and Development. Bush depended heavily on Conant's talent for coolly assessing people and projects. Conant, who remained president of Harvard throughout the war, soon found himself spending half his time and three-quarters of his government work on the fledgling atomic bomb.[5]

One of the projects funded by Briggs and the Uranium Committee was at the University of Chicago and directed by the physicist Enrico Fermi. His research confirmed that graphite slowed down neutrons, and he demonstrated the usefulness of graphite as a neutron absorber. Impressed, Briggs authorized the purchase of eight tons of uranium oxide and forty tons of graphite for Fermi. Graphite was relatively easy to get—but what about uranium, which was suddenly required in substantial amounts? Fortunately, the African Metal Corporation had 1,200 tons of 65-percent-pure uranium sitting in a warehouse in New York and another three thousand tons at its mines in the Congo. After some sleuthing, another seven hundred tons were located in Canada.

The greatest challenge facing Briggs's committee, however, was producing fissionable material like U235 on an immense, industrial scale. A potential atomic weapon would need substantial amounts of fissionable uranium—kilograms, not micrograms. Most uranium (including that sitting in the New York warehouse) was of the far more common U238 variety. In fact, only .07 percent of U238 contains the U235 isotope. Stockpiling U235 required separating it from U238. The Uranium Committee considered at least four options.

One possible method for separating uranium would employ high-speed centrifuges. Such a device had been built in 1939 at the University of Virginia, where minute amounts of U235 were separated using a gaseous mixture of uranium and fluorine gas known as uranium hexafluoride. Because the process produced only insignificant quantities, its development was assigned a lower priority than the alternatives, a seemingly sensible decision at the time but in fact shortsighted. It took five years and huge investments in alternative methods of production to determine that centrifuges were the fastest and cheapest method.

Another possibility was gaseous diffusion, a process promoted by the chemist and Nobel laureate Harold Urey, in which the uranium hexafluoride gas was forced through filters, or barriers, over and over again. In May 1940, the Harvard chemist George B. Kistiakowsky's experiments for the

Bureau of Mines seemed to hold promise for isolating U235 with this process, and he agreed to concentrate on developing barriers with holes small enough to filter the uranium gas. The idea was that at each stage in the diffusion process, the gas would become increasingly purified and concentrated as U235; the heavier U238 was collected at the bottom of the stages and the lighter U235 was collected at the top. Hundreds of miles of pipe were needed, as were thousands of barriers, each barrier containing billions of holes less than 1/1,000 of a millimeter in diameter.

A third possibility was liquid thermal diffusion. This process, similar to petroleum refining techniques, involved forcing gases to cool at differing rates. There was considerable uncertainty within the committee as to how effective such a process would be with uranium.

But the most promising method by far appeared to be the electromagnetic separation process under development by Ernest Orlando Lawrence at Berkeley. Lawrence had joined the University of California physics faculty in 1928 and two years later had been named full professor. Tall, blond, and social, he cut an attractive figure at Berkeley. He began work in the early 1930s on rudimentary particle accelerators he called cyclotrons, the first of which was less than five inches in diameter. The device was successful and led to a series of larger, more sophisticated machines that used giant magnets to keep charged particles accelerating in spirals within an electrical field. For this work, he was awarded the Nobel Prize in 1939. Lawrence and his staff continued to improve the process and by 1940 were regularly separating miniscule quantities of U235 from U238.

Although the electromagnetic process seemed the most promising approach to separation, Bush and the Uranium Committee believed that all four methods of uranium production had to be pursued. The alternatives were prioritized, however: Lawrence's electromagnetic process was given top priority, followed by gaseous diffusion, the centrifuge, and finally thermal diffusion, the last two considered distant bets.

It was granted that Briggs was dealing with unprecedented scientific and technological challenges, but by 1941 there was growing dissatisfaction that Briggs had achieved so little. Many of the recipients of grant money expressed no sense of urgency, and research projects seemed poorly coordinated. Inevitably, scientists complained that their funding was inadequate, limiting the pace and productiveness of their research. With Hitler's empire growing, and with continuing intelligence reports that the Germans were working steadily on fission research, more needed to be done, and quickly. Lawrence, who had recently been appointed director of the new Radiation Laboratory at the University of California, spoke for many critics when he urged a more aggressive and better-funded program of research.

There had been some good news in the spring of 1940. Working under Lawrence, the physicist Edwin McMillan discovered Element 93—soon named neptunium—while experimenting on fission fragments. A few months later, the chemist Glenn T. Seaborg produced Element 93 and evidence of still another element. On August 20, a day that Seaborg described as the "most exciting and thrilling day I have experienced," he and his team produced a tiny amount of Element 94, which they named "plutonium," or Pu239. It was only one microgram and existed as a precipitate, but it was the first time the new element, in Seaborg's words, "has been beheld by the eye of man."[6] Shortly thereafter, Seaborg and his colleague Emilio Segre reported that plutonium was 1.7 times more likely than U235 to undergo fission with slow neutrons, offering an alternative material for an atomic bomb.[7]

Shortly after the confirmation that plutonium was fissionable, Bush ordered a review of the work of the Uranium Committee and asked Arthur H. Compton, the recipient of the 1927 Nobel Prize in physics and the chairman of the department of physics at the University of Chicago, to lead it. He was instructed to assess the work underway, to report on the probability of developing a bomb, and, if a bomb seemed to be a realistic prospect, to suggest a timeline for its development.

Compton's preliminary report to Bush, dated May 17, 1941, suggested that it would take from three to five years to separate enough U235 to make a bomb. Pu239, however, could be produced in greater amounts in a chain-reacting pile like that envisioned by Fermi, and enough plutonium might be available as early as twelve months after the first chain reaction. "Atomic explosives" were probably some years away—perhaps by 1945. Working with Fermi, Compton suggested that somewhere between twenty to one hundred kilograms (forty-four to 220 pounds) of U235 would be needed for a critical mass, the smallest amount of fissionable material that will support a chain reaction.[8]

In July, Britain's Military Application of Uranium Detonation Committee, or MAUD, speculated that a much smaller amount of U235 would be required for a bomb, perhaps as little as 11.4 kilograms (twenty-two pounds), and that such a weapon could be produced in less than two years at a cost of some twenty-five million dollars.[9] This was welcome news.

On June 8, 1941, President Roosevelt issued Executive Order 8807 creating the Office of Scientific Research and Development (OSRD). This new organization was to initiate and direct a wide range of scientific and technical efforts, including the development of advanced bombs and missiles, radar, the proximity fuse, even medical treatments. Its most secret project was the atomic bomb, however. OSRD was placed within the Office for Emergency Management but reported directly to the president. Bush was named the director of OSRD and led the Uranium Committee (now renamed for security purposes the S-1 Committee), while Conant took over the National Defense Research Committee. OSRD eventually supported the research of more than twenty-five thousand people, including two-thirds of America's physicists. Six months after the creation of OSRD, America was officially at war.

On December 7, 1941, a combination of Japanese bombers, torpedo planes, and fighters attacked the U.S. naval base at Pearl Harbor, Hawaii.

In only ninety minutes, 2,008 sailors, 218 soldiers and airmen, and 218 civilians were dead. Simultaneously, the Japanese struck the Philippines and British Malaysia, Singapore, and Hong Kong. Four days later, Germany and Italy declared war on the United States. Suddenly, the atomic bomb took on urgent importance.

On December 16, Vice President Henry Wallace called a high-level meeting to review the progress of fission research. It was increasingly apparent during the discussions that some larger organization would soon have to take over the rapidly expanding fission program, particularly to manage the production of nuclear materials. Not surprisingly, the most appropriate organization was the U.S. Army, particularly its Corps of Engineers. Coordinating research would be difficult enough, but building and overseeing the uranium separation plants and plutonium reactors required special experience.

At the same time, Bush was even more convinced that it was necessary to explore all the various methods of obtaining large quantities of U235. He sent Roosevelt a copy of Compton's report along with a letter stating that he was forming an engineering group to look at plant designs. He closed by saying that he would wait for presidential approval before committing any further resources to production. On January 19, 1942, Roosevelt returned the letter with a handwritten notation: "V. B. OK— returned—I think you had best keep this in your safe. FDR."[10]

Bush moved quickly. He selected Eger V. Murphree, a vice president of the Standard Oil Company and a man with useful experience in the construction of large chemical plants, to look into the requirements of large-scale uranium production. He then made three additional assignments within the S-1 Committee. Lawrence would continue to head the electromagnetic work at Berkeley, and Arthur Compton would lead chain reaction research and plutonium production in Chicago. Harold C. Urey took charge of diffusion and centrifuge separation. Urey had been awarded the 1934 Nobel Prize in chemistry for the discovery of deuterium and had pioneered the development of the gaseous diffusion method of separation.

At an early meeting of S-1, Lawrence reported that Pu239 had a spontaneous fission rate no higher than that of U235,* and theoretically at least,
could be produced on a large scale with reactors, a less complicated production process than gaseous diffusion.

Compton prepared a timetable. The possibility of a successful chain
reaction must be demonstrated by July 1, 1942, the actual test of a chain
reaction concluded by January 1943, the first production of Pu239 in a pile
by January 1944, and a final bomb by January 1945.[11] Reviewing the report,
Bush came to believe in the desirability of centralizing all fission research
at one location; he was spending a great deal of time traveling from project to project and holding meetings. Not all work could be centralized, of
course, but the principal actors and projects could be brought together.
As a partial solution, Bush created the Metallurgical Laboratory at the
University of Chicago at the end of January 1942, and asked Compton to
serve as director.

On May 23, 1942, Bush brought together Compton, Conant, Briggs,
Murphree, and Lawrence in Washington, D.C., to review their programs
and make recommendations for plant construction. Murphree recommended that at least one centrifuge and one gaseous diffusion plant be
built as soon as possible to determine their effectiveness, but he also
reminded the S-1 Committee that sufficient quantities of uranium oxide
were needed as the raw material for a nuclear reactor: it was during the
operation of the pile that uranium would be transmuted into Pu239. Other
decisions quickly followed in the afternoon. The committee approved the
construction of gaseous diffusion, electromagnetic, and heavy water plants
by the end of 1943 and a centrifuge plant and one or more plutonium piles.
All in all, they authorized eighty million dollars in expenditures, a huge
increase from the previous year's funding on fission.[12] Building and managing

---

* Some nuclear materials, such as U235 and Pu239, occasionally begin fissioning
without being artificially bombarded by neutrons. When this "spontaneous fission"
occurs, an explosive chain reaction cannot take place.

the industrial plants was going to require experience and skills that Bush and his scientists simply did not have, but that the U.S. Army did.

On June 17, 1942, Bush met with Roosevelt and recommended that, for the moment, work on the bomb officially be divided between OSRD and the Army Corps of Engineers. OSRD would continue to do nuclear research, and the army would build the plants. At some later point, the army would take full control. The president agreed and initialed Bush's proposal with a simple "OK. FDR."

―――――――――――

In early March 1942, the army chief of staff General George Marshall had appointed Brigadier General Wilhelm D. Styer, to be the principal liaison between the army and the S-1 Committee. Styer was a 1916 graduate of West Point with a long history in construction and engineering. As a young officer, he had served in the army campaign against Pancho Villa before being sent to France during the First World War. In 1942 he was deputy chief of construction for the War Department when Marshall chose him as liaison. A few months later, on June 10, Bush met with Styer and Marshall to discuss the transfer of uranium and plutonium production to the army and to make the first of a series of important decisions. The Stone and Webster Company was awarded a contract for the construction of a pile in Oak Ridge, Tennessee, to produce commercial quantities of plutonium. But when Bush urged that all four methods of separating uranium be explored, Marshall resisted, arguing that bankrolling four expensive experiments was unaffordable, given the other demands of the war effort. He initially gave tentative approval to the plutonium pile and the uranium electromagnetic programs. The impasse was resolved with a compromise. Bush persuaded Marshall to approve all four methods with the provision that priority be given to the methods requiring the least draw on critical materials and offering the greatest promise of success. The army would finance 60 percent of the program in 1943 and all of it in 1944.[13]

Styer quickly appointed Colonel James C. Marshall (no relation to General George Marshall) of the army's Syracuse Engineering District to head the new fission program, quickly named the Development of Substitute Materials, or DSM, District. James Marshall was a West Point graduate with good field experience in construction, including a $250 million project for the Syracuse Corps of Engineers. But he lacked two qualities necessary for the job. He was not decisive, because he, like almost everyone else, knew little about uranium and plutonium production, and he was not a Washington insider, which turned out to be critical to managing the new project. Colonel Marshall took command on June 18 and shortly thereafter secured offices in New York City in the headquarters of the North Atlantic Division of the Corps of Engineers. But his office needed to be within the War Department, where the important decisions were being made. In August 1942, Colonel Leslie Richard Groves, a member of Styers's staff, suggested renaming the Development of Substitute Materials District—a name that might arouse curiosity—"Manhattan," following the Corps of Engineers' practice of naming a new district for the city in which its offices were located. The name stuck, and the project was renamed the Manhattan Engineer District, or MED.[14]

Colonel Marshall ran into trouble soon after taking command. Briefings by Bush and members of the S-1 Committee gave him little hard information on which to act. He was uncertain what to do: build plants for all four methods or build the electromagnetic plant because it seemed likely to deliver first? And to complicate matters, he had taken command of an army project lacking both rank and experience with the army's high-level bureaucratic procedures. A fine field officer, he now found himself hampered at every move by army regulations and bureaucratic fiefdoms. More damaging, he was unable to obtain a priority rating for procurement higher than A-3, whereas nothing less than AAA, the highest priority rating, was needed. Marshall's only good fortune was to have assigned to him Colonel Kenneth D. Nichols, who had experience in both scientific research and engineering. Nichols, thirty-two and balding, had a Ph.D. in hydraulic engineering from Iowa State University. He was, however, just one man, and his assignment did nothing to resolve the many problems facing the project. The MED seemed dead in its tracks, hampered by both indecision and inertia. Bush was dismayed and felt compelled to ask General Marshall personally to approach the War Production Board for a priority change. Quietly, he prodded General Styer to replace Colonel Marshall with someone more aggressive and experienced.

In late September 1942, to Bush's considerable relief, there was a sea change in the army's lumbering Manhattan Project. Colonel Marshall was replaced as director of the Manhattan Engineering District. Its new leader would be none other than a very unhappy Colonel Leslie R. Groves.

Chapter Three

GENERAL AND PHYSICIST

Although the two men who would do the most to shape America's wartime atomic program came from different backgrounds, they shared several important experiences. Leslie Groves and Robert Oppenheimer both witnessed World War I and the revolutionary weapons it introduced to warfare: tanks, airplanes, submarines, zeppelins, and poison gas, among others. They both lived through the Depression, although only one of them ever had to worry about money. And by the beginning of World War II, they were both married with families and enjoying successful careers. Those careers, apparently so dissimilar, brought them together for the first time in 1942, and their similarities allowed them to work together productively for the next three years.

Leslie Richard Groves Jr. was born on August 17, 1896, in Albany, New York. Always known as Dick and never Leslie, he was his father's favorite son. The elder Groves was a seventh-generation American who practiced law for a few years before becoming a Presbyterian minister. The year Dick was born, Groves joined the U.S. Army as a chaplain and moved from one distant assignment to another—from China to the Philippines—during the first five years of the boy's life, leaving his wife, Gwen Griffith Groves, at home to raise the children by herself.

By 1901, the family was together again, and Dick spent the next decade and a half moving with his parents and siblings from one state to another—Washington, New Jersey, Michigan, Montana, California, Oregon, and back to Washington. An army chaplain's salary was never generous, and Dick, who helped out with part-time jobs, never forgot how hard it was to spend day after day picking fruit in California. The family was not exactly poor, but there was little extra money, and his childhood austerities made Groves financially careful for the rest of his life. He was a quiet, shy boy who spent more time with his family than with outsiders.

The constant moving shaped Groves's character. He loved riding trains and discovering new places in America. In Montana, Dick was befriended by the post commander, Colonel Richard H. Wilson, who exposed him to classical music, the great books, and baseball. And Dick made the acquaintance of the commander's young daughter, Grace, whom he quietly resolved to marry one day.

In 1913, Groves entered the University of Washington. He really wanted to go to the U.S. Military Academy, though his father did not approve. The elder Groves had become disenchanted with the army, which, as he saw it, was filled with drunkards and gamblers. Dick took the West Point entrance exam but failed. Disappointed, he vowed to try again—an early but telling sign of his determination. He transferred to the Massachusetts Institute of Technology, took the West Point exam again—successfully this time—and in 1916 reported to the academy. It was exactly what he wanted. Later he wrote, "Entering West Point fulfilled my greatest ambition. I was deeply impressed with the character and devotion to duty of the Army officers I knew, and I was imbued with the idea that West Point graduates were normally the best officers."[1]

Groves excelled at the academy, although the experience was not altogether a happy one. He was older and more experienced academically than all the other plebes. He had little money and felt compelled to write down each expenditure and report it to his father. He didn't mix easily, and others saw him as a loner. One classmate, Willard Holbrook, thought Groves was unhappy throughout all four years at West Point: "He was unpopular, and he was lonely."[2] Groves spent much of his time studying by himself, an effort that paid off with excellent grades. He became an outstanding cadet, won his sergeant stripes, and began to demonstrate an ability to size a man up quickly, assessing his strengths and weaknesses—a talent that would prove invaluable throughout his career. He graduated fourth in his class in 1918, too late to serve in World War I. Resigned to a peacetime commission, he chose the Army Corps of Engineers as his branch of service.

His first two years out of West Point were spent in engineering school at Fort Humphreys in Virginia. Groves considered the experience "top notch," and it prepared him for his long career. He was especially proud that the school "included not only undergraduate work but also something in graduate work."[3]

His next assignment couldn't have suited him better. In early 1921, he was sent to Fort Worden in Washington, near Puget Sound, where his first social call was at the home of Grace Wilson. He courted her, persuaded her to cancel her engagement to another young man, and married her the next February. They were a good fit, and their successful marriage produced two children, Richard and Gwen. It didn't hurt that Grace had grown up in a military family and had no illusions of what life with an army officer would be like.

The next two decades were, predictably enough, a series of moves. Groves was assigned to the Presidio in San Francisco; Schofield Barracks in Honolulu; Galveston, Texas; and Fort DuPont, Delaware, where a grenade accident killed one of his enlisted men. The incident produced the only negative entry in Groves's personnel file and left him even more determined to control the events and people he supervised.

He fared much better in his next assignment, Nicaragua, where his team explored an alternative to the Panama Canal. His performance in Central America earned him a promotion and an assignment to the Military Supply Division in Washington, D.C., where for the first time he worked with scientists, an experience that would shape his thinking in the future. He was involved with a large, well-funded project searching for more sophisticated methods of detecting aircraft in flight. In the early days of aviation, the military relied on sound to detect an approaching aircraft, but as planes flew higher, that method became useless. The project turned its attention to infrared detection, a method that was eventually eclipsed by radar.

In 1940, Groves was promoted to colonel and made special assistant to the quartermaster general, chief of operations, and deputy chief of construction. He soon found himself overseeing thousands of contract employees and more than eight billion dollars in expenditures. His performance was flawless, and his superiors quickly took note of his talents. In 1941, he was assigned to oversee the Corps of Engineers' largest construction project at the time—the new War Department building that became known as the Pentagon.

Groves had a reputation for competence, but he had other traits that were less becoming. He was demanding, rough, and sometimes brutal with his staff, intolerant of delay, of mental slowness, and even of what he considered unmilitary behavior or minor infractions, such as telling jokes in the office. He was the same with his civilian staff, and was known for hiring and firing secretaries. On the other hand, he never swore, rarely lost his temper, and never raised his voice. He was also prepared to let subordinates disagree—if their arguments were sound. And he disliked people who groveled. The scientist Robert Bacher, who would work closely with Groves during the war, quickly realized that the man "didn't like being kowtowed to.... In fact, the more people kowtowed to him, the worse they got along with him. I think he liked a demonstration of spirit and independence in the people he worked with."[4] Groves's style, said General William Wannamaker, was "to delegate whatever he could and then put the screws to the delegees." Even his son-in-law, Alan Robinson, later remarked, "He was a taskmaster. He was proud of the fact that people were scared of him."[5]

Colonel Kenneth Nichols, who worked with him throughout the war, observed that most people who came in contact with Groves found him "abrasive and often very critical. He seldom indulged in casual conversations, and in fact he usually appeared aloof. As a result, many people considered him unfriendly." Nichols remembered inspecting a construction site with Colonel James Marshall and Groves. The general criticized the project at every stage. When Marshall asked him if he ever praised anyone for a job well done, Groves said no. "I don't believe in it. No matter how well something is being done, it can always be done better and faster." But Nichols was smart enough to see through Groves's gruff persona to the results he was achieving. In a frank assessment of his boss after the war, he called him

> the biggest S.O.B. I have ever worked for. He is the most demanding. He is the most critical. He is always a driver, never a praiser. He is abrasive and sarcastic. He disregards all normal organizational channels. He is extremely intelligent. He has the guts to make timely, difficult decisions. He is the most egotistical man I know. He knows he is right and so sticks by his decision. He abounds with energy and expects everyone to work as hard or even harder than he does.... [I]f I had to do my part of the atomic bomb project over again and had the privilege of picking my boss I would pick General Groves.[6]

Groves was also fortunate that to his immediate superior, General Styer, his talents were more compelling than his flaws. Styer protected him from the brutal, internecine politics of the army, offering a simple reason for his support: "He knows what he wants, and he knows how to get things done."[7]

This powerful combination of experience, talent, and personality, and the entry of America into the war, brought Leslie Groves the assignment that would secure his place in history.

In 1942, Groves worked in the same building as Colonel Marshall and was familiar with the Manhattan Engineer District, which he knew was supposed to produce a super weapon. Groves even assisted Marshall with site locations and purchases. And because some responsibilities between their two offices overlapped, Groves asked in mid-August for a weekly report of Marshall's activities to be completed within three or four days after the close of each week. From a distance, he watched Marshall stumble trying to get the program moving. Part of the problem, as Groves saw it, was that Marshall "was too deferential, and he wasn't demanding enough of his subordinates. He did not have the drive and ability to push the project at the speed needed."[8] Another problem, in Groves's view, was that Marshall "would also defer to the scientists on all scientific matters even if as was usually the case they were merely guessing."[9] Groves tried to keep his distance, but it didn't work. At age forty-six, he found himself in charge of the program he had named: the Manhattan Engineer District.

Groves got the job because General Styer, General Marshall's and Vannevar Bush's first choice, did not want it. He already held an attractive position in the War Department, and the proposed fission project appeared to involve complicated construction on a gigantic scale. Styer proposed Groves, and the appointment was quickly approved by General Marshall, Secretary of War Stimson, and President Roosevelt. Groves did not want the job, but he understood how he got it:

They originally wanted Styer whom they [Bush and other scientists] knew and had worked with on this Project in the preliminary stage to see whether the Army should go into it. There was no question that they wanted him.... [General Brehon B.] Somervell [head of the Army Services of Supply] didn't want to lose Styer, who was his chief of staff, and Styer didn't want the job because he saw what it was like. You see at that time nobody thought it would succeed. Nobody with any brains at all could possibly think it would succeed.[10]

Later, after the war, Groves would soften his explanation by pointing out that he not only possessed unmatched experience in large construction projects but also knew how to navigate his way around Washington.

Whatever his own motives, Styer believed that if anyone could handle the Manhattan District, with all of its vagaries and difficulties, it was his subordinate. Groves was not asked for his opinion. Instead, he learned of his new appointment in the hallway of the New House Office Building where he had just testified before the House Military Affairs Committee. Running into General Somervell, who reported to Marshall, he was casually told that the secretary of war had a new assignment for him and that the president had approved. When told the job was in Washington, Groves guessed it was the faltering Manhattan District. "Oh, that thing," he said. Groves protested but to no avail. Somervell simply said, "If you do this job right, it will win the war."[11]

Groves turned to Colonel Marshall's assistant, Colonel Nichols, to learn more of the scientific details of the project. They met Saturday morning, September 17, and Groves later recalled, "I was not happy with the information I received; in fact, I was horrified. It seemed as if the whole endeavor was founded on possibilities rather than probabilities. Of theory there was a great deal, of proven knowledge not much. Even if the theories were correct, the engineering difficulties would be unprecedented."[12] What particularly disturbed him was the prospect of constructing huge and expensive plants for developing a previously unknown substance even though there was no clear evidence that the process would work on a grand scale.

Later that same day, at three o'clock in the afternoon, Groves and Nichols charged into Vannevar Bush's plush offices in the Carnegie Institution's Beaux Arts building on P Street. Groves had barely introduced himself when he announced that he was now in charge of the Manhattan Project. It was quickly apparent that Bush had no idea who these men were. Groves had a small edge at the meeting, in that he was aware that Bush was involved with the fission effort at a high level. Groves asked for up-to-date reports on the outstanding work, but Bush either declined or gave evasive answers. He was not about to give secret information to a man he had not met or even heard of before. After Groves and Nichols left, Bush immediately sought a meeting with Styer, who apologized. Bush thought Groves "too aggressive" and feared he would offend scientists. Styer agreed that there might be difficulties but stated his belief that Groves would get the job done. Bush then wrote to Harvey Bundy, an assistant to Secretary Stimson for atomic energy affairs, and reiterated that Groves lacked tact. His letter ended forlornly, "I fear we are in the soup."[13]

On September 19, Groves met with Colonel Marshall to explain how the MED would be run, including the news that Marshall would now report to him. Marshall made a note of the meeting: "He allowed me to read copy of secret letter to the Chief of Engineers.... Groves states that the Manhattan District status and, particularly, my job as district Engineer were not affected by the change in Groves' status."[14]

Groves, Nichols, and Colonel Marshall met again with Bush on September 21. By this time, Bush had met with General Styer and understood that Groves was in charge. An apology was made, and Bush gave a brief history of the project and answered questions. Bush changed his mind about Groves, and the two men began a respectful and productive association. Groves quickly proved himself with his unflagging energy and ability to make decisions. Moreover, he now realized that he had the assignment of a lifetime and sprang into action.

Groves was promoted to brigadier general on September 23, the same day he attended a meeting with Generals Marshall, Somervell, and Styer, along with Bush and Conant. Groves asked for his appointment officially to take effect that very day. "I thought that there might be some problems in dealing with the many academic scientists involved in the project and I felt that my position would be stronger if they thought of me from the first as a general instead of as a promoted colonel."[15] They established a Military Policy Committee to oversee the military's participation in the atomic bomb project. Groves insisted that the committee have only three members. Bush, representing the scientists, would serve as chairman. Conant would be his alternate and would sit in on all meetings. Admiral William R. Purnell, the assistant chief of naval operations for materiel, would represent the navy, and General Styer would represent the army. Groves would report directly to the committee and would serve as executive officer. Groves then announced to the startled group that he had to catch a train to visit several Manhattan project sites and asked to be excused. That impressed Marshall.

Groves visited the Metallurgical Laboratory in Chicago for the first time on Monday, October 5. Arthur Compton, the lab's co-director, gave him a tour, with a lunch and briefing to follow. Groves's arrival and the news that he now directed the Manhattan Project, which included the Met Lab, were met with more suspicion than enthusiasm. Many scientists were unhappy with the army's involvement in what had been their exclusive domain. Leo Szilard was an outspoken opponent, but even Compton wrote to Conant to question the "desirability" of putting the fission projects under military control. Conant felt it necessary to warn Groves of Szilard's attitude. "Szilard will be very opposed to your being here," he told Groves, "because he want[s] to have a committee in which he would be the dominant character running this whole project with the government just pouring in money." Szilard managed not to offend Groves during his visit, but once the general left he asked how anyone could work with such a man.[16]

After lunch, meeting in wood-paneled Room 201 of Eckart Hall, Groves was introduced to fifteen of Compton's senior scientists, including Szilard and three Nobel laureates: Compton, Enrico Fermi, and James Franck. Groves was particularly interested in learning how much uranium or plutonium would be needed for a bomb. Given a broad range of figures, he asked the scientists how accurate they thought these numbers were and was told that they were accurate within a factor of ten. Groves was stunned. "Ten kilograms" could mean anything from one to a thousand kilograms. Was that really what they meant, he asked them, and the scientists assured him it was. Groves was unhappy with the lack of specificity, but he was also impatient with what he perceived to be their narrow approach to problem-solving. At one point, he told the group that if there were two possible solutions to a problem, they should try them both. Unfortunately, his sense of urgency collided with their traditional scientific practice. Compounding the problem, Groves asked Compton to make a decision by the end of the week on which of the four methods of separation he thought would be most successful. The general concluded the meeting by saying that while he did not have a Ph.D., he did have ten years of formal education beyond college. He left with a "very high opinion of the scientific attainments of the Chicago group" but disappointed that he did not have concrete information to inform the decisions that had to be made concerning the various separation plants under consideration.[17]

The scientists at the Met Lab were equally disappointed, if not shocked, by their visitor's behavior. Groves seemed to confirm their worst fears about army involvement and control. Their collective sense of the man was that he was both bumptious and ignorant of the scientific process. This unfavorable sentiment, unfortunately, spread among scientists, often encouraged by Groves's own off-the-cuff comments, as when he told Lawrence, "I'm not the least bit interested in the scientific knowledge of the world, except insofar as it gets the job done."[18] Interestingly, Lawrence agreed.

Groves's visit to Chicago changed the way he thought about the project. He realized that dealing with scientists—especially this type of scientist—was going to be difficult. It would not be like his experience in the Military Supply Division or on the aircraft detection project years before. The scientists he had worked with at that time were men with tangible, concrete ideas, not vague, theoretical ones. Assembling competent men to design, build, and operate the huge gaseous diffusion plant and plutonium reactors would be a challenge, but Groves felt fully prepared to undertake it. After all, he had spent his whole career on increasingly complex construction projects. But finding scientists who understood how to design a bomb was going to be a far greater challenge. He would need a certain kind of scientist to help him, a man who could comprehend the theoretical considerations but also lead the effort to convert theories into practical, deliverable weapons.

Groves set up his offices in the War Building in Washington in rooms 5120 and 5121. He preferred to keep his headquarters as small as possible, and during the war they never occupied more than seven rooms. His personal office was purely functional: a green carpet, two big desks, an oak conference table, a leather sofa, and two large safes for classified papers. Two outside doors were bolted shut as were the louvered shutters on one. The only entrance into a conference room was through an inner door in the room immediately outside Groves's office.

He also brought with him his secretary, Jean O'Leary, who had worked for him since the summer of 1941. Unlike all of her predecessors, she was not intimidated by Groves and met his sarcasm and barbs with her own. They quickly formed a close working relationship. Promising her that it would be a "very quiet and easy job," he put her at one of the two desks in his office. A widow raising a ten-year-old daughter, O'Leary quickly rose to be one of the general's most trusted aides. She was exceptionally well organized and ran the office with an efficiency and firm hand that earned her the nickname "Major O'Leary." The initials "JOL" on any memo meant business.[19] Groves trusted her implicitly. She had access to all the secret codes, correspondence, and reports and was the only one of his staff to attend meetings of the Military Policy Committee with him.

Groves was taking on far more responsibilities than had been entrusted to Colonel Marshall, whose Manhattan Engineer District was absorbed into Groves's portfolio of projects. Marshall was reassigned overseas the following year, and Nichols was named to succeed him. Groves was happy to have Nichols. The two of them had served in the same battalion in Nicaragua a dozen years earlier.

Within two days of his promotion, Groves personally persuaded the War Production Board to grant the Manhattan District an AAA priority rating and made a decision to locate the gaseous-diffusion plant at Oak Ridge, Tennessee—a decision that had stalled under Colonel Marshall for three months. Like Bush, he also began to consider centralizing the various research projects scattered around the country. His quick assessment was that coordination was haphazard and that precious time and resources were probably being duplicated and wasted. The idea of a central weapons laboratory suited him. It would provide better security and be easier for him to manage. But who could lead such an organization? The general had not yet met the man he thought could do the job.

Julius Robert Oppenheimer was born in New York City on April 22, 1904. He was named after his father but later called himself J. Robert Oppenheimer because he disliked the name Julius. Unlike his fellow New Yorker Leslie Groves, whose family had been established in America for many generations, Oppenheimer was of immigrant stock. His father came from Germany in 1888 and started a textile import business, and over the years he became quite wealthy. Robert's mother, the American-born Ella Friedman Oppenheimer, was a painter. Their home was eventually adorned with paintings by van Gogh, Renoir, Picasso, and Vuillard. In 1912, Julius and Ella had a second son, Frank, and moved to a roomy, expensive apartment that occupied the entire eleventh floor of a building on Riverside Drive.

If some children are loved by their parents, Robert was adored. Delighted, even awestruck, by their precocious son, his parents did whatever they could to nurture his intellect and feed his interests, which even at six or seven included mineralogy and chemistry. They sent him to the progressive Ethical Culture School, where he completed the third and fourth grades in one year and skipped much of the eighth. It was no surprise when he was accepted by Harvard University.

Robert's privileged childhood included trips to Europe and luxuries unavailable to most children, but there were disadvantages as well, especially for a young man so intellectually gifted. Making friends, learning boundaries, and developing the social skills necessary to move successfully into adolescence and then adulthood were among the fruits of a conventional childhood that were denied him. Even in his twenties, Oppenheimer displayed surprising immaturity in his relations with others, and he was given to fits of depression. The novelist and historian Paul Horgan, who met Oppenheimer in the early 1920s, saw that "Robert had bouts of melancholy, deep, deep depression as a youngster. He would seem to be incommunicado for a day or two at a time."[20] The depression lingered well past adolescence.

At Harvard, he excelled until he became ill with trench dysentery and his parents brought him home. As a further measure, Julius Oppenheimer engaged a man named Herbert Smith to take his son to New Mexico to recuperate in the high, clear air of the Pecos Mountains. This trip was the beginning of Oppenheimer's love affair with New Mexico.

Once recovered, he returned to Harvard, changing his major from chemistry to physics, and finished his undergraduate degree with honors.

He left for Europe to work on a doctorate, first at Cambridge University, where he was hopelessly incompetent in a laboratory, and then at the University of Göttingen in Germany, where he studied under Max Born. Along the way, his social immaturity displayed itself on a number of embarrassing occasions. He purportedly left a "poisoned apple" on a teacher's desk and on another occasion suffered something close to a nervous breakdown. Still, he completed his Ph.D. in 1927 at the age of twenty-three. The center of theoretical physics at the time was Europe and England, and Oppenheimer found himself in demand at universities in America and Europe. After fellowships at the California Institute of Technology and Harvard and further studies in Europe, he accepted a position at the University of California at Berkeley in 1929.

Before he could assume his teaching duties, however, he contracted a mild case of tuberculosis, so he returned to New Mexico to heal, this time taking his brother Frank with him. They rented a small ranch high in the Pecos Mountains near Cowles and spent their days hiking or riding horses. During one of these long rides across mountain chains he discovered Pajarito Plateau and a private boys school that occupied one end of it. Oppenheimer recovered after several weeks and returned to Berkeley to resume his career. His students adopted the nickname for their young professor that he had acquired in Europe, "Oppie," and it stuck. He grew to accept it, and soon even his colleagues were calling him by the nickname. Years later at Los Alamos, he was, to scientist and technician alike, simply Oppie.

Oppenheimer thrived both personally and professionally. In the fall of 1932, he wrote to Frank, "The work is fine: not fine in the fruits but in the doing. There are lots of eager students, and we are busy studying nuclei and neutrons and disintegrations; trying to make some peace between the inadequate theory and the absurd revolutionary experiments."[21] Decades later, Oppenheimer fondly recalled those productive years:

> Starting with a single graduate student in my first year at Berkeley, we gradually began to build up what was to become the

largest school in the country of graduate and postdoctoral study in theoretical physics, so that as time went on, we came to have between a dozen and 20 people learning and adding to quantum theory, nuclear physics, relativity and other modern physics. As the number of students increased, so in general did their quality; the men who worked with me during those years hold chairs in many of the great centers of physics in this country; they have made important contributions to science, and in many cases, to the atomic-energy project.[22]

Within a few years, his reputation was solidly established, and having studied under Oppenheimer became the highest recommendation for young theoretical physicists.[23] Hans Bethe, himself a respected physicist, captured Oppenheimer the teacher: "Probably the most important ingredient he brought to his teaching was his exquisite taste. He always knew what were the important problems, as shown by his choice of subjects.... [I]n one afternoon, [he and his students] might discuss quantum electrodynamics, cosmic rays, electron pair production, and nuclear physics."[24]

Oppenheimer and his friend and colleague Ernest Lawrence were both bachelors at Berkeley and much sought after for faculty parties. Oppenheimer's charm and wit always made him a welcome guest. The two men were physically different. Lawrence was tall—well over six feet—and blond, while Oppenheimer was an inch or two shorter, much thinner, with wispy, dark hair. Lawrence spoke confidently, in a tenor voice; Oppenheimer in a slightly deeper voice, but hesitantly. Despite their different temperaments they became good friends. They spent Thanksgivings together in Yosemite and rode horses on the weekends in the Berkeley hills.[25] Lawrence married in 1932 and subsequently named one of his two sons Robert. Both were intelligent, but Oppenheimer's intelligence was deeper, quicker, and more facile. Lawrence always appreciated his friend's brilliance and would be the man to bring Oppenheimer into the fast-growing fission movement.

Another friend and Berkeley colleague, Haakon Chevalier, described the Oppenheimer of the early 1930s as

> tall, thin and angular. His physique suggested both delicacy and strength, and in his movements grace combined with an occasional odd stiffness in gesture or posture. He always wore a gray suit and blue shirt, and old-fashioned round-toed black shoes, worn but well-polished. His favorite outfit was a blue work-shirt and a pair of faded, old blue jeans. His fine curly hair, which he let grow rather long, formed a misty halo on his head. He was an inveterate smoker. Much of the ritual of his movements was dictated by this addiction, and his long fingers were deeply stained with nicotine. His teeth were ravaged. But it was the structure of his face and its expressiveness that arrested attention, and they made one forget all the rest.[26]

But not everyone was taken with the brilliant and charming physicist, including Chevalier's wife, who found Oppenheimer "selfish and ruthless, for all his affability, charm and generosity. He was spoiled ... by his superior intelligence and his wealth." She predicted that he would get Chevalier into trouble, and as it turned out, she was right.[27] The "wealth" she referred to came from gifts of cash from his father and later from an inheritance of two hundred thousand dollars. Molly Lawrence, Ernest's wife, also saw a darker side of the man. She acknowledged his brilliance and charm but found him, at heart, "a poseur."[28]

Oppenheimer's mother died of leukemia in 1931 and his father from a heart attack six years later. Their deaths changed him, as did living in Berkeley, a cauldron of political and social unrest of the 1930s. Oppenheimer himself recalled,

> My friends, both in Pasadena and in Berkeley, were mostly faculty people, scientists, classicists, and artists. I studied and

read Sanskrit with Arthur Ryder. I read widely, mostly classics, novels, plays, and poetry; and I read something of other parts of science. I was not interested in and did not read about economics or politics. I was almost wholly divorced from the contemporary scene in this country. I never read a newspaper or a current magazine like *Time* or *Harper's*; I had no radio, no telephone; I learned of the stock market crash in the fall of 1929 only long after the events.... Beginning in 1936, my interests began to change.[29]

It was during the 1930s that Oppenheimer discovered politics and the larger world. At Berkeley especially he was drawn to the vibrant and voluble world of left-wing politics and causes. While he joined few organizations, he supported a great number with his time and money. He gave, for example, gifts of cash that rarely exceeded one hundred dollars to the Spanish Relief Committee. This was hardly unusual for both the time and place: a nation still struggling to recover from a terrible depression and a liberal campus alive with demonstrations, marches, and protests. He met a younger woman, Jean Tatlock, the daughter of a Berkeley professor, who stirred his consciousness of a world beyond physics and introduced him into the intense political atmosphere of the campus. Their relationship became serious, and at least twice they thought of themselves as engaged. Tatlock was attractive and socially adept, although she had a dark side, which some, like Oppenheimer's post-doctoral assistant Robert Serber, thought stemmed from being manic-depressive.[30] Tatlock's politics were of the far left, as Oppenheimer knew:

> She told me about her Communist Party membership; they were on again, off again affairs, and never seemed to provide for her what she was seeking. I do not believe that her interests were really political. She loved this country and its people and its life. She was, as it turned out, a friend of many fellow travelers

and Communists, with a number of whom I was later to become acquainted.[31]

Oppenheimer never joined the Communist Party, but within a year, he was involved with a number of leftist organizations and groups, including the American Committee for Democracy and Intellectual Freedom, the Western Council of the Consumers' Union, the Teachers' Union, and Friends of the Chinese People.[32]

In September 1936, Oppenheimer's brother Frank married a Canadian student at Berkeley, Jacquenette Quam, known as Jackie. Oppenheimer did not approve of Jackie, and tried to discourage the marriage. He was even more upset when he learned that both Frank and Jackie had joined the Communist Party within a few months of marrying. He blamed Jackie and thought Frank a "fool."[33]

By early 1940, Oppenheimer's relationship with Jean Tatlock had cooled, evolving into an off-and-on-again affair. That spring he met Katherine "Kitty" Puening at a garden party hosted by his friend Charles Lauritsen. Born in Germany in 1910, Kitty moved to America with her parents when she was two and grew up in Pittsburgh. Her first marriage, to a musician, was annulled after a few months, and in 1934 she married Joe Dallet. The son of a wealthy Long Island silk merchant, Dallet had dropped out of Dartmouth, joined the Communist Party, and was organizing steelworkers when Kitty met and married him. She subsequently joined the Communist Party herself. They separated after a few years but reunited briefly in Paris in June 1937. Dallet was on his way to Spain, where within the month he was killed in the civil war. Devastated, Kitty returned to the United States and resumed her college studies in biology at the University of Pennsylvania. There she renewed a friendship with Richard Harrison, a British physician. They married and moved to Los Angeles, where Harrison began interning at a Pasadena hospital.

Kitty was small and slender, with brown eyes and a wide mouth. She was pretty but not beautiful. Intelligent and witty, she could and did display great charm when she chose to, and men found her intriguing and attractive. As an adult, her friendships were almost always with men, and she related emotionally to few women.

Married less than a year to her third husband, Kitty met Oppenheimer in Berkeley and, according to her, "fell in love with Robert that day."[34] Oppenheimer was similarly attracted, and the relationship was, by all accounts, intense. They married on November 1, 1940, the day Kitty's Nevada divorce was final. Both the divorce and marriage were timely; their first child, a son named Peter, arrived seven months later.

The brief courtship and marriage stunned Oppenheimer's friends. Many expected that he and Jean Tatlock would work out their differences and eventually marry. Some of Oppenheimer's old friends viewed Kitty as "too flirtatious and manipulative." Even Oppenheimer himself later remarked that "there was among our friends much concern."[35]

But now married, the two began to pull away from their political friends—not all at once, but slowly, particularly as events unfolded overseas. The Nazi-Soviet Pact and the Russian invasions of Poland and Finland were particularly unsettling to Oppenheimer. Perhaps it was also his new wife and family or the accelerating developments in nuclear fission, scrutinized more closely by the government, or the combination of both, but Oppenheimer clearly sensed that the world was changing and his personal behavior had to change with it. Even his family had to fall in line. In the autumn of 1941 he asked his brother Frank if he and his wife were still members of the Party. Frank said no. Oppenheimer himself later described the moment he made the break. "I went to a big Spanish relief party the night before Pearl Harbor; and the next day, as we heard the news of the outbreak of war, I decided that I had had about enough of the Spanish cause, and that there were other and more pressing crises in the world."[36]

Oppenheimer was certainly aware of a growing distrust of left-wing causes within the university and off campus as well. Newspapers, for example, seemed less indulgent in their coverage of the left than even the year before. Oppenheimer also knew that the FBI was investigating everyone associated with some government-sponsored research projects. Lawrence, among others, made it clear to Oppenheimer that he had to cease his political activities and end certain associations. Oppenheimer agreed, writing to his friend, "I assure you there will be no further difficulties."[37] For the moment, at least, Lawrence was satisfied. And although he didn't yet know it, Oppenheimer would soon be introduced to the man who would change his life. A visit to Berkeley by Brigadier General Leslie Groves was not too far in the future.

Chapter Four

THE EXTRAORDINARY
PARTNERSHIP

R obert Oppenheimer became aware of Hahn's and Strassmann's
fission breakthrough at the end of 1938, long before Leslie Groves
began his search for a director of a secret laboratory. Like everyone
else, he was stunned by the development. "The U business is unbelievable,"
he wrote to a colleague in January 1939. "We first learned of it in the papers
... and have had a lot of reports since."[1] Oppenheimer corresponded with
a number of his friends on the subject and even undertook some theoretical studies on his own or with his students. He also witnessed the
resulting rush of experiments to further explore the fission process. His
colleagues, Lawrence among them, were receiving increasing financial
support from the federal government or private foundations. In March
1940, for example, Lawrence proposed building a new 184-inch cyclotron
with a 4,500-ton magnet at an estimated cost of more than 2.5 million
dollars, and the Rockefeller Foundation had already pledged the first million.

Much of this support was prompted by the war in Europe and the frightening prospect of the eventual involvement of the United States.

Oppenheimer lamented that many of his friends and colleagues were being drawn into defense-related research. He wrote to a friend in May 1941, "The situation in Berkeley & here in Pasadena is in some ways very gloomy.... [A]lmost all the men active in physics have been taken away for war work."[2] In September, Lawrence hinted at the findings of the MAUD report.

But it was a meeting in Schenectady, New York, a few months later that marked Oppenheimer's first real involvement in America's fission movement. Arthur Compton's committee on fission research was meeting for the last time, and Lawrence had asked Compton for permission to bring Oppenheimer along: "I have a great deal of confidence in Oppie, and I'm anxious to have the benefit of his judgment in our deliberation."[3] Lawrence recognized early on that Oppenheimer had much to offer the fission effort and wanted him involved as soon as possible.

In January 1942, at Lawrence's invitation, Oppenheimer and a small team of graduate students undertook a series of theoretical calculations of fast neutrons. They made enough progress to report to Lawrence that all further theoretical problems associated with a bomb could be solved with "a total of three experienced men and perhaps an equal number of younger ones."[4]

At the end of March, Lawrence wrote Conant, "One other matter I should like to bring to your attention is the desirability of asking Oppenheimer to serve as a member of S-1. I think he would be a tremendous asset in every way. He combines a penetrating insight of the theoretical aspects of the whole program with solid common sense, which sometimes in certain directions seems to be lacking, and I am sure that you and Dr. Bush would find him a useful adviser."[5]

Lawrence's intercession worked. In May 1942, Arthur Compton appointed Oppenheimer to replace Gregory Breit, a physicist at the University of Wisconsin, on the S-1 Committee. Breit had been serving as the coordinator of what S-1 was calling "fast-fission programs." These included overseeing a number of projects of varying ambition at universities, all studying the fission process. Breit had suddenly resigned, complaining of breaches in security: "Compton's project," as he called it, was riddled with scientists who deliberately flouted the need for secrecy. Among the worst offenders was Enrico Fermi.

Few of Breit's colleagues were upset. Abrasive by nature, he was a poor manager and had become obsessed with secrecy. Not only was Compton relieved—he had realized earlier that Breit needed to be replaced but hesitated to fire him—but he had come to believe that Oppenheimer was the man to replace him. Compton was struck by Oppenheimer's quick mind and ability to work with others. Although he did not have the prominence of Vannevar Bush or even Ernest Lawrence in 1942, he was well known among physicists and, because of his theoretical work on fission, also to a larger audience of scientists and policy makers. Everyone who knew him admired his remarkable intelligence and ability to synthesize complex problems. An old friend, Robert Edsall, spoke for many when he said that Oppenheimer possessed an "extraordinarily brilliant and rapidly moving and scintillating mind that was beyond the power of most of us to follow. He could reach and see intuitively things that most people would be able to follow only very slowly and hesitatingly, if at all."[6]

When Compton offered him Breit's position, Oppenheimer was doing fission research as a theoretician. He had spent a decade without any practical experience in the laboratory or workshop, and it was jokingly said of him that he hardly knew how to flip a light switch. While that particular jab wasn't fair, he did need help bridging the gap between his theoretical world and that of applied physics. Therefore, as a condition of accepting Compton's offer, Oppenheimer asked for the assistance of someone familiar with the current work in experimental physics. Compton agreed to assign him an applied physicist, John Manley, who was using the Cockcroft-Walton accelerator at the University of Chicago's newly created Metallurgical Laboratory.

Manley, however, told Compton that he had reservations about working with Oppenheimer. Several years earlier, Manley had heard Oppenheimer deliver a lecture, and although he had been impressed with the presentation, he had been put off by the man's detachment.[7] Compton asked him to meet with Oppenheimer. Manley did and changed his mind. The men became friends and a good working team.

Within weeks, the two met in Chicago and agreed that Oppenheimer would continue his theoretical work at Berkeley while Manley would take over the direction of several geographically scattered projects, including the work of John Williams at the University of Minnesota, of Joseph L. McKibben at the University of Wisconsin, and of Norman P. Heydenburg at the Carnegie Institute. This meant a lot of travel for Manley, but Oppenheimer also felt a responsibility to visit each project site, spending long hours in tedious travel during the next few months. Manley, with a family to care for, found the work fascinating but exhausting. The so-called fast fission projects were spread among universities in California, Texas, Illinois, Wisconsin, Minnesota, New Jersey, New York, and Washington, D.C.

Oppenheimer seized the chance during a break in his own travels to invite a small group of theoretical and experimental physicists to join him and a colleague, Robert Serber, for a joint meeting to assess the fission landscape. They met first in Chicago on June 5 and 6, 1942, and then in Berkeley in July. Serber had been a postdoctoral assistant under Oppenheimer for a few years but had moved on to join the physics faculty at the University of Illinois. In April, he was lured back to California. For the first full week of meetings, Oppenheimer secured the use of several attic rooms on the fourth floor of Berkeley's LeConte Hall. Security needs were met by covering each window with heavy steel mesh and fitting the door to the suite with a special key, which only Oppenheimer possessed. LeConte Hall was the home of the physics department and the site of the first cyclotron designed and built by Lawrence in 1930s. Oppenheimer's personal office was on the second floor, in Room 219.

The July meetings produced the consensus that few theoretical gaps were left in fast-neutron research, although no one was sure just how much fissionable material was necessary for a bomb. The best guess was that a ball of uranium some six inches in diameter and weighing about fifteen kilograms (thirty-three pounds) would be needed. Plutonium would require less—a two-inch ball weighing around 4.5 kilograms (ten pounds).[8] The discussions were promising enough for Oppenheimer to write to Manley that while there was a lot to do, he had hopes of getting some "exciting" questions settled while he still had a "galaxy of luminaries" available.[9] Teller was one of the participants, as were Emil Konopinski of Indiana University, Felix Bloch of Stanford, Van Vleck of Harvard, and Oppenheimer's former students Stanley Frankel and Eldred Nelson.

Hans Bethe was also invited. Born in Strasbourg, Germany, to a Protestant father and Jewish mother, Bethe demonstrated extraordinary versatility as a theoretical physicist. Dismissed from his teaching post at the University of Tübingen because of his Jewish mother, he left Germany for England in 1933 and for America in 1935. Bethe became an American citizen and by the war was working at the Radiation Laboratory at MIT. In 1939, he married the daughter of one of his physics professors in Stuttgart, Rose Ewald. One of the leading theoreticians of his time, he would receive the Nobel Prize in the 1960s for his explanation of the production of energy in stars. He was grandfatherly and slow speaking but at the same time brilliant and droll. Assessing his own position in physics in the United States in a letter to his mother, he wrote, "I am about the leading theoretician in America. That does not mean the best. [Eugene] Wigner is certainly better and Oppenheimer and Teller probably just as good. But I do more and talk more and that counts too."[10]

In the summer of 1942, Serber saw plutonium as the main challenge— "getting light element impurities low enough to keep the neutron background down and getting a high enough velocity gun to assemble larger masses."[11] The scientists assembled with Oppenheimer also discussed blast damage and made predictions from scaled-up data. In 1945, they proved to be surprisingly accurate. "We missed two things at Berkeley," Serber later remembered: "The fireball and consequent flashburns, but that was studied at Los Alamos during the first summer in 1943. The only surprise at Hiroshima and Nagasaki was the x-rays from the fission fragments in the fireball. That I don't think anyone thought of."[12] It was also clear that a weapon would require much larger amounts of fissionable materials than small university laboratories could produce. Since large-scale operations were needed, the four industrial options for producing uranium and plutonium under consideration by Groves's Manhattan Project were more important than ever.

The concept of implosion—using explosives to "compress" solid material—apparently came up during the conference. Richard Tolman seems to have mentioned the possibility first, although there is no official record of the idea. Tolman, however, did write to Oppenheimer in March 1943 suggesting that an ordinary explosion could "blow the shell of active material into the center. I think that would be an easy thing to do." Two days later, Tolman wrote to Groves with the same thought: "In the case of the mechanism on the deformation of a shell of active material ... it might be possible to bring this about by explosive charges which would blow fragments of the shell into the interior."[13]

The informal discussions also considered the chilling possibility that a larger, more powerful thermonuclear, or fusion, bomb could be produced with the heat from a uranium fission bomb. Teller and Fermi had first recognized this possibility earlier in the spring during a conversation over lunch at the faculty club at Columbia University. Teller had further discussed the idea with Bethe and Konopinski on the train from Chicago to Berkeley. That possibility was startling enough on its own, but there was also the prospect that a thermonuclear bomb could ignite the atmosphere. Teller raised the matter by asking if a fission bomb, which could ignite deuterium, might not also ignite the nitrogen in the atmosphere. His calculations suggested that a fission bomb igniting twelve kilograms (26.5 lbs.) of liquid heavy hydrogen would equal eighty-five thousand tons of

Leslie R. Groves (1896–1970). Intelligent, ambitious, and a gifted administrator, Groves was perhaps the perfect choice to lead the Manhattan Project. His abrasive personality didn't win him friends, but his ability to make difficult—and correct—decisions was crucial for the project's success. (Los Alamos National Laboratory)

J. Robert Oppenheimer (1904–1967). Brilliant, inspiring, and, like Groves, ambitious, Oppenheimer was America's preeminent theoretical physicist. Not yet forty when he became director of Los Alamos, he was an unexpected choice because he lacked administrative experience. Groves, however, valued his intelligence and ability to lead other scientists. (LANL)

General Groves and Jean O'Leary. Widowed and in her early thirties, O'Leary became Groves's secretary in June 1942. She refused to be intimidated by him and returned his barbs and sarcasm. They quickly developed a close and productive relationship. Known as Major O'Leary by Groves's staff, she knew almost as much about the Manhattan Project as her boss. (U.S. Army)

Robert Bacher (1909–1997). The scientist Oppenheimer believed most crucial to the success of the new laboratory and one of the few senior leaders with administrative experience. He helped convince Oppenheimer not to put scientists in uniform. In 1944, he took over the Gadget Division and played a major role in developing the implosion, or Fat Man, bomb. (LANL)

Norris Bradbury (1909–1997). Along with William Parsons and George Kistiakowsky, Bradbury was one of the few scientists at Los Alamos with experience in explosives. Self-assured and competent, he was given responsibility for the final assembly of Fat Man at Trinity. Groves appointed him director upon Oppenheimer's retirement. (LANL)

James B. Conant (1893–1978). President of Harvard and chairman of the National Defense Research Council, Conant was an advisor to Groves and a member of the Military Policy Committee that oversaw the Manhattan Project. Conant later said that he spent three-quarters of his government work during the war on the atomic bomb. (LANL)

Edward Teller (1908–2003). Brilliant but irascible, Teller was a Hungarian refugee from the Nazis. Invited to work at Los Alamos, Teller quickly lost interest in fission weapons and demanded to work on the thermonuclear, or hydrogen, bomb. It was said that he had a hundred ideas a day, but only one was good. (LANL)

Enrico Fermi (1901–1954). Winner of the 1939 Nobel Prize for Physics, Fermi was forced to flee Italy because of his Jewish wife. He produced the world's first sustaining chain reaction in a nuclear reactor under Columbia University's unused squash courts. Brilliant and intuitive, it was said of Fermi that he was "almost always right." (LANL)

Kenneth Bainbridge (1904–1996). One of the first arrivals at Los Alamos in 1943, Bainbridge was in charge of the experimental test of the implosion bomb. After the successful detonation of Fat Man, he said that his strongest reaction was relief that he would not have to climb the tower to see what had gone wrong with the bomb. (LANL)

Hans Bethe (1906–2005). A refugee from the Nazis and an extraordinarily versatile physicist, Bethe directed the Theoretical Division at Los Alamos. He was awarded the Nobel Prize for Physics in 1967. (LANL)

George Kistiakowsky (1900–1982). "Kisty" was one of several men at Los Alamos who had experience with explosives. The leader of X (Explosives) Division in 1944, Kistiakowsky was largely responsible for developing the implosion bomb's explosive lenses. (LANL)

USN Captain William "Deak" Parsons (1901–1953). Parsons was Groves's personal choice to oversee weapons development and serve as unofficial associate director. His work was eventually concentrated on the gun weapon, and he personally armed Little Boy on *Enola Gay*'s flight to Hiroshima. (LANL)

One hundred tons of high explosives were stacked on this twenty-foot wooden tower a few miles southeast of Ground Zero at Trinity and detonated on May 7, 1945. The explosion, heard sixty miles away, was used to calibrate instruments for the Fat Man test. (LANL)

Aerial photograph of the Los Alamos Laboratory's Technical Area. This photograph was taken in 1946, but with the exception of the white metal water tower (upper right), the buildings are essentially the same as in 1945. Two covered walkways connecting separate high-security areas are visible in the upper right quadrant of the photograph. Two-story apartment buildings can be seen in the upper left-hand corner. (LANL)

The hastily built Base Camp at Trinity, containing sleeping barracks, administrative offices, storage and meeting areas, and a cafeteria. The dark structures with the white peaked roofs (upper left) are sleeping tents set up for visitors such as Groves and Oppenheimer. This photograph was taken from a second windmill. (LANL)

Norris Bradbury with the implosion "gadget"—also known as Fat Man—atop the one-hundred-foot tower at Ground Zero. The cabin's corrugated metal sides were temporarily removed to aid air flow and the delivery. (LANL)

An early version of the implosion bomb. The large hemisphere in the center of the weapon is the aluminum pusher. The two rows of explosive lenses are visible in the upper right-hand corner. Later versions used a simpler design. (LANL)

TNT. Bethe didn't think so and even produced a study that suggested otherwise. Teller was adamant, however, and Oppenheimer took the prospect seriously enough to make an urgent trip to Compton to tell him the news. Bethe thought Oppenheimer's concern as well as his trip to be premature. His analysis suggested that at best no ignition would occur and at worst far more research was necessary. This was an early display of the differences between the excitable Teller and the cautious Bethe. Compton remembers Oppenheimer's visit to his vacation home in northern Michigan:

> I'll never forget that morning. I drove Oppenheimer from the railroad station down to the beach looking out over the peaceful lake. There I listened to his story. What his team [at Berkeley] had found was the possibility of nuclear fusion—the principle of the hydrogen bomb. This held what was at the time a tremendous unknown danger.... To set off such a reaction would require a very high temperature. But might not the enormously high temperature of an atomic bomb be just what was needed to explode hydrogen? And if hydrogen, what about the hydrogen of seawater? Might the explosion of an atomic bomb set off an explosion of the ocean itself?[14]

Compton's response was practical: he asked if such a weapon could be produced in time for use in the war, as did Bush when he was informed of Teller's concern. Oppenheimer told both men that it was not possible until a fission weapon was developed. That settled the matter for the time being. The fission bomb was the first and most important priority. It seemed sensible to allow Teller to continue his theoretical calculations on a superbomb, but America needed a fission bomb as soon as possible for use in the war.

Although there was tight security surrounding the meeting—locked doors, sealed windows, and a campus policeman downstairs—there was one minor and unintentional breach. Priscilla Green, a recent graduate from Berkeley, was on loan to Oppenheimer from Lawrence as a secretary. She knew from the correspondence she typed for Oppenheimer that the secret meetings were related to defense. But one day she found the door of the empty meeting rooms open and the blackboard covered with calculations and drawings. Cigarette smoke still lingered in the air. "Somebody had drawn a spherical shape and, from the various scribbles, well, it was obviously a bomb. So I knew then. I was glad to know what we were doing. Almost immediately after that, everyone started calling it 'the gadget.'"[15] She kept what she saw to herself.

The conference began to slow down after an intense week. Some people returned to their teaching posts, others left and returned as time permitted. The meetings ceased by the end of the summer. Oppenheimer was satisfied that most of the theoretical issues had been settled, but they still did not know precisely how much critical material was necessary for an explosion. He and Serber traveled to Chicago several times over the following months to meet with Bethe, Teller, and Konopinski, as well as with members of the Met Lab.

In September, in response to security concerns, Oppenheimer prepared a list of persons who had worked with him in the past few months and knew something of the work so far on the bomb. He sent three lists to Conant the following month. The first group knew the "whole story," the second group had performed "technical calculations which do in fact concern the military application [the bomb]," and the third group had conducted only mathematical computations and "have essentially no knowledge of what it is all about."[16] Oppenheimer, of course, knew the whole story, and he was beginning to experience the secret pleasure that comes from being an insider.

―――――――――――――

Although the Metallurgical Laboratory in Chicago was momentarily the center of bomb design, Groves and his Military Policy Committee came to believe that the fission projects scattered across several universities and laboratories must be collected in one location at some distance from a large city. Groves felt strongly that work needed to be compartmentalized for reasons of security as well as efficiency. He had already learned of leaks at the Met Lab, and shortly after the Berkeley summer conference, word had leaked out that work on a "superbomb" was underway. Bush argued that an open exchange of information—at least at the top level—was in large part responsible for the successes achieved so far. Bush himself was scrupulous—he kept many of his project leaders in the dark about work at other institutions—but he and Groves both had the advantage of coordinating information and projects from the top. He thought that a similar principle should be employed for bomb development.

Just as these concerns were being discussed, Groves made his first visit to the various fission projects on the West Coast and met Lawrence and Oppenheimer for the first time. After discussions with Lawrence, Groves became convinced that as many production alternatives as possible should be pursued, and he decided that Lawrence was the "ablest" of the directors he had met so far.

Oppenheimer recalls that he and Groves first met on October 8, at a party at the home of Berkeley's president, Robert Sproul.[17] The general was taken with the intelligent, articulate physicist. Oppenheimer's mind was like quicksilver, but it was his remarkable ability to explain complex concepts clearly and without condescension that most impressed Groves. His unambiguous answers to the general's questions were markedly different from what Groves experienced in Chicago. Not surprisingly, they discussed the idea of a secret, central laboratory where all fission projects could be conducted and coordinated. A few days later, Oppenheimer was asked to fly to Chicago to join Groves, Nichols, and Marshall on the train to New York, and they continued the conversation. Crammed into a compartment designed for a single person, the four men talked through the night on subjects that ranged from creating a special laboratory to whether scientists should serve as officers in the Corps of Engineers. Nichols was as impressed with the Oppenheimer as Groves was: "There remained no doubts in my mind that he should direct the new lab."[18]

Oppenheimer went on to Washington with Groves. They met again in the general's office at nine o'clock on the morning of October 10, and Bush joined them for a second meeting in the afternoon. The visit signified Oppenheimer's new status with Groves and his new authority as well. It was also Jean O'Leary's first glimpse of the cerebral scientist.

The three men talked about the concept of a new, secret laboratory. Oppenheimer argued strongly that "we needed a central laboratory devoted wholly to [work on the bomb], where people could talk freely with each other, where theoretical issues and experimental findings could affect each other, where the waste and frustration and error of the many compartmentalized experimental studies could be eliminated, where we could come to grips with chemical, metallurgical, engineering, and ordnance problems that had so far received no consideration."[19]

Oppenheimer was now Groves's leading candidate for director of the new laboratory, but he had several disadvantages. He had no administrative experience, and unlike Lawrence, Urey, and Compton, he had no Nobel Prize, so Groves asked for other suggestions. Compton initially favored Carl Anderson of Pasadena, a winner of the Nobel Prize in physics, but Anderson was unconvinced of the prospects for the atomic bomb and rejected a tentative offer. Lawrence was another choice. Groves favored him, but the vast electromagnetic plant at Oak Ridge needed his full attention for the next few years. Harold Urey was still another possibility, but Groves considered him a chemist and not a physicist. And Lawrence, acting on his own, offered the job to Edwin McMillan, a move that irritated Groves.

Several others were named, but one by one Groves rejected them.[20] It came down to Oppenheimer. His rapport with his colleagues, his solid performance as a replacement for Breit, and his leadership of the Berkeley summer conference convinced Groves that Oppenheimer was the right choice: "Outside the project there may have been other suitable people, but they were fully occupied on essential work, and none of those suggested appeared to be the equal of Oppenheimer."[21] Bethe didn't think Oppenheimer was the most obvious candidate. He had no experience directing a large organization, and much of the work would involve experimentation and engineering. Even Isidor Rabi, one of Oppenheimer's closest colleagues, found "it a most improbable appointment. I was astonished."[22]

Groves thought otherwise. Shortly after the war he told an interviewer about Oppenheimer, "He's a genius.... A real genius. While Lawrence is very bright he's not a genius, just a good hard worker. Why, Oppenheimer knows about everything. He can talk to you about anything you bring up. Well, not exactly. I guess there are a few things he doesn't know about. He doesn't know about sports."[23] Groves was captivated by the physicist. When Anne Wilson, a young secretary in Groves's Washington office, asked the general, somewhat inappropriately, what he thought of Oppenheimer, he said, after a lengthy pause, "He has the bluest eyes I've ever seen. He looks right through you. I feel like he can read my mind."[24]

Oppenheimer was hardly known to the members of Groves's Military Policy Committee except Bush. When the general put his name before them they were hesitant, so Groves asked them for other candidates. None was put forward, so he once again asked for Oppenheimer, and they approved.

Oppenheimer, who desperately wanted the job, accepted without hesitation. He had told his wife that he was "courting" Groves like a lover. He was almost forty and had published few important papers. In fact, he was better known as a co-author on papers written by his students. He doubted that he would ever win the Nobel Prize, and it was increasingly clear that his career had stalled. He had seen many of his colleagues leave their teaching posts to take important positions in war-related research projects such as radar. His career needed a boost, and the directorship of a new laboratory vital to the war could provide that. He had another, deeply personal reason—members of his family in Germany were victims of Nazi persecution. Since the late 1930s, Oppenheimer had used his own money to help family members escape to America. Leading the effort to construct a war-winning and world-changing weapon would be a way of fighting back.

It was abundantly clear to Groves that a special weapons laboratory would serve no practical purpose without an adequate supply of a fissionable material. At the end of October 1942, he, Conant, and Bush again reviewed the problem of separating uranium. Of the four methods, the centrifuge still seemed the weakest and Lawrence's electromagnetic process the most promising, although Groves had authorized a gaseous diffusion plant to be built in Tennessee. But what of plutonium? A nuclear reactor was the most direct and least expensive way to produce Pu239. Groves decided that if plutonium could be produced in sufficient quantity, the new element might be the key to the quicker delivery of a usable weapon. Recognizing the usefulness of a reactor was one thing; building it was another. Fermi's prototypical reactor was still under construction at the University of Chicago.

Conant and Bush agreed that such a pile might mean faster production, and they immediately began a search for an industrial corporation capable of building one. That fall, Groves and Conant met with representatives of the DuPont companies, their first choice to assist the Manhattan Project's major contractor, Stone and Webster, in the design and operation of an atomic pile. Only after three days of intense, internal considerations did DuPont come to believe that there was a reasonable chance it could deliver plutonium by late 1944. If the federal government covered all costs for construction, maintenance, staffing, and the like, DuPont would charge only one dollar in fees. It was their contribution to the war effort.

Groves gave Oppenheimer major responsibility for planning the new laboratory in November 1942, and Oppenheimer quickly brought his

Berkeley colleague Ed McMillan and the Chicago Met Lab's John Manley onto the project. Both men would play important roles in the early development of the laboratory. Three months later, in February 1943, Oppenheimer's position became formal with a letter from Groves and Conant.

But as soon as Groves appointed Oppenheimer, the man's political past provoked an intense and prolonged security investigation. Not only were his own political activities well documented, but his former girlfriend Jean Tatlock, his wife Kitty, and even his brother and sister-in-law all had been members of the Communist Party.[25] Arthur Compton came away from a frank exchange with Oppenheimer about his Communist associations persuaded that the man was only trying to learn about different political philosophies: "He felt that a responsible citizen ought to have reliable knowledge of this growing new movement."[26]

Despite Oppenheimer's troubling connections, Groves thought his loyalty was never in question. This unlikely assessment was yet another example of Groves's remarkable flexibility in order to get a job done. He ordered security investigations for all major Manhattan project participants as a matter of course, but Oppenheimer's clearance was held up for months while investigators pried into his past. He provided all the information requested and submitted to several long, probing interviews with the project's security officers. Many of his colleagues wrote letters of endorsement. In a memorandum "For Whom It May Concern," Lawrence wrote, "I have known Professor J. Robert Oppenheimer for fourteen years as a faculty colleague and close personal friend. I am glad to recommend him in highest terms as a man of great intellectual caliber and of fine character and personality. There can be no question of his integrity."[27]

Oppenheimer's lengthy investigation was conducted by Lieutenant Colonel Boris T. Pash, who took a particularly zealous interest in his subject's past. Pash had fought the Bolsheviks in Russia as a youth but escaped to America with his wife and child. He was a reserve officer in the army when he was recalled to duty in 1940 and served as a security officer in Los Alamos. Early in his examination, Pash decided that Oppenheimer was a security risk. Despite the lack of evidence of disloyalty, he wrote to Lieutenant Colonel John Lansdale Jr., the director of G-2 (intelligence and security) for the Manhattan Project.[28] Lansdale was not unsympathetic to Pash's anti-Communist stance, but he did not believe that Oppenheimer was the risk that Pash made him out to be. A series of conflicting reports made their way to Groves, who, as he would later say, found "much" that was not to his liking but nothing that clearly established the man as a security risk. Oppenheimer had been de facto director for half a year and was doing an exceptional job, and there was no other candidate for the directorship. In July 1943, Groves finally issued the following order to the security office of G-2:

> In accordance with my verbal directions of July 15, it is desired that clearance be issued for the employment of Julius Robert Oppenheimer without delay, irrespective of the information which you have concerning Mr. Oppenheimer. He is absolutely essential to the Project.[29]

Pash was subsequently removed from the investigation and placed in charge of a secret program to gather intelligence on German atomic bomb activity.

The order by Groves to clear Oppenheimer did not end the scrutiny. FBI and Manhattan Project security agents continued their investigations, spurred on at least in part by two incidents that would haunt Oppenheimer long after the end of the war.

The first incident took place early in 1943. Shortly before moving to Los Alamos, Robert and Kitty Oppenheimer invited his university colleague Haakon Chevalier and his wife, Barbara, to dinner at their Eagle Hill home. At some point Oppenheimer went into the kitchen, perhaps to make another round of his famous martinis, and Chevalier joined him moments later. He told Oppenheimer about a conversation he had had with George Eltenton, a British scientist working with Shell Oil in Berkeley who was known to both of them. Eltenton apparently offered to pass along any technical or scientific information to the Soviets and, according to Chevalier, suggested that Oppenheimer be approached with this opportunity. Oppenheimer immediately rejected the idea and no more was said.

That might have been the end of the matter, except that on August 23, 1943, Oppenheimer chose to visit with Manhattan Project security officials while on a recruiting trip to Berkeley. Meeting on campus, Oppenheimer mentioned that the officials might want to investigate Eltenton. This news necessitated a second meeting the next day, this time with Pash participating. During the conversation, which was recorded without Oppenheimer's knowledge, Oppenheimer revealed that there was a man in the Soviet consulate who could pass scientific information back to Russia and added that "approaches" had been made to other people Oppenheimer knew. When pressed by Pash for their names, Oppenheimer declined on the basis that he did not want to jeopardize innocent people. Inexplicably, however, Oppenheimer then added that he was aware of "two or three" cases in which other scientists had been approached not by Eltenton but by another party. An alarmed Pash, under the impression that as many as three people had been contacted by an unnamed intermediary, immediately reported the interview back to Washington.

The matter of the mysterious contact was raised again during a train trip with Groves and Lansdale. Oppenheimer again declined to name the person but said he would do so if Groves ordered him. Groves did not press the issue at that time. On December 12, 1944, however, Groves asked Oppenheimer to drive with him—alone—from Los Alamos to Albuquerque. During the winding trip Groves ordered his director to reveal the contact, and Oppenheimer told him it was Chevalier. Unfortunately, Oppenheimer failed to clear up the mistaken impression he had left with Pash that three men had been approached.

At the time, Groves wasn't unduly concerned. In fact, both he and Lansdale assumed that Oppenheimer was covering for his brother Frank. "It was always my impression," Groves later testified, "that [Oppenheimer] wanted to protect his brother, and that his brother might be involved in having been in this chain, and that his brother didn't behave quite as he should have.... He always felt a natural loyalty to him." The reluctance to name names was the "typical American schoolboy attitude about telling on your friends."[30]

The second incident occurred later in 1943 during another trip to Berkeley. In June, Oppenheimer received word that his former girlfriend, Jean Tatlock, wanted to see him. She was severely depressed, and he felt an obligation to meet with her. Although he knew he was being shadowed by security men, he nonetheless took a cab to her apartment on Montgomery Street and spent the night there. The agents who trailed him parked outside the apartment through the night and reported the incident back to Washington. Once again, Groves did nothing, even if he found the episode personally distasteful. Oppenheimer's behavior, however, encouraged the suspicion of Pash and others that he was not only a security risk but perhaps a Soviet agent.

A few months later, in January 1944, Tatlock committed suicide. She left a note saying, "I wanted to live and to give but I got paralyzed somehow."[31] Between his ever increasing duties and his marriage to Kitty, Oppenheimer could express nothing publicly. He kept his grief to himself.

At the end of November, Groves, Bush, and Conant learned that Fermi was nearly ready to put his latest uranium pile into operation at the University of Chicago.

Enrico Fermi was one of the leading figures in physics in the decade before the war. Originally interested in mathematics, he gravitated to physics and made important contributions to quantum theory and nuclear and particle physics. He was at the Sapienza University of Rome when he received the Nobel Prize for his work on induced radioactivity in 1938. Although he had earlier joined the Fascist Party, his wife, Laura, was Jewish, and growing anti-Semitism drove him from Italy that same year. He came to the United States, like so many other European refugees, and accepted a position at Columbia University.

On the evening of December 1, 1942, Fermi and his helpers completed the assembly of nearly four hundred tons of graphite, six tons of uranium metal, and fifty tons of enriched uranium oxide into a large cube. The team had taken possession of Stagg Field, the University of Chicago's unused squash courts in an abandoned stadium on the city's South Side. The enriched oxide was uranium ore that had been processed to remove as many impurities as possible and then prepared in metal form. Since early November, the team had been laboriously making graphite blocks, pressing the uranium into small pellets, and arranging both into a large block-like structure of alternating graphite blocks and uranium of differing concentrations. The men assembling the pile were covered in a black dust from head to foot. A large cloth balloon had been prepared to enclose the entire pile, but it was not used.

Shortly after four o'clock p.m., the last layer of graphite and uranium bricks was put down and measurements were made. Penetrating the pile were three sets of cadmium control rods. These long tubes absorbed the neutrons and made a chain reaction impossible. Fermi was convinced that when the rods were removed a reaction would take place.

At 8:30 the next morning, Fermi, his staff, and invited guests gathered for the first test of a nuclear pile. Fermi, Columbia University physicist Walter Zinn, and Arthur Compton arranged themselves around a panel of instruments at the east end of a small balcony at the north end of the courts. Several of the manual control rods were placed so that they could be dropped if the pile became too radioactively hot. A few staff members were prepared in an emergency to flood the pile with a liquid solution of cadmium salts to retard the exchange of neutrons.

At 9:45 Fermi ordered the cadmium rods withdrawn, one by one. Fifteen minutes later the emergency rod was withdrawn. During the next hour the final rod was withdrawn by stages. At each stage Fermi accurately predicted the neutron intensity as measured by dials and by a recording instrument. Shortly after 11:30, the automated safety rod suddenly dropped into the pile and shut it down. It took several minutes for the startled audience to realize that someone had set the safety level too low, triggering the shutdown.

Everyone broke for lunch and returned to watch Zinn slowly extract the last rod. With all eyes straining to watch the dials, the drama continued until the late afternoon. Then Fermi suddenly broke into a smile and announced that the reaction was self-sustaining. The time was 3:53 p.m. Man had just produced the first controlled nuclear chain reaction.

While Fermi and the others celebrated the achievement with a bottle of Italian Chianti, Compton telephoned Conant at Harvard. "You'll be interested to know that the Italian Navigator has landed in the New World." Asked how the natives were, Compton replied, "Very friendly."[32]

———

Developments in all quarters were accelerating. In the middle of November 1942 word arrived from Chadwick in England that plutonium appeared more likely to produce spontaneous fission—the unpredictable emission of neutrons—than uranium. This news meant that a bomb would need plutonium of a higher purity than the researchers had thought. At the end of November, Oppenheimer, Manley, Serber, and Teller authored a reappraisal of what was known about atomic bombs and shared it with Groves, Bush, Conant, and others. Using a code in which the material 23 referred to U233, 25 to U235, and 49 to Pu239, they reported three main findings:

A. According to present data there is strong reason to believe that any one of the known possible materials, 23, 25, 49, will produce the same energy per gram as any other.

B. The minimum amount of material required probably differs, however. Our present tentative results suggest that 2 to 3 times less 49 will be needed than 25; of 23 even somewhat smaller amounts may be sufficient. The exact amount is uncertain because of the uncertainty of experimental data on fission and total cross-sections.

C. The most frequently considered method of detonation is to shoot together with high velocity ... two subcritical masses. The success of this method depends on a sufficiently low neutron background.... [T]his in turn requires that the 49 be purified to a very high degree of certain light elements.[33]

The Military Policy Committee welcomed the report and conducted its own project-wide review before sending its findings to Roosevelt on December 16, 1942. The report contained what members now believed were reasonable predictions of delivery dates for weapons. The chance of having a weapon by June 1944 was small, somewhat better by January 1945, and good by mid-1945.[34] The president approved the committee's request for additional funding quickly, on December 28. But even before receiving approval, Groves authorized contracts with American corporations for nearly half a billion dollars, and Bush approved the final transfer to the army of all contracts covering nuclear research held by OSRD and NDRC.

Conant, mindful of the very real possibility that the Germans were ahead of the Americans in atomic developments, wrote to Groves with a sense of urgency:

It is quite possible that the Germans are a year ahead of us, or perhaps have even eighteen months head start.... I would judge there was an even chance that the Germans would produce a number of effective bombs by the middle of 1945 and a slight chance (perhaps 1 in 10) of their achieving the same result by the summer of 1944.... To my mind, it is this fear that the Germans may be near the goal which is the prime reason for an all out effort now on this gamble. This being so, it is clear that nothing short of a full-speed, all-out attempt would be worthwhile.[35]

Essential to this "full-speed, all-out" effort was the partnership emerging between Leslie Groves and Robert Oppenheimer. Groves, for all of his experience in construction, budgeting, and negotiating army politics, was an engineer charged with the enormous task of delivering atomic weapons to be used in the war against Germany and Japan. He had the expertise and skills necessary for the construction and management of giant industrial plants to deliver uranium and plutonium but not for the construction of the bombs themselves. That was a scientific and technological task beyond him. He needed a scientist to lead that effort, and he found the right man in Oppenheimer, who was more than willing to leave his ivory tower to work under an army general. Groves also keenly sensed the man's "overweening ambition" and gave him an extraordinary opportunity impossible in any circumstances except war. The general viewed the relationship pragmatically:

> Dr. Oppenheimer was used by me as my advisor ... not to tell me what to do, but to confirm my opinion. I think it is important for an understanding of the situation as it existed during the war to realize that when I made scientific decisions ... that outside of knowing all the theories of nuclear physics, which I did not, nobody else knew anything either.... So Dr. Oppenheimer was used in many ways as a chief scientific advisor on many problems which were within his bailiwick.[36]

Groves intended to manage the new laboratory himself—it was that important to him. Colonel Nichols remembers that "in the case of Los Alamos, Groves made it clear that he personally would do all the direct supervision of the work."[37] As Groves himself said, "Due to the magnitude of the District I retained personal direction of the Los Alamos bomb laboratory and took personal charge of the development of the weapon from the point where fissionable materials were supplied through and including the military operation."[38]

In his personal supervision of the Manhattan Project, with his high standards and expectations, Groves was often heavy-handed, rude, and even brutish with his subordinates—but not with Oppenheimer. Their collaboration was marked by a cautious respect and a shared commitment to success, and each man knew that the other was totally committed to developing a weapon of war. "That combination made the thing work," explained Rabi.[39] Their ambitions and need for one another brought these very different men together, united them, and sealed what would become an extraordinary partnership.

Chapter Five

A MILITARY
NECESSITY

By mid-November in New Mexico the autumnal gold is gone; high in the Jemez Mountains, the bright yellow aspens have faded as have the buttery leaves of the cottonwoods in the valleys. Everywhere there are only leafless trees waiting for the first heavy snow to turn their world white.

A light, gentle snow was falling when Groves, Oppenheimer, and three companions made their way up Highway 4 to the Los Alamos plateau on November 16, 1942. They stopped short of the complex of buildings that constituted the Los Alamos Ranch School, the center of which was the two-story wood and stone building called Fuller Lodge. Even as it snowed some boys were outside in their regulation year-round shorts pitching balls in a field. Oppenheimer had been to New Mexico many times as a youth, crisscrossing the Jemez Mountains on horseback and occasionally finding himself on this mesa, where the young sons of wealthy parents were taught Latin and Greek as well as how to handle a horse.

Their car displayed no military markings except for a government license plate, and the men wore civilian clothes. Accompanying Groves and Oppenheimer were Edwin McMillan, a colleague of Oppenheimer's from Berkeley (and Ernest Lawrence's brother-in-law), Lieutenant Colonel William Dudley, and the driver, an enlisted man stationed in Albuquerque with the Army Corps of Engineers. Conversation centered on the suitability of the geography for a proposed highly secretive army installation. Oppenheimer had suggested the location several weeks earlier.

Los Alamos had a long and colorful history. The landscape had been forged in volcanic fire and violence millions of years before. The Jemez Mountains rimmed a giant eye-shaped caldera. This ancient lake slowly wore away part of the rim to form the Jemez River gorge. Pajarito Plateau, created by several large ash flows five million years ago, resembles an outstretched hand, each finger a mesa. Between the mesas are canyons two hundred to four hundred feet deep, with precipitous multicolored cliffs eroded from the volcanic tuff. The mesas rise gently to the west, where they abut the Sierra de los Valles. The western edge of Pajarito Plateau is over eight thousand feet above sea level, and the peaks of the Jemez Mountains rise another two thousand feet.

Although men arrived there as early as ten thousand years ago, Pajarito Plateau was probably settled in the thirteenth century by Indians. Within a hundred years or so, they moved to lower elevations and built the larger nearby settlements of Tshirege, Otowi, and Navawi. The Spanish found all these sites abandoned and in ruins when they arrived in the sixteenth century.

In the early twentieth century, the plateau was occupied mostly by homesteaders, the exception being a private school for boys founded in 1916 by Ashley Pond. Originally from Detroit, Pond had visited New Mexico to recuperate from a nearly fatal case of typhoid picked up while serving with Theodore Roosevelt's Rough Riders in Florida. Like so many others, Pond was captivated by New Mexico. He envisioned a school where boys from the harsh climates of the East could enjoy the advantages of an outdoor life without sacrificing a superior education. Drawing its head-master and teachers from the Ivy League, the school eventually offered a sophisticated program of academics, athletics, horsemanship, and camp-ing.[1]

Despite the high tuition of $2,400 a year—a huge sum during the Depression—the school was at its peak enrollment of forty-five students plus faculty and their families in the late 1930s. World War II first threat-ened the school's success when young teachers were drafted and could not easily be replaced, and its prospects darkened further as the pool of pro-spective students dwindled. The students and faculty watching the low-flying airplanes making repeated passes over the school in late October 1942 did not realize that the flights heralded the end of the school itself.

———————————

General Groves was not impressed with the scenery or the history as he surveyed the location. He wondered how much labor and money would be needed to convert this mountainous landscape into a military post housing a scientific laboratory. Would it be possible to quarter scientists and their families here? Could the development of an atomic weapon be kept secret from nearby communities? Groves felt great pressure to get the laboratory functioning quickly. The United States had entered the war almost a year before, and now in November the situation on all fronts was critical. German troops were deep in Russia resisting the renewed Soviet attack on the Stalingrad front. Allied Expeditionary Forces had just landed in French North Africa, U.S. Marines in the Pacific had recaptured Gua-dalcanal at a terrible cost, and American naval forces were preparing for a decisive battle in the Solomon Islands.

Groves and Oppenheimer had established criteria for a laboratory site some weeks before and were now about to make a decision. Groves felt that the most important requirement was isolation. Security leaks at the University of Chicago's uranium project had convinced him of the need for tight control. The two men were looking for other things as well. In addition to isolation, the prospective site needed adequate space for laboratory buildings and for testing. No one thought that an actual bomb test would be conducted near any laboratory, so ample rather than unlimited space would suffice. A favorable climate, as well as access by road and railway, would also be necessary. Construction materials, water, and power had to be readily available. Groves also wanted the laboratory to be some distance from civilian populations. He didn't want scientists, whom he regarded as undisciplined, to be tempted by the attractions of nearby cities. And the site should be far enough from the East and West coasts to deter enemy attack.

At first, Oppenheimer thought a location near the plant in Oak Ridge was a possibility, or perhaps in Cincinnati. Groves rejected Tennessee because he feared that concentrating too much Manhattan Project activity in one location would increase the danger of sabotage. Cincinnati was also rejected.

Colonel Dudley had conducted much of the early scouting, traveling widely throughout the Southwest in the previous weeks. His first choice was Oak City, Utah, but building a laboratory in what he called an "oasis" would require evicting a number of families and destroying productive farmland. Two locations in California had been considered and also eliminated. The first, in San Bernardino, lacked suitable laboratory and living facilities, and Groves also thought it was too close to Los Angeles. The second option lay to the east of the Sierra Nevada Mountains near Reno, where heavy snows could inhibit work during the winter.

Dudley then narrowed his search to several locations in New Mexico. The federal government owned large sections of the state that fulfilled the requirements of isolation and distance from the coast. Albuquerque was a major rail center, and its airport had one of the newest and longest runways in the country. The search came down to five New Mexico towns: Gallup, Las Vegas, La Ventana, Jemez Springs, and Los Alamos. Groves rejected the first three before leaving Washington because his representatives in

New Mexico reported that building space was extremely limited. That left Jemez Springs and Los Alamos. Groves wanted to see the locations for himself and agreed to meet Oppenheimer and McMillan in Albuquerque and drive north.

Oppenheimer strongly favored Los Alamos and had promoted the site at a meeting in Berkeley in early November with Groves and Dudley. Their reaction was favorable enough for Oppenheimer to write to John Manley, "Dudley and Groves were here and the question of the site is well along toward settlement. [Los Alamos] is a lovely spot and in every way satisfactory, and the only points which now have to be settled are whether the human and legal aspects of the necessary evacuations make insuperable difficulties. Ed [McMillan] and I plan to go down and have a look next week."[2]

Groves and his companions first visited Jemez Springs, but as they discovered, it was a long, thin valley dramatically hemmed in on three sides by cliffs. Existing buildings left much to be desired, and even though the laboratory population was projected to be small, Groves could see at once that perhaps 70 percent of the housing needed would have to be constructed. Worse, an army study ordered earlier by Groves had revealed that the entire valley was subject to flooding. Groves, Oppenheimer, McMillan, and Dudley all agreed that the site was unacceptable. McMillan remembered the general's reaction and the decision to move on to Los Alamos: "As soon as he saw the site he didn't like it; he said, 'This will never do.'"[3] Oppenheimer then reminded him that Los Alamos was not far away. Everyone got back in the car and headed for the mesa, stopping along the way to eat a few sandwiches.[4]

From the reports compiled by the Army Corps of Engineers, Groves knew that Los Alamos, at least on paper, generally met all the preliminary criteria he and Oppenheimer had set. Isolated high on a mesa, Los Alamos could be reached by only one road, so access could be controlled easily. A preliminary count of school buildings had suggested that at least some of the required physical facilities already existed. And it appeared from the survey report that, at least for the moment, there was an adequate supply of both water and electrical power.

Groves's own observations at Los Alamos confirmed these reports. From the car he noted several large buildings and a number of small houses. He was pleased to learn that nearly forty-seven thousand of the estimated fifty-four thousand acres of land required were already owned by the government. The private land was used primarily for cattle grazing, and Groves knew that this kind of land generally had a lower purchase price than cropland. The openness of the plateau provided what then seemed to be more than adequate room for expansion and safe spacing of buildings. There were two difficulties: the road into Los Alamos was rough and dangerous and would not sustain heavy traffic, and water was limited. These problems could be solved, however. The road could be rebuilt, and conservation could probably take care of the limited water supply.[5]

Groves decided that day to locate the special weapons laboratory in Los Alamos. The group returned to Albuquerque, and Groves flew back to Washington to request formal approval through the secretary of the interior and the War Department. In less than a week, after a brief trip to Washington, Oppenheimer returned to Los Alamos with McMillan and Ernest Lawrence. They walked the property and inspected all the main buildings as well as the small cluster of residential bungalows. Although they used aliases, one clever student named Sterling Colgate, heir to the Colgate toothpaste fortune, recognized Oppenheimer and Lawrence from photographs he had seen in science textbooks and magazines.

The government moved quickly to acquire nine thousand acres of privately owned land on the mesa. To avoid the lengthy legal complications of normal land proceedings, War Department lawyers seized the private acreage using special procedures that removed title defects in acquiring private land. There was surprisingly little resistance to the seizure; only two families on the mesa objected to the cash settlement offered by the government. A government clerk's discovery that the designated land included an ancient, sacred Indian burial ground within Bandelier National

Monument occasioned a brief delay, but the Bandelier land was eventually excluded from the acquisition. The government acquired right of entry on November 23, 1942, but agreed to let the school to operate until February 8, 1943. The land acquisition was completed in March 1943, when Secretary of War Henry Stimson requested transfer of the government-owned land on the mesa from the United States Forest Service to the Department of War. In his request, he stated that "there is a military necessity for the acquisition of approximately 54,000 acres of land for the establishment of a demolition range."[6]

The director of the Los Alamos Ranch School, A. J. Connell, was saddened when the government sent word that his school and the mesa would be needed for a wartime installation. His board of directors, however, were not. Enrollment was falling, and there was little prospect of improvement with the war underway. The government's purchase of the land would allow the school to sell its assets and move to a more convenient and less expensive facility, perhaps in nearby Taos. Connell demanded and received in December a personal letter from Stimson stating that the prosecution of the war necessitated the appropriation of the school and accompanying land. Connell read Stimson's letter to a special meeting of all the students and faculty in the school's largest academic building, the Big House. He posted Stimson's letter where everyone could read it for himself and sent copies to the students' parents.

Classes were accelerated, and arrangements were made for most students to attend other schools. As much as possible of the year's remaining work was compressed into the two months that the government gave the school to wrap up its affairs at Los Alamos. Seniors graduated in February and went on to college.[7] Oppenheimer himself, standing in front of the huge fireplace in the Big House, addressed the graduating class.

Classes ended and the school closed on schedule in February. Peggy Pond Church, whose father had founded the school and whose husband taught there, was shocked as the army arrived in force, its bulldozers throwing the formerly quiet mesa into chaos. "Civilian visitors were conducted on tours of inspection everywhere, even through our homes.... I was introduced to a young looking man by the name of Oppenheimer. Cowboy boots and all, he hurried in the front door and out the back, peering quickly into the kitchen and bedrooms. I was impressed, even in that brief meeting, by his nervous energy and by the intensity of the blue eyes that seemed to take in everything at a glance, like a bird flying from branch to branch in a deep forest."[8]

A new chapter in the history of Pajarito Plateau, one never anticipated by any of its previous occupants, was about to begin.

Chapter Six

LARGE-SCALE EXPERIMENTS

———————◦———————

J ohn Manley, one of the first arrivals at Los Alamos in early 1943, wryly
described the new laboratory as a ship that was sailing even as it was
being built. The destination was known, even if the route there was
not.[1]

There was a great deal of activity, however. Both Groves and Oppenheimer moved quickly to get the laboratory going, Groves acquiring the
land and beginning construction, Oppenheimer organizing the project
and recruiting staff.

Groves acquired fifty-four thousand acres of land in just weeks at the
cost of only $415,000, very likely one of his smaller expenditures. He then
established a military post in Los Alamos with a contingent of 254 officers
and enlisted men, 190 of them assigned to the new post as military police.
He was determined not only to secure his new project but also to send a
clear message to all who came there that this was a military installation.
He then put the construction of buildings, roads, and other infrastructure

under the charge of the army's Albuquerque Engineering District, a unit of the Army Corps of Engineers and not part of the Manhattan Project. The Los Alamos operation was to be formally called Project Y.

Organizing his new laboratory was a challenge for Oppenheimer. When he discussed it with John Manley in the fall of 1942, Oppenheimer promised to draw up a broad organizational scheme, indicating major groups or divisions, how they would be structured, and who would report to whom. Groves wanted to see a plan as well. After several months and multiple requests, however, Manley had received nothing. "I started needling him about the assignment of responsibilities. Here we had a new laboratory coming along; who would look after the procurement, the stock room, the personnel, how would the parts of the project and so forth, be arranged. It wasn't until February when I walked into his office on the top floor of La Conte Hall in Berkeley, quite bedraggled and groggy after a DC-3 flight from Chicago in the wintertime, that he threw some sheets of paper at me and said, 'Here's your damned organization chart.'"[2]

An organizational chart was one thing, but Oppenheimer also needed to create a program of research and development, a list of priorities, even work assignments for those scientists who would soon be arriving in Los Alamos. Robert Wilson, who was coming to the laboratory from Princeton with a cyclotron and several men, visited Los Alamos in early March 1943. The foundation for the building to house his cyclotron had not been laid, and even more disturbing, no one he talked to had any idea of what the research program was going to be like. Wilson flew on to Berkeley, where he joined Manley for a meeting in Oppenheimer's office. The two men complained about the lack of planning and aggressively pushed for decisions. Oppenheimer listened patiently while an embarrassed Priscilla Green took notes. Later that evening Wilson and Manley joined Oppenheimer at a dinner party at his house on Eagle Hill. As Wilson remembered it, the evening consisted of "the driest of dry martinis mixed by the hand of the master, sophisticated guests, gourmet food (but on the scant side) and an amorphous buzz of conversation, smoke, alcohol . . . the inevitable ingredients of an evening at the Oppenheimers." Once again, the two men confronted Oppenheimer with their complaints, but this time, Oppenheimer reacted angrily. "He exploded in a fit of cursing, acrimony and hysteria that left me aghast. I departed, fearing that the end of my relationship to the project had come, that all was lost. It wasn't."[3] Oppenheimer later apologized, but Wilson never forgot the incident.

The new laboratory needed the administrative expertise of an institution that could provide accounting, purchasing, and other such services, just as the Met Lab, for example, was managed by the University of Chicago. Both Groves and Oppenheimer believed that the University of California was the best choice for Los Alamos. The arrangement took shape in a preliminary agreement of January 1, 1943, and was finalized on April 20. Oppenheimer's former employer assumed the responsibility—with "the utmost dispatch"—for the conduct of "certain studies and experimental investigations at a Laboratory located at a site which has [been] or will be informally made known to the Contractor."[4]

Oppenheimer had compiled a primary list of people he wanted at Los Alamos, but he knew that considerable recruiting was still to be done and that it would not be easy. "The prospect of coming to Los Alamos aroused great misgivings. It was to be a military post; men were asked to sign up more or less for the duration [of the war]; restrictions on travel and on the freedom of families to move about would be severe."[5] To overcome these objections, he had to frame the invitation as both a great scientific adventure and an act of patriotism.

Groves believed that one of Oppenheimer's strongest talents was communicating and working with his scientific colleagues. At a meeting in Chicago in September 1942, Oppenheimer, Manley, Fermi, McMillan, and Lawrence gathered to look more closely at the projected laboratory. Their first conclusion was that the organization would consist of six theoretical physicists with six assistants, twelve experimentalists, fourteen assistants, and five secretaries.[6] These projections were soon heavily revised. They expanded their estimates to a laboratory with one hundred scientists. Although Groves had originally discouraged families, Oppenheimer argued that staff would be hard to recruit if families could not be brought along.

But just a month after the September meeting, a frustrated Oppenheimer wrote to Manley from his offices in Berkeley, "I did see General Groves when he was here and we discussed the problem of the laboratory rather fully, and by this means managed to undo such certainty as had before been reached."[7] The new director was beginning to learn that the general had his own ideas about how the new organization was to be structured and operated. And one of those ideas almost derailed the operation from the start.

Groves wanted all Los Alamos scientists to be in uniform. Perhaps he had the Met Lab in mind, but from his perspective, militarization would provide discipline and a measure of control over unruly and talkative scientists. This was not an unreasonable position—the nation was at war, and many of the prospective employees of the laboratory were of draft age and would soon be in uniform anyway. In fact, over sixteen million men and women would serve in uniform by war's end. In this, Groves had support from Conant, who said he had no objections and cited his own experience in military laboratories during World War I.

The preliminary plans called for Oppenheimer to be made a lieutenant colonel, and all division leaders were to be majors. Oppenheimer did not object, and his early acceptance of the proposal no doubt endeared him to Groves: "I would have been glad to be an officer. . . . I thought maybe the others would."[8] He met with officials at the Presidio, the army base on the northern tip of the San Francisco Peninsula, and underwent a complete physical by army doctors, which he failed. Groves ordered the examining physician to pass him anyway.[9] But some of the scientists important to the proposed laboratory objected fervidly, especially Isidor Rabi and Robert

Bacher, well-known scientists whom Oppenheimer was eager to have join him. Oppenheimer tried to convince the scientists to acquiesce, but after a meeting in Washington, D.C., at the end of January 1943, Rabi, Bacher, McMillan, and Luis Alvarez all rejected the idea, and Rabi even threatened to stop helping to recruit. Oppenheimer was forced to give in, and he passed along to Groves his colleagues' concerns, the chief one being that open decision-making would be difficult if scientists and technicians were working together as officers and enlisted men. A rigid military organization, the scientists argued, would be inimical to the free exchange of ideas. How, for example, would an army officer admit to being wrong or change a decision? Recruitment would also suffer.

Oppenheimer wrote Conant an urgent letter on February 1, now making the case against militarization:

> [T]he arguments here were first that a divided personnel would inevitably lead to friction, and to a collapse of Laboratory morale, complicated in our case by social cleavage, and, more important, that in any issue in which we were instructed by our military superiors, the whole Laboratory would be forced to follow their instructions and thus in effect lost its scientific autonomy.[10]

He hoped that Conant would broker a deal with Groves and permit the laboratory to remain a civilian enterprise, at least for some time. This would be of immeasurable help in recruitment. Groves reluctantly agreed but reserved the right to induct the staff into the army at a later date, although not before January 1944. This was another example of Groves's flexibility; militarization had to be subordinate to getting the new laboratory organized and underway. Bacher admired this characteristic of the general. "I think Groves knew himself that a military project wouldn't work, because he'd had sufficient trouble with the military people, and he saw the same kind of trouble that we were trying to show him. I've always had a very high opinion of Groves, in part for that reason."[11]

In one of Oppenheimer's memoranda to new staff he affirmed that Los Alamos would be a civilian operation for the moment but clarified the role of security:

> You will have noted from the War Department letter of February 25 ... that the project will not be militarized earlier than January 1944. During its civilian period, admission to the Post will be by pass only, and to the laboratory by special pass. In general, no restrictions will be placed on the entrance or exit of personnel holding permanent passes. Visitors' passes to the Post or laboratory will be issued only to persons with an essential contribution to make to the project.[12]

Groves did insist on making Los Alamos itself a military post. Oppenheimer's laboratory would operate under the auspices of the University of California, but its staff would work within the barbed wire fences of a military installation where the army controlled every aspect of security.

For Oppenheimer to recruit scientists for what was still a very uncertain project, Groves and Conant believed he needed a statement of purpose, and on February 25, 1943, they sent him a letter that became a loose charter for the Los Alamos Laboratory. It served as a framework for his responsibilities as director and, at his discretion, could be shared with the scientists he was trying to persuade to join him.

The letter referred simply to the "development and final manufacture of an instrument of war." Even more ambiguously, it stated that Oppenheimer and the new laboratory would conduct "certain experimental studies in science, engineering, and ordnance." At some unspecified future date, the laboratory would conduct other large-scale experiments in "difficult ordnance procedures and the handling of highly dangerous material."[13] Oppenheimer, who was responsible for the conduct of all scientific work and the "maintenance" of secrecy, was urged to take the advice of his colleagues. The letter also stressed the importance of close cooperation between the commanding officer—Groves and his military representative in Los Alamos—and Oppenheimer, an indisputable affirmation of the military's key role in the project.

The same day, writing on War Department stationery from Washington, D.C., Oppenheimer forwarded the Groves-Conant letter to John Manley, who was visiting the Met Lab, along with a two-page document written by the laboratory manager, J. H. Stevenson, titled "First Memorandum on the Los Alamos Project." Oppenheimer asked Manley to read Stevenson's memorandum and circulate it among those who had already agreed to join the project. The memo dealt primarily with salaries but also stated that Los Alamos expected its new employees to arrive between March 20 and May 1, 1943, and reassured them that "personnel would not be militarized." The memo contained basic information about Los Alamos and the expected working conditions.

Between conferences with Groves, overseeing the construction at Los Alamos, and beginning work with his small staff, Oppenheimer set out on long recruitment trips to attract the best people he could find. Given the times, almost all of the scientists and engineers he was looking for were men, of course, but as the laboratory matured a few highly talented women joined them. In any case, recruitment was not an easy task for the new director. The Manhattan Project—brand new, somewhat nebulous, and shrouded in secrecy—was invisible in the academic world. It had neither the cachet of Lawrence's lab in Berkeley nor the high profile of the Radiation Laboratory at MIT. The years a man spent at Los Alamos would not count toward later promotion or tenure at a university. Many eminent scientists were already engaged in war work, and the cadre of physicists and chemists associated with Chicago and Berkeley were already part of the Manhattan District. Although Oppenheimer had few budget constraints—indeed, the urgent demand for a bomb gave him a blank check—his preeminent concern, as he would later recall, always was personnel:

The program of recruitment was massive. Even though we then underestimated the ultimate size of the laboratory, which was to have almost 4,000 members by the spring of 1945, and even though we did not at that time see clearly some of the difficulties which were to bedevil and threaten the enterprise, we knew that it was a big, complex and diverse job. Even the initial plan of the laboratory called for a start with more than 100 highly qualified and trained scientists, to say nothing of the technicians, staff, and mechanics who would be required for their support, and of the equipment that we would have to beg and borrow since there would be no time to build it from scratch. We had to recruit at a time when the country was fully engaged at war and almost every competent scientist was already involved in the military effort.[14]

Oppenheimer's enthusiasm was often met with skepticism, and his powers of persuasion were not always sufficient. Despite his prestige in scientific circles, he did not have the stature of Ernest Lawrence or Vannevar Bush. His unknown project in a place no one had heard of would be a laboratory on a military post. And the prospect of being isolated in New Mexico for the duration of the war, with travel and family freedom severely restricted, was nearly as unappealing as the real possibility of the project's failure and the consequent damage to the reputations of everyone associated with it. Leo Szilard, when he heard about the new lab and its location, was appalled. "Nobody could think straight in a place like that.... Everybody who goes there will go crazy."[15] It was not a challenge for the timid or for those who could not live without the comforts and freedoms of a modern city.

Even Teller was persuaded to help recruit scientists. In a promotional "prospectus," Teller, who had not yet been to Los Alamos, described the setting as a combination of existing ranch school facilities and new laboratories built around "a small lake." Only after he arrived in Los

Alamos did he discover that the lake was actually a small, often dry, pond.[16]

Oppenheimer stayed busy. "I traveled all over the country talking with people who had been working on one or another aspect of the atomic energy enterprise, and people in radar work, for example, and underwater sound, telling them about the job, the place that we were going to, and enlisting their enthusiasm."[17]

There were several men who Oppenheimer believed were crucial to any future success. On February 26, 1943, he wrote to his friend Rabi, "There are two men whom I should be more than reluctant not to have on the project: Bacher and Bethe.... You have a great deal of influence with these two men, and they in turn on many others who are involved in the project. I am asking that you use that influence to persuade them to come rather than to stay away."[18] Oppenheimer might have added that he wanted Rabi himself to come just as badly as the other two.

Oppenheimer had first met Hans Bethe in June 1940 at a meeting of the American Physical Society in Seattle, where he gave the opening presentation, "The Present Crisis in the Quantum Theory of Fields." Bethe was in the audience and that evening attended a small party at which Oppenheimer conveyed his concerns over the events in Europe and expressed his deep conviction that nothing less than Western civilization was at stake. Bethe was deeply impressed. After a more intimate exchange between the two, the relationship developed, and Bethe was invited to Oppenheimer's select summer conference at Berkeley in 1942.

In December 1942, Oppenheimer wrote a letter to Bethe and his wife, Rose, answering questions the two of them had posed and trying to allay their concerns. He expressed the hope that all problems could be addressed, and he cited the "great effort and generosity that [Colonel] J. M. Harmon*

---

* Colonel John Harmon was the first commander of the Los Alamos Army Post, although he served only briefly. After four months, Groves replaced him with Colonel Whitney Ashbridge.

and Groves have both brought to setting up this odd community and in their evident desire to make a real success of it." Oppenheimer closed with a wry observation: "In general they [the army] are not interested in saving money, but are interested in saving critical materials, in cutting down personnel, and in doing nothing which would attract Congressional attention to our hi-jinks. I found that there were 1800 people working at the school to get the thing built fast."[19]

He wooed Robert Bacher just as assiduously. Bacher was working at the Radiation Laboratory at MIT but was a close collaborator with Bethe, whom he helped to write the three-volume series *Nuclear Physics. A: Stationary States of Nuclei*. Bacher had also researched the nuclear cross sections of cadmium, and his results had garnered considerable praise from Fermi. He was directing part of the Radiation Lab's extensive radar program. Oppenheimer, who valued not only his scientific expertise but also his administrative skills, thought Bacher was the "only physicist in the country who could replace Fermi...."[20]

In April, he wrote to Bacher, "You know that I am extremely eager to have your help in this work. I think perhaps that you have not fully realized how much I appreciate your administrative experience and obvious administrative wisdom, nor how aware I am of our need for just this in the present project.... I believe it is essential [for you to] work in this laboratory, that you accept without further delay."[21] Oppenheimer finally made a similar pitch to Isidor Rabi, who declined to come permanently, but eventually agreed to visit as a consultant.

The new director sold the Hill—what locals called Los Alamos—as best he could and emphasized that the resources available to the project were virtually unlimited. He didn't always mention the level of security Groves intended, including the early possibility of being in uniform. Long after the war, Oppenheimer reflected that "the last months of 1942 and 1943 had hardly hours enough to get Los Alamos established. The real problem had to do with getting to Los Alamos the men who would make a success of the undertaking."[22]

Pushed by Groves, and with the ranch school still in session, the Albuquerque engineers moved forward through the winter with the construction of an administrative building and several laboratories and shops. Civilian contractors were hired to build housing, and Groves kept up with nearly every aspect of construction through ceaseless phone calls and letters from Washington. The early, sparse plan for the laboratory and housing for staff was quickly discarded. As more and more young men, many with their wives and children in tow, swamped the mesa, the true scope of the project emerged. Groves insisted on approving every major building and structure: laboratories and office buildings, one new housing area after another, a school, a hospital, dorms for single scientists and dorms for male and female members of the military, and cafeterias.

Groves decided to keep the ranch school's Fuller Lodge, a beautiful two-story log structure designed by the famous New Mexico architect John Gaw Meem, as a dining room and hotel for visitors. A special room was always reserved for the general when he visited. An even larger school building, the Big House, served as a temporary dormitory. Infested with termites and deemed irreparable, it was torn down, despite protests, in late 1943.

Just south of Fuller Lodge was Ashley Pond, the "lake" mentioned by Teller, and next to it a stone building that had once been an icehouse; the army kept the small structure although no one at the time knew what it would be used for. Mysteriously, a small flock of ducks took up residence on the pond one day where none had ever been seen before. The explanation turned out to be that an Army officer with previous experience at a military hospital for shell-shocked soldiers had requisitioned six ducks from Santa Fe as part of a rest-and-recreation effort. The flock prospered and the ducks were quickly adopted by residents as community pets.

The nomenclature of the buildings at Los Alamos was functional and unimaginative. Across the dirt road from the old icehouse, engineers built the Main Technical Building, or T Building, which would serve as headquarters for Oppenheimer, his administrative staff, and the Theoretical Physics Division. It eventually contained an auditorium and library with a vault for classified documents. Plans called for the construction of U Building for the chemistry and physics laboratories just behind T Building and connected to it by a covered walkway. On either end of U Building were to be separate laboratories for the Van de Graaff and Cockcroft-Walton accelerators. These huge machines and their ancillary components were shipped by rail in two boxcars and laboriously trucked to the mesa top. Shops were to be located in V Building. Almost on the edge of Los Alamos Canyon were Y and X Buildings, for the cryogenics laboratory and the cyclotron. This rambling complex was known as the Technical Area, or simply the Tech Area.

Most of the technical buildings were constructed in what euphemistically was called modified mobilization style—a drab lapboard exterior topped by a simple pitched roof of asphalt or wood shingles, with acoustical tile ceilings inside. Few of the Tech Area buildings were air conditioned or dustproof. Buildings for the army personnel were even less attractive.

During the construction of the Tech Area, the need for more housing became painfully apparent. Some men were taken off Tech Area construction and set to building houses. A letter to new recruits called "Third Memorandum" inaccurately reported, "About twenty percent of the new housing at Los Alamos should be completed before April first. All construction should be completed by May first."[23] In reality, very little was ready at Los Alamos when Oppenheimer and a few hearty staff members arrived in Santa Fe in mid-March.

The largest contingent of early arrivals came from Princeton University, where the cancellation of Robert Wilson's isotron and uranium separation projects had freed more than thirty scientists for transfer to Los Alamos. Others came from the fast-neutron projects at the University of California, the University of Minnesota, Stanford, and Purdue.

Groves asked for a status report on all fission work, and Oppenheimer, Robert Serber, and Richard Tolman met in Berkeley in early March 1943 to review uranium and plutonium research related to the development of weapons. In less than a week all but Tolman would move to Los Alamos. Their findings were sent to Groves, but the review also helped Oppenheimer formalize the initial organization of the laboratory and provided the basis for a series of orientation lectures for the staff assembling in Los Alamos. In keeping with the plan he shared with Manley, he formally proposed creating four divisions—Experimental Physics, Theoretical Physics, Chemistry and Metallurgy, and Ordnance—all reporting to a central administration. Within each division were operating units or groups. Group leaders were responsible to division leaders, and division leaders were responsible to Oppenheimer. And Oppenheimer was responsible to Groves.

On March 16, Robert and Kitty took the train from San Francisco to Lamy, New Mexico, a small whistle stop about twenty miles southwest of Santa Fe. Their son, Peter, and a nurse would follow a few days later in a car driven by Robert Serber and his wife. Oppenheimer's temporary office was in the La Fonda Hotel in Santa Fe, and Priscilla Green joined him as his personal secretary. When Oppenheimer needed secretarial help for his summer conference in 1942, Lawrence had kindly "loaned" Green to his colleague. Green found Oppenheimer "unbelievably charming and gracious," and the two worked well together. When Oppenheimer asked to have her as his secretary in New Mexico, Lawrence acquiesced with regret. Green was thrilled: "And what secretary wasn't going to be absolutely overwhelmed by somebody who in the middle of a letter—we all smoked in those days—whipped his lighter out of his pocket and lighted your cigarette while you were taking dictation and he was talking?"[24] She was paid $250 a month.

Green was given a room in the La Fonda next to the Oppenheimers. There was a connecting door between the two rooms, which Oppenheimer used sometimes when he wanted to conduct business. That ended abruptly a few days later when Kitty sternly informed Green that the adjoining door was to be locked at all times.[25] Green also came down with the measles while waiting for offices in T Building to be completed. When she was better, she made her first trip to the Hill with Oppenheimer. It was a mess: few buildings were complete and there was mud everywhere.

Once the administration offices at Los Alamos were available, the new director selected a small corner office on the second floor of T Building, with an adjacent office for Green. The room was furnished in standard-issue army furniture, with large blackboards on the walls and a view of the parking lot and construction sites. Green handled Oppenheimer's correspondence and attended meetings in the director's office as recorder. For a while she ran the mailroom and, when installed, the laboratory's switchboard. She was also responsible for "fending off" Teller when he insisted on meeting with Oppenheimer.

To make the most of their precious time, Oppenheimer often took Green with him on his drives to and from Santa Fe so she could take dictation as they traversed the harrowing road. He seemed particularly interested in having records made of his conversations with Robert Underhill, the University of California representative, and with General Groves. Despite protestations from the general, Oppenheimer had Green take notes of all his telephone conversations, though an exasperated Groves would sometimes insist, "I'll answer that if she [Green] will get off the phone." Of course, Groves had his own secretary, Jean O'Leary, quietly taking notes of his telephone calls. Where they could, both Green and O'Leary adopted the caller's nickname: in their notes, for example, Oppenheimer was "Oppie" or "Dr. O;" scientist George Kistiakowsky was "Kisty." Conant was "Uncle Jim."

Green observed Groves closely during his visits and witnessed his boorish behavior. One day Groves walked out of Oppenheimer's office and noticed that the pocket door between their offices was dirty around the handle. Groves glared at the secretary and asked, "Don't you ladies ever wash your hands?"[26] Oppenheimer was quick to defend the general, however, and always said that Groves wasn't as mean as he appeared to be. Green did see the respect that the two obviously had for each other, and it was clear to her that Groves valued Oppenheimer's ability to work with scientists.

T Building was the main administration building within the Tech Area. Several dozen buildings had been constructed, or were under construction, to house the generators and cyclotron, chemistry and physics laboratories, plutonium purification, ordnance and other groups, a library, and various other labs and offices. The entire complex was surrounded by a nine-and-a-half-foot-high wire fence with concertina wire on top. Military police guarded the gates. Three sides of the complex hugged the canyon rim, with a security road following the fence perimeter. The fourth side faced a road that ran northwest to southeast. When additional technical buildings were needed on the opposite side of the road, a new area was fenced in with its own guard gate. An enclosed walkway running from the second story of one building, over the road, to the second story of the opposite building allowed staff to move easily and securely between fenced-in areas.

While the director traveled, organized the lab on the run, and issued memoranda, men continued to arrive daily with their families. A few men from the Metallurgical Laboratory in Chicago had been encouraged to go to Los Alamos, and others had been recruited from MIT, Columbia, Iowa State University, and the National Bureau of Standards. For the first few months, staff members and their families had to be housed at remote and crowded guest ranches, where they often had to share kitchens and bathrooms. Some of these charming but dated tourist enclaves were in spectacular settings like the Frijoles Canyon, but their temporary occupants described them as rustic or primitive.

Oppenheimer's official offices in Los Alamos, and indeed the offices for all the administrative staff, were not yet complete when they arrived, and for the moment he and others moved into five rented rooms at 109 East Palace Avenue in Santa Fe. For security reasons, Groves had ordered that no laboratory staff were to stay in Santa Fe, but because of the disarray on the plateau, he made a temporary exception for this small suite near the city's ancient square. The Santa Fe office was managed by Dorothy McKibbin, a congenial and patient woman in her fifties who had come to New Mexico years before for her health and to raise her young son after the death of her husband. She answered delivery queries, greeted confused scientists with calm assurances, and dispensed practical recommendations about where to buy toiletries and which restaurants offered the best blue plate specials.

The first two months of the laboratory's operation were a chaotic and exhilarating time for McKibbin, who played a particularly helpful role:

> When the Technical Area administrative staff arrived in March 1943, they ... took over five offices at 109 and functioned there in full blast until the end of April. Army guards crept around these offices and stood in the shadow of the portals day and night. The Director's office, the offices for the business manager, procurement, and personnel were hives of activity. Telephones rang constantly, and since few connected inter-office, secretaries were chasing from office to office to bring the person being called to the waiting telephone.[27]

From Santa Fe, everyone made the tortuous forty-mile trip to Los Alamos by car or truck. The few official vehicles were mostly old, and they frequently broke down on the road to Los Alamos, which not only had dangerous switchbacks but was layered with sharp rocks. The roads to the guest ranches were even worse. To protect the natural state of the mesa, the Los Alamos Ranch School had kept road building to a minimum. There were few paved roads on the mesa in early 1943, and houses were connected by dirt trails. Later, residents learned that roads put down in the winter when the ground was frozen turned to mud in the spring. When it rained, the mire slowed vehicular movement to a crawl. Newcomers worked their way up the hill in cars and buses and arrived at a security checkpoint and their first view of what would eventually be miles of barbed wire fences. For the hearty and open-minded, it was the beginning of an adventure. For others it was a depressing glimpse of how they would live "for the duration."

From his office in Washington, Groves came up with procedures to expedite construction in Los Alamos. For nontechnical buildings such as housing and community buildings, he arranged for the Albuquerque Corps of Engineers to submit their requirements directly to the architectural and engineering firm of Willard C. Kruger in Santa Fe instead of going through the University of California. Kruger, in turn, worked with various subcontractors to develop cost estimates and proposals that were submitted to the Albuquerque Engineering District under a lump-sum contract.[28]

Groves was keen on monitoring construction costs. Although the laboratory's staff and their families were growing by leaps and bounds, Groves and Oppenheimer saw Los Alamos as a temporary war project for which investments in infrastructure should be kept to a minimum. Many of the telephone calls in 1943 between Groves and Oppenheimer and between Groves and Lieutenant Colonel Whitney Ashbridge, who had replaced Harmon as base commander at Los Alamos, dealt with construction. On May 31, for example, the general authorized Ashbridge to build quarters for up to 1,500 military personnel and members of a special engineering detachment at a cost not to exceed one hundred thousand dollars. On June 24, he assured Oppenheimer that Ashbridge had a "free hand" to build a school and pave roads. Groves even authorized the expansion of rooms in Fuller Lodge for visitors and for scientists waiting for a permanent housing assignment. Construction progressed so quickly that it often outstripped supplies. Oppenheimer and Ashbridge reported that the delays were often more a matter of materials than men.

Except for the site's isolation, the original assessment of Los Alamos as ideal for a secret laboratory appeared to be proved wrong at every turn. No sooner did men and machines arrive than the water supply ran short. In the winter, pipelines froze and shattered. Teams were sent to tap water in Los Alamos Canyon and later in nearby Pajarito and Guaje canyons. The reservoir on the Hill grew algae. One huge water tank and then another were built. As soon as the scientists began their work and understood what equipment, resources, and space they needed, they requested new construction that quickly added to the backlog. The first building contractor had been able to complete 54 percent of its contract in two months; the remaining 46 percent took a year because each new request for expanded or new facilities delayed progress while construction teams were shifted from project to project. Oppenheimer's only solution to this problem was to urge Groves to hire more contractors.

To help with both administrative and technical issues, Oppenheimer organized an informal committee known as the Planning Board. It included himself, Wilson, McMillan, Manley, Serber, and Edward Condon, whom Oppenheimer had hired as an assistant on recommendation from Groves. Condon, one of the few native New Mexicans in the early laboratory, was director of research at the Westinghouse Electric Company and a consultant to the NDRC when he was recruited for the laboratory. The group first met on March 6, 1943, in Berkeley to consider arriving staff, facilities, and support services. It met again on April 2, this time in Los Alamos, and expanded to include Robert Christy, who had been hired by Oppenheimer, Richard Feynman from Princeton, and a member of the 1942 summer conference, Emil Konopinski. Once again the committee delved into the problems of facilities and space, procurement, and housing allocation, but they also planned a series of lectures to be given by Serber to the organization's leadership. At their last meeting, on April 8, they could note with some pride and some surprise that Los Alamos had now attracted 150 scientists.

In early March, Richard Tolman, the vice chairman of the NDRC, met for several days in Berkeley with Oppenheimer and Robert Serber. Tolman was able to prepare a briefing paper on the state of fission research for General Groves and to assemble a list of questions for a proposed "review" committee to help Oppenheimer determine the scope of work for the new laboratory. The idea of a review committee ostensibly originated with Conant, who thought that the general could improve his relations with scientists by involving an outside consultative body. Groves had come to value Conant's insights and advice:

> He [Conant] pointed out that these people were accustomed to making their views known to similar committees appointed by their university administrations.... A further advantage which we both recognized was that a review committee, with its fresh outlook, might be able to make a suggestion that would be eagerly seized upon, whereas if the same suggestion came from me, it might be regarded as interference.[29]

Groves had another, more practical motive in mind. He saw that his new director was struggling with the dual tasks of creating and staffing a new organization as well as setting its priorities. Based on his own experience with large projects, Groves could see that Oppenheimer not only underestimated the number of scientists and engineers he needed, but that he had not yet grasped the full complexity of the task of making an entirely new kind of weapon. Even at this stage, it was clear to Groves that a hundred men and a few laboratory buildings were not going to be enough. On March 8, he called Oppenheimer in Berkeley to discuss the proposed committee and announced that he would be in Los Alamos the following week, his first visit since selecting the area the previous November. Oppenheimer agreed to work with Tolman on a list of potential committee members. He favored Tolman as chairman but also thought that Warren Lewis of MIT and Condon would be good members.

A few days later, Groves dispatched a member of his staff, Major Stanley Stewart, to Los Alamos to check on progress. Stewart dutifully reported back on construction and hiring snags, adding, "This matter brings up a point I believe worth mentioning. From my observations, it appears that Dr. Oppenheimer has been quite busy on other matters and has not had time to do much about organizing the Scientific Staff."[30] Groves moved quickly and pushed again for the review committee, establishing a pattern of assisting, mentoring, and gently prodding his director. Later he would write, "Oppenheimer was my first selection for Los Alamos. All of the people he brought were brought in under my direction. This decentralized Oppenheimer. Others like Ernest Lawrence in California I didn't have to worry about because he was an executive and driver from way-out. Compton's organization was pretty well set. It just needed a few people."[31]

Urged by Groves, Oppenheimer and Tolman quickly prepared a list of potential review committee members. On March 20, Tolman sent Groves the names:

> As a theoretical physicist, familiar with nuclear problems, we suggest Dr. E. Fermi, Dr. G. E. Uhlenbeck, or Dr. E. B. Van Vleck, in the order named. As an explosives expert, familiar with the mechanism of detonation, we suggest Dr. E. B. Wilson, Jr., Dr. J. G. Kirkwood, or Dr. G. B. Kistiakowsky, in the order named. As a chemical engineer, familiar with production methods, we suggest, Dr. W. K. Lewis. As a mechanical engineer, familiar with ordnance problems, we suggest Mr. E. L. Rose.[32]

Groves chose Lewis of MIT; Edwin Rose, the director of research for Jones and Lamson Machine Company; and Van Vleck. Tolman would be the committee's chairman.

Tolman prepared a briefing paper for Groves and the members of the review committee titled "Memorandum on Los Alamos Project as of March 1943," summarizing the physics behind fission, the primary nuclear materials to be used, and the current thinking on how to detonate such a device. He also created a series of questions that could "appropriately be asked of the project": What did scientists know at the moment about critical masses, the conditions that affect nuclear reactions and detonation, the chemistry and metallurgy of uranium and plutonium, and the possibility of a thermonuclear, or hydrogen, bomb? What did Los Alamos need to know about the production and delivery schedules of uranium and plutonium? And it was not too early to consider the military's logistical requirements for the bomb itself, which almost certainly would be air dropped and therefore had to fit within the fuselage of an existing or planned aircraft.[33]

On April 4, Tolman chaired the first meeting of the review committee —an all-day affair—in Washington, D.C., in Groves's conference room. Groves attended in the morning but left for lunch with Vannevar Bush, then returned to the meeting. Late in the afternoon, Groves called Oppenheimer to tell him that the review team would visit Los Alamos on April 24, and that he himself would visit the laboratory the week before, on April 18 and 19. The committee delivered its final report in early May, proposing an agenda for the laboratory that covered the spectrum from metallurgy to engineering. Their recommendations irrevocably expanded the work of the lab far beyond what Oppenheimer and others had originally imagined. Nonetheless, Oppenheimer was glad for the guidance.

Groves now wanted to know what steps Oppenheimer would take to meet the recommendations of the committee. Oppenheimer responded on May 27, with a long letter detailing the measures underway. First, he admitted that he had not yet selected an associate director, although three men were under consideration: Sam Allison, Bob Bacher, and Deak Parsons. Oppenheimer favored Allison for his overall expertise and his "remarkable personal qualities." There were still gaps in personnel, however, particularly in the areas of recruitment and procurement. The review committee's recommendations for theoretical studies, especially in the area of critical masses, were already underway, and as suggested, the laboratory would undertake the purification of Pu239 and increase and strengthen the metallurgical staff. And last, the creation of an "engineering division" had been "enormously facilitated by the appointment of Commander Parsons." Moreover, key department heads within engineering had been named: "Dr. Brode for the problems of arming safety and firing; Dr. Bainbridge for the problems of instrumentation; Dr. Rose and Dr. Critchfield for problems of internal ballistics and gun design; Dr. Ramsey for problems of delivery, [and] Dr. Thompson for problems in the H.E. [high explosives] method as well as a general aide to Commander Parsons."[34]

Oppenheimer subsequently sent a memo to the staff announcing new hires and the creation of a governing board, but most importantly,

> The Reviewing Committee has recommended and General Groves has accepted in principle, that the staff be increased to between four and five hundred. The additions will be largely in the fields of engineering, engineering-physics and chemistry, but some additions to the theoretical and experimental staff for nuclear physics are also contemplated. We are planning to build [as a result of the committee's recommendations] ... a new chemical and metallurgical laboratory, an office and drafting building for design and ordnance, and a large shop and service building for the engineering side. These will probably be built immediately to the west of the present technical buildings.[35]

The idea of a small laboratory with a hundred scientists disappeared amidst the roar and rattle of bulldozers and falling trees.

———————————

Groves and Oppenheimer were in daily communication during the spring and summer, and the new director quickly learned that no item of business was too small for his army boss. While many of these exchanges were technical or scientific in nature, others dealt with personnel, security, logistics, and the mundane matters of creating a new community on a mountaintop. There were many conversations about housing, or the lack of it, construction, the availability of cooking ranges, power capacity and diesel units, sprinkler systems, the need for an army truck with a crane rated at sixteen thousand pounds capacity, the pavement of roads, and a request for binoculars. (Groves said no to the binoculars.) Security issues concerned the availability of telephones, scramblers, teletypes, detailed lists of visitors and their purpose for being on the Hill, the use of compartments on train trips, and security at the guard gates. Groves wanted justifications for hiring a physicist named Norman Ramsey and a pediatrician named Henry Barnett. Oppenheimer complied.[36]

Many of these conversations were directly between Groves and Oppenheimer, but some calls to the director came from Jean O'Leary. Oppenheimer—and everyone else at Los Alamos—quickly learned what everyone on the general's staff in Washington already knew: a call from O'Leary was a call from Groves. During any given day, calls to the laboratory might come from one or the other. It was an effective strategy—as if Groves had managed to "clone" himself.

Chapter Seven

THE LOS ALAMOS PRIMER

———————◦———————

General Groves's tolerance for Oppenheimer's open organization of the laboratory was about to be tested.

Earlier in the year, Oppenheimer had persuaded Groves to permit a free exchange of scientific and technical information among staff. It was the antithesis of the compartmentalization that Groves enforced on every other Manhattan Project activity. The challenge played out in a series of important lectures given to the laboratory's leadership in April and subsequently to all new arrivals in the spring and summer. The idea was to share with listeners what was known about fission at the time. The information would be based on the numerous research projects in universities and laboratories around the country. Up to this point, information was compartmentalized, and security dictated that an individual staff member know only about his own project. Oppenheimer scheduled the lectures for April 5, 7, 9, 12, and 14, 1943, and asked Robert Serber to start with a general overview. Oppenheimer believed Serber had the best overall view of the challenges facing Los Alamos.[1] The participants met in the small auditorium at one end of the first floor of the newly constructed T Building.

Serber's background was in engineering physics. When by chance he had heard Oppenheimer speak at the University of Michigan, he had been impressed and decided to do postdoctoral research under Oppenheimer at Berkeley. He quickly became an assistant, and the two men developed a remarkably fruitful professional relationship. In fact, Serber shuttled between Berkeley and Cal Tech with Oppenheimer every semester for four years, and he and his wife, Charlotte, rented the small apartment above Oppenheimer's garage. In 1938 he took a position at the University of Illinois, where he taught until invited to Los Alamos.

Serber was shy and spoke with a slight lisp, but he was a brilliant physicist and held his audience's attention throughout. He had even adopted Oppenheimer's habit of lecturing with a lit cigarette in one hand and a piece of chalk in the other. The challenge for Los Alamos, Serber said, was to make a "practical military weapon." That pronouncement was intended to reassure Groves, who was suspicious that the mostly academic members of the new staff would continue to think of the bomb as simply another scientific experiment instead of a weapon. To some degree, Groves retained that suspicion throughout the war despite all that Oppenheimer did to assure him otherwise.

There were three alternative ways to make a bomb, Serber told the audience. The first was the "gun" method, in which one subcritical mass of fissionable material is fired rapidly into another, causing a supercritical, or explosive, reaction. The gun would have an explosive charge and a subcritical mass on one end and a second subcritical mass at the other. He drew a circle with a much smaller circle inside on the blackboard. The subcritical mass could be crafted, Serber explained, as a sphere with a hole bored into the center. The other subcritical mass, shaped like a cylinder to fit the cavity, would be fired into the sphere.

The second alternative was the "autocatalytic," or self-assembling, process, in which "clusters" of neutron-rich materials imbedded into the

U235 or Pu239 are compressed or expulsed. Serber voiced some skepticism about this method. Preliminary calculations suggested that the assembly of such a device, as it was then understood, would require large amounts of fissionable material and would yield a relatively low explosive force. It was the least attractive of the three possible designs.

The third possibility was an "implosion" bomb, in which a slightly sub-critical amount of fissionable material in the shape of a sphere is surrounded by high explosives. When the explosives are detonated and part of the blast wave flies inward, the subcritical mass is compressed into a supercritical mass and releases extraordinary energy. Serber called the implosion bomb the "gadget," and while it was clever in concept, he said such a device would be difficult to construct.

If any of these designs worked, the damage would be considerable. Radioactive materials generated in the explosion would contaminate everything within one thousand yards of the detonation point, and Serber estimated that five kilograms of U235 would produce a destructive radius of two miles: "The one factor that determines the damage is the energy release, [and] our aim is simply to get as much energy from the explosion as we can. And since the materials we use are very precious, we are constrained to do this with as high an efficiency as is possible."

Serber revealed to the audience that he and Oppenheimer had theorized that the energy released from one kilogram—about 2.2 pounds—of U235 equals the energy released from the detonation of twenty thousand tons of TNT. And it would take only a little more than eighty generations of neutrons hitting the nuclei of atoms to "fish the whole kilogram," as the thin, fey speaker described it. The best guess was that some fifteen kilograms (thirty-three pounds) of U235 or five kilograms (eleven pounds) of Pu239 would be required for a bomb. The uranium, Serber emphasized, had to be more than 90 percent pure. But these amounts, even if accurate, could vary depending on the shape, density, and surroundings of the nuclear material.

While the scientists had a basic understanding of the fission process, many theoretical and practical challenges and questions faced the laboratory.

For example, the bomb needed what Serber called a "tamper"—a metal cover of some kind that would develop an "economy of neutrons" by returning escaping neutrons back into the critical mass. The tamper would also prevent expansion of the fissionable material, if only briefly. This was important because if the material were allowed to expand, becoming less dense, it would lose its critical mass and the chain reaction would fizzle and die.

The laboratory also needed to find out how likely it was, under various conditions, that neutrons escaping during fission would strike another nucleus, sustaining the chain reaction. These calculations of probability were called cross sections, and they had to account for neutrons of different speeds and for nuclear material containing various impurities.

Serber compared the problem of cross sections to the carnival game in which the player throws a baseball at a row of milk bottles. If the surface of a bottle is one square foot, then the area that a player can hit with a ball—the cross section—is one square foot. But the cross section changes if a beer bottle is substituted for the milk bottle, if a ping-pong ball is substituted for the baseball, or if the pitch is faster or slower. The player is more likely to score a hit throwing a baseball slowly at the milk bottle than throwing a ping-pong ball hard and fast at the beer bottle. In fission, the uranium or plutonium nucleus is the bottle and the neutron is the ball. It wasn't the size of the nucleus that mattered but the probability of scoring a hit.

Particle accelerators known as atom smashers, which could bombard samples of potential bomb materials with neutrons of varying speeds, would be used to gather these data. Some neutrons are slow and some fast. A bomb requires fast neutrons, and it also needs a predictable source of neutrons that can be released at the right instant. That internal source, which Serber called an "initiator," must release hundreds of thousands of neutrons in a single burst at precisely the right instant. Serber suggested they might use the elements polonium and beryllium—the polonium as an alpha source to interact with the beryllium to initiate neutrons.

Sitting in the audience was Seth Neddermeyer, a tall, thin, thoughtful thirty-six-year-old who had been quiet throughout most of the lectures. The concept of implosion captured his imagination, especially the idea of inward forces acting in three dimensions. He wondered, why not wrap high explosives around a spherical combination of tamper and hollow core? He remembered reading something about two bullets fired into each other—"It may have been a photograph of two bullets liquefied on impact. That is what I was thinking when the ballistics man mentioned implosion."[2] His thoughts were not fully formed at that moment, but he began to see how implosion had the advantage of bringing nuclear material together more quickly: the velocities in implosion were simply higher than in a gun. And there was something else: What if the bomb used a hollow, spherical shell of uranium or plutonium? Such a design would conserve precious material.

The lectures also raised the concern that the gun method might not work with both U235 and Pu239, although at the time no one could be sure. In fact, no one knew with certainty whether plutonium emits neutrons during fission. Unfortunately, neither uranium nor plutonium would be immediately available in quantities sufficient to conduct any of the experiments scientists anticipated, much less to make a weapon. Serber told the audience that a plant for large-scale production of U235 was under construction at Oak Ridge, Tennessee, and another for plutonium at Hanford, Washington.

Teller also spoke, and for those who had not yet encountered him, his speaking style and heavily-accented English made a deep impression. So did his thick set of highly animated eyebrows. He raised the possibility of a thermonuclear weapon, or superbomb, much as he had done the year before at the secret Berkeley conference. It was clear that this possibility continued to excite him. A fission bomb that used heavy nuclei, he told the audience, could generate the necessary and astronomically high temperatures for igniting a lighter substance like deuterium in a thermonuclear device.[3]

Deuterium is an isotope of hydrogen, the lightest element, and is twice as heavy as the hydrogen nucleus. Teller suggested that deuterium in a "Super," as he nicknamed the potential thermonuclear bomb, has obvious advantages. It has the lowest ignition temperature—about four hundred million degrees Fahrenheit—and once ignited it would be five times as explosive, or energy-producing, as U235. The bomb's destructive potential would be vastly greater than that of the fission bomb. To Teller, the possibility could not be ignored by Los Alamos.

At the end of the lectures, listeners were left with the daunting prospect of converting theory into practice—workable bombs that could be dropped on Germany or Japan. It was obvious that while considerable theoretical understanding of the fission process had been achieved, many more problems of applied physics and engineering remained. Throughout the talks, Oppenheimer's crew-cut new assistant director, Edward Condon, took notes. These were quickly transcribed and assembled into a twenty-four-page booklet, *The Los Alamos Primer*, which was subsequently handed out to new arrivals.

The Los Alamos Laboratory formally opened on Thursday, April 15, 1943, with the first of the mandatory morning orientations that would continue until May 6. The weather on the mesa was cool. Winter still lurked in the shadows in the daytime, and coats and blankets were called for at night.

One by one or in small groups, the newly hired staff walked into the first-floor conference room in T Building, the smell of fresh wood and paint still lingering in the air.[4] They sat in rows of wood frame and canvas chairs facing a small stage. Oppenheimer greeted and mingled. Many of the participants were men he had personally recruited. General Groves was also present to assist in the orientation. Oppenheimer appeared calm and reassuring, betraying none of problems plaguing him at the moment. The few men who had not met Oppenheimer before or had spent little time with him caught their first glimpse of his ubiquitous cigarette or pipe and his slightly disheveled tweed jacket. He had a curious manner of speaking. While articulate and often eloquent, his speech was punctuated by pauses in which he voiced a soft "nim-nim-nim" with his lips. And he was thin. His hips were so small that he could slip easily into the child's highchair in John Manley's kitchen. Sometimes as he spoke he swayed like a reed in a gentle wind.

The reaction to General Groves was considerably more mixed. Many of the men had no experience with the military, and Groves's officious behavior put them off. One young scientist remembered, "We were all herded into one room.... It turned out the reason was that this General wanted to come talk to us. A rather portly gentleman came into the room. He stood in front of us and said, 'Perhaps you don't know who I am, but I am General Groves, and I am in charge of this project.'"[5]

Outside T Building there was chaos. Priscilla Green found it "a pretty appalling place,"[6] and Hans Bethe was equally disappointed. "I was rather shocked by the isolation, and I was shocked by the shoddy buildings.... [E]verybody was afraid that a fire might break out and the whole project might burn down."[7] Few buildings were completed, and mud was everywhere. Some buildings were crammed with people; others waited empty for ceiling tiles to be installed and wall sockets connected to electrical mains. Oppenheimer could not afford to be discouraged. Indeed, he had decided that the series of orientation lectures and discussions designed to bring the technical staff up to date on nuclear weapons research would take place regardless of the state of construction.

After introductions and the somewhat splenetic speech from Groves, Oppenheimer began the meeting with an overview of current work, repeating the more important elements of Serber's lectures and including Teller's recent thinking on the Super. He also optimistically announced that as much as one hundred grams of U235 would be shipped to Los Alamos every day beginning in early 1944 and perhaps as much as three hundred grams of Pu239 every day in early 1945.[8]

The topic changed every morning. On the second day, Manley reviewed the upcoming experimental program for the cyclotron, the Cockcroft-Walton generator, two Van de Graaf machines, and a proposed nuclear reactor nicknamed the "water boiler." On the third day, Bethe addressed the fission process, including cross sections and critical mass. Serber discussed the tamper in the fourth session. The remaining six sessions covered a wide range of theoretical and experimental issues, including the development of detectors, the properties of natural uranium, design of the gun weapon, experiment for the water boiler, and methods to determine critical mass.

As the men filed out of the auditorium, trying to absorb what they had just heard or talking among themselves, there was a palpable sense of excitement. They were part of what Don Hornig called "a very live-wire intellectual organization." The atmosphere in the auditorium had been electric at times, even intoxicating, and it was matched outside by the crackling spring air of the high mesa. There was a sense that the physics they had been taught in school was about to explode and that these young men would rewrite the old textbooks with their experiments and discoveries. Oppenheimer made them feel special:

> Almost everyone realized that this was a great undertaking. Almost everyone knew that if it were completed successfully and rapidly enough, it might determine the outcome of the war.... Almost everyone knew that this job, if it were achieved, would be a part of history. This sense of excitement, of devotion and of patriotism in the end prevailed.[9]

The review committee delivered its final report on May 10, advising that although many research schedules would be determined by the availability of uranium and plutonium, the design of the bomb must proceed, and that whatever weapon emerged needed to fit into an airplane.

Theoretically and practically, Los Alamos had much to learn. Which of three fissionable materials—U235, Pu239, and a uranium hydride—would be most satisfactory in a nuclear weapon? What was the average number of neutrons per fission in both U235 and Pu239? Was it wise for Groves and his Military Policy Committee to produce plutonium in quantity? On the engineering side, chemists and metallurgists had to find ways of casting and shaping large amounts of U235 and Pu239, while ordnance men needed to bring subcritical masses together with enough speed to prevent predetonation.* And finally, the critical mass, tamper, explosives, and firing mechanisms needed to fit conveniently into a shell for airborne delivery by the military.

The review committee provided Groves with what he wanted: a relatively clear path for Oppenheimer and his scientists to follow. This was the first and certainly the most important intervention by Groves to guide his director and shape the direction of the organization. Oppenheimer's organizational naiveté was obvious. The committee's report also irreversibly broadened the scope and depth of operations at Los Alamos. It called for more money, more staff, and a larger facility.

The prospect of going to work immediately on the material specifications of a bomb without the benefit of experimental data on U235 and Pu239 was daunting. The best guess at the moment was that it would be at least two years before the cyclotron in California and the plants in Washington and Tennessee could deliver any appreciable quantity of

---

* A nuclear explosion occurs when the uranium or plutonium core passes through a series of stages—virtually instantaneously—from subcritical to critical to supercritical. A preliminary chain reaction can start when the core reaches the critical stage, however, and if the supercritical stage is not reached quickly, the chain reaction may die out or produce only a minimal explosion—a result called "predetonation." Stray neutrons from cosmic rays and spontaneous emission can also disrupt the chain reaction. The most efficient explosion occurs only when the core becomes supercritical.

uranium and plutonium. If they were lucky, tiny specks for experimental purposes would arrive later in 1943.

Just a few weeks after the laboratory's official opening in April, Oppenheimer found himself regretting his original estimate of "perhaps a hundred scientists." Groves was not surprised. In his experience, large projects had a tendency to balloon over time. He had guessed from the beginning that designing and building a bomb was going to take more men and a lot more money. Oppenheimer now realized that the tasks ahead demanded far more scientists and technicians as well as a larger physical plant. Suddenly the mesa seemed very small. When the needed men arrived with their families, where would they live? Where would they build the huge plant for purifying plutonium? How would trained technicians—metal workers, plumbers, welders—be found and persuaded to move to New Mexico? Had Oppenheimer appreciated the scope of the project earlier—even as recently as six months ago—he might not have promoted Los Alamos Mesa for Project Y.

Groves and Oppenheimer were in regular contact, often by telephone, and many of the conversations in the spring concerned housing, recruitment, and planning problems. Groves listened, but the conversations confirmed the general's assessment that his director's greatest weakness was a lack of administrative experience. Groves took the initiative and recommended Edward Condon to assist Oppenheimer with administrative matters for the laboratory. Oppenheimer willingly obliged and hired Condon, who would also serve as liaison with the military commander of the Los Alamos Post. As it turned out, Condon was a poor choice. He clashed almost immediately with both military and scientific personnel and stayed only six weeks. Groves took responsibility for the appointment. Condon, he wrote later, "did little to smooth the frictions between the scientists and the military officers who handled the administrative housekeeping details."[10] Groves pressed Oppenheimer to request a written letter of resignation from Condon, in part to prevent recriminations later. He suspected that Condon had left because he feared the project would fail and damage his reputation, and Groves believed it was Condon who pushed Oppenheimer to "open" the laboratory instead of compartmentalizing it. Condon saw it differently: "The thing which upsets me most is the extraordinarily close security policy.... I only want to say that in my case I found that the extreme concern with security was morbidly depressing—especially the discussion about censoring mail and telephone calls."[11]

It took six months to find a suitable replacement for Condon. In the meantime, Oppenheimer chose to appoint special assistants to take charge of administrative duties. One of his best was David Hawkins, who came from the University of California to serve as the liaison between the civilian organization and the military post. Hawkins later became the laboratory's first unofficial historian. Oppenheimer then asked Arthur L. Hughes, former chairman of the Department of Physics at Washington University in St. Louis, to become personnel director.

Next, Oppenheimer set about selecting his division leaders. Each of these crucial positions required prestige in one's field as well as some managerial skill. Oppenheimer relinquished his temporary directorship of the Theoretical Division and formally placed Hans Bethe in charge. Robert Bacher came to Los Alamos to assume leadership of the Experimental Physics Division. Captain William S. Parsons of the navy took directorship of the Ordnance Division somewhat later in the year. Joseph Kennedy, only twenty-six years old, came from Berkeley and took over the Chemistry and Metallurgy Division.

Oppenheimer decentralized the organization's government by creating a Governing Board to help plan and conduct the technical effort and act as a directorate for cooperative decision-making. In addition to Oppenheimer, this would be the group that Groves would seek counsel from during his many visits to the laboratory. The first members of the board were Oppenheimer, the four division leaders, and Hughes and Dana P.

Mitchell, representing the administrative offices. Later, Edwin McMillan, George Kistiakowsky, and Kenneth Bainbridge were added as liaisons with the technical units.

The Governing Board met on Mondays and Thursdays at 7:45 p.m. in Oppenheimer's second-floor office. The first few meetings hardly touched on research and development but dealt with frustrating details of housing, construction, security, morale, and personnel. Realizing that the board should not be preoccupied with such matters, Oppenheimer announced on June 17 the establishment of the Laboratory Coordinating Council. Not a decision-making body, the council would handle policy matters referred to it by the Governing Board. Most of its twenty members were at least group leaders. Bacher was asked to prepare the agendas, and either he or Oppenheimer presided over the meetings.

At Bethe's suggestion, a third group was established that month— a colloquium in which scientists could freely exchange ideas. The group would develop a broad sense of the laboratory's activities, and young men would participate in the discussions on an equal footing with their seniors. The Governing Board set the agenda for the first colloquium: discussion of the three or four most promising methods of uranium and plutonium production, questions of precise measurements of nuclear processes, and various ordnance characteristics of explosives.[12]

General Groves was nearly apoplectic when he heard about the colloquium. To his way of thinking, it gave every participant a full view of the work at Los Alamos and, to some extent, the work of the Manhattan Project. His concept of security demanded compartmentalization. The more someone knew, the more he could disclose, accidentally or otherwise. In the general's entire operation, only Jean O'Leary came close to knowing what he knew. As he said long after the war, he didn't bring Oppenheimer "into the whole project," but then, he didn't bring Lawrence and Compton and others as well.

Colonel Nichols, who instituted compartmentalization early on at Oak Ridge, understood Groves's concerns:

Groves ardently supported compartmentalization of the atomic bomb project. He did not want too many individuals having complete knowledge of all the work. He believed compartmentalization was the only way to maintain secrecy to the maximum possible extent. Moreover, knowing the inquiring minds of scientists, he felt that they would spend too much time prying around into other parts of the project, and he wanted to keep everyone's nose to the grindstone.[13]

Groves pressed Oppenheimer hard to drop the idea, but Oppenheimer stood firm. It was critical, he argued, that scientists in each division and group know of the work in other units. Bethe saw that "this free interchange of ideas was entirely contrary to the organization of the Manhattan District as a whole.... Oppenheimer had to fight hard for free discussions among all qualified members of the laboratory. But the free flow of information and discussion, together with Oppenheimer's personality, kept morale at its highest throughout the war."[14]

The colloquium was the subject of heated discussion at the August 5 Governing Board meeting. Lieutenant Colonel Whitney Ashbridge, the military post commander, spoke for Groves in voicing concerns over security. In the end, the board stood by Oppenheimer:

The following recommendations are made by the Board: (1) that all work done in this laboratory can appropriately be discussed in the colloquia; of work done elsewhere which reaches us in the form of classified reports, all questions which have a presumptive bearing on the work of the laboratory may be discussed; (2) that Dr. Teller again be asked to operate the colloquia on this basis without further discussion; and (3) that if this is not possible, Dr. Oppenheimer be requested to clarify at Mr. [*sic*] Teller's request the policy governing the running of the colloquia at the next meeting of the coordinating council on making the above statements.[15]

To placate Groves, Oppenheimer agreed to enforce a strict honor system and to limit participation in the colloquium to "staff members"—persons with scientific degrees or equivalent experience, who, in contrast to other laboratory staff, were regarded as "contributors to or beneficiaries from an exchange of information." Although a major departure from military custom, the colloquium was well worth the risk because of the cross-fertilization of ideas and the *esprit de corps* fostered among scientists—or so Oppenheimer argued.

To further mollify Groves, Oppenheimer established a three-man committee—composed of Hawkins, Manley, and Kennedy from the Chemistry Division—responsible for security within the Tech Area. They made sure that office safes were locked and that classified documents were properly secured. When someone was caught violating the rules, he had to roam the offices the following evening to catch similar violations.

Groves was not satisfied. In late June he quietly raised the question of the colloquium with his Military Policy Committee. Although the committee members could not dispute its value, they urged tight control. Vannevar Bush was asked to persuade President Roosevelt himself to write to Oppenheimer about the importance of security. Before Bush had an opportunity to make an appointment with the president, Roosevelt called him in for a review of the fission project. Bush asked him to write to Oppenheimer, and the president agreed. Roosevelt's letter encouraged Oppenheimer to advance the work of Los Alamos and implored him to remember the need for security and for living under unusual restrictions:

I have therefore given directions that every precaution be taken to insure the security of your project and feel sure that those in charge will see that these orders are carried out.... Though there are other important groups at work, I am writing only to you as the leader of the one which is operating under very special conditions, and to General Groves.[16]

Years later, Groves was still rankled by what he regarded as the "breakdown" of compartmentalization at Los Alamos, although he wasn't sure whom to blame for it. "[Condon] did a tremendous amount of damage at Los Alamos in the initial setup.... I could never make up my mind as to whether Dr. Oppenheimer was the one who was primarily at fault in breaking up the compartmentalization, or whether it was Dr. Condon."[17]

There were other, less heated, disagreements over security measures. In May 1943 Groves instructed Colonel Ashbridge, Harmon's replacement, to issue orders that no one was to enter or leave Los Alamos without signing his name at the guard house, with the exception of men employed by contractors. This order caused friction between civilian and military personnel, and Oppenheimer was forced to write to Groves in protest: "By placing the emphasis on post rather than laboratory security the effects of this measure would tend to weaken the only security which we can effectively carry out at this time." Groves's order had been issued in violation of an earlier agreement that residents would be advised of any new security measures before they were put in place. Oppenheimer therefore asked Groves to "rescind" his order[18] and the general backed down.

Oppenheimer's security concerns extended beyond Los Alamos. The task of developing a weapon depended heavily on the other projects of the Manhattan District. The Hill relied not only on the huge plants at Hanford and Oak Ridge for nuclear materials but also on the smaller laboratories—such as the Metallurgical Lab at Chicago and the Radiation Lab at Princeton—for the results of ongoing experiments. Without information from these other sites, the Los Alamos lab was operating in a vacuum. Oppenheimer and his staff found the shroud of secrecy covering Manhattan laboratories frustrating.

The pressing need for communication among the labs was only partially resolved in June. Groves accepted the need for some exchange, but he considered the demands of security so great that only the most critically necessary information should be shared. Accordingly, he drafted a set of liaison procedures stipulating that the exchange of information between Los Alamos and, for example, the Met Lab at Chicago be conducted between specified representatives and limited to questions of chemical, metallurgical, and certain other properties of nuclear materials. On June 17, Groves sent both Oppenheimer and Compton a four-page letter that set out the "principles" that should govern the exchange of information between Los Alamos and Chicago. Some information was strictly prohibited: "For reasons of military security, certain kinds of information as to production piles, military weapons, and time schedules ... are not to be interchanged even though this would be of benefit to the work."[19]

Oppenheimer felt these procedures were too strict, and on July 2 he wrote to Groves that division heads in the laboratory must be kept "adequately" informed about production schedules. Scientists at Los Alamos needed to know in what form they would receive the uranium as well as what kind of processing it would have undergone. Groves partially relented, insisting that visits to other sites were justifiable only if they benefited both organizations.[20]

Only a handful of scientists were given substantial access to the entire MED enterprise. The short list included Conant, Tolman, Compton, Lawrence, and Oppenheimer.[21]

Complaints inevitably found their way to Oppenheimer. Many had to do with human relations: security, censorship, transportation, commissary access, and the like. Condon's arrival and abrupt departure had done little for civilian-military relations, which in any case had never been smooth. Army security personnel—saddled with the difficult task of administering and securing a civilian enterprise located within a military setting—were as much in the dark about the work of Los Alamos as any outsider and tended to overreact in matters of security. And all GIs resented the higher salaries paid to scientists as much as they envied the comparative freedom and privileges of their civilian neighbors.

Groves was repeatedly bothered by what he regarded as the outrageous behavior of the scientists and their families. To him, they seemed incapable of discipline and unaware that many other Americans, as part of the war effort, were doing with much less. Demands for babysitters, maids, better stoves, and similar luxuries frustrated him. Groves referred to Los Alamos civilians, young and old, as children. Hill residents, as the scientists began to refer to themselves, in turn called the general many equally unflattering names, including Dorothy McKibbin's favorite, "Goo-Goo Eyes."

On one issue, Groves remained unflagging: security. In February 1943, the general, always vigilant, ordered Ashbridge to exercise "complete censorship" of communications in order to maintain the secrecy of the project.[22] At the time, censorship did not apply to personal correspondence. Ashbridge occupied a unique position at Los Alamos: he was actually a graduate of the Ranch School and delighted in showing new residents his former haunts. His security duties, however, became more difficult as Los Alamos grew and increased its contact with other MED projects.

Groves found it necessary to remind Oppenheimer to "tighten up" security and frequently wrote brief letters or memos citing specific security breaches. The contingent of visiting foreign scientists dismayed him with their carelessness. He was equally disturbed by the use of the telephone. In a burst of letters, Groves reproved Oppenheimer for the phone habits of the scientists working with Kingman—the code name for the army's Wendover Air Field in Utah—several of whom had been secretly monitored over telephone lines tapped by Post Intelligence:

> I've always been disturbed at the length of telephone conversations between Kingman and Y, although I knew we couldn't do without them.... I understand that a teletype machine and scrambler have now been installed at Kingman. That should enable a reduction in the number and length of essential telephone calls and result in improvement in our security. I wish you would remind our people that while we hope and pray that scramble teletypes are secure we can't be sure and therefore we must be on our guard in writing of our messages.[23]

When he learned that there was a telephone in Fuller Lodge, Groves called Oppenheimer and asked him to explain. The phone, Oppenheimer responded, was there in case he or any other laboratory official was urgently needed.

Security was not Oppenheimer's only headache. He also had to deal with contention over salaries. Initially, scientists were paid according to one of two pay scales. The first was that of the Office of Scientific Research and Development, a fairly crude system based on scientific degrees held and the number of years since the degrees had been conferred. Those with a simple bachelor's degree would earn two hundred dollars a month; those with master's or a bachelor's with one year of experience, $220; a doctor-ate with one year of experience, $305; and a doctorate with four years, $380. The maximum salary on this scale was four hundred dollars a month.[24] The second scale, for those who had come to Los Alamos from a university, was based on a "no loss, no gain" principle. Persons who had been paid for the nine-month academic year were now paid at twelve-tenths of their academic rate.

There were difficulties and inequities in both systems. Those who came to Los Alamos from industry got higher salaries than their academic colleagues, some of whom resented being paid less for doing work of equivalent or greater importance and difficulty. Technicians—men with considerable technical skill but usually with no college degree—had to be paid at rates consistent with the current labor market. In numerous cases, technicians who ranked lower in responsibility than many of the young scientists were paid more. And because of its youth, the laboratory had no formal system for granting service or merit increases. Groves, unfortu-nately, was of little help in resolving the problem.

When Oppenheimer finally asked Hughes, the personnel director, to prepare some sort of institutional policy, Hughes devised a plan based on OSRD scales and submitted it to Groves and the University of California. Its approval was delayed in Washington until February 1944. Although tentative salary proposals were drawn up and followed to one degree or another while the laboratory waited for formal approval of its salary schedule, there were no promotions at Los Alamos until the war was nearly over.

Oppenheimer tried to draw attention to the problem in a personal way. In September 1943, he wrote to Robert Sproul, the president of the University of California system, requesting that his salary of ten thousand dollars a year be reduced by two hundred dollars a month. He justified the reduction by "applying" the salary rules currently in place. Sproul replied that it was ultimately for the War Department to decide, although he and colleagues thought the salary fair given the level of responsibilities.

Groves received a copy of Oppenheimer's letter to Sproul, and he wrote to his director, "I do wish to tell you how much I personally approve of your attitude."[25]

It was a small gesture, but it was the sort of act that Oppenheimer knew would please his boss.

Chapter Eight

FORTUNATE CHOICES

O nce Leslie Groves accepted his new assignment, he embraced it
completely. From his appointment in September 1942 until the
end of the war, he worked at full speed, often fourteen hours a day
or more in Washington, D.C., and even longer on the road visiting the
installations of the Manhattan Project scattered from one end of the con-
tinent to the other. His remarkable energy and stamina frequently
exhausted those who worked and traveled with him.

When he was in Washington, he rose early, made his own breakfast,
and drove a green Dodge from his two-story home on Thirty-fifth
Street, N.W., to his offices in the New War Building in Foggy Bottom
(now part of the State Department). Sometimes he would pick up one
of the young secretaries in his office, Anne Wilson, and together they
would drive downtown. With Jean O'Leary, he was always one of the
first in the office. At six in the evening, he typically received a call from
his wife regarding dinner. If he could spare the time, he drove home,

joined his wife and daughter briefly, and then returned to work. If that wasn't possible, he ate in the War Building cafeteria or at a diner less than a block from his office. This was the pattern six days a week and sometimes Sundays. On the rare weekend day the general had off, he liked to get in several sets of tennis, a game at which he was surprisingly competitive.

Early in their marriage, Groves told his wife never to ask what he did at work; he wanted to be able to say that he never talked about work at home. Grace complied, and she knew nothing about the Manhattan Project until the end of the war. She assumed what he did was important, and, as a good army daughter and wife, she dutifully accepted her husband's outrageous schedule. The unspoken understanding between Grace and Dick was that this was how military families lived, especially during wartime. From time to time, Grace and the children visited the general's offices. They became quite friendly with a few members of the staff, particularly O'Leary, who often passed along messages from Groves to his wife or children or mailed checks to his son Richard at school. At no time, however, did she reveal even the smallest detail about what the office and the general were doing.

Grace made her own life. With her daughter, Gwen, in high school and her son, Richard, in his last year at West Point, she had time to volunteer at the Soldiers and Sailors Canteen, and she even worked part-time at Garfinkel's department store to earn extra money. The Groveses didn't socialize a great deal. It wasn't in the general's character to give or attend parties, and his schedule during the war precluded many of the activities they might have pursued together in peacetime. In 1943, following the death of her mother, Grace suffered something of an emotional breakdown, but she sought help and worked her way back to health.

One thing was clear to Groves—the urgency of his mission. It was the basis for his management of the Manhattan Project, and he knew that the vast sums of money he was spending in pursuit of that mission would inevitably have to be justified:

My mission as given to me by Secretary Stimson was to produce [the atomic bomb] at the earliest possible date so as to
bring the war to a conclusion. That was further emphasized by
his statement that any time that a single day could be saved I
should save that day. The instructions to the project were that
any individual in the project who felt that the ultimate completion, insofar as he understood it, was going to be delayed by as
much as a day by something that was happening, it was his
duty to report it direct to me.... [U]rgency was on us right
from the start.[1]

Groves's days were a lively mixture of meetings with staff and visitors,
appointments elsewhere in Washington, and phone calls—typically dozens of them. Scientific visitors might include Oppenheimer, Tolman
(always one of Groves's favorites), Sir James Chadwick, Bush, or Conant,
perhaps his most useful scientist ally in the endeavor. Military visitors
might include General Styer or General Tom Robbins, Groves's immediate
superior, or any number of the younger officers who worked for him in
all parts of the country. Frequently he had to rush to the Pentagon for
meetings with George Marshall, Secretary Stimson, and his aides Harvey
Bundy and George Harrison. And there was the occasional meeting at the
White House.

Groves communicated extensively by letter and memorandum, sent
and received by secure courier, as well as by telex, but he was addicted to
the telephone. Arthur Compton in Chicago and Ernest Lawrence in Berkeley called or received calls daily, and Groves could be on the phone with
Oppenheimer in Los Alamos four or five times a day. Many of his conversations were with the officers who managed the project's laboratories and
plants: Major Arthur Peterson at the Met Lab in Chicago, Major Harry
Fidler at the electromagnetic separation plant in Berkeley, Lieutenant
Colonel James Stavers in the MED offices in New York City, Colonel
Franklin Matthias at the reactors in Hanford, and—perhaps more than

anyone else—Colonel Kenneth Nichols at the gaseous diffusion operation in Oak Ridge. Groves used the phone so often that his arm, especially his elbow, began to hurt. His staff acquired a telephone operator's headset for him in 1944, although publicity photographs always show him with a conventional receiver, never a headset. Many times, O'Leary, who shared his office, would listen in on the calls from her own phone and take notes.

Security was pervasive. Teletypes were sent in codes that were changed regularly. There were special codes for communications with key persons like Oppenheimer and Nichols, who were expected to carry their code with them at all times and report its loss immediately. Only Groves and O'Leary had access to all of them. A collection of "shorthand" words and phrases was employed in telephone conversations.

With the exception of the general himself, no one was allowed to keep a diary or a record of his work or the operations of the office. O'Leary kept his calendar and records of his phone calls, which were locked up every night. In fact, all paperwork was collected, even personal calendars, at the end of the day and secured in office safes, along with a box of the general's favorite chocolates. Nothing was left to chance. In late 1943, when Groves suspected that foreign agents were following him, he had two of his own security men shadow him throughout an entire day in Washington. They detected nothing.

From Washington, Groves darted back and forth to every part of the country at a pace that would have drained many others. He occasionally traveled by commercial aircraft, usually TWA, and in 1945 Secretary Stimson put a military plane at his disposal. But most of Groves's travel was by rail. His private drawing room on the Santa Fe Super Chief, the B&O Capitol Limited, or the Southern Pacific Streamliner served as a second office. Sometimes O'Leary or another aide would accompany him for a few hours of work on board before leaving the general's train and returning on another to Washington. If Groves was traveling to California or Los Alamos, O'Leary would ride with him as far as Baltimore and then get off and take another train back to Union Station. Others, including

Oppenheimer, Lawrence, and Nichols, rode with Groves partway on trips to snatch time with their overcommitted boss.[2] Lawrence recalled one overnight ride with Groves on which, after hours of conversation, Lawrence decided to get some sleep. When he woke at dawn, he was surprised to see his companion still at work. The general was determined to use every moment he could.

In order to not draw attention to himself as a general officer, Groves traveled in civilian clothes, and he instructed Colonels Nichols and Marshall to do the same. But he always changed into uniform when he reached his destination. He did not carry a briefcase—again, to avoid attracting attention—but instead carried a simple brown envelope that he kept with him at all times. When he slept on the train, he slid the envelope underneath the mattress and blocked the door. Later in the war, when he traveled by military airplane, he kept the envelope in his hand or sat on it. Groves even carried a pistol with him—sometimes a .32 caliber, other times a .25—but never in a holster, just in his pocket.

Groves's prodigious energy surprised many people, especially those who mistook his overweight frame for a sign of indolence. No one ever questioned his drive or determination, but his manner, often rude and brusque, and his perpetual frown were hardly endearing. The overwhelming majority of the Manhattan Project's employees—from Oak Ridge to Hanford—never met Groves or even knew his name. The exceptions were in the smaller installations, such as Los Alamos and the Met Lab, where the general's interactions with scientists and engineers often reinforced an unfavorable opinion. Groves sensed their unfavorable reaction but dismissed it:

> A lot of [the younger scientists] were resentful about being held down during the war; because their opinions had not been asked for. There had been no "faculty" meetings. If I went to Los Alamos, for example, I would see Oppenheimer and his group leaders. We might be in a meeting. We might go around

and see things and talk to various individuals who were way down on the scale. But they weren't asked for their views on how to solve these problems or what we should do.[3]

Many of the scientists disdained the military, especially the army. Priscilla Green observed, "The scientists felt they were an elite group. They didn't consider the military helpful; anything the soldiers had done to get the post started could have been done better by a scientist."[4] For the scientific rank and file, Groves was the personification of the military.

Oppenheimer and his senior leaders, on the other hand, soon came to see Groves as an extremely intelligent man who quickly grasped many of the intricacies of physics, chemistry, and explosives and did homework to learn more. His personality could be jarring, and his tongue was often sharp, but there was no doubting his intelligence and his capacity for getting things done. And this appreciation was not limited to Los Alamos. Colonel Matthias at Hanford noticed a change in those who regularly came in contact with Groves: "Scientists were amazed that he could absorb all that technical theory, then express it in terms anyone could understand."[5]

Groves's management style reflected his experiences in the military. He learned early on to look for the best people and companies and to hire them. Lines of authority were vertical and clear. To the extent he could, he assigned responsibility to those below him. And he avoided being swamped by detail. Robert Bacher thought that "Groves was a very fortunate choice to head this project. He was energetic and forceful but very blunt. He was a good judge of people, knew when to trust advice and when he did, he backed that advice without wavering."[6]

Groves could also be flexible in his dealings with people, although on a case-by-case basis. While he had no tolerance for error or stupidity, he tolerated disagreement from subordinates—to a point. Colonel Nichols, for example, confronted Groves early on about the general's treatment of him in public. Afterward, Groves exercised restraint, and the relationship was less strained.[7] Although never friends, they managed to establish a working détente that benefited both men.

The most important example of Groves's flexibility was his relationship with Robert Oppenheimer. Groves valued the man's intelligence and ability to work with and motivate other scientists—indeed, he depended on this—and he was prepared to overlook Oppenheimer's political associations and those of his family. Groves took great care to treat Oppenheimer with respect and deference, and Oppenheimer returned the favor. He accepted Groves's assistance and what some might have taken as intrusion into the management of the laboratory, and a genuine collaboration grew between them. When they were together, they addressed each other as "General Groves" and "Dr. Oppenheimer," but their letters often began with "My Dear General Groves" and "My Dear Dr. Oppenheimer." They met frequently and stayed in contact constantly. Groves recalled,

> I saw him on the average ... of anywhere from once a week to once a month. I talked to him on the phone about anywhere from 4 to 5 times a day to once in 3 or 4 days. I talked on all possible subjects of all varieties. During the time I spent a number of days, for example, on trains traveling where we might be together for 6 or 8 or 12 hours at a time.[8]

No one, whether in Washington or Los Alamos, ever heard the two men argue or exchange harsh words. If Groves displayed his less attractive qualities, Oppenheimer would genially rise to his defense. When Groves complained in front of Priscilla Green about missed deadlines and apathy among the scientists, Oppenheimer took it in stride and later explained to his secretary with a wry smile that the general was just letting everyone know who was in charge.

Oppenheimer's appointment as director surprised many of his colleagues. There was no question about his brilliance or charm, when he chose to display them, but as academics were fond of observing, a good professor does not necessarily make a great university president. Yet Oppenheimer—the theoretical physicist, the aesthete, the lover of Baudelaire and the Bhagavad Gita—emerged as an effective, even charismatic, organizational leader despite his lack of managerial experience.

Los Alamos was not a university, although its denizens often thought of it that way, and certainly not a large corporation or Wall Street bank. It was a rather odd collection of persons living temporarily in wartime isolation and charged with developing a new and extraordinary weapon before the enemy did. Subject to no budgetary bottom line, they were told to spend what was needed to get the job done.

In the spring of 1943, Robert Oppenheimer, not yet forty years old, found himself at the center of this grand enterprise, which even twelve months earlier he could not have imagined. An early riser like Leslie Groves, he could be seen walking from his home—Oppenheimer was one of a handful who were assigned a real house with a tub instead of a shower—to work at 7:30 in the morning. Instinctively responding to the New Mexico climate, he quickly traded the relatively formal attire common to universities of the time for loose, tweedy jackets and narrow ties that accentuated his slenderness. When he was casual, he was in jeans with a blue cotton shirt and a massive Navajo silver buckle on his belt. His porkpie hat became emblematic of his presence throughout the laboratory; one tongue-in-cheek memorandum to the Maintenance Group requested a single nail installed in Oppenheimer's office for the "Director's hat." Everyone knew what that meant. He toured the scattered offices, interacting with staff, listening to ideas and complaints, cajoling when necessary and encouraging when he could. Some thought the small crowd of animated, talkative young men who often followed him around made Oppie look like a mother duck with her ducklings. He came to know hundreds of men and women by their first names.

Despite the rapid growth of the laboratory, Oppenheimer remained accessible to his staff. Charles Critchfield of the Engineering Division found Oppenheimer quite approachable:

> [H]e kept his door, the hall door and his secretary's office door open, so when you went by, he would greet you if he wasn't busy. Sometimes he would say, "Do you have a minute? I'd like to talk to you." ... So I'd go in and he'd close the office door to the secretary and to the hall. Then he would start discussing— maybe things about work—but it always ended up in a lecture of some kind.... But he didn't talk about weapons or physics. He talked about the mystery of life.[9]

Oppenheimer became effective in mediating differences among his luminous and diverse staff, and he could sense when he could be useful in surmounting a theoretical or developmental obstacle. John Manley likened Oppenheimer's ability to manage his complex staff to that of a ballet director. Oppenheimer was both generous and occasionally abrasive, deftly leading his colleagues but sometimes irritating them with his intellectual superiority. He was perfectly willing to let them take credit for success but rarely gave a direct compliment. On a few occasions—when he was piqued or exasperated by slow thinking or perceived obstinacy or, later in the war, when he was near exhaustion—he could be caustic. Manley's impression was that Oppenheimer "had an impatience with stupidity, which was understandable, and an impatience with fumbling: fumbling in expression, thinking. In no case was it deliberate to cause pain."[10] Harold Agnew disagreed. He was shocked when Oppenheimer unexpectedly lashed out at someone so harshly that nearby staff members had to look away, stunned and embarrassed. Norris Bradbury never saw this darker side with laboratory staff but did see it directed at the military.

Colonel Nichols, Groves's aide, was particularly the butt of "strong language" from the director.[11]

Oppenheimer was at his best leading meetings among his colleagues, settling differences, and acting as a buffer between the civilian staff and General Groves and the military. In meetings, Oppenheimer, having set the agenda, listened carefully as participants rambled, and then he skillfully pulled together a dozen alternatives into a coherent plan. He looked forward to his informal visits to the Hill's many offices and labs. These took more and more time as buildings spread across the mesa and into the canyons. It was easy enough in the early days to walk to nearby buildings, such as those in the Tech Area, but more difficult as the laboratory expanded and his schedule grew more demanding.

The visits allowed him to listen quietly from the back of the room before offering a new interpretation or solution. Although his presence intimidated some staff members, most appreciated Oppenheimer's ability to see quickly many dimensions of a problem. His understanding was not restricted to his own specialty, theoretical physics, but embraced all the fields represented in the project, from metallurgy to explosives. According to a favorite, if apocryphal, story told at Los Alamos, Oppenheimer walked into a room where a group of physicists, having wrestled all day with a particularly difficult problem, had filled a large blackboard with their elaborate calculations. Oppenheimer observed for a moment, then walked to the board, corrected a figure, and walked out without saying a word. The myth of Oppenheimer had a foundation in fact. As Bethe later acknowledged, he "was intellectually superior to us."[12]

Priscilla Green watched her boss mature as a leader week by week, month by month. "It's a real mystery that he rose to this so fast, considering that he was a very diffident, shy person to begin with," she recalled.[13]

Yet for all of his intelligence, magnetism, and newly found administrative skills, Oppenheimer harbored his own insecurities. Could he truly direct such an enormous undertaking as the laboratory? Driven by ambition, had he overreached? Could he make the tough decisions necessary to deliver an atomic bomb in time for use in the war? Groves sensed this lack of confidence early on and tried to bolster Oppenheimer when he could, for example, by establishing the review committee. Robert Bacher came face to face with Oppenheimer's insecurity when the director confessed during the summer of 1943 that he didn't know if he was up to the job.

> During that first summer…Robert often expressed privately his real doubts about his suitability for the director's job and his concern as to whether he could really do it. In a sense he was riding the tiger and he felt very heavily pressed by the many problems of the project and doubtless also by his difficulties with the security people.[14]

Bacher spent many hours with Oppenheimer, reassuring him, during long walks into the Jemez foothills, that he was not only capable of leading the laboratory but perhaps the only man who could. Despite this reassurance, Oppenheimer's self-doubts continued throughout the war.

While Oppenheimer loved the mesa, his wife, Kitty, did not. At Berkeley, she had been the wife of a charming, brilliant, wealthy professor who moved in eclectic circles and lived in a city of some sophistication. And there, especially in the early years of their marriage, she was the center of her husband's world. In Los Alamos, she was still Robert Oppenheimer's wife, but the small town was squalid, the mix of people different from what she had known, and, more troubling for her, she was no longer the focus of her husband's life: she had been replaced by his work.

Kitty was a gracious hostess when she needed to be, especially when VIPs were involved. But her husband's late nights, his long absences, her growing family—a daughter, Katherine, nicknamed "Toni," was born in December 1944—and the pressure of being "first lady" took their toll. She was far more comfortable with men than women and had few female friends, a pattern throughout her life. She was solicitous of those she liked and dismissive of those she didn't. She did not care for Rose Bethe, for example, who, like her husband, Hans, was admired by everyone. She turned against the equally popular Charlotte Serber and stopped inviting the Serbers to dinner, despite their association that went back almost a decade.

Priscilla Green saw Mrs. Oppenheimer up close. "Kitty was impossible," she recalled. "She was not friendly, she was the boss's wife, and she could really be mean. She could also cause trouble for you, so you had to be very careful."[15] Anne Wilson, who replaced Green in 1945 as Oppenheimer's secretary, initially had her own difficulties with Kitty. Wilson was young and attractive, and rumors that she and her boss were "involved" inevitably circulated in the small community. Kitty heard the talk and confronted Wilson, who, dumbstruck by the question, denied any involvement. Kitty apparently believed her and backed off.[16] Green remembered that a number of men and women unabashedly, but mostly under their breath, called Oppenheimer's wife a "bitch." Those who were more forgiving simply found her "very difficult to handle." It seems that Robert never intervened in his wife's relationships or tried to change her behavior. Some, like Louis and Elinor Hempelman, thought he was intimidated by his wife. Others assumed that he simply didn't want the confrontation.

Kitty kept to herself at home or left the mesa to shop in Albuquerque or made visits to California, sometimes staying for weeks. She also began to drink heavily. Some days she shut herself in her house and drank by herself, and other times she invited a small number of women to join her. Occasionally, after drinking excessively at parties, she would reveal deeply intimate information about her married life. Her sister-in-law, Jackie Oppenheimer, was invited to cocktails one afternoon. When she arrived at four o'clock, "there was just Kitty and four or five other women—drinking companions—and we just sat there with very little conversation—drinking. It was awful and I never went again."[17]

Who came to Los Alamos? When congressional committees put that question to Groves and Oppenheimer after the war, they could answer simply, "Everyone." They meant everyone with a reputation in physics. For most of its wartime history, Los Alamos was aglow with a galaxy of eminent scientists. Five men had already won the Nobel prize.* Five more would win it after the war.

Los Alamos also attracted a younger but well established generation of prominent scientists.[18] Hiring one senior scientist often meant acquiring a bright team of young graduate students. Robert Wilson brought a staff with him from Princeton, as did Bacher from Cornell and the Radiation Lab at MIT. Wilson's experience was typical. When his isotron project at Princeton ended, he and his team were "without a problem to work on." Yet they had experience and spirit, and "like a bunch of professional soldiers we signed up, en masse, to go to Los Alamos."[19]

Oppenheimer even managed to attract Niels Bohr, a scientist-god of sorts, who arrived with his son and assistant, Aage. Bohr, who became known as Uncle Nick, was a living legend to most young men at Los Alamos. He had performed ground-breaking work in quantum physics and received the Nobel Prize for his theoretical work in 1922. He was also the man to whom Meitner and Frisch had rushed with the news that the Germans had discovered fission.

Bohr had barely escaped the Germans in October 1943. Fleeing Copenhagen, he reached Sweden hidden aboard a fishing boat. His young granddaughter followed him in the shopping case of a friendly diplomat. From Sweden, the British flew him to England in the bomb bay of a Mosquito fighter, but he arrived unconscious because of a poorly fitting oxygen mask. Within a few weeks, Bohr left for America and Los Alamos. He

---

* The five Nobel laureates at Los Alamos at one time or another were Niels Bohr, James Franck, James Chadwick, Enrico Fermi, and Isidor Rabi; other laureates served in other parts of the MED.

brought with him a diagram of a nuclear device given to him earlier in the year by the man leading the German nuclear effort, Werner Heisenberg. The diagram was soon judged not to be a bomb but a rudimentary reactor.

Bohr met with many of the laboratory's staff but spent considerable time on the theoretical considerations of fission. Oppenheimer felt his work was not only insightful but valuable to morale. After Bohr's visit to Los Alamos in January 1944, Oppenheimer wrote to Groves to allay his distrust of foreigners. Using Bohr's code-name, he wrote that "Dr. Baker has done everything he could to support this project and to indicate that he is sympathetic not only with its purposes and general method of procedure, but with the policies and achievements of this project's overall direction. I should like to make it clear that the effect of his presence on the morale of those with whom he came in contact was always positive and always helpful."[20]

Groves did not share Oppenheimer's elevated view of Bohr, however. By chance, Groves rode the same train from Chicago to Lamy, outside of Santa Fe, with Bohr on the Dane's first trip to Los Alamos. "I got through talking to Niels Bohr on the train going to Los Alamos for the first time. I think I talked to him about 12 hours straight on what he was not to say. Certain things he was not to talk about out there. He got out there and within 5 minutes after his arrival he was saying everything he promised he would not say."[21]

For help with explosives research, Oppenheimer readily accepted Groves's de facto hire, Captain William S. "Deak" Parsons of the U.S. Navy. Groves, who had met Parsons in the 1930s while working on antiaircraft defense, liked him and invited him to his office one morning. Within minutes the general "was sure he was the man for the job."[22] Oppenheimer interviewed Parsons that afternoon, and he and Groves offered him the posting on the spot. Coming from the U.S. Naval Proving Ground, Parsons was one of the few men at Los Alamos with experience in explosives, and he had been involved with the development of the navy's MK 32 proximity fuse. He was put in charge of the Ordnance Division. He read textbooks and articles on physics at night, quickly earning the respect of his scientific colleagues for his quick mind and willingness to learn. Within a year, the laboratory added two other men with experience in explosives, George Kistiakowsky and Norris Bradbury.

After two years of negotiations between Winston Churchill and President Roosevelt, the British sent a team to Los Alamos. In the summer of 1942, Oppenheimer and his group at Berkeley had been impressed with the results that researchers in several British universities had achieved, but the war had channeled much of Britain's scientific effort into other endeavors, particularly radar, and Churchill reluctantly admitted that only the United States had the resources to undertake the research and development of atomic weapons. In the fall of 1943, the two countries established a Combined Policy Committee in Washington. Conant favored restricting or at least compartmentalizing British access to America's atomic effort, a position Groves strongly endorsed, though he would have preferred no British involvement at all. Among other concerns, he found their security vetting of scientists questionable. But with the agreement between Roosevelt and Churchill, some participation was inevitable.

In November 1942, Oppenheimer, with Groves's reluctant approval, sent a report to Rudolf E. Peierls, the German-born director of Britain's fission project, codenamed Tube Alloys. The twenty-page memorandum reflected Oppenheimer's diplomatic style: "In the last months a group of theoretical physicists has been investigating some of the questions involved in the design of a fast fission bomb.... [W]e thought it might be helpful to communicate to you in an informal way some of the findings of our group."[23] The report was reasonably frank, although it did not mention American theoretical speculations on the hydrogen bomb. By December 1943, several teams of British scientists arrived in the United States for placement in various Manhattan District laboratories. A twenty-member group was dispatched to Los Alamos.

Oppenheimer originally considered asking Sir James Chadwick, discoverer of the neutron, to lead a separate British division but changed his mind; the Britons' expertise was needed in all groups. Members of the team were dispersed throughout the laboratory, and each man reported to his American group or division leader. When Chadwick returned to Washington, Peierls assumed command of the mission. British scientists like Otto Frisch, Ernest Titterton, Philip Moon, Carson Mark, William G. Penney, and James Tuck brought with them valuable experience in nuclear physics, electronics, and explosives.

The British didn't come all at once but rather in small groups. A few arrived in December 1943, and more came in the spring. To their surprise, the first arrivals were met outside under some pine trees by Oppenheimer, wearing his porkpie hat and smoking a pipe. "Welcome to Los Alamos," he said through nicotine-stained teeth, "and who the devil are you?"[24]

Groves refused to allow five French scientists working in Canada to enter the United States and even insisted there be no contact between them and men in Los Alamos. He saw them as a security risk. On the other hand, he deferred to Oppenheimer's insistence that George Placzek and his team, all native-born Canadians, be allowed to come to work at the laboratory.[25]

One member of the British team, Klaus Fuchs, would become infamous after the war. A German Jew, he escaped from the Nazis, became a British subject, and was part of the British contingent at Los Alamos. After the war, it was learned that even before his arrival in Los Alamos, Fuchs had turned over to the Russians American and British plans for uranium separation. Strongly sympathetic to the socialist cause, he believed that atomic secrets belonged as much to the communist countries as to the United States or Britain. Working for Soviet intelligence under the code name "Charles," Fuchs methodically submitted to Russian agents detailed information and drawings on the implosion bomb.

Several times during his stay in Los Alamos, Fuchs met the American-born Soviet spy Harry Gold in Santa Fe. At the Castillo Bridge or driving through the outskirts of town, Fuchs briefed Gold, a chemist, on the implosion developments and occasionally turned over a packet of papers written in small, tight script. Leading a quiet life in Los Alamos, Fuchs talked little, remained conscientious in his work, and mixed carefully with his colleagues. He was, as one person described him, bright and productive but bland and seemingly innocuous. He occasionally baby-sat for his married friends, and one wife dubbed him Poverino—the poor one.

Fuchs's boss, Hans Bethe, was as surprised as anyone when the news of his betrayal broke in 1950. Bethe told the FBI, "If he was a spy, he played his role beautifully. He worked days and nights. He was a bachelor and had nothing better to do, and he contributed very greatly to the success of the Los Alamos project."[26]

It is possible to guess the sort of information Fuchs provided to his Soviet contact, although not its extent. As an angry and embarrassed Groves said after the war, "we do know ... what he knew and consequently what he could have told them."[27] That knowledge included the design of the Oak Ridge gaseous diffusion plant, the designs for both the gun and implosion bombs, what improvements could be made to both weapons, the initiator, and the wartime thinking on the Super.

Unknown to Fuchs—and to government security—two other men were also passing information to the Russians. David Greenglass, a corporal stationed at Los Alamos as part of the army's Special Engineer Detachment, worked at S Site with the group designing and fabricating explosive lenses for the implosion bomb. In 1944 his in-laws, Julius and Ethel Rosenberg, gave Greenglass's wife, Ruth, $150 to visit her husband in Santa Fe. During their brief reunion, Ruth suggested that David might pass along information on the laboratory's work. The information in turn would be passed to Soviet agents. Like Fuchs, Greenglass was sympathetic to the communist philosophy, but unlike Fuchs, he accepted money for the information he supplied. By the end of the war, Greenglass—given the code name "Bumblebee" by his Soviet handler—had met several times with Julius Rosenberg and Harry Gold to pass along fairly complete sketches of the molds used to fabricate explosive charges for the implosion bomb.

The third spy was Theodore Hall, an exceptionally bright young physicist who graduated from Harvard at age eighteen. Quickly recruited for the Manhattan Project, Hall arrived at Los Alamos in January 1944, barely two months after his nineteenth birthday, the youngest scientist employed there during the war. Fearing an American monopoly of the atomic bomb, he contacted the Soviets in New York City on a brief visit in October and volunteered to pass along details about the weapons under development. Hall—code named "Mlad"—confirmed for the Soviets that the laboratory was developing two types of bombs and provided details of the plutonium implosion design—exceptionally valuable information that confirmed the accuracy of what Fuchs had told them.[28]

Despite the contribution of foreign scientists, the ranks at Los Alamos were overwhelmingly American. Many, like Joseph Kennedy, left attractive positions at major universities to join the new laboratory as group leaders. Kenneth Bainbridge, who was working on radar at the Radiation Laboratory, agreed to join the new venture after an afternoon with Oppenheimer and Bacher at the National Academy of Sciences Building in Washington. Norris Bradbury, who would succeed Oppenheimer as director, came from the U.S. Naval Proving Ground, where he worked for Parsons. Seth Neddermeyer arrived from the National Bureau of Standards. Donald Hornig left the Underwater Explosives Research Laboratory at Woods Hole, Massachusetts, after telephone calls from both Kistiakowsky and Conant. His boss asked him if he wanted to leave Woods Hole for another job, but he could not tell him what or where the project was. Hornig declined, but within twenty-four hours Conant called with a bit more information. "Remember, Hornig," Conant told him, "Uncle Sam is pointing his finger at you."[29]

During the first year, many of the young men came because they were already part of a project supported by the Manhattan program or some other research project. Others had been students of someone now on the Hill, and some were serving in the military but had relevant skills and scientific or technical backgrounds. It is safe to say that none would have guessed that the work he was engaged in would lead him to Los Alamos.

These young men would begin their careers at Los Alamos. Harold Agnew, twenty-one years old, came directly from working with Fermi and the reactor at Chicago. Oppenheimer seemed equally interested in employing Agnew's wife, Beverly, who had served as assistant to Richard Doan, director of the Metallurgical Laboratory. Skilled secretaries were highly prized, and she went to work for Robert Bacher. Raemer Schreiber left a small Manhattan District project at Purdue University, and Berlyn Brixner an engineering job in Albuquerque. Al Van Vessem, an army GI, had been told that only summer clothing was needed in New Mexico; he arrived during a major snowstorm in March 1944. William Popham was brought to Los Alamos because someone with plant management experience was needed to run S Site; when he arrived, everyone but Popham was surprised to learn that his Ph.D. was in botany. And Richard Feynmann, perhaps the brightest of the young men, came with a new Ph.D. from Princeton. He worked with Hans Bethe, who said he would rather lose two other men than lose Feynmann.[30] Even Frank Oppenheimer joined the staff in 1945 after having helped to plan the uranium separation plant at Oak Ridge and to make it operational. At Los Alamos, Frank was assigned to work with Bainbridge, who in 1945 directed preparations for the test of the implosion weapon, Fat Man.

Bob Krohn was typical of many young recruits. In 1942, he had just received his bachelor's degree in engineering physics at the University of Wisconsin and decided to join the navy. Serendipitously, his professor offered Krohn a job as a research assistant on a fission-related project being funded by the University of Chicago with OSRD money. The offer meant not only employment but an opportunity to take graduate courses and a temporary draft deferment. Krohn accepted, and less than half a year later, he was asked to meet with two visiting scientists—Ernest Lawrence and John Manley—who were recruiting for Los Alamos. They offered Krohn a job, which he accepted. He arrived in Los Alamos on opening day, April 15, 1943.[31]

Security clearances were a problem, at least at first. They could not be processed quickly enough, and for those with complicated social or political backgrounds, it could take even longer. Meanwhile, men were arriving every day on the Hill, bringing along wives and children, bags and furniture, dogs and cats, and cars. Groves reluctantly relaxed the rules so that scientists could vouch for one another. There were simply too many men with too much to do and too few security officials personally to investigate each new hire. Oppenheimer vouched for his senior men; they in turn, vouched for those working for them.

It was also necessary to establish a unit of military personnel with scientific and technical backgrounds, the Special Engineer Detachment (SED). Some of these men had degrees—a few even had doctorates—and others had been draftsmen or technicians before the war. The SED numbered thirty-nine men in 1943 but grew to over 1,600 by the war's end, accounting for 42 percent of the overall workforce at Los Alamos. Unlike their civilian colleagues, SED personnel were paid the smaller army salary and subject to military regulations. George L. Williams's story was typical. A graduate in engineering from the University of New Mexico, Williams was a master sergeant working at the army's Aberdeen Proving Ground in Maryland when he was told to pack his gear and prepare for reassignment. When he asked where he was going and what he would be doing, he was simply told he would learn everything later.

Val Fitch was another SED man assigned to Los Alamos. Having completed three years of his undergraduate course in electrical engineering before being drafted, he was assigned to work with the British physicist Ernest Titterton. He felt the discrepancies between military and civilian life immediately:

> I was assigned to an upper bunk.... We lived in single floor barracks, roughly 60 men to a unit. Our mail was censored, both incoming and outgoing. We ate in an army mess hall, but there was no KP.... Reveille came at 6 am, and we had calisthenics from 6:30 to 7:00. We could not leave our barracks for work on Saturday morning until after inspection of quarters.[32]

There was also a detachment of Women's Army Auxiliary Corps* at Los Alamos. The first seven WAACs arrived from Fort Sill, Oklahoma, on April 21, 1943, led by Captain Helen Mulvihill, who found Los Alamos "mind-boggling." Like everyone else coming to the Hill, she had no idea what to expect, having been told only that the posting was in New Mexico and she and her girls should report to an address in Santa Fe. In less than a month, though, she was hooked: "The country is very beautiful.... I've ridden all over it in a jeep.... [T]he climate is wonderful—clear, cool and light."[33] More women arrived and were dispersed throughout the organization. Those with college degrees were sent into laboratories. Myrtle Bachelder, with a B.S. degree as well as a master's in education, went to work in the Chemical and Spectrographic Analysis Section. Mary Miller, a Ph.D. in chemistry, was assigned to the Chemical and Metallurgical Division, where she ultimately became an alternate group leader. And Skip Green Richie, an assistant to Deak Parsons's secretary, doubled as a part-time babysitter for the Oppenheimers. Her most memorable moment was discovering that a bottle of indelible ink in her pocket had leaked down

---

* The Women's Army Auxiliary Corps (WAAC), which was not part of the U.S. Army itself, was replaced by the Women's Army Corps (WAC), which was part of the regular army, in July 1943.

her leg to her shoes and finally to the Oppenheimers' white carpet. She was quickly forgiven by the director himself.[34]

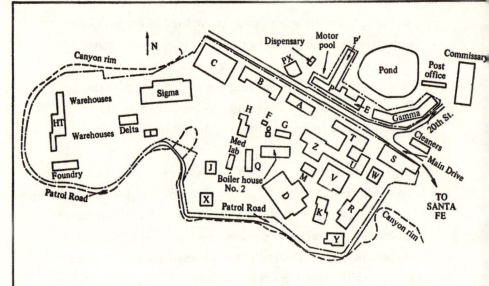

MAP OF TECHNICAL AREA – 1945

LEGEND

A - Director's Offices
B - Offices and Conference Rooms
C - Shops
D - Plutonium Purification Plant
E - Theoretical Division Offices
F - Storage
G - Graphite Fabrication
H - Offices & Laboratories
HT - Heat Treatment Plant
J - Research Laboratories
K - Gas Stock
M - Chemistry Supplies & Storage
P - Theoretical Division Offices & Personnel Offices

Q - Medical Offices
R - Laboratories
S - Stockroom
T - General Offices & Library
U - Chemistry & Physics Laboratories
V - Shops
W - Van de Graaff Machines
X - Cyclotron
Y - Cryogenics Laboratory
Z - Cockcroft-Walton Generator
Delta - Auditorium
Gamma- Research for M Division
Sigma - Metal, Plastic, & Ceramic Fabrication

Chapter Nine

ALL POSSIBLE
PRIORITY

———◦———

L os Alamos was a gamble.

As commanding general and the man with the most to lose—or win—Groves pushed and bullied his Manhattan Project as hard as he could. He wanted the atomic bomb delivered in time for use in the war. Oppenheimer also understood that Los Alamos was a gamble, and he too wanted to win. His tactics were less brutal and more circumspect. Where Groves commanded, Oppenheimer inspired. But there were barriers that both men had to overcome: a series of fundamental scientific and technological unknowns. No one knew for sure whether the fission of Pu239 emitted enough neutrons for an explosive chain reaction. Theoreticians had calculated reasonably accurate but not precise numbers for the amount of critical material necessary for a bomb. But what would a gun bomb look like? Was it possible to adapt the kind of gun barrel already in use by the army or navy? How would they produce a simultaneous, uniform explosion in an implosion device? Lack of knowledge in one area held back work in another. During the first few months, many groups within the laboratory were waiting on one another for baseline information they needed to proceed with their own experiments or developments.

After his orientation in T Building, every staff member knew that two basic types of weapon were envisioned: gun and implosion. The gun option seemed the more likely alternative, and the use of uranium differed from that of plutonium only in the speed with which the first piece needed to be shot into the second. Uranium required velocities of around one thousand feet per second, whereas plutonium, it was thought, required perhaps three thousand feet per second or more. Plutonium required a higher speed because of its high neutron "background." If it were fired at a slower speed, it would not connect with its other half in time to prevent predetonation.

The implosion bomb was a far more difficult design, both theoretically and technically. If the active material was compressed symmetrically and with great force, the super-dense core would—in theory, anyway—become supercritical and result in a powerful explosion. On April 28, 1943, Serber presented a series of new calculations demonstrating that implosion would achieve higher speeds during the explosive process. He based his work on the choice of a spherical shell of either uranium or plutonium. Skeptics countered that spherical implosion would not be achieved, because the inward explosive force would not be uniform but instead would flatten out. Teller described the problem succinctly: "Even a small deviation from the initial symmetry of the shock wave may grow exponentially, in which case it quickly produces a dramatic distortion."[1] Only practical tests would tell.

The implosion possibility was of interest to Groves, even if he did not quite understand the challenges of achieving perfect simultaneity and symmetry. He regularly questioned Oppenheimer and Parsons about the idea during his visits to the laboratory. He understood that implosion was a likely alternative to the gun, and in his mind, having two chances to win was better than having only one.

The first experiments using TNT to compress hollow steel cylinders were conducted in an arroyo on South Mesa, and began, appropriately, on the fourth of July, just two months after the laboratory's official opening. It was a hot day, and only those familiar with the sun at high altitudes understood how quickly you could sunburn at 7,300 feet. Parsons gathered some TNT, Primacord—a brand of detonating cord used in dynamite blasting—and a small selection of kitchen stovepipes and two-inch cast-iron sewer pipes. With him were Neddermeyer, McMillan, Hugh Bradner, Charles Critchfield, and John Streib. Critchfield remembered that they took the explosives and pipes to the distant mesa and "packed the TNT around the sewer pipe, inside the stove pipe, equipped it with the detonating system including 50 yards of Primacord to a sheltering rock where the six of us took cover and set off the experiment. By coincidence, this 'haywire' experiment proved just the correct combination to blow the iron pipe into a solid mass and keep it that way. A lovely demonstration of Seth [Neddermeyer]'s idea."[2]

It was only a piece of two-inch pipe, but it was a start, and the experiment worked. Parsons left for Pecos, New Mexico, to buy a saddle for his wife's horse. The remaining five men decided to have a bit of fun, and as soon as Parsons was out of sight, they grabbed what was left of the TNT and stuffed it into another piece of stovepipe, making a giant firecracker. It was the fourth of July, after all. This ensuing explosion was larger than the earlier one and reverberated over the mesa.

The compression test was at the heart of the laboratory's interest in implosion. The process had two advantages over the gun method: implosion worked with either uranium or plutonium, and plutonium promised to be available in quantity before U235. Implosion also accelerated the fission process, lessening the chance of a misfire. Yet there were serious obstacles. It was one thing to crush a pipe, but a hollow metal sphere the size of an orange? Neddermeyer and his team repeated this experiment over and over, changing the material, the size, the explosives, and as many variables as they could study. It was the "Edison approach": crude, repetitive experiments repeated many times, each time with a slight modification. The goal was to increase their understanding of the implosion process with each experiment.

Oppenheimer was continuously under pressure from Groves to pursue both weapons in order to deliver at the earliest possible date. The Theoretical Division strengthened the case for the implosion design in the summer of 1943 when it confirmed that a large part of the kinetic energy caused by implosion would be transferred to potential energy or compression. This energy would in turn squeeze dense matter, hollow or solid, even further. At several governing board meetings in September and October, Oppenheimer threw open the discussion. Neddermeyer's latest work suggested that the right kind and arrangement of explosives would generate the appropriate forces to compress or implode a ball of either uranium or plutonium. He pointed out that the gun worked in only one dimension, whereas implosion worked in three. The idea could not be discounted. In fact, the more Oppenheimer heard about implosion, the more promise he thought it had. He approved an implosion program, though it would remain secondary to work on the gun weapon. This satisfied Groves, who, as Oppenheimer reported to his governing board, was very much in favor of alternative approaches.

The first minute speck of plutonium arrived July 10, 1943, from the Metallurgical Lab in Chicago. Glenn Seaborg personally brought 150 micrograms of Pu239 in a bottle in his suitcase, but only on "loan"—the Met Lab wanted it back. When the time came to return the small sample, Robert Wilson and a friend, armed with a Winchester .32 deer-hunting rifle, drove it in a pickup truck to Santa Fe, where Seaborg was waiting at the La Fonda Hotel.[3]

One of the most important discoveries made with this tiny sample was that Pu239 produced 1.27 times more neutrons than U235 did. This revelation suggested the use of plutonium in both types of weapons,[4] promising news that Oppenheimer forwarded to Groves. Later that fall, another tiny amount of Pu239—one milligram—arrived by rail from Berkeley in a liter of uranyl acetate solution. The radiochemist Art Wahl, accompanied by an armed guard instead of packing his own rifle, picked it up at the station in Lamy.[5] Polonium, the source of neutrons, also began to arrive—slowly. The production process was agonizingly protracted. At the test reactor at Oak Ridge for example, five bismuth slugs, weighing 440 pounds, irradiated for a hundred days produced only ten curies of polonium.[6]

Despite the pressing needs of the Theoretical Division, Teller insisted on devoting as much time as he could to studying what he and everyone else now called the "Super," a diversion that came at the expense of work on the gun and implosion weapons. Teller's work consisted of long calculations by hand on note pads and was only theoretical at this stage, but some interesting discoveries emerged in late 1943. A member of his staff, Emil Konopinski, who had participated in the Berkeley summer conference in 1942, had just calculated that the ignition temperature for the detonation of liquid deuterium could be lowered by adding the artificially produced isotope tritium. With a lower ignition point, the probability of the deuterium's undergoing fusion when ignited by a fission bomb increased.

Citing the tritium discovery, Teller asked Oppenheimer and the governing board in September for more independence and additional staff for his research. He argued that the Germans' interest in deuterium and heavy water, the subject of recent intelligence reports, was evidence of their work on superbombs. In a memo to Oppenheimer on July 21, Teller wrote, "The Germans may be in possession of a powerful new weapon which is expected to be ready between November and January. There seems to be a considerable possibility that this new weapon is tuballoy [uranium].... It is possible that they will have a production let us say, of two gadgets a month."[7] What no one guessed at the time was that the "powerful new weapon[s]" were the V-1 missile and V-2 rocket under secret development at Peenemunde, Germany. And the German interest in heavy water was actually in its use as a moderator in a reactor.

One building away from the Theoretical Division was Robert Bacher's Experimental Physics Division. Its office space and experimental laboratories were only partially completed when Bacher and his staff began to arrive in March and April, and the division had no completed facilities in which to set up the equipment that was arriving every day from Harvard, Princeton, Wisconsin, and Illinois. The machinery, shipped in large wood containers, was stacked in the open air and had to be covered by tarps while it waited for a home. The Harvard cyclotron finally found a permanent location in X Building in April, the two Van de Graaff generators from the University of Wisconsin were ultimately installed a month later on the ground floor of W Building, and the Cockcroft-Walton in Z Building a month after that.

Each of these hand-crafted machines had its own peculiarities. The largest of the Van de Graaff generators, a horizontal tube twenty feet long and five feet high, contained a series of pressurized pipes and other equipment. Someone had to check all the pipe connections periodically to make sure they were airtight. A scientist—usually one of the smallest men on the team—climbed inside and, with the pipes pressurized, sprayed alcohol on all connections and seams. If bubbles appeared there was a leak. Because of the confined space and the alcohol, the man typically became inebriated and had to be pulled out and allowed to sleep it off in the lab or sent home in a car.

In the late summer, Bacher's team received one extremely thin piece of U235 metal foil with which to conduct experiments. Somewhat larger samples of low-enrichment uranium arrived in early 1944 from Lawrence's electromagnetic plant at Berkeley. Groves and Oppenheimer were disappointed with the quality of the material. Despite the heavy investment in these gigantic machines, they were producing relatively small amounts of U235, and it was of low concentration. On a visit to Berkeley in March 1944 to investigate, Oppenheimer telephoned Groves and told him that although the concentration of U235 was improving, "we will probably settle for less than the right thing."

There was some good news despite these difficulties. The discovery, made with Wilson's Van de Graaff generator, that plutonium emitted neutrons in numbers slightly greater than U235 was highly reassuring. Now the laboratory knew with certainty that plutonium could be used in an implosion weapon. Groves was relieved to learn the news as well, for it helped to justify his planned construction of massive plutonium reactors in Hanford, Washington. In November 1943, Wilson's men also confirmed that most of the neutrons emitted from fissioning U235 were "fast" neutrons. These neutrons were generated in less than a millionth of a second, making the gun a reasonable certainty.

During this same period, Bacher took up the design of the implosion weapon's "tamper." This was nothing more than a reflecting mechanism, a large ball of heavy metal that surrounded the core and bounced neutrons back into the plutonium or uranium. Manley's team ran numerous experiments on a dozen metals as potential tampers, among them lead, tungsten, uranium, platinum, and even gold. Visitors to Manley's office were surprised to see a large disc of gold on loan from the U.S. Treasury serving as a doorstop.

Bacher, like every other division director, found himself perpetually short of staff. In addition to needing scientists and engineers, he was desperate for trained machinists and a large, well-equipped machine shop. He went to Oppenheimer, who telephoned Groves on May 4. The shop would probably cost around $150,000, and they also needed machinists to man it. Could the general help? Groves approved the building and said he would look for enlisted men with machinist backgrounds.

Bacher also wanted to construct a small experimental nuclear reactor to be operated by Donald Kerst and his team. But even a small reactor was going to be expensive and would require the general's approval. Oppenheimer made the appeal by letter, and on June 10, 1944, Groves replied, approving the undertaking only half-heartedly, worried that the scientists were losing their focus. He reminded Oppenheimer that their "sole interest" at this time was in procuring "the necessary but small number of the final gadgets.... This, as I know you agree, is at the present time far more important than getting a more refined gadget at a later date."[8]

Oppenheimer and Bacher went ahead with the construction, drawing on Fermi's Chicago reactor design to guide them. For safety in case of a malfunction or accident, it was located in the isolated Los Alamos Canyon at a spot dubbed Omega Site. Bacher's original plans called for a reactor that would operate at about ten thousand watts and produce some three thousand curies of radiation—the "curie" was the standard unit for measuring radiation at the time. The reactor did not actually "boil" water; fission fragments interacted with the water and caused it to bubble, giving it the appearance of being heated. The water temperature was actually a temperate seventy-three degrees. The apparatus was remarkably simple, consisting of a hollow stainless steel ball one foot in diameter filled with a mixture of U235 and water and surrounded by heavy shielding.

Fermi came from Chicago in September for consultation and found a number of problems waiting for him. As planning for construction progressed, Bacher's team began to suspect that the reactor, at least as currently designed, would produce a gas that could hamper or prevent operations. Moreover, no one knew what to do with the radioactive residue that would form after the reactor had been in operation for a few months. Fermi recommended even heavier shielding around the reactor and urged that the reactor's power be cut back considerably, thus reducing the gas. He also suggested additional means of disposing of radioactive waste. The prospect of having to reduce power was disappointing, since less power would limit the boiler's usefulness in a wide range of experiments.

In December, Niels Bohr visited Los Alamos to give a presentation at the weekly colloquium. His habit of dropping the last syllable of words could make him difficult to understand. The room was perfectly silent as he spoke, many people leaning forward in their chairs and cupping their ears to hear better. During the discussion that followed, Fermi quizzed Bohr on the content of his presentation but apparently wasn't satisfied with the answers. He turned to a colleague sitting next to him and said, "People come to hear Bohr like they go to church: not that they will learn anything, but only that it is the thing to do."[9]

But the admired Dane served another purpose: he had what Oppenheimer called a "salutary" effect on Los Alamos. "He was marvelous," Oppenheimer told scientists after the war. "[He] made the enterprise which looked so macabre seem hopeful."[10] It didn't go unnoticed that Bohr's visit had just as much of a "salutary" effect, if not more, on Oppenheimer himself.

All of the laboratory's divisions grew wildly the first year, accelerating with every conundrum or breakthrough, each division adding qualified men as quickly as they could be identified and cajoled into coming to New Mexico. But none grew faster than Joseph Kennedy's division. For most of the first year, the Chemistry and Metallurgy Division had been loosely organized around its three primary functions—purification, radiochemistry, and metallurgy—but in April 1944, Kennedy faced institution-wide pressure to provide additional services. As a result, he expanded and reorganized his division, creating new groups to deal with health and safety, high-vacuum research, and the analysis and recovery of uranium and plutonium. He pleaded continuously with Oppenheimer for help. As usual, the director turned to Groves for the reassignment of scientists and enlisted men with relevant skills, especially those at other Manhattan sites whose talents were more urgently needed at Los Alamos. To the displeasure of Compton, Groves ordered the production and purification teams at the Metallurgical Laboratory to Los Alamos, as well as men from the chemistry laboratories at Berkeley and Iowa State College. By the end of the war, Kennedy's division, which had begun with twenty staff members, had over four hundred scientists and technicians.

Metal purification became Kennedy's most extensive and demanding program. Neutrons are formed when alpha particles collide with nuclei containing impurities, particularly in light elements—the alpha particle emission rate for plutonium is a thousand times greater than that for enriched uranium—and those neutrons increase the chance of a fast-fission chain reaction's beginning before supercriticality has been achieved. Kennedy, therefore, had to eliminate or considerably reduce impurities, a project that required a huge investment in infrastructure.[11] While most of the buildings in the Tech Area were indistinguishable on the exterior, with the same drab siding and red roofs, Kennedy's buildings were more substantial, constructed with air conditioning and special ventilation systems in order to eliminate dust and small particles from the air. The largest was the massive D Building for plutonium research, located at the far edge of the Tech Area.

In the purification process, the uranium and plutonium went through what metallurgists called wet and dry stages. In the wet stages, precipitants of the metal were obtained through chemical procedures; in the dry stages, the precipitant was ignited, oxidized, and heated in the presence of several other chemical compounds. Considerable effort was made to recover every scrap of the extremely scarce metal. Scientists had estimated that, for use in a bomb, uranium needed to be only one-third as pure as plutonium needed to be.

Working with plutonium presented many health hazards, for the powdery particles were easily inhaled. Trying to prevent plutonium poisoning, Kennedy and Dr. Louis Hempelmann, the laboratory's medical director, sought methods of detecting it in the human body. When someone had been exposed to plutonium, it was often difficult, if not impossible, to measure the extent of his exposure. Nose dabs were one possible test, but Hempelmann believed that the most satisfactory method was an examination of the person's feces.[12] Early on, no one was certain how much exposure was dangerous. Hempelmann determined in January 1944 that a harmful dose was two micrograms; a month later, he reduced that number to one microgram. As a precaution, Oppenheimer ordered that all new staff should have blood tests as soon as they arrived on the Hill. The results would establish a baseline of existing radiation levels in the body.[13]

Deak Parsons arrived in Los Alamos with broad experience that included working on radar and serving as a gunnery officer on a destroyer, but it was his work on the proximity fuse that made him particularly valuable to Los Alamos. At forty-three, he was older than most of the men there, trim and balding and all "spit-and-polish," and universally regarded as inventive and cool under pressure. Born in Chicago, he had grown up in Fort Sumner, New Mexico, where Pat Garrett gunned down Billy the Kid, and attended high school in nearby Santa Rosa on the original Route 66 (now Interstate 40). He and his wife often hosted an "open house" on Sundays, and everyone was invited. He acquired his nickname early in his naval career—"Deacon," a play on his last name, had quickly become "Deak." His staff quickly learned that Parsons wasn't afraid to challenge the rules.

In keeping with the Review Committee's recommendations, Parsons's Ordnance, or "O," Division, focused during the first year primarily on developing the gun. The most obvious design simply fired one piece of uranium or plutonium into another. A variation of that design employed two guns joined at the muzzle, each firing fissionable material at the other at the same time. The challenge, as with implosion, was to achieve simultaneous firings. Teller humorously suggested firing two guns, each with subcritical masses, from different locations. The two guns would be mathematically programmed so that the subcritical parts would meet in midair above the target. As they met, they would become supercritical and explode. A more serious suggestion was to use jet propulsion, but that idea proved impracticable. The two-gun approach was eventually scrapped in favor of a single barrel, and the gun soon took on the nickname "Little Boy."

Many of Parsons's experiments were conducted at on a firing range at Anchor Ranch, a large, flat site adjacent to a small canyon not far from the laboratory. Under Ed McMillan's direction, the staff test-fired a wide variety of projectiles. The shots were controlled from a large concrete building covered with dirt in the canyon, from which they were viewed through a periscope.

The Ordnance Division at first occupied only three small rooms in U Building, directly behind Oppenheimer's offices. Space was so limited that Parsons, his secretary Hazel Greenbacher, Charles Critchfield, and Ed McMillan shared a single twelve-foot-by-twelve-foot room stuffed with five desks. But Ordnance, along with the other divisions at Los Alamos, saw its responsibilities mushroom, and it rapidly expanded into multiple buildings. Work in one area or division inevitably meant additional or entirely new work in another. As theoretical physicists generated insights into implosion dynamics, for example, ordnance engineers incorporated their findings into the design of new explosives, which in turn required new techniques to produce them. It was possible to trace an invisible although not always direct line from calculations on blackboards to experimental tests at Anchor Ranch to the milling of metal components. By the end of 1943, Parsons had reorganized his division to include three new groups: Engineering, High Explosives, and Detonators.

Groves took particular interest in Parsons's work, and the two of them frequently exchanged telephone calls and telex messages. Parsons also made regular, almost monthly, visits to Groves in Washington. The two men shared a military background, but Groves also appreciated Parsons's "get-it-done" personality; it contrasted with what the general saw as a lackadaisical attitude among many at Los Alamos. In subtle ways, Groves counterbalanced Oppenheimer with Parsons, whom he trusted to be more practical than his director. More than anything else that first year, Parsons, like all division heads, needed help with staffing. Groves obliged, but Parsons also peppered him with requests for money to pave roads, replace laboratory equipment, construct bunkers for explosive testing, and, increasingly, to acquire and set up a series of test sites in Utah and California for testing prototypical bomb casings in flights. Groves was particularly helpful in negotiating the acquisition of B-29 bombers.

Parsons needed not only more men but men with experience. Someone he knew and respected was Norris Bradbury, a navy officer working at the Naval Proving Ground in Dahlgren, Virginia. Bradbury was a full professor in physics at Stanford University until called up for service. Parsons tried to recruit him, but Bradbury was reluctant to leave, considering his work to be vital to naval interests. Parsons turned to Groves for help. In his inimitable style, the general picked up the phone and personally called Admiral Purnell, who served with him on the Military Policy Committee, and pressed for Bradbury's transfer. Purnell looked into the matter but called Groves back in June 1944 to tell him that it wasn't likely that Bradbury could be released. He was too important. Parsons would not back down, however. He was adamant that Bradbury was critical to the Ordnance Division, telling Groves his division's chances of success without Bradbury were 30 percent but 50 to 60 percent with him. Groves continued to push Purnell until on July 4 he got word that Bradbury would be transferred.

Groves also arranged, at Parsons's request, for Thomas Olmstead, a navy ordnance technician, to be transferred to Los Alamos. Olmstead had considerable experience loading and firing large cannons, and while his expertise was greatly needed, so were his human relations skills. He served as a buffer between Parsons and his teams of scientists, known as the

"Black Powder Society." Parsons, like Groves, was always unhappy with the civilians' pace of work. Olmstead kept testing on schedule while always remaining pleasant and approachable.[14]

With approval and money from Groves, Parsons set his staff to improving and expanding Anchor Ranch. Larger and more solid buildings were constructed with gun emplacements, sand butts, and bombproof control rooms and magazines. As the testing program grew and gun requirements became better understood, walls and roofs were reinforced, and some buildings were moved to ravines for better protection. Anchor Ranch was still not entirely safe, however. The range ran along a main road that had to be blockaded during firings. Metal fragments were known to fly as far as seventy-five yards, and as Anchor expanded, controlling the area became a greater challenge.[15] Explosive tests, which were conducted mostly during the day, rocked the canyon walls of the plateau and reverberated throughout Los Alamos. New arrivals always needed a period of adjustment before the crack and thunder of explosions blended into the Hill's daily cacophony of trucks churning in the mud, voices, and the incessant hammering and sawing of construction.

Explosives research was only one of the Ordnance Division's lines of work. Fuse design was another. Robert Brode was charged with developing dependable detonators and electronic systems to trigger them. Brode had been a professor of physics at Berkeley but, with the war, went to the Applied Physics Laboratory at Johns Hopkins, where he helped to develop the proximity fuse. In 1943, there were several existing types of detonators to consider. One was the so-called "bridgewire" detonator, in which an electrical charge heated a small wire, which in turn set off a small amount of explosives. Another was known as the "spark-gap" type, in which an electrical spark ignited the explosives. It was obvious that neither type was useable in its present form.

Brode also needed a device to trigger an electrical system that in turn would send a bolt of sufficiently high voltage to set off whatever kind of detonator was eventually chosen. Whatever the device, it had to reliably activate itself at the right altitude in order to maximize the destructive force of the bomb. There were at least two approaches to triggering the electrical system: adapting barometric switches already on the market or perfecting more complex devices such as the radio proximity fuse, radio altimeter, and tail-warning radar. Clocks were still another method of firing, but they were suspect because of the opportunity for human error; an operator would have to select the right setting just before releasing the bomb. Although a barometric switch was the simplest device, there was no assurance that it would be reliable in a falling bomb. Parsons arranged for airplanes to drop model bombs with radio transmitters to compare barometric readings and actual elevation. The tests were conducted at the Muroc Army Air Force Base in California, one of the laboratory's offsite locations that Groves acquired. Test results ruled out the barometric fuse as a primary system; it would serve as a backup.

Independently of Los Alamos, the Radio Corporation of America had developed a radar-based tail-warning device, nicknamed "Archie," that Brode hoped could be adapted to his team's needs. The device was actually a small radar system in the tail of an airplane that alerted pilots to nearby enemy aircraft. A substantial number of RCA pilot models were made available to Brode for experimentation. If the Archie could be adapted, it would alert the bomb's electronics when it was within a certain distance of the ground. But these would have to be tested at Muroc to determine if they would work in a weapon.

As Brode's team struggled with detonators, they found themselves in desperate need of an expert in porcelain, particularly someone familiar with the material as it was used in automobile spark plugs, which in many ways resembled detonators. As it turned out, the nation's leading expert on spark plug porcelain was working on a war-related project at General Motors. When all attempts to convince GM to make this man available for a few days of consultation failed, Oppenheimer asked Groves to intercede. The general immediately placed a call to Henry DuPont, a member of the GM board of directors whom he knew personally. "I told him that my people had asked General Motors for this expert and were turned down on the grounds that this man was just overwhelmingly busy on very important warwork."[16] Groves insisted the man was even more crucial to work at Los Alamos. Thirty minutes later, DuPont called back and said the expert was ready to go.

In March, there was an unintended breach of security, one that in retrospect is almost funny. On March 13, 1944, the *Cleveland Press* ran an article by the reporter John Raper headlined "Forbidden City," which not only identified Los Alamos but placed it near Santa Fe and gave the population as between five thousand and six thousand persons. The story said that the "mysterious" place was led by Dr. J. Robert Oppenheimer and reported that "tremendous explosions" were often overheard by those traveling in the vicinity. "The most interesting story is that Prof. Oppenheimer is working on a beam that will cause the [airplane] motors to stop so that German planes will drop from the skies as though they were paving blocks."

The article came to the attention of a horrified Colonel Ashbridge, who hurried to let Groves know that the "leak" was not something the laboratory could have prevented. Ashbridge also informed Oppenheimer and then telexed the article to Groves, explaining that "the reporter had doubtless picked up some local gossip and put it together with information on Dr. Oppenheimer in Who's Who." Groves already knew about the article and immediately shut down its further circulation. He also apparently considered drafting Raper and sending him to the Pacific, but the reporter turned out to be in his sixties.[17]

While Brode and his men struggled with the fusing and detonating systems, Norman Ramsey was asked to head a new Delivery Group, whose task was to design an aerodynamic housing for the new weapon. A physicist from Columbia University and the son of an army general, Ramsey began in the summer of 1943 to investigate military airplanes that could be adapted for an unusually large payload. This work required an estimate of the final size and weight of the atomic weapons, which he received in the fall. The gun bomb was expected to be seventeen feet long, including its metal shell or casing and set of stabilizing fins. Among American planes, only the B-29, then under development, could handle a bomb of that size, and it was speculated that even then both bomb bays would have to be joined. The British Lancaster was rejected, even though the B-29 might not be immediately available for testing purposes. A British bomber would require a British crew, and that was something Groves was unwilling to consider for security reasons. In late September, using the latest data from the Theoretical Division, Ramsey calculated that the implosion weapon would be a large sphere, at least five feet in diameter and encased in an egg-shaped shell with fins for stability. Such a weapon would also work in a B-29.

Despite all the progress, Parsons was concerned about the pace of work at the laboratory. At an April 21, 1944, meeting with Oppenheimer and others, he reported that there were serious gaps in what the laboratory needed to know, including the "nuclear and mechanical" properties of plutonium and the ability of a thin gun barrel to survive pressure of seventy-five thousand pounds per square inch. He felt these voids were holding back development of the plutonium gun. And he had concerns about the implosion gadget as well.

Following a meeting on May 19 in Washington with Groves, Oppenheimer, Bush, and Conant, Parsons followed up with a four-page letter to the general recapitulating the most important "assumptions" that he and his ordnance team were working under: an implosion bomb of low yield might be ready by the end of 1944; the B-29 could be modified to accommodate a large sphere like Fat Man, as the implosion bomb was nicknamed; the bomb would be designed to be dropped from an altitude of thirty thousand feet; and, as a precaution, the bomb would be enclosed within an armor case and assembled with explosives near the take-off site.[18]

Work continued on the plutonium gun as well, despite growing suspicions that impurities in plutonium might generate too many neutrons and cause predetonation. Glen Seaborg wrote to Oppenheimer about this possibility, suggesting that light element impurities would have to be less than one in one hundred billion in order for Pu239 to be useable in a gun weapon.[19] Oppenheimer quickly shared this alarming news with Parsons and Groves, and everyone realized that it strengthened the argument for perfecting Neddermeyer's implosion design.

Seth Neddermeyer was indomitable. His implosion team consisted of fewer than a dozen men and was the smallest within the ordnance division. He set up a work area on South Mesa, one canyon over from the Tech Area. In the first crude attempts at implosion, hollow cylinders were wrapped with explosives and detonated, similar to the first test the previous July. The experiments grew in sophistication, but achieving a uniform implosion remained elusive. Results were slow in coming and ultimately mixed.

There was simply no outside experience or research that Neddermeyer and his men could draw on. They were breaking new ground at every step. Inevitably there were mistakes and even a few dangerous moments. During an investigation of the explosive Pentolite in April 1944, for example, a particle of charcoal embedded in a Pentolite cylinder ignited when someone removed it from the cylinder. If the entire charge had exploded, it would have killed all the men in the room.

Pressed to report on his group's work, Neddermeyer presented some early data at a weekly meeting of the colloquium. No one was particularly impressed. The theorist Feynman said simply, "It stinks," and Parsons gently mocked his subordinate: "To my mind he [Neddermeyer] is gradually working up to what I shall refer to as the Beer-Can Experiment... The point to watch for is whether he can blow in a beer can without splattering the beer."[20]

Unexpectedly, Neddermeyer—and implosion—gained vital support in the form of a visit from John von Neumann, a gifted mathematician and highly regarded scientist. After meeting with Neddermeyer in late September and early October 1943 and performing some calculations, von Neumann voiced his belief that implosion could work. His idea was to use "shaped" explosives—explosives configured in specific physical forms— to fit spherically around the plutonium or uranium. His idea was a more sophisticated version of what Neddermeyer had proposed earlier in the year. The detonation of shaped explosives would quickly assemble, or compress, the active material. Based on his own experience with shaped charges used by the military, von Neumann was convinced that the regularity of collapse improves as the ratio of charge to mass goes up. Furthermore, the time necessary for passing from critical to final assembly was close enough to the time required for the chain reaction to evolve and avoid predetonation. Teller quickly made his own calculations and concurred.[21]

Von Neumann's idea was a breakthrough. Charles Critchfield, a scientist in the Ordnance Division, understood its implications immediately: von Neumann's suggestion "woke everyone up.... Johnny...was a very resourceful man, at least twenty years ahead of his time.... I remember Edward [Teller] calling me and saying, 'Why didn't you tell me about this stuff?' I said...Seth [Neddermeyer], Hugh [Bradner] and Sreibo [John Streib] have been working on this, and nobody paid any attention to it."

Critchfield remembers that Groves, after being told of von Neumann's suggestions, scolded Parsons for not keeping him fully informed of this implosion possibility.[22] Groves then ordered Parsons to attend a meeting of the Military Policy Committee in Washington on November 3 and to bring with him a "written statement explaining the advantages and difficulties of the implosion method, including an outline of the organizational set-up proposed [to work on implosion] and the personnel needed, if possible with names, and certainly with the qualifications desired."[23] Neddermeyer quickly prepared a detailed outline, which Parsons reviewed and edited, and the final version was sent to Groves on October 29. On November 4, a day after the Military Policy Committee's meeting, Oppenheimer reported to his governing board that Groves and Tolman supported "pushing" the implosion method and that Groves wanted the work completed in six months, a period the board felt was a "little optimistic."[24]

The episode also illustrates the nature of Groves's involvement with the laboratory. He did not hesitate to call Parsons directly, something he did quite frequently, instead of going through Oppenheimer. Another director might have regarded the move as demeaning or intrusive, but Oppenheimer accepted it as part of their working relationship. Groves's intention was not to undermine his director but to use his commanding position to intervene at a point where he could force a decision or move the project along.

The fear that Pu239 would not work in a gun bomb was reinforced when a disquieting report about the spontaneous emission of neutrons reached Oppenheimer in June 1944. Compton had forwarded a report compiled by Tolman describing the most recent work by Frederic Joliot-Curie in France. Joliot had noted a spontaneous emission of neutrons from fissioning polonium, an element lighter than either uranium or plutonium, and therefore reasoned that spontaneous emission might therefore be expected from plutonium. Fermi, who had read the report in Chicago, agreed with Joliot's speculation. Because of the discovery's tremendous implications for the work at Los Alamos, Oppenheimer called his governing board together on June 17.

This was potentially bad news. The board gloomily agreed that if Joliot's findings were accurate—and many on the board did not trust the quality of Joliot's work—plutonium would almost certainly emit neutrons spontaneously as well, making it ineffective in a gun weapon unless highly purified plutonium became available or some technological breakthrough occurred. Unless the Pu239 was virtually "pure," the neutron background would trigger predetonation and prevent a nuclear explosion.

Oppenheimer could not entirely discount the plutonium gun design, however. Considerable staff time already had been spent on the project, and Groves was insistent on pursuing multiple alternatives with the hope that at least one could be developed and delivered quickly. Research was still being conducted that might reveal spontaneous emission to be a smaller problem than feared. But Joliot's discovery was another boost for implosion, whose advocates pointed out that if plutonium could not work in a gun design, it could work in an implosion weapon. With Groves's approval, Oppenheimer decided to continue both the uranium and plutonium gun alternatives, at least for the moment, and implosion would still take a lower priority. Neddermeyer would continue to manage the effort.

Oppenheimer turned to Emilio Segrè to settle the question of spontaneous fission in Pu239 as soon as a sample of the metal could be obtained. Segrè, who had been a student of Fermi's in Italy, had been forced like so many others to emigrate. Before he came to Los Alamos he worked with Lawrence at Berkeley. Segrè and his team searched for an appropriate site for their experiments. They wanted quiet but also shielding from cosmic rays and radiation generated during various experiments in the Tech Area. They eventually chose an old Forest Service cabin in Pajarito Canyon, at least fourteen miles from the Hill, which Segrè found both useful and charming: "It was a log cabin that had been occupied by a ranger and it was located in a secluded valley a few miles from Los Alamos. It could be reached only by a jeep trail.... The cabin-laboratory, in a grove shaded by huge broadleaf trees, occupied one of the most picturesque settings one could dream of."[25]

––––––––––

Jim Tuck, a young member of the British team from Oxford—tall, perpetually disheveled, with a wide gap between his two front teeth—had a provocative idea based on von Neumann's theories. He suggested assembling a number of cone-shaped charges—like those in armor-piercing shells—around a core and detonating them all at once. Each charge would produce a converging wave that would focus on the nuclear core and compress it. Tuck imagined something like a modern soccer ball composed of hexagonal and pentagonal patches, each patch an inverted, explosive pyramid.

Tuck's idea inspired research into what happens when heavy and light materials are forced against each other during an explosion. It seemed clear that the force must produce stability or the explosion would fail. Mathematical studies by another Englishman, Geoffrey Taylor, suggested that heavy materials pushing against light ones would result in stability, while light materials pushing against heavy ones would produce the opposite effect. To ensure stability, therefore, heavy material must push against light, and the explosives in an implosion bomb would need to be correctly adjusted for the weight and quality of the tamper and core.

Neddermeyer had been convinced from the beginning that the implosion design would work. A former student of Oppenheimer's, he had come to Los Alamos from the National Bureau of Standards at the director's personal invitation and had been given considerable latitude to explore implosion with a small staff. But as interest in implosion rapidly grew within the laboratory, so did demands on Neddermeyer to produce results. Bright, imaginative, and dedicated as he was, Neddermeyer was a poor manager. As work intensified, decisions stalled and priorities fell behind. He demanded more people while his existing staff languished in repetitive or dead-end pursuits. He became frustrated and often contentious, offending Parsons and other group leaders. Despite his role as the champion of implosion, Neddermeyer was becoming a liability.

Complaints about Neddermeyer's performance reached Oppenheimer, who felt compelled to recognize the "stagnation," as he put it at a meeting of the governing board. At the same time, Oppenheimer dutifully recognized that Neddermeyer's group was too small. The situation was sufficiently critical for Groves to make a personal visit to Los Alamos for a special implosion review scheduled for October 28; he was prepared to force action. Groves, Oppenheimer, and the board reviewed the history of implosion and decided the implosion bomb must be given a higher priority. Despite Neddermeyer's lack of progress, the board was impressed with von Neumann's recommendations from September, including the prospect that implosion could be accelerated by increasing the amount of explosives, not necessarily their number.

Von Neumann, who would go on to play an important role in the development of computers after the war, was a mathematical genius whose interests extended to physics, statistics, economics, and computational devices. He was greatly respected, even revered, and his endorsement carried considerable weight. Oppenheimer had tried from the beginning to get von Neumann to come to Los Alamos, which he described at the time as a "somewhat Buck Rogers project." As always in such circumstances, Oppenheimer had turned to Groves, who appealed to Tolman and Admiral Purnell, for permission to release von Neumann at least part-time from his job at the navy's Bureau of Ordnance. The appeal worked: von Neumann could serve as a consultant.

Von Neumann's support for implosion was raised again at the November 4 meeting of the governing board. Oppenheimer passed along the news that both Groves and Tolman favored "pushing" the implosion weapon, partly because it justified Lawrence's massive electromagnetic separation program, which had produced disappointingly little U235 despite its huge investment.[26]

Unfortunately, there was little progress over the next five months. Oppenheimer was receiving daily reports on the deteriorating implosion program. Close scrutiny by the governing board aggravated Neddermeyer's self-consciousness and poor management, and Oppenheimer was unable to galvanize both the man and the program. Oppenheimer might have allocated more men to the effort but under the circumstances elected not to do so. Groves, Tolman, and Conant met with Oppenheimer in

Chicago in early 1944 and urged him to intensify work on the implosion weapon even if its efficiency was low. The pressure inevitably intensified concerns about Neddermeyer's leadership. Conant also wanted the laboratory to consider using both U235 and Pu239 in an implosion bomb, even if a force of only several hundred tons of TNT was achieved.[27] Oppenheimer disagreed—such a weapon would hardly justify the expense in both dollars and time.

For all of his talents, Oppenheimer was prone to hesitate in making critical decisions, particularly when he had to confront his own scientists. In 1944 he faced a laboratory divided: different and often competing constituencies within the organization fought over turf, hence over resources, and many felt that the weapons alternatives they were pursuing deserved support regardless of other priorities. But now, with several thousand employees working for him, Oppenheimer stalled because he couldn't decide what to do. He feared failure, and he feared failing Groves. Isidor Rabi, one of Oppenheimer's closest colleagues, appreciated his friend's weakness: "Oppenheimer was brilliant, but he was not a strong character. He was indecisive, and definitely not a fighter. If he couldn't persuade you, he'd cave in, especially to group opposition. Groves, on the other hand, could provide him with strong backbone in the form of consistent policy."[28]

The situation reached its nadir in the late spring of 1944, when Oppenheimer was finally forced to take long-delayed action, in no small part because of pressure from Groves. The implosion effort was stalled, and someone more aggressive and with better management skills was needed to manage the program. To minimize ill will among the implosion team, Oppenheimer decided not to replace Neddermeyer with someone already on the project. Groves favored George Kistiakowsky, a chemist and expert on explosives who had been visiting the laboratory as a consultant for over half a year and was respected by everyone at Los Alamos. Kistiakowsky was not easily convinced to come, however. He doubted that a bomb could be developed in time for use in the war and had an attractive overseas assignment in the works. Oppenheimer wrote to Conant for help, knowing that his call would also reach Groves: "We have come to the conclusion that the only step which offers any real immediate promise is the assignment to the [implosion] work of Kistiakowsky." The appeal worked. Kistiakowsky reported for full-time work on February 16, 1944, "a reluctant bride throughout the life of the project," as he put it. He found himself in the middle of a battle of management styles and personalities, between the conservative, military Parsons and the loose, fragmented Neddermeyer:

> I found that my position was untenable because I was essentially in the middle trying to make sense of the efforts of two men who were at each other's throats. One was Captain Parsons who tried to run his division the way it is done in military establishments—very conservative. The other was, of course, Seth Neddermeyer, who was the exact opposite of Parsons, working away in a little corner. The two never agreed about anything and they certainly didn't want me interfering.[29]

Kistiakowsky quickly realized that he could not work with Neddermeyer, either. It was impossible to administer the implosion program if Neddermeyer was responsible for the scientific work. Kistiakowsky didn't think it appropriate to ask Neddermeyer to resign, so he offered to do so. Oppenheimer rejected the offer and instead asked Kistiakowsky to take charge of the floundering effort and quickly to submit a plan for reorganization within the Ordnance Division. Oppenheimer privately assured his governing board that Neddermeyer would be given a role in a less sensitive position.

On June 13, Kistiakowsky, nicknamed "Kisty" by both laboratory staff and Jean O'Leary, submitted his reorganization plan. Implosion would be under his direction as an associate division leader, and Neddermeyer would continue as a senior technical advisor. A steering committee was formed with Kistiakowsky as chairman and Luis Alvarez, Bainbridge,

Neddermeyer, and Parsons as members.[30] Oppenheimer approved the plan and undertook the personally distasteful task of informing his friend and former student of the changes.

In a painful, exhausting meeting on June 15 with Neddermeyer, Kistiakowsky, and others, Oppenheimer reviewed the haphazard progress of the implosion program and then presented Kistiakowsky's plan and announced that he had approved it. It was unspoken but obvious that the plan had Groves's consent as well. The meeting started late in the afternoon and went through part of the evening; Oppenheimer's office reeked of cigarette smoke and stale coffee. Neddermeyer left the meeting unhappy and feeling abandoned. Oppenheimer was left to prepare a memorandum to his colleague to formalize the new structure.

"The only alternative which has appeared possible to me," he wrote to Neddermeyer, "is to ask Kistiakowsky to undertake the direction of E-5 [the implosion program] himself. He has been asked to accept full responsibility for the operation of the Group." To soften the blow, Oppenheimer reminded Neddermeyer that he would be a technical advisor attached to the Ordnance Division and as well as a member of the high explosives (H.E.) program. He added, "I am asking you to accept the assignment.... I believe that they are the only ones which have promise of working, and on behalf of the success of the whole project, as well as the peace of mind and effectiveness of the workers in the H.E. program, I am making this request of you. I hope you will be able to accept it."[31]

Neddermeyer had no choice but to accept. His demotion—and that is what it was—hurt. A few of his colleagues rallied around him, blaming Oppenheimer for mishandling the situation, but to no avail. After the war, Neddermeyer reflected on the experience: "From my point of view, he [Oppenheimer] was an intellectual snob. He could cut you cold and humiliate you right down to the ground. On the other hand, I could irritate him.... He became terribly, terribly impatient with me ... because I seemed not to push things for war research but acted as though it was just a normal research situation."[32]

The change in staffing reinvigorated the laboratory, but Oppenheimer ought to have acted earlier. Just a few weeks later, news arrived that provoked the laboratory's greatest crisis, one that prompted Groves's decisive intervention and ultimately Oppenheimer's most vigorous restructuring of the organization since its inception.

By chance, Kistiakowsky's assumption of leadership of the implosion program coincided with the arrival of plutonium from the reactor in Oak Ridge. Minute as it was, the sample was sufficient to allow Segrè to confirm that an impurity in plutonium—the isotope 240—was the source of spontaneous fission. Segrè's findings indicated that plutonium could be used in a gun only if extraordinary velocities or an extremely high level of purity could be achieved. A high-velocity gun, however, was simply not possible for the foreseeable future.

Although Oppenheimer wanted to keep the bad news quiet, too many people had already heard. He was forced to announce Segrè's findings to the staff at the July 4 colloquium, and he also informed Groves and Conant at the same time. There were now two alternatives for pursuing a plutonium bomb. The first was to build additional facilities to "purify" plutonium by separating out the 240 isotope, an enormously costly undertaking that would take perhaps take a year. Oppenheimer advised Groves by telex, "My opinion is that [further purification of Pu239] is not a job which can be developed within any reasonable time scale but that it should be referred to [Lawrence] for more expert consideration."[33] The second alternative was to see if Lawrence's electromagnetic program could produce purer Pu239. Both alternatives involved delays that Groves and Oppenheimer simply could not afford.

Groves was scheduled to visit Los Alamos on Monday, July 17, but immediately canceled his plans. Instead, he summoned Conant, Charles Thomas, Oppenheimer, Fermi, and Colonel Nichols to an emergency meeting in Chicago at the Met Lab. Oppenheimer repeated the bad news: Impurities in the sample of Pu239 provided by the Oak Ridge reactor precluded its use in a Little Boy weapon. Worse, the Pu239 expected from the Hanford reactors now under construction in Washington would be even more contaminated because the reactors would be operated under greater radiation. Implosion was the only alternative. Groves had to decide whether to complete the Hanford reactors or to wait for proof that implosion would work.

Conant once again argued that Los Alamos should concentrate on a low-yield implosion bomb using a mixture of uranium and plutonium. Any success with such a weapon, he believed, would pave the way for a more powerful, sophisticated weapon later. Oppenheimer still opposed the idea of a less powerful weapon, objecting that following that path would waste resources and achieve little to justify the cost. He argued for a full-scale implosion bomb using plutonium. It was a risk but a sensible one. In the end, Groves yielded to his director. Back in Los Alamos, Oppenheimer wrote to Groves, confirming the lab's new priority:

> It appears reasonable to discontinue the intensive effort to achieve higher purity for plutonium [in a gun bomb] and to concentrate attention on methods of assembly which do not require a low neutron background for their success. At the present time the method to which an overriding priority must be assigned is the method of implosion.[34]

Groves decided to move ahead with construction of the reactors at Hanford, authorizing Colonel Matthias to accelerate the effort whenever possible. Nichols admired the courage behind the decision:

> Not to continue building Hanford ran the obvious risk of determining that an implosion bomb was feasible, but then not having plutonium to fuel it. On the other hand, continuing to

build would make our loss that much greater if implosion proved impossible. Groves again demonstrated guts by approving continued construction at the HEW [Hanford Engineering Works] at the same urgent pace.[35]

Oppenheimer and his staff now had to regroup—again. Shaken by the plutonium gun debacle, Oppenheimer considered resigning. But on more long walks with the director, a calm and reassuring Bacher convinced him that he was indispensable to the project.

Groves knew that Oppenheimer, whatever his weaknesses, worked harder and longer than anyone, and he began to worry that the director was approaching exhaustion. After the war, Groves recalled his concern:

> He worked harder at times than I wanted him to, because I was afraid he would break down.... That was always a danger in our project.... I had a physical taken of him when we were talking about making [the laboratory] a militarized affair, and I knew his past physical record, and I was always disturbed about his working too hard. But I could never slow him down in any way.[36]

Much of the first year's work seemed in vain. As agreed in Chicago, Oppenheimer ordered the laboratory to stop work on the plutonium gun bomb: "Essentially, all work on the [plutonium] 49 gun program and the extreme purification of 49 should be stopped immediately.... All possible priority should be given to the implosion program."[37] He wistfully added that perhaps a later discovery might redeem the previous year's work, and as a precaution, he asked that none of the abandoned work be destroyed.

After a year of operation, the Los Alamos Laboratory was a very different organization from the one envisioned on that chilly day in November

1942 when Groves and Oppenheimer first visited the Ranch School. The original staff of one hundred scientists had grown to more than two thousand, scattered over Pajarito Plateau. Their goal of delivering an atomic bomb was still months away, perhaps a year or more. The uranium gun bomb would almost certainly work, but implosion, although promising, still faced difficult hurdles. On the other hand, the implosion program had grown from a small band of determined men under Neddermeyer to a far better organized and multidisciplinary program of fourteen groups in the Ordnance Division, expanding as well to two new divisions, Gadget and Explosive. After some organizational difficulties, the laboratory at Los Alamos was hard at work on multiple fronts, and considerable theoretical progress had been achieved.

For Groves, who had been promoted to major general in March, it was also a year of struggle and small successes. None of the huge U235 production plants were up and running yet, nor were the plutonium reactors. These would be operational later in 1944, and their construction was in competent hands. Los Alamos had reorganized, but Groves realized that Oppenheimer would need closer supervision in the months to come. Privately, he had to wonder if he and the Manhattan Project would be successful in time to help end the war. And he wasn't the only one.

Far beyond Groves's offices in Washington, beyond the uranium and plutonium production plants and the mesa and canyons of Pajarito, in a thousand battlefields, airfields, and encampments scattered over Europe, Africa, Asia, and the Pacific, millions of men were fighting their own war. Their battles, their hopes, their fears were very different from those of the men of Los Alamos. But they could hope that someone, or something, would come to help them win the war.

The question on everyone's mind was, would they be in time to help?

Chapter Ten

SPLENDID ISOLATION

———◆———

I t was a reflection of the times—when people got their information from newspapers, movie newsreels, and radio—that most Americans were unaware of the real purpose of the secret "atomic cities" that were part of the Manhattan Engineer District, all created and managed by an army general who was virtually unknown to the sixteen million men in uniform.

Two of the MED's largest sites—Oak Ridge, Tennessee, and Hanford, Washington—were well known. The size of their operations and the number of people involved made them conspicuous. Oak Ridge, formally known as the Clinton Engineer Works and named after a small nearby town, occupied fifty-two thousand acres and employed fifteen thousand construction workers and another fifty thousand production staff in the generation of U235. What was not known was the purpose behind all this work. Most assumed it was war-related, and that sufficed. The secrecy was reinforced by continual reminders to all residents and employees not to talk about what they saw or did. In Washington, where the Hanford Engineer Works sat on almost 450,000 acres straddling the Columbia River and employed 132,000 construction workers and production staff, the government could hardly hide the giant buildings that housed the plutonium reactors. But again, most employees and residents of these communities, except those who worked directly with the reactors, did not know the purpose of the plants. They, like the residents of Oak Ridge, simply assumed the work was related to the war. No one knew that the buildings they worked in and the communities they occupied were part of a larger, national effort to manufacture an atomic bomb.

But the jewel in the crown, the most secret of all General Groves's operations, sat on a mountaintop in northern New Mexico, isolated amid spectacular scenery and known to comparatively few. And those outsiders who did know of the small community on Los Alamos Plateau were mostly the residents of nearby Indian pueblos or towns like Santa Fe and Albuquerque, who, like the residents of Oak Ridge and Hanford, assumed the quirky residents of the plateau were engaged in some esoteric war work. Which is why the Hill was a unique and extraordinary place to live and work during World War II.

Almost everyone coming to Los Alamos passed through Santa Fe, although those arriving by rail quickly learned they could not reach the small town directly. Trains let their passengers off at Lamy, eighteen miles south of Santa Fe, where travelers bound for Los Alamos were greeted by old friends or bored GIs in casual clothing sent to drive them in unmarked cars and dark green buses. Others arrived in Albuquerque and were picked up and driven north. Oppenheimer's instructions to newly recruited staff were cryptic but precise: Report to Room 8 at 109 Palace Street in Santa Fe.

The small city beside the Sangre de Cristo foothills and east of the Jemez Mountains, home to barely twenty thousand residents in the mid-1940s, has the honor of being the oldest state capital in the United States. Founded in 1610 by the Spanish, Santa Fe over the centuries had seen Indian revolts, conquest by United States and Confederate troops, and lately the coexistence of Indian, Spanish, and Anglo cultures. Its low, graceful buildings drew strength and character from the sun-dried adobe bricks from which they were made. The city's streets were narrow, many of them crooked and of cobblestone. Around its central public square were the Palace of the Governors, built in 1610, rows of small shops, a Woolworth's, and one of Fred Harvey's hotels, the La Fonda. During the day, Indians from nearby pueblos sat under the portal of the palace to sell their pottery and jewelry.

Less than a block from the Governor's Palace was the laboratory's Santa Fe office. It consisted of five rooms in an old adobe building reached by passing through an archway of carved wooden lintels called *vigas* into a courtyard. Dorothy McKibbin managed the ceaseless activity in the office, which was identified simply as "U.S. Army Corps of Engineers." As the laboratory grew and more employees and families arrived, the courtyard filled with boxes, suitcases, and crying babies. Everyone received a warm welcome from McKibbin, who soothed agitated feelings and tried to answer questions. Buses from Los Alamos made several round trips each day to take newcomers to the Hill. Those with cars were given yellow maps with red markings to guide them out of the city toward Espanola and then to Los Alamos.

Dorothy McKibbin, a graduate of Smith College, had first come to Santa Fe in 1925, at the age of twenty-nine, to recuperate from tuberculosis. She recovered and after eleven months was pronounced cured. During that stay she fell in love with the city and the eccentric artistic crowd that lived there. She returned home to Kansas City, married, and had a son. Life seemed promising until her husband was diagnosed with Hodgkin's disease and died in 1931 after a long and difficult illness. She returned to Santa Fe six months later with her son and found a job. One day in March 1943, she ran into a friend, Joe Stevenson, who had just taken a new job and knew of a secretarial position that would soon be open. Was she interested? Dorothy agreed to meet Stevenson's boss, who turned out to be Robert Oppenheimer. The interview lasted only a few minutes, and when Oppenheimer offered her a job, she accepted without hesitation.

The lab's office at 109 East Palace, said McKibbin, "served as a reception desk, information center, and travel bureau. Scientists arrived there breathless, sleepless, and haggard, tired from riding on trains that were slow and trains that were crowded, tired from missing connections and having nothing to eat, or tired from waiting out the dawn hours in railway stations."[1]

Those who were driving took their maps and went "up." They passed the edge of San Ildefonso Pueblo and crossed the Rio Grande at Otowi on a suspension bridge. The floor of the bridge was made from wooden planks, and cars and trucks made a distinctive "bump-bump-bump" sound as they passed over it. Across the river the difficult ascent to Los Alamos began.

State Highway 4 was formidable. The Ranch School had done nothing more than having it cleared and leveled every few years. The edges of the sharp switchbacks looked like they might crumble into the canyons with every vehicle that passed. The rugged beauty of the terrain was lost on some new arrivals, who feared for their lives. Groves ordered the road paved, but the steady traffic of heavy trucks pulverized the surface within weeks, and the larger vehicles could barely make the switchback turns. He was forced, therefore, to undertake the major project of widening and strengthening Highway 4. An alternative route, often used by Oppenheimer and other scientists in early 1943, was State Highway 30 from Espanola, which joined Highway 4 before the ascent. It was another tortuous, unpaved road strewn with rocks that ranged from pebbles to boulders.

Once atop the mesa, the road leveled and straightened, and after a mile or so, arrived at a three-story wooden watchtower. Across the road stood a small, white clapboard guardhouse with a green asphalt roof, a miniature version of the administrative and technical buildings a few miles ahead.

Here newcomers had their first taste of the laboratory's security system. They were asked to leave their vehicles by military police, who carefully checked their names against a roster of those expected and scrutinized their identification. When cleared, each adult was issued a temporary pass—it would take a day or two to prepare permanent identity cards for an entire family—and the party was sent to the next checkpoint up the road. There they had their first unobstructed view of the new town. The picturesque log and stone buildings of the Ranch School were now hidden by ugly, colorless, prefabricated structures. Unnamed dirt roads led to unmarked buildings of one or two stories. New residents had to memorize the names of buildings and, until they learned their way around, locate them in relation to some landmark, such as the town's water tower.

Dazed new arrivals found their way to a housing office in a converted garage. Most couples had been advised beforehand in a "Second Memorandum on the Los Alamos Project," written by Oppenheimer, that housing would be "extremely simple." He warned:

> There will be no individual houses, as such. Couples without children will live in three-room apartments (bedroom, living room, kitchen and bath), which are built two to the house. Four- and five-room apartments will be unfurnished; the commissary, however, will have very plain furniture on hand which may be drawn as needed. Floors are varnished and waxed hardwood, except for the kitchen floor which is linoleum. The rooms are fairly small; the entire design and construction simple but adequate.[2]

Housing assignments in hand, families searched through several residential areas, some resembling mining camps, before they found their own house or apartment complex. Robert and Bernice Brode, who arrived with their two sons in September 1943, were assigned Apartment C in Building T-124. After some confusion, they found their apartment in a fourplex on the far end of a slope looking into the Jemez Mountains. They were immediately greeted by the wives and children of the Bacher, Cyril Smith, and Teller families, who shared the fourplex. The Tellers stood out because they had arrived with both a grand piano and a new Bendix washing machine. Edward Teller was just as interesting a character outside the Tech Area as he was within. A talented musician, he often played his piano late into the night. He adored his young son and could be seen with the boy perched on his shoulders walking in his neighborhood, easily recognizable by the distinctive gait occasioned by his artificial foot.[3]

Not all new arrivals fared as well as the Brodes. Phyllis and Leon Fisher, who had been mailed a floor plan of their promised new home, immediately learned that domestic life at Los Alamos could be full of surprises:

> Our belongings were unceremoniously dumped in the wrong house, a smaller place (classification: garage style) at about six o'clock this evening. Our chosen home, we were told by a WAC in the housing office, had been assigned by mistake to someone else. Instead, after a great deal of scurrying around, we were deposited here to remain until another batch of houses can be built.[4]

Most new arrivals wanted to get settled quickly. Unmarried men and women were assigned to dormitories, separated by sex, where they had college-style single rooms that shared a bath with a neighbor. Groves thought such accommodations were more than adequate for bachelors. They were, after all, a considerable step-up from the open barracks assigned to the army. But civilian housing at Los Alamos, which was utilitarian at best, was a liability in recruitment. Oppenheimer wrote to Groves on June 21 pleading for better facilities, especially for single male scientists. "These dormitories will house not, as you seem to think, primarily or exclusively college students, but men who under normal circumstances would be living in faculty clubs or small apartments, and who have enjoyed for some years past a fairly high standard of living." Most of all, Oppenheimer wanted more space—"at least 100 square feet."[5]

Groves reluctantly complied, but only to a degree. By mid-1943, he had already spent hundreds of millions of dollars and had committed to the expenditure of at least a billion more. He was prepared to spend whatever it took to produce an atomic bomb, but he was uncomfortable spending money on permanent facilities, because the laboratory's future after the war simply was not clear. And there was something else—he disliked having to pamper Oppenheimer's scientists when the workers and residents of Oak Ridge and Hanford had settled for equally unattractive prefabricated quarters.

Calls and telexes between Groves and Los Alamos frequently concerned housing. In June 1944, for example, Groves, pressed again by Oppenheimer for not only more housing but a greater variety of it, telephoned Ashbridge and demanded a tabulation of available apartments and houses, who lived in the occupied houses, and any exceptions to existing rules by which housing was assigned. He also wanted to know the "types" of personnel (that is, their trade) requiring their own houses. Groves believed that most new arrivals were going to have to accept "demountable" housing, which could be moved. These were not trailers, but something more like today's prefabricated homes. The results of the survey were passed along to Oppenheimer, who in a follow-up call from Groves said he would "study" the report. For Oppenheimer, housing was more than just providing shelter. Living accommodations increasingly were an issue in recruitment.

Housing was not an issue for Oppenheimer and his family, however. A row of small, beautifully built stone and log cabins that had been used as faculty homes and for student activities during the days of the Ranch School were assigned to the laboratory's senior leaders, among them Oppenheimer and Parsons. The Oppenheimers and their children lived in the house formerly occupied by the school director's sister. For a while this row of homes behind Fuller Lodge had the only bathtubs in Los Alamos, and the neighborhood was enviously nicknamed Bathtub Row. Parsons and his family lived next door to Robert and Kitty and were given a slightly larger house because they had two young daughters; a third daughter had died from polio in the 1930s.

Robert and Ruth Marshak were among those assigned half of a duplex called a "Morgan" after its builder. It consisted of a bedroom, a small living room, a tiny kitchen, and a bathroom with a shower but no tub. Later, the McKee Company built single-family houses with flat roofs. Pre-furnished with GI furniture, they had an oil furnace, an auxiliary oil heater, and an oil-burning water heater. The auxiliary unit didn't give off much heat but "roared and belched at night like a bilious dragon." And all the McKees had cracks around the windows and doors that let in the cold during the winter and dust throughout the year.[6] Another type of prefabricated house, built toward the end of the war, was modeled after box-like units at the Hanford Plant in Washington.

Most of the apartments and houses were heated by coal, which generated clouds of soot. When the weather turned cold in the fall, men hired from local pueblos went from building to building starting the heaters, taking breaks along the way to smoke and occasionally surprising residents with songs from their pueblos. The heating system worked but could be dangerous. Bob Krohn and his wife were awakened one morning when a fireman's foot suddenly came through the ceiling of their bedroom. It turned out that one of the pueblo workers had inadvertently turned off the fan and the furnace had overheated, starting a fire in the unit above the Krohns'.

For the women arriving in Los Alamos, accustomed to modern conveniences like gas cooking stoves, the cast-iron wood-burning stoves they found in their kitchens were a shock. These "Black Beauties" were slow to start and, once lit, generated so much heat that kitchens became saunas. Robert Wilson's wife, Jane, struck a blow for all the homemakers one evening when she got General Groves himself to demonstrate how to light a stove. After an hour's labor that covered his uniform with soot, Groves produced a small flame. Within days, army-issue hot plates were sent to each home in Los Alamos.

There was another challenge to cooking: the altitude. Wives from the East and West coasts were surprised to learn that cooking in the mountains took much longer. Elinor Hempelmann, the wife of the laboratory's medical director, learned the hard way. Soon after arriving on the Hill she gave a party and planned to serve a roast. Unmindful of the high-altitude cooking time, she put the meat into her Black Beauty just before guests began to arrive, thinking she would give everyone a chance to enjoy a drink or two before eating. But as the roast refused to cook, the cocktail hour dragged on and on, and the distraught hostess eventually found herself with a houseful of inebriated guests before anyone had had a bite of dinner.

Inexpensive rent and medical care were two bright spots at Los Alamos. Unmarried men and women paid no more than thirteen dollars a month for rent, and families paid rent based on the husband's income. Someone making less than $2,600 a year paid only seventeen dollars in rent; those making over six thousand dollars paid no more than sixty-seven. The barracks-style hospital was staffed with several full-time doctors and nurses whose services were free. Hospital stays cost one dollar a day.

There were no residential telephones. In the beginning, there was only an old Forest Service line between Oppenheimer's office in the Tech Area and Santa Fe. After a while, a second line for use by the army post was laid. By June 1944, switchboards were added so that calls could be made between the various technical sites and the army post. Army WACs eventually took over managing the telephone system. For security purposes, they were instructed not to call men with a Ph.D. "Doctor," although that title was permissible for physicians, such as Louis Hempelmann. Single telephones were assigned numbers: Oppenheimer was 146; Parsons, 147; and Procurement's Harry Allen, 37. The La Fonda Hotel was Santa Fe 500. Anyone needing to talk to General Groves required the switchboard operator to dial Republic 6500 in Washington, D.C., or confidential numbers at Oak Ridge and Hanford. In 1944, three additional lines to Santa Fe were added by laying twenty miles of wire by hand, either directly on the ground or strung from short poles, as the terrain dictated, and cutting into exist-ing telephone lines in Pojoaque.[7]

Schooling for Los Alamos children was another early challenge. A school had to be built, teachers hired, and a curriculum planned. Deak Parsons, one of the first members of the school board, made sure that the school building, unlike the housing, was a model of sound construction and fairly attractive. Built of cinder block, with beautiful views of the Jemez Mountains, the school was intended to serve as a community center in the evenings. Groves thought it was too expensive and told Parsons he would hold him "responsible" for it. There were many young families at Los Alamos with preschool children whose mothers worked in offices and laboratories, so Oppenheimer had a nursery school built as well. He insisted that the new grade school be open to the children of the mesa's native population.[8]

Water was a constant problem—there was either too little or too much. When it rained, the streets turned to mud, forcing many drivers to abandon their cars until the weather cleared and streets dried out. Water pipes tended to freeze in the winter. When water was available, it was occasion-ally too heavily chlorinated. Sometimes residents had to haul their water from trucks parked in front of the hospital, taking care to note which water was potable and which was suited only for flushing toilets. They frequently found at their doors mimeographed circulars with information about water. A circular dated November 4, 1943, is typical:

> For the next few days, until additional water supplies are avail-able from Guaje Canyon, the water situation in this camp is critical. This is brought about by the freezing of flumes and in-takes in both the Anchor Ranch and Los Alamos supply areas. Every effort is being made to provide the camp with ample water, but the cooperation of the entire population to

conserve the supply must be obtained in order that drastic restrictions may be avoided.[9]

For all its privations and inconveniences, life on the Hill offered one unexpected advantage: there was virtually no serious crime. There were minor incidents, of course, such as the one noted in the April 17, 1944, *Daily Bulletin*:

> One night last week, the MP's endeavored to stop an automobile by driving their weapons carrier crossways in the road. However, the car took to the ditch, went around the weapons carrier, and kept on going. For the information of all concerned, 45 slugs make a rather large hole, and the MP's have been directed to shoot in cases of this nature. It cannot be over-emphasized in the interest of preservation of life, limb, and property that all individuals either afoot, mounted or in vehicles STOP whenever it appears that the guard indicates such a desire either by action or order.[10]

In spite of difficulties, the residents of Los Alamos achieved a semblance of normality in their daily lives. Wives greeted startled newcomers to the neighborhood with smiles and coffee. A thriving network of baby-sitters emerged. Neighbors learned to help, or at least accommodate, one another: a woman who kept her friend's children one day could expect the favor to be returned the next, and apartment dwellers restricted their playing of radios and pianos to agreed-upon hours. There was radio reception in Los Alamos, although not from stations in nearby Santa Fe or Albuquerque. Instead, residents got their news and music from the powerful signals of WMAQ and WGN out of Chicago. Trips to Espanola and Santa Fe were coordinated to limit the number of cars and gas coupons required.

The sense of isolation at Los Alamos declined as the community came together for hikes and picnics in their majestic surroundings. Almost everyone came under the spell of New Mexico and Pajarito Plateau.

Although the physical setting was enough to give life in Los Alamos a character distinctly its own, another factor set the Hill apart—security. After accepting a position, each new employee received the "Memorandum on the Los Alamos Project," an introduction to life on the Hill that was twice revised during the war. The first memo, prepared under the supervision of Groves and reflecting his concern with security, provided the bare minimum of information. As complaints about the memo's insufficiency increased, the laboratory found it necessary to give new arrivals more background information.

With a warning that it was "restricted" and a citation of the Espionage Act, the memo introduced the reader to Los Alamos. The town was situated on a strip of land two miles wide, eight miles long, and 7,300 feet above sea level. Most construction would be by the U.S. Army, and schools, commissaries, beer halls, and theaters would be available, as would community services like water, electricity, and sewerage. The weather was said to be pleasant—an average of 67.7 degrees Fahrenheit and rarely hotter than ninety-five degrees in the summer or colder than fourteen degrees in the winter. The reader was instructed to supplement his wardrobe with "rough country clothes."

Oppenheimer included a "Note on Security" in the memorandum in which he cited the need for secrecy. He optimistically stated that travel to and from the Los Alamos Post was not restricted, but "travel" outside Los Alamos and the immediate area meant movement related to laboratory work or perhaps personal emergencies. The note concluded with a warning and a plea:

> The extent to which we shall be able to maintain this comparative freedom will depend primarily on our success in keeping the affairs of the Laboratory strictly within the confines of the Laboratory, on the cooperation which the project personnel

affords us in its discretion on all project matters, and on our willingness to rupture completely our normal social associations with those not on the project.[11]

Not only were laboratory personnel and their families confined to Los Alamos except for brief excursions to Santa Fe, but they were not permitted to have visitors or friends on the Hill. Everyone had the same mailing address: Post Office Box 1663, Santa Fe, New Mexico. Only close family members could be told that the project was in New Mexico. Professional magazines and journals could not be mailed directly to Los Alamos but had to be forwarded through former university or job offices. If that was not possible, the employee could use a blind post office box in Los Angeles. Groves hoped that this circumspection would prevent enemy agents from compiling lists of persons at Los Alamos.

Censorship of the mail did not begin until late in 1943. It had not occurred to Groves and Oppenheimer that mail needed perusal, but rumors began to circulate that all mail was secretly being opened and read by army officials. Groves ordered an investigation, which revealed no censorship but raised the question of need. He decided that censorship was required and persuaded Oppenheimer to accept it. At a governing board meeting late in October 1943, Oppenheimer asked his senior staff if they had any objection to censorship of the mail and, if not, if they felt they were speaking for the organization as a whole. No one objected, and the board reached the consensus that, while censorship would be an additional hardship, the laboratory would accept it.[12] Oppenheimer notified Groves, who initiated the laborious process of having all mail read in cramped offices above a bank in Santa Fe. Captain Peer de Silva oversaw the censorship process.

A list of mail regulations prepared by the army was circulated to each staff member and his family. Scientists were forbidden to enclose personal mail with official correspondence to other Manhattan laboratories. Private mail was to be placed in unsealed envelopes and dropped in special mailboxes. Sealed mail would automatically be returned to the sender by the censors. Objectionable content would not be excised or obliterated, but the mail would be returned to the sender with notations on the offending content. Incoming mail would be opened, read, and resealed with official censorship stamps and seals. Among topics never to be discussed were: "(a) Your present location except that it is in New Mexico; (b) the names of your associates and the personnel employed on the project both military and civilian; (c) the professions of personnel employed at the project; (d) the nature or any details of your work; and (e) the number of people at the project either military or civilian."[13]

Oppenheimer tried to avert unfavorable staff reactions by presenting the new regulations as a preventive measure. The intention, he said, was to prevent the Los Alamos laboratory from being connected with other projects in the United States and to obscure details of its size, physical characteristics, and the identities and number of staff members. He emphasized that details that were insignificant in themselves could be pieced together with others to form a picture of Los Alamos that could be of interest to the enemy.

There were also discussions on how to "explain" the laboratory to outsiders. At the end of April 1943, Oppenheimer sent Groves a letter with a suggestion that had been approved by the governing board: "I have given some thought to the question of a story about the Los Alamos Project which, if disseminated in the proper way, might serve somewhat to reduce the curiosity of the local population, and at least delay the dissemination of the truth. We propose that it be known that the Los Alamos Project is working on a new type of rocket and the detail be added that this is a largely electrical device."[14] This suggestion and a later one for a story about an "electromagnetic gun" went nowhere.

Despite precautions, unintentional, almost comical breaches of security occurred. Ruth and Robert Marshak were on their way to Los Alamos from their home in Montreal when they stopped for gas in Colorado, not far from the New Mexico border. The attendant, seeing their license plate, asked where they were headed. When, as instructed, they said New Mexico, he replied, "Oh, you folks must be going to that secret project." Apparently he had seen enough travelers with unusual license plates heading south that he had guessed something "secret" was going on in New Mexico.[15]

On another occasion, new arrivals Ed Hammel and his wife, Caroline, were met at Lamy by a WAC driver and driven first to Santa Fe, and then with other couples to the Hill. Halfway up, Caroline stunned everyone when she announced that she knew where they were going, even though no one—not the WAC, not even Dorothy McKibbin—had actually used the name. "We're going to Los Alamos," she said brightly. "I've got a picture taken from this very spot." It turned out that she had spent the summer of 1937 at the Brush Ranch Resort near Tererro and had taken a field trip to the Los Alamos Boys School and Bandelier National Monument.[16]

Security had other light moments. Letters sent to commercial firms were occasionally returned by army censors with a note that the sender had failed to enclose a check. Letters with drawings or doodles were also returned. When Richard Feynman's wife was in a hospital in Santa Fe with a serious illness, he devised simple codes to amuse her and wrote her cryptic letters every day. The censors quickly reacted. When de Silva cross-examined Feynman, the scientist explained the purpose of the codes and offered to supply de Silva with a deciphering table. Not amused, De Silva ordered him to stop.

The post's Security Office arranged for driver's licenses to be made with code numbers instead of addresses. More than a few puzzled policemen encountered traffic offenders with foreign names and no address or occupation forthcoming. Senior staff were assigned code names to avoid attention. Enrico Fermi became "Henry Farmer;" Niels Bohr, "Nicholas Baker;" Hans Bethe, "Howard Battle;" Edward Teller, "Ed Tilden;" and Oppenheimer, "James Oberhelm." Everyone became an "engineer" and, if pressed by local policemen or officials, could say he worked for the Army Corps of Engineers. ID numbers instead of names were used on automobile registrations, bank accounts, income tax returns, food and gasoline rations, and even insurance policies.

Security arrangements were particularly burdensome for the leaders of the Manhattan Project. As early as 1943 Groves had discouraged Oppenheimer and Ernest Lawrence from traveling on airplanes. On July 29, he forbade flying and even driving under some circumstances. Flying was "not worth the risk," and Oppenheimer was instructed to have "protection" with him when he drove to Santa Fe as well as when he drove around Los Alamos at night.[17] It wasn't until the war ended that Groves withdrew this restriction. Security shadows were assigned to Oppenheimer and Parsons, and Groves ordered special MPs to guard their homes. This surveillance was hard on wives and families, who would occasionally forget identification badges and be forbidden entry to their own homes until proof of identity could be produced.

The Oppenheimers suffered more than anyone. Even though the MPs were asked to be inconspicuous, in such a small community everyone knew who they were and what they were doing. By 1944 fences had been erected around their home and the Parsons' on Bathtub Row for additional security. Oppenheimer was followed everywhere he went, as was his wife, and their phone calls were monitored. His bodyguard and occasional driver was a security agent who regularly reported his movements.

Colonel John Lansdale, the member of Groves's security team who had investigated Oppenheimer, took an interest in Kitty because of her earlier membership in the Communist Party. He interviewed her on a number of occasions, both in California and at Los Alamos. Lansdale found her fascinating: she clearly didn't like her interrogator but played along. He noted years later,

> She was trying to rope me, just as I was trying to rope her. The thing that impressed me was how hard she was trying. Intensely, emotionally, with everything she had. She struck me as a curious personality, at once frail and very strong. I felt she'd go to

any lengths for what she believed in.... I got the impression of
a woman who'd craved some sort of quality or distinction of
character she could attach herself to.... She didn't care how
much I knew of what she'd done before she met Oppenheimer
or how it looked to me.

The interviews with Kitty influenced Lansdale's report on her to
Groves. "[H]er strength of will," he wrote, "was a powerful influence in
keeping Dr. Oppenheimer away from what we would regard as dangerous
associations." Lansdale detected something else in his interviews with
both Robert and Kitty—ambition. "It was perfectly evident that both he
and his wife regarded this project as his outstanding career opportunity."[18]

The work day in Los Alamos began at 7:30 a.m. with a shrill siren
sounding from the Technical Area. Another blast of the siren sounded half
an hour later as a reminder. Except for the hottest days in summer and
when it rained or snowed, the mornings were crisp and the mountain air
electric. The workdays were long, often extending into the evening hours.
Sunday was an official day off, but early in 1945 the workweek shifted to
seven days.

The Tech Area was cluttered with mostly two-story buildings thrown
up with little regard for the activities that would actually take place in
them. Some buildings were connected by elevated, covered walkways running from one secure area to another. Charlotte Serber, who became the
laboratory's scientific librarian and whose husband, Robert, also worked
within the Tech Area, thought the place had a "disorderly, academic air.
The offices were simple enough, though incredibly dirty, overcrowded,
and badly equipped.... The Area was in a state of continuous crisis."[19]

A few wives worked for the laboratory from the very beginning, but
by 1944 more than two hundred women were employed, and even more

by 1945. Many of the women had secretarial jobs, but others had technical work or served as human "computers" of long mathematical problems. Bernice Brode, like dozens of other women, worked part-time in the Tech Area as a statistician. Everyone who worked for the laboratory had a color-coded identification badge that admitted him to various buildings or areas. White badges were the most encompassing and the most prestigious, giving access to the entire Technical Area, all of the remote locations like Anchor Ranch or S Site, and, to Groves's dismay, the colloquia. A blue badge limited the bearer to a specific site, and orange was for support staff such as secretaries and typists. The one exception was Priscilla Green, the secretary to the director—she wore a white badge.

Wives kept busy. Kay Manley directed the town's choral society. Eleanor Jette and Peg Bainbridge took on the Cub Scout pack, and Dorothy Hillhouse ran the Brownie troop. Jean Bacher and Eleanor Jette served on the housing committee of one of Oppenheimer's creations, the town council. Several wives taught in the Los Alamos schools—Alice Smith taught social science, Betty Inglis mathematics, and Peg Bainbridge French.

In the beginning, the town council was appointed by Oppenheimer, but later it was elected. The six members typically met on Monday evenings, at first in a private room of Fuller Lodge, but later, as Los Alamos grew, in the main dining room. Although it had no real power, the council discussed community problems and made recommendations to Oppenheimer, the army post commander, and eventually to Groves. It determined speeding fines on the Hill, planned festivities, and investigated a charge that prostitutes were propositioning young men outside the PX. The propositioning wasn't happening at the PX, the council learned, but in one of the women's dormitories. The army wanted to close the dorm because of a rise in sexual diseases, but there were protests, particularly from single men. In the end, the town council did nothing, and the dorm stayed open.

Parties at Los Alamos were unmatched for gaiety and alcohol. As Jean Bacher put it, "We worked hard and we played hard." Square dancing, a bit of local color, became popular. Choral and drama groups were organized, and after a few months, a small symphony orchestra was assembled. The parties given by the single men and women were the loudest, most crowded, and most alcohol-saturated events on the Hill. Each dorm had a large lounge that could accommodate a small band and tables for food and drinks. The focus of the party was the punch bowl, a huge five-foot glass chemical reagent jar borrowed from one of the nearby laboratories. The punch itself was a mixture of whatever liquor could be purchased in Santa Fe for the occasion. A fifth of liquor typically cost around $1.50, although the more desirable brands, such as Old Grand Dad, cost two or three dollars. Just as often the punch bowl was filled with two-hundred-proof alcohol snatched from laboratory's chemistry supplies. It tasted like vodka but had to be diluted with water in order to avoid poisoning drinkers. The parties lasted until dawn, and when couples tired of the noise or dancing, they drifted into the rooms for quieter socializing.

On weekends, residents could explore New Mexico's striking landscape and archeological sites. They could go east into the Santa Fe National Forest or west into the Jemez Mountains for hiking and picnicking. The Oppenheimers and others kept horses in the old school stables. On a Sunday morning, Oppenheimer might be spotted on his horse, Chico; Kitty might be with him on Dixie. Oppenheimer gave a horse to Robert Christy and John Williams to share, and the two men carried on a debate over who owned which half. Fermi hiked year round and often organized outdoor sessions for scientists, combining walking and work. Emilio Segrè favored fishing over hiking and unsuccessfully tried to get Fermi, his former professor, to join him in one of the many mountain streams.

In the valleys below Los Alamos, nestled against the Rio Grande, lived the descendants of the ancient Indian tribes. San Ildefonso, the nearest and one of the largest pueblos, became a source of labor for the laboratory. Its most famous resident was Maria Martinez, whose careful cultivation of Indian pottery techniques revived the art form from near-extinction. Her son, Popovi Da, worked on the Hill, where he was known by his Anglicized name, Julian Martinez. Like other pueblos, San Ildefonso combines Indian and Spanish cultures. The Spanish had come to the valley in 1598, bringing their customs and religion. While the Indians adopted Christianity, they continued to revere a nearby mesa called Tunyo, or Black Mesa, as the home of their ancestral gods. Not far from San Ildefonso are the pueblos of Santa Clara, Nambe, Santo Domingo, Zia, and San Juan. And sixty miles north is the multistory pueblo of Taos, the oldest continuously inhabited dwelling in North America.

The pueblo residents took the burgeoning Los Alamos population in stride. For some, Los Alamos meant jobs as construction workers or maids; for others, the newcomers added to the market for pottery and other crafts. The Indians found Los Alamos residents no brasher than the general lot of tourists, although they did seem to have more money to spend. The reaction to Los Alamos in Santa Fe was somewhat different. Residents of the ancient city were at first amused by the new arrivals and considered them, as did the Indians, as tourists. Their loud voices, copious baggage, and unruly children seemed to confirm suspicions about the decadent East and West coasts. As Los Alamos grew however, so did the demands on Santa Fe's gasoline, food, home items, and the like. The money Hill people spent in Santa Fe barely compensated for the invasion of laboratory buses that congested their streets. Speeders and other misdemeanants seemed above the law because the U.S. Army was inclined to intervene on their behalf. And it was a mystery why everyone had the same post office box address in Santa Fe.

It was inevitable that someone would turn to verse to try to capture life on the Hill. One clever ditty was attributed to a GI:

> Some folks live in the city.
> Some folks live in a town.
> Some folks live out in a suburb.
> But we—well, listen now:
> We're just a P.O. number.
> We have no real address

Although we were selected,
I wonder—for the best!
We're not like other people,
No one knows what we do:
So, P.O. Box 1663,
Here's to you.[20]

Los Alamos was undoubtedly a strange place: temporary, makeshift, always incomplete. There were deprivations and shortages, erratic municipal services, and, no matter how expansive the landscape, fences and security that constrained the residents, if only psychologically. But the town had a school, hospital, churches, and food at the commissary to buy with ration coupons. This at least was like home. For people set in their urban ways, the mesa held little appeal. Young couples with children did not have the comfort of their childhood neighborhoods or the support of their families; they either made families of their neighbors or they were on their own. Most coped, and for many it was a memorable experience. It seemed exceptional at the time, but perhaps the experience was only unusual. Maybe life was no better and no worse for the men and women of Los Alamos than for millions of other ordinary people in wartime America. Except, as Oppie was fond of saying, everyone lived in splendid isolation.

He meant the land and sky. It was this magical combination of mesa and mountain—deep, riveted canyons and multihued cliffs, and virtually unlimited sky—that had so enchanted Oppenheimer in his youth and drew him back again and again in the decades before the war. It was why he wanted his secret laboratory located here.

There were moments in Los Alamos that were breathtakingly beautiful. One newly married couple in the winter of 1943 found themselves walking from Fuller Lodge back to their tiny apartment on a still, cold night, hand in hand, with large, leafy snowflakes drifting down from a dark sky, not in torrents, but sparsely, as if dropped one by one by hand, each snowflake gently illuminated by the light from a window or the glow of the Tech Area. In that luminous moment, they were the only two people alive on the mesa.

Phyllis Fisher, having survived her family's earlier housing troubles, quickly fell in love with the landscape. She wrote to her family, "Today is lovely. Skies are clear and the snow glistens so that without dark glasses, I am dazzled. The field behind our house sparkles in the winter sun and, across the valley, the mountains appear to be topped with fluffy whipped cream. They look so near that I feel I could almost reach over, dip my fingers in and lick the delicious stuff."[21]

Everyone experienced those rare early mornings when the air was so crisp, so crystalline and fragile, that it seemed a careless breath might shatter everything. And everyone lived through the storms, large and small, that struck the mesa or gathered in dark clouds with a hundred shades of gray in the distance and then rolled from one end of the horizon to the other with thunder and lightning, like nature executing a drama on a vast stage. These were majestic displays of raw power and dark beauty. Occasionally smoke would billow up from a spot where lightning had struck and ignited a fire. And lightning was an unpredictable danger, especially in the summer, and sometimes lethal. When a storm hit the mesa, its crack and thunder rattled windows, frightened children, and sent residents caught outside scurrying for cover.

Some Los Alamos residents wondered if perhaps this was a reminder that whatever the laboratory thought it could do with the atom, nature could do more.

Chapter Eleven

A NECESSARY REORGANIZATION

G roves knew instinctively that the decision to halt development of the plutonium gun required a reorganization of the laboratory, and he encouraged Oppenheimer to take the appropriate measures as quickly as possible. The message was clear: implosion had to be given the highest priority without jeopardizing completion of the uranium Little Boy.

On July 17, 1944, Oppenheimer announced two new divisions: the G, or Weapons Physics, Division, and X, or Explosives, Division. Bacher had shown strong leadership all along and was appointed to head G Division, which soon became popularly known as "Gadget" Division. It incorporated units of the old Experimental Physics Division as well as several small groups from Ordnance. Oppenheimer wrote to Bacher on August 14 detailing the fundamental functions of G Division:

1. To develop methods and to apply them for the determination of the hydrodynamics of implosion with particular emphasis on symmetry, compression and the behavior of materials in a gadget.

2. To conduct semi-integral and integral studies of the materials to be used in implosion gadgets from the point of view of their multiplication properties.

3. To be immediately responsible for the design specifications of the tamper, active material, source, etc., to be used in implosion gadgets, and for the appropriate correlation of the results obtained by work under 1 and 2 above....

4. To collaborate whenever possible in providing instrumentation for studying the problems of the Explosive Division.[1]

In a move that surprised some, Kistiakowsky was given leadership of X Division, a position equivalent to Parsons's. Bacher's and Kistiakowsky's responsibilities overlapped to some extent, but Bacher's division emphasized experimental studies, while Kistiakowsky's was focused on development of the implosion bomb itself. The Experimental Physics Division was renamed R, for Research, and given to Robert Wilson, and Parsons continued with his remaining Ordnance staff.

Kistiakowsky's appointment to lead X Division did not sit well with Parsons. Kistiakowsky tried to soothe his colleague's feelings but never really succeeded. "Parsons was furious," he recalled, "...he felt that I had by-passed him and that was outrageous. I can understand how he felt.... From then on Parsons and I were not on good terms. He was extremely suspicious of me."[2] Parsons, who had led the implosion effort *despite* Neddermeyer, with all of his stumbles and setbacks, felt betrayed by Oppenheimer. He also feared that splitting responsibility for weapons between divisions would waste manpower and make coordination difficult if not impossible. Parsons sent Oppenheimer a memorandum asking that he once again be given control over both the Little Boy and the Fat Man weapons. Oppenheimer refused: "The kind of authority which you appear to request from me is something I cannot delegate to you because I do not possess it. I do not, in fact, whatever the protocol may suggest, have the authority to make decisions which are not understood and approved by the qualified scientists of the laboratory who must execute them."[3] Disappointed but a team player, Parsons had no choice but grudgingly to accept the new organization.

As he had done for Bacher with G Division, Oppenheimer formally laid out the five primary functions of X Division in a letter to Kistiakowsky on August 14:

1. To investigate promising explosives, methods of initiation, boosting, detonation, etc. for implosion.

2. To develop methods for improving the quality of [explosive] castings.

3. To develop lense [*sic*] systems and methods for fabricating and testing them.

4. To develop a suitable engineering design for the assembly of the explosives and of the initiating systems to be used with them in an actual gadget.

5. To cooperate closely with the Gadget Division in providing the necessary charges for their investigations.[4]

With the establishment of these two new divisions, implosion had grown from Neddermeyer's small team in 1943 to more than fourteen groups operating within T Division and the newly created X Division. Of the six hundred people now working for Kistiakowsky's X Division, almost four hundred were army personnel sent to Los Alamos as members of the Special Engineering Detachment. The laboratory had Groves to thank for these soldiers. From his powerful position in the military, he was able to have the records of millions of men searched for applicable skills—no small task in the age before computerized records. Though these men performed professional work at Los Alamos, they were treated as enlisted men. Kistiakowsky thought their treatment was unfair, but he was powerless to change it:

> They were kids mostly, with partial college education, but there were even a few PhDs. Now Groves ... [who] deferred to the living comforts of civilians because he knew he couldn't get them there [Los Alamos] otherwise, took it out on these enlisted personnel, who lived in barracks built to a minimum permissible standard by the army, forty square feet [per] person.[5]

Oppenheimer's proposed reorganization had been sufficiently important for Groves to make two quick trips to Los Alamos in less than two weeks. On July 26, he flew to Albuquerque, was driven to the Hill for a day of meetings centered on implosion, and was back in his office in Washington by the afternoon of July 28. He returned to New Mexico on August 1, spending the day in discussions with Parsons, Kistiakowsky, and others and in intense private meetings with Oppenheimer. Groves was determined to keep the laboratory focused on completing a weapon.

The reorganization revealed that Oppenheimer, his division leaders, and even the governing board were seriously overburdened. In addition to their responsibilities for research and development, these men had numerous administrative tasks—for example, mediating housing disputes, contending with complaints about water and food, drafting policy for the laboratory—not directly related to scientific and technical matters.

Oppenheimer discussed the tremendous increase in the workload of the board with his leadership and then with Groves, who agreed that changes should be made. Explaining that technical and administrative issues needed to be handled separately, Oppenheimer established a division for administration, and on June 29 he dissolved the governing board, replacing it with two smaller boards, administrative and technical.[6] Despite its drawbacks, the laboratory's committee structure remained vital to its success and was the forerunner of today's "committee-run" big science endeavors.

While the administrative board was organized informally to handle problems like housing, the technical board was charged with overseeing immediate scientific and technical concerns and to assess progress throughout the organization. Oppenheimer made sure that the committee's membership reflected a mixture of senior men—including Bacher, Bethe, Fermi, and Parsons—and younger scientists, such as Bainbridge, McMillan, and Ramsey.[7]

Despite the good intentions, the reorganization did not resolve all the problems facing Groves and Oppenheimer. Managers complained of being overtaxed. There was confusion over responsibilities and, as a consequence, discontent in some groups. As tension increased and the work accelerated, Oppenheimer's office received numerous complaints about wages, housing, working conditions, excessive hours, and the like. From Washington, Groves ordered Colonel Ashbridge to institute a fifty-four-hour work week for all military personnel at Los Alamos and to cancel all leaves. His order carried the implication that Oppenheimer would do something similar with civilians.

When Oppenheimer met with his new administrative board on August 3, he acidly complained that the situation at the laboratory was one of "laxity" more than discontent.[8] Accusing staff members of slacking was an unusual attack from the normally tolerant director. Oppenheimer cited the example of "certain" chemists whose lackadaisical attitude had come to his attention after their involuntary transfer from other divisions to Kistiakowsky's unit. Despite the pressing need for reassignment, the men in question had objected. Some were unconvinced of the feasibility of the implosion alternative and wanted to stay with what they perceived to be the more promising gun program. When the administrative board meeting degenerated into another round of complaints, Oppenheimer was forced to identify several people within the organization to whom complaints could be brought.

Two weeks later, Oppenheimer reported to the administrative board that "too much time was being spent in the PX by employees." It was a small matter, but it was symptomatic of the overall malaise he observed. In the spirit of Groves's order to his military post, Oppenheimer announced that the Tech Area siren would now sound at 7:25 a.m., 7:30, 8:25, 8:30, 12:00 noon, 12:55 p.m., 1:00, and 5:30. Frequent soundings of the siren were intended to "induce" people to be at work on time and to remind them of the lunch hour and closing.

Amid the discontent, Cyril Smith's Chemistry and Metallurgy Division remained desperate for useful amounts of U235 and Pu239. They were responsible for receiving, processing, and casting the metals, and while they had tiny amounts of both substances by mid-1944, there was not enough for more than experimental purposes. The problem was especially acute with U235—Lawrence's electromagnetic separation machines were not delivering meaningful quantities of it, and the gaseous diffusion plant at Oak Ridge was not yet running at full capacity. The laboratory's research program would face serious difficulties without more U235. Oppenheimer now believed that failing to pursue thermal diffusion as a means of producing U235 had been a "blunder." "I think he was right," Groves would acknowledge after the war. "It is one of the things I regret the most in the whole course of the operation. We failed to consider [thermal diffusion] as a portion of the process as a whole."[9] Fortunately, Oppenheimer was able to convince him to pursue it now.

Philip Abelson had developed an experimental diffusion system earlier in the war, but Groves, advised that thermal diffusion was less likely to produce substantial quantities of bomb-grade U235 than other methods, had declined to make it a priority. By 1944 Abelson had assembled a more sophisticated operation with the support of the Naval Research Laboratory, and he let Oppenheimer know that his new plant could produce up to five grams of enriched U235 a day. Oppenheimer in turn informed Groves, who took quick action, and in less than a month a contract was awarded to the H. K. Ferguson Company to build a thermal diffusion plant at Oak Ridge. With access to nearly 230,000 kilowatts of power coming on line at Oak Ridge, more than enough to generate the steam necessary for an enormous thermal diffusion plant, Groves acted with characteristic boldness. The new plant, nicknamed S-50 or, more colloquially, "Fox's Farm," would eventually consist of 2,142 thermal columns, each forty-eight feet high.

The contribution of the thermal diffusion process was considerable. At 23 percent U235, the enriched uranium that emerged from S-50 was still less than what was required for a bomb, but it could be fed into the electromagnetic plant in California, where the U235 was enriched to 84 percent. In March 1945, Groves informed Oppenheimer that Los Alamos would receive slightly more than eleven kilograms of enriched U235 by June 1.[10] This was the batch of uranium that eventually went into Little Boy.

In the summer of 1944, Groves and his intelligence staff still believed that the Germans might produce an atomic bomb, although the prospect was diminishing as the Allies pushed into France and liberated Italy. Military strategists were now speculating that the war against Germany could be over by Christmas 1944, and Japan emerged as the more likely target of any Los Alamos weapon. Planners began to take a closer look at potential targets in Japan—all urban centers—and particularly those whose destruction might forestall the need for an Allied invasion in 1945 or 1946. Groves desperately wanted to use the bomb in at least one theater of war to justify the two billion dollars spent so far.

In the hope of expediting work at Los Alamos, Oppenheimer made additional organizational changes. Fermi and Parsons were appointed associate directors. Fermi was given responsibility for F Division, which included research, theory, and nuclear physics, and Parsons was placed in charge of ordnance, assembly, delivery, and engineering.

Fermi, who had been making regular visits to Los Alamos, formally disengaged from his work at Chicago and joined the staff on the Hill full-time in August 1944, his arrival reflecting Oppenheimer's strong belief that Fermi was invaluable to Los Alamos. Groves, however, had questioned the advisability of Fermi's involvement at Los Alamos, even as a consultant, and had asked Oppenheimer to discontinue Fermi's visits altogether. Oppenheimer could only assume that the general's objections stemmed in part from Fermi's purported carelessness about security in Chicago, an attitude he considered indefensible, and he raised the issue with his governing board on June 17. He was frank: he could neither explain Groves's position nor support it. On the contrary, he wanted Fermi at Los Alamos as soon as possible. The board strongly concurred.[11]

The new technical board, which was supposed to streamline the scientific operations at Los Alamos, proved to be a disappointment. Almost as soon as it was established, it began to falter under the increasing pressure and momentum of the implosion program and the need for tighter scheduling. The board was never formally dissolved, but Oppenheimer now assigned more and more responsibility to special committees and temporary task forces, such as the Intermediate Scheduling Conference, formed in August 1944. Its purpose was to coordinate the activities, plans, and schedules of groups whose work would culminate in what was beginning to seem inevitable: a test of the implosion bomb. Parsons acted as chairman, and the membership—which included Bainbridge, Bacher, Kistiakowsky, and Bradbury—was confirmed in November. Very shortly the committee extended its oversight to the gun bomb program as well.

The establishment of specialized committees further decentralized the governing structure of the laboratory but allowed more flexibility in the allocation of resources, particularly scientific and technical staff. At the same time, almost all divisions needed more men. Oppenheimer reported to Groves that recruitment had fallen off, and he believed the organization had a poor hiring program. Recruiting was still conducted by direct communication with potential candidates or the reassignment of army draftees, procedures that were inadequate for the growing personnel requirements. Recruitment also suffered because Los Alamos salaries were not competitive with those of private industry.[12] Men like Bacher and Shane undertook lengthy trips to find new personnel in other units of the Manhattan District. These efforts were little more than "raids" on the other projects, and they generated ill will. Compton's Met Lab, whose work was winding down in late 1944 and early 1945, was particularly vulnerable, and Groves received many angry calls from Compton complaining about Los Alamos's depredations. Despite the urgency of the need, however, only a few men from Oak Ridge, the Metallurgical Laboratory, and laboratories in New York were convinced to move. Groves, meanwhile, continued to look for military projects he could loot of staff.

———

In a letter of August 7, 1944, to General George Marshall, who shared it with Secretary of War Stimson, Groves wrote that the nuclear bomb depended on the production of uranium and plutonium and on implosion "experiments yet to be conducted" in Los Alamos. Drawing on reports from Hanford, Oak Ridge and Los Alamos, he described three weapons under development. The MARK I was a low-yield, low-power uranium gun bomb. Its blast would be the equivalent of several thousand tons of TNT, producing what Groves called "Class B" destruction: extensive damage beyond repair to perhaps 75 percent of the buildings in an area of five or six square miles. The MARK II was a more sophisticated uranium gun with twice the explosive power of the MARK I. The MARK III was an implosion weapon requiring relatively little fissionable material but having comparatively greater explosive force. Groves promised Marshall that a MARK II weapon would be available by August 1945. And if implosion experiments underway at Los Alamos were successful, then between five and eleven MARK III bombs might be ready between March and June 1945. He even predicted that twenty to forty implosion bombs might be available by the end of 1945.[13]

Unfortunately, Groves's projections once again proved to be overly optimistic.

A week later, Groves sent Conant to Los Alamos to independently assess the situation. Conant reported back that the gun weapon was on schedule and would require between thirty-nine and sixty kilograms (eighty-six to 132 pounds) of U235. The amount required for an implosion weapon depended on the design. A U235 weapon might require as little 7.5 kilograms (16.5 pounds), while a Pu239 weapon might need as much as nine kilos (19.8 pounds).[14] All of these weapons depended on the delivery of fissile material. Conant was not optimistic about any of the implosion designs, however. There "is not more than a 50–50 bet that Mark IV [a low-yield implosion weapon] can be developed at all before the summer of 1945," he reported.[15]

While much of the laboratory found itself in the throes of reorganization or embroiled in disputes over responsibilities and personnel, Hans Bethe's Theoretical Division remained somewhat outside the whirlwind. More academic scientists were in his division than in any other, and their work employed paper, pencils, chalkboards and chalk, the new IBM calculators, and desks and tables, in contrast to the men at Anchor Ranch and S Site with their explosives, bunkers, revetments, and explosions. Although the men of T Division arrived like everyone else at 7:30 or 8:00 in the morning, they sat at their desks or conducted what appeared to be casual and unrelated conversations, filling blackboards with long calculations that were carefully scrutinized and corrected, sometimes over a period of days. Bethe and his theoreticians frequently posted "Do Not Erase" signs for the cleaning crews.

Bethe himself was universally liked, certainly within his own division, and everyone thought him an effective leader. One reason for this broad acceptance was his demeanor—that of a kindly uncle or grandfather—and another was his careful, considered approach to problem solving. He had a first-rate mind and was exceedingly well organized. Christy, who was assigned to work with Bethe, found him "a prodigious worker.... He was just an absolutely amazing person. He wasn't such a brilliant thinker offhand, but nevertheless a very, very solid person."[16] Mildred Richards, whose physicist husband, Hugh, worked for Robert Wilson, substituted once as Bethe's secretary. She was accustomed to taking dictation, but she had never worked for someone whose "dictation was so smooth and flawless. He slowly paced back and forth while he dictated at a steady rate, with perfect grammar, with no changes or corrections. It was hard to believe that he wasn't reading from a polished manuscript."[17]

The theorists gravitated from concentrating on efficiency and critical mass to gaining a better understanding of the many forces involved in implosion. They did not completely turn away from the former questions but more and more tried to grasp the hydrodynamics of the process. The IBM calculators greatly extended the range of their work. Serber's Diffusion Group, for example, assisted McMillan in calculating Little Boy's expected efficiency and the probabilities of detonation. Peierls and his staff sought to develop a mathematical model for an "ideal" explosion. During a visit as a consultant, von Neumann drafted Stanisław Ulam—a Polish refugee who taught mathematics at the University of Wisconsin before coming to Los Alamos—into determining the hydrodynamics of implosion using the new IBM computers.

To verify the accuracy of the new machines, some calculations were checked by making parallel computations by hand. Nick Metropolis and Richard Feynmann were placed in charge of a group of women with conventional, hand-operated mechanical Marchant machines. Each woman was assigned a particular step, for example multiplying or dividing a set of numbers. "We worked out all the numerical steps ... *she* was the multiplier, and *she* was the adder, and this one cubed, and we had index cards, all she did was cube this number and send it to the next [woman]." Feynmann noted that the new machines didn't get tired but the women did.[18] The calculations by hand confirmed those by machine.

One of Christy's first assignments was to calculate the critical mass of the small nuclear reactor proposed by Bacher's experimental group. To keep the design simple and feasible, Christy proposed using an enriched salt of U235 in water, surrounded by beryllium cubes. As it turned out, his predicted critical mass was almost perfect. "So I acquired tremendous fame—here is a theoretical physicist who calculated the right number.... [N]ow I will confess that anytime you hit something within a percent, it's largely luck. But I didn't go round telling people it was luck"[19]

Other questions arose during the course of T Division's work: how could shock waves be made to converge simultaneously on the plutonium core? The problem of simultaneous convergence is analogous to trying to crush an egg uniformly with only two hands. The division had to rely on indirect evidence from explosive experiments on a variety of objects at

Anchor Site and, at times, a lucky guess. The real proof of their work would be a successful test of the implosion gadget.

After the reorganization and the arrival of Fermi, Edward Teller was placed in charge of an independent unit, the Super and General Theory Group. A man of considerable intellectual capacity but a complex personality, Teller did not always work well with others members of the staff. It was said that he had a hundred big ideas a day, but only one was good. As much as Teller's skills were needed for fission work, he was often difficult, and over time it was easier for Oppenheimer put him in an independent position—what some of his colleagues began to call a sinecure—which he did in June 1944. Oppenheimer revealed the difficulty he experienced in dealing with Teller when he organized a welcoming party for new members of the British delegation at Los Alamos. At some point he realized that he had forgotten to invite the delegation's head, Rudolf Peierls. When he recognized his mistake, he rushed to Peierls to apologize and was reassured that no offense had been taken. Oppenheimer expressed relief but then said, "Can you imagine what would have happened if I had forgotten to invite Teller?"

Teller's ego was a match for Oppenheimer's, as was his ambition, and their relationship grew increasingly strained as the war wore on. It didn't help that Teller's wife, Mici, had not wanted to come to Los Alamos and wasn't fond of Oppenheimer.[20] Bethe, who worked with both men, observed that they shared several characteristics: "Teller had an extremely quick understanding of things, so did Oppenheimer.... They were also somewhat alike in that their actual production, their scientific publications, did not measure up in any way to their capacity. I think Teller's mental capacity is very high, and so was Oppenheimer's but, on the other hand, their papers, while they included some very good ones, never reached the top standards."[21] Luis Alvarez disagreed. Oppenheimer's early work on black holes and neutron stars, he believed, was worthy of a Nobel Prize. Nonetheless, Oppenheimer grew weary of Teller's machinations and increasingly relied on Priscilla Green to keep him away. His private view of Teller was bitter: "In wartime he is an obstructionist, and in peacetime he will be a promoter."[22]

Teller's relationship with Bethe also reached the breaking point despite their long friendship. At one point, Bethe asked Teller to undertake a mathematical study of implosion hydrodynamics, a critical issue at the time. Teller started the complex calculations, stopped, started again, and finally refused to do more. Bethe was stunned. Teller refused to lead a team charged with making crucial calculations on implosion and as a result, new men had to be brought in—not an easy task when the laboratory as a whole was suffering from a lack of trained personnel. Bethe was angry, particularly as Teller was assigned his own group at a very difficult moment: "Only after two failures to accomplish the expected and necessary work, and only on Teller's request, was he, together with his group, relieved of further responsibility for work on the wartime development of the atomic bomb."[23]

Teller saw himself and his role at the laboratory in different terms:

> I enjoyed Bethe's company and conversation on any number of topics, and most certainly on physics. But as physicists, we approached problems differently. Bethe enjoys turning out what Fermi called "little bricks," work that is methodical, meticulous, thorough, and detailed.... Although I have made a few tiny little bricks, I much prefer (and am better at) exploring the various structures that can be made from brick, and seeing how the bricks stack up. Oppenheimer, in my view, also approached physics in a manner more like a bricklayer than a brick maker.[24]

Oppenheimer was forced to ask Rudolf Peierls to step in and take over Teller's responsibilities. Oppenheimer had to justify the move to Groves:

"These calculations were originally under the supervision of Teller who is, in my opinion and Bethe's, quite unsuited for this responsibility. Bethe feels that he needs a man under him to handle the implosion program."[25]

Stan Ulam had been recruited by Bethe to work in the Theoretical Division, specifically to help relieve the burden on existing staff who at the time were in the middle of intense calculations. On his very first day in T Building, Ulam was cornered by Teller and engaged in a lengthy discussion on the Super.[26] Bethe had told Ulam that understanding the fission process had the highest priority and that the Super was a weapon for the future, and Ulam was bewildered at Teller's intense interest in such a remote possibility.

Teller was, as one colleague who knew him well said, "visibly ambitious." He did not like having Bethe as his boss, and Bethe knew that his appointment to be head of the Theoretical division "was a severe blow to Teller." Bethe believed that Oppenheimer chose him instead of Teller because his "more plodding but steadier approach to life and science would serve the project better at that stage of its development, where decisions had to be adhered to and detailed calculations carried through, and where, therefore, a good deal of administrative work was inevitable."[27] Bethe and Oppenheimer understood that brilliant ideas and brilliant leadership are not the same thing.

Teller's explanation for his refusal to complete the implosion hydrodynamics study was that he had other contributions to make to the war effort:

> The task Bethe was discussing seemed far too difficult. Not only were there other people more capable than I of providing such work, but I also suspected that a job that formidable might not be completed in time to have any influence on a bomb that could be used during this war. Although I began explaining all those reasons to Bethe, he was convinced that I needed to tackle the job; I was just as convinced that if I did, I would

make no contribution to the war effort. We talked for almost an hour without coming to an agreement.... Fortunately, we never had to resume that conversation.[28]

Still, outside Los Alamos, Teller continued to draw supporters. The prospect of a Super continued to be of interest to Groves and Tolman, who thought that the possibility of a massively powerful weapon could not be ignored, even if it was work for after the war. Groves himself said, "The Super cannot be completely forgotten if we take seriously our responsibilities for the permanent defense of the U.S.A."[29]

In the beginning, Teller was limited to developing theoretical concepts. Only in 1944 was his team able to speculate on such applied concerns as methods for using a combination of liquid deuterium and ordinary fission bombs as a source of the high temperatures and pressures necessary for ignition. Interest in the Super grew in the spring of 1945 when Teller announced that it might be capable of generating a force as great as ten megatons (ten million tons) of TNT. Teller thought that if an ordinary fission bomb could produce a blast equivalent to ten kilotons of TNT over an area of ten square miles, a Super could produce a similar effect over one thousand square miles. The blast of such a weapon would easily be sufficient to devastate New York City.*

Inspired by the prospect of seemingly endless destructiveness, Teller turned his attention to determining how the blast might be increased or diffused over a larger area by altering the site or altitude of detonation. He and his team speculated that extensive damage would occur if a Super were placed underground or underwater near a continental shelf, where the blast

---

* While a Super would be enormously destructive, it would not be the largest explosion ever witnessed on earth. The laboratory had combed historical records for large explosions, such as volcanic eruptions and meteorite impacts. The eruption of the Krakatoa volcano in 1883 was thought to have generated an explosion many megatons in size and heard three thousand miles away. The large meteorite crater in Arizona gave evidence of an explosion larger than that of a ten-megaton Super.

would have the effect of a large earthquake. Even more chilling was the prospect that if a Super burned a ten-meter cube of liquid deuterium at a height of three hundred miles, the blast would equal a thousand "ordinary" Supers detonated at the height of ten miles. The potential damage staggered even Teller, for such a weapon would lay waste to over a million square miles.

Provocative as these possibilities were, Los Alamos was still relentlessly focused on implosion. Its directive was clear and unalterable: it had to deliver a weapon that could be used against the Germans or Japanese.

The many problems besetting implosion in the late summer of 1944 revived interest in the "autocatalytic" assembly bomb. This approached had been shelved in 1943 when its efficiency seemed considerably lower than that of the gun or implosion. In the autocatalytic process, small pieces of material in the active core would absorb neutrons at the right moment. Fermi's staff now explored the possibility of coating small pieces of paraffin with boron, a high absorber of neutrons used in reactors, and placing them within the fissionable plutonium to keep the entire assembly subcritical. To force a chain reaction, the boron bubbles would be compressed, thereby reducing their capacity to absorb neutrons and raising the level of criticality. Experimentation revealed the process to be lethargic at best. The explosion—if it occurred at all—would be minimal. Once again, the process was dropped, this time for good.

Kistiakowsky and his X Division continued to grapple with perfecting explosives and detonators for the implosion bomb. In November, Kistiakowsky reported to Parsons that his groups would concentrate on testing explosives on a small scale. "In the beginning all the three research groups will work on small charges for which the techniques are simpler and are better worked out, so that more shots can be made each day and unsatisfactory designs more rapidly eliminated."[30]

Producing sturdy, reliable detonators that could be fired at the same time with great precision remained a challenge. Even as early as 1943 it was understood that the detonators in an implosion bomb had to fire simultaneously to ensure that all the explosive lenses—which focus the explosive force just as an optical lens focuses light—were ignited at the same moment. In April 1944, Kistiakowsky learned that the British were having success with advanced detonators, but their experiments were quickly superseded by a new approach proposed by Luis Alvarez. He suggested vaporizing a bridgewire using the discharge from a powerful capacitor, producing a small shock wave that would detonate the explosive charge. Alvarez and one of his former students, Lawrence Johnson, quickly conducted some experiments on South Mesa in late May that confirmed simultaneity. Over a two-year period, Alvarez and his staff prepared thousands of detonators of different styles, but it was not until May 1945 that Alvarez found the right materials and the correct configuration for dependable units. The device, moreover, was safe because it was not subject to accidental discharge—a major concern when a live bomb was placed inside an airplane.

Reliable detonators required an electrical system to ignite them. A five-thousand-volt pulse of energy had to be delivered in less than a millionth of a second. To achieve this, scientists designed an apparatus that used the energy stored in a charged capacitor and released it through a high voltage device called a "spark gap switch." Where the typical residential electrical switch handles 110 volts, the spark gap handles thousands if not millions of volts. Once the switch was flipped, five thousand volts sped to the detonators along special electrical cables. Los Alamos cleverly adapted an existing voltage and capacitor system invented by the Raytheon Corporation that was part of a powerful flash unit used by the Army Air Force in nighttime aerial photography. Ordinary car batteries drove a generator known as a dynamotor, which in turn provided the five thousand volts.

The system was developed by Don Hornig and was simply known as the "X-unit."[31]

Kistiakowsky and his men were working on the assumption that the implosion weapon would employ some number of explosive charges, or lenses, configured around a spherical core, the heaviest weighing approximately 125 pounds. But another alternative was to use only two charges, large hemispheres of explosives with cavities in the center of each for the nuclear core. They would effectively "wrap" the plutonium or uranium. Parsons had pursued this option earlier and had a member of his team, David Busbee, a civilian brought in from the Naval Ordnance Bureau, build a small plant at S Site for pouring large explosive castings. Kistiakowsky rejected this approach. In his experience, it would be difficult if not impossible to produce a homogeneous and defect-free hemisphere of such size. And even if it were possible, each hemisphere would weigh a metric ton and require a heavy lift to move around. Smaller castings were easier to produce, more likely to be defect free, and safer to handle.[32] Fortunately, experiments with various castings were sufficiently successful for Kistiakowsky to announce, "The results to date have been exceedingly encouraging, in that it has been possible to produce convergent waves of predicted spherical curvature and in that two adjacent lenses have been shown to form a single convergent wave without disturbances at the point where a wave from one lens joins that from the other."[33] Kistiakowsky's most immediate problem was that the machines that produced lenses could not manufacture them in the necessary quantity, particularly those with intricate shapes. More equipment was urgently needed.

Parsons remained considerably less optimistic about lensed weapons, seeing too many difficulties and obstacles to overcome. He pointed out that only top-quality lenses could be used, and even with new molds, truly reliable explosives lenses might not be developed any time soon. In August 1944, he felt it necessary to warn Oppenheimer and Groves that "with extremely good breaks ... this development [of lenses] might be ready for

field development at full scale by February 1945. With reasonably bad luck
... this development could well occupy most of 1945."[34]

Parsons also viewed the increasing interest in an experimental test of
an implosion bomb as delaying completion of the gun design, the one
weapon that everyone agreed was most likely to succeed. As he saw it, more
engineering support for the gun was still required. Parsons also suspected
that too many men were advocating the test merely as a scientific experiment and, worse, that they saw a "controlled test" as the culmination of
the work of the laboratory. This alarmed Groves, whose focus was always
on delivering a weapon. Parsons prepared a report reflecting his views for
Oppenheimer, who in turn was expected to submit it to Groves. Oppenheimer did so on October 9, 1944, but in a cover letter he stated that on a
"few points" he disagreed with Parsons. "I believe that Captain Parsons
somewhat misjudges the temper of the responsible members of the laboratory.... For the most part these men regard their work here not as a scientific adventure, but as a responsible mission which will have failed if it is
let drop at the laboratory phase." Oppenheimer then justified the test:

> The laboratory is operating under a directive to produce weap-
> ons; this directive has been and will be rigorously adhered to.
> The only reason why we contemplate making a test, and why I
> have in the past advocated this is because with the present time
> scales and the present radical assembly design this appears to
> me a necessary step in the production of a weapon.[35]

Parsons, who bore the final responsibility for delivering weapons to
the military, was no doubt sincere in his concerns. Still, his apprehensions,
genuine or not, encouraged a trace of rancor among some who suspected
that Parsons's pessimism was inspired by his feelings about Kistiakowsky.

Parsons continued to fuel the debate over lensed versus non-lensed
designs until November 2, when a special meeting was called to settle the
issue. He still favored using two large, hemispherical explosives instead of

a multitude of small ones, the design under development by Kistiakowsky. Oppenheimer, perhaps reflecting lessons he had learned from Groves about hedging his bets, decided the laboratory would pursue both methods. On February 19, 1945, Parsons once again sent Oppenheimer a memorandum stating his concerns: "It is difficult in cold blood to look for an adequate tested lens implosion gadget in 1945." Kistiakowsky said nothing.

Parsons had his own heavy load of responsibilities. The reorganization freed him from implosion research, and he could now focus on producing field weapons. Delivering these weapons, however, particularly an implosion bomb, presented challenges, and Parsons expressed his concerns in a meeting in May 1944 with Groves, Oppenheimer, Bush, and Conant, and he later wrote a detailed four-page letter to Groves, with whom he continued to maintain a close relationship.

> I believe that it is necessary to start action along certain lines fairly soon, because unless plans have been made which will permit certain highly desirable delivery conditions to be met, we may find, perhaps this Christmas, that these conditions cannot be met either by us or by the High Command; in which case a much less positive gadget or method of delivery will have to be accepted.[36]

He then listed a number of "assumptions" under which his division was operating, the chief one being that an implosion bomb with the equivalent force of at least a thousand tons of TNT could be developed, with "good breaks," by the end of 1944. It would be in the form of a large sphere, at least sixty inches in diameter, stabilized with a box tail, and weighing over ten thousand pounds—a size that would require a B-29 bomber. The bomb would be dropped from a high altitude—at least thirty thousand feet above sea level—and it could be dropped day or night. In order to ensure "positive delivery," the airplane would be equipped with APQ-13 navigational and bombing radar and preferably with the latest

LORAN equipment to assist in navigation. And last, because of the weapon's size and weight, "it is planned to develop a gadget which will be assembled near enough to the point of take-off so that transportation and unloading operations can be minimized."[37]

All of Parsons's assumptions proved correct except one: the bomb would not be ready by the end of 1944, although the implosion weapon that finally emerged would be far more powerful.

In September 1944, Groves sent Colonel Elmer Kirkpatrick, a member of his staff, to Los Alamos to assess personnel and make recommendations that might increase efficiency. Ostensibly, Kirkpatrick was there to study the army's post operations, but his review naturally took in activities within the Tech Area. He presented his findings first to Groves and then to members of the administrative board on September 28. He felt that a large part of the personnel was "lacking in a sense of urgency," as reflected in the working hours. He suggested increasing hours and using a siren or whistle to announce the beginning of the workday, lunch, and closing time. The board agreed to that recommendation but turned down Kirkpatrick's recommendation that every office install a time clock.[38]

An unexpected bit of luck came in the fall of 1944 when Oppenheimer learned that a rocket research project at the California Institute of Technology was nearing completion. Because its staff had experience useful to Los Alamos, Oppenheimer quickly conferred with Charles Lauritsen, the project's director and a friend and colleague from before the war, about the possibility of collaborative work. The Cal Tech program, code-named Project CAMEL, was half the size of Los Alamos, but it nevertheless had more than three thousand staff members. Groves found the potential

collaboration attractive as well, especially the prospect of relieving personnel pressures at Los Alamos. Oppenheimer excitedly told the administrative board on November 24 that working with Cal Tech offered three
important and immediate advantages to Los Alamos. First, the project
had considerable contracting and subcontracting experience with some
three hundred shops in southern California, many of which could provide
services to the laboratory. Second, CAMEL had experimental proving
grounds that could supplement those in Los Alamos. Third, they had on
staff a "few extremely competent chemists, physicists and engineers." The
only downside was that Oppenheimer believed security was lax, but he
thought it could be beefed up. He was particularly pleased that Lauritsen
and one of his key associates, William Fowler, planned to spend most of
their time on the Hill if the collaboration was approved.[39]

Approval came quickly from Groves, along with support from Conant
and Bush. CAMEL was quickly established as an arm of the Los Alamos
Laboratory at Cal Tech. The organization would now take over some of the
problems with bomb assembly and delivery, and it would manufacture Fat
Man mockups, called "pumpkins," to be dropped from airplanes in tests for
stability. More importantly, CAMEL would work independently on implosion assembly, lens mold design, fusing, and assembly of the high-explosives.

Fortunately, the arrangement would leave the CAMEL staff in California, for even as the McKee Construction Company finished its third
phase of housing construction in Los Alamos in December 1944, the need
for more housing went unsatisfied. Groves still believed that Los Alamos
was only temporary, a place for the "duration," and he was reluctant to
invest more in housing. In fact, he purposefully began to delay all Los
Alamos requests for additional housing appropriations. To some extent,
his decision backfired: one-third of the more than two hundred men
recruited in November and December 1944 resigned by January because
of hardships and poor housing in Los Alamos. And this was at a time when
the laboratory was offering technicians a one-hundred-dollar bonus if
they came without their families.

Work gathered momentum in the fall but at the same time increased in complexity. In December, Oppenheimer established another committee, the Technical and Scheduling Conference, for scheduling experiments, shop time, and the use of active material. Oppenheimer arranged for Samuel Allison at the Met Lab in Chicago to come and head the new advisory body. Allison, an experienced physicist, brought a fresh outlook to the staggering demands for coordination within the divisions and units. Having no fixed membership or agenda, each conference addressed a current problem such as the development of explosive lenses or experiments with the small amounts of U235 that had begun to arrive. These topical conferences discharged many of the duties of the weakened Technical Board.

The summer of 1944 brought an urgently needed bonus: both uranium and plutonium shipments began to increase. At the end of August Oppenheimer was able to telex Groves that the laboratory had received some fifty-one grams of what for security purposes he called X-10 stock—Pu239. With some pride, he was also able to report that some 2,500 separate experiments had been conducted with this material and the loss rate was only 1 percent.

Working directly with such potentially dangerous substances required great care. The division followed advanced laboratory procedures for working with radioactive materials. Workers operated in special closed cubicles in designated "hot" areas, with washable walls and no furniture. Everyone wore protective hoods, facemasks, and protective clothing, which was either discarded or washed after each use. All potential outlets for materials led to reservoirs, partly to prevent contamination but also to permit recovery.

The small quantities of uranium and plutonium available were precious. For over a year, what little nuclear material Los Alamos possessed was stored in the old stone icehouse built by the ranch school. Later, as more material arrived and was processed into spheres or cylinders, it was stored at Omega Site. In the meantime, when Kennedy raised the question of who would be responsible for the loss of U235 or Pu239, Oppenheimer suggested that it was up to every person who released the material to another worker to be convinced that the recipient was trustworthy. Although he was less concerned with theft than with disasters such as fire, Kennedy also asked for guards at storage centers. The post military complied, but no provisions were made at the time for fire protection.

Fire, however, was a serious threat. Most structures in Los Alamos, including living quarters, were made of wood. Cooler temperatures and snow diminished the hazard in the winter, but it was greater in the summer, particularly during dry spells. Always vigilant, Groves recognized the possibility in a visit in July 1944. It seemed to him that the Tech Area was particularly vulnerable because of the large number of cars and trucks parked in the narrow spaces between buildings. He ordered Colonel Ashbridge to build other parking areas, but the essential risk remained.

That changed in January 1945, when a fire destroyed the C-Shop building in the Tech Area. Groves, in Washington, was alarmed, and everyone suddenly realized that a fire in the plutonium facilities next door would be catastrophic. For greater protection, a new building—DP site—was built on the east side of the mesa. It would be a prototype of future buildings. All construction would be of noncombustible materials—steel walls and roof, rock wool insulation, metal lathing, and plaster lining. A revolutionary new ventilation system would not only clean air from the outside but process it a second time internally before releasing it outside.

Trouble approached from other quarters as well. Congress was beginning to question the vast expenditures of the Manhattan Project. When Congressman Albert Engel learned of another major request from the War Department for the Manhattan District, he wrote Secretary Stimson a long letter of protest. Stimson appealed to Engel's loyalty, temporarily quieting congressional interest, but the war mobilization chief, James F. Byrnes, independently wrote a memorandum for President Roosevelt suggesting an impartial review of the overall project by scientists not associated with the Manhattan District. This review, he felt, might convince Congress that the money was being well spent. He noted that "the expenditures for the Manhattan Project are approaching two billion dollars with no definite assurances yet of production." While the impartial review might offend some scientists, such as Bush, he felt that "two billion dollars is enough money to risk such hurt."[40] Roosevelt sent a copy of the memo to Stimson, who joined the president for lunch and was able to defeat the suggestion for a review by pointing out that the Manhattan Project included every physicist of major standing as well as multiple Nobel Prize winners.

Despite fire and the threat of a congressional investigation, the work at Los Alamos whirled ahead at a frantic, almost dizzying pace. Dispersed throughout the mesas and canyons, work was never more intense or complicated than in the first half of 1945. Spirits rose, and even Oppenheimer, drawn and tired, sensed progress and an improvement in morale. Conant, who was regularly apprised of the work at Los Alamos and frequently visited in person, believed in late October that there was now at least a fifty-fifty chance that an implosion bomb would be ready for a test on May 1, 1945, and a three-to-two chance by July 1.[41]

By the end of January 1945, the estimates of critical mass for both uranium and plutonium had been theoretically refined. Fermi and his staff were able to answer many previously unresolved questions through ingenious experiments with the water boiler. In one of these, a beam of thermal neutrons from the boiler was fed onto a small target of U235 placed within a sphere of uranium. Activity within the sphere was carefully measured and the results brought the laboratory closer than ever before to specifying the critical mass of U235 necessary to sustain a supercritical reaction. It appeared that some sixty-four kilograms (141 pounds) would do it.

Those working on implosion were further encouraged when Fermi announced results from a series of experiments with a small sphere of plutonium from the Clinton reactor. The sphere itself was less than one inch in diameter, but experiments confirmed earlier estimates that at least six kilograms (13.3 pounds) of Pu239 would be needed in a bomb.

Throughout the early months of 1945 Groves paid particular attention to improving production at the uranium plant in Oak Ridge and the plutonium plant in Hanford. He pushed his deputy, Colonel Nichols, to expedite the U235 separation process as much as possible. Groves similarly ordered his Hanford director, Colonel Franklin Matthias, to increase shipments to Los Alamos with all speed.[42] Delays in plutonium production at the Hanford plant in 1944 were overcome by increasing the number of uranium rods feeding into the reactor, which in turn accelerated the fission process during which uranium was transmuted into plutonium. By May, production at Hanford had been quintupled. Unless a major disaster occurred, Groves felt that the deadlines reported to Secretary Stimson and hence to the president could still be met.

Uranium from the Y-12 plant in Tennessee arrived at Los Alamos as a purified fluoride called uranium hexafluoride. Groves had forbidden the transportation of the precious substance by air as too risky, so delivery was primarily by train and finally by truck. At 10:30 a.m. on predetermined days beginning in late 1944, army couriers in civilian clothing left Oak Ridge with the uranium packed carefully in ordinary luggage. At 12:50 p.m., the men caught the Southland Express for Chicago, where they were met by members of the Manhattan District Office. At noon the next day, another team of army couriers boarded the Santa Fe Chief for Lamy, where they were met with trucks from the Hill. In Los Alamos, the fluoride was finally reduced to metal through a tedious extraction process.

Everyone working with radioactive materials wore around his neck a film badge, which was basically dental x-ray film with a protective covering. Each badge bore a numbered assigned to a specific person. At the end of the day or of a work session, someone from the radiation chemistry department would collect the badges and analyze them for exposure. Radiation could also be monitored without a Geiger counter by using a device about the size of a fountain pen called a dosimeter.

Because little was known about handling large quantities of uranium and plutonium, and much less about critical masses, experimentation with these materials required a certain devil-may-care attitude. One of the most bizarre and dangerous experiments was conducted by Otto Frisch's Critical Assemblies team at Omega Site, an area they shared with Fermi's water boiler. Using a contraption nicknamed the Pit Assembly, the team prepared and tested U235 and Pu239, first as small cubes, and later, when more material was available, as small spheres. Richard Feynmann dubbed the experiment the "dragon" because it was so capriciously dangerous that it was like tickling the tail of a sleeping dragon. In the experiment, a small slug of uranium hydride was dropped through the open center of a larger piece of similar material and guided by four metal rails. Frisch had nicknamed the device "Lady Godiva." For a hundredth of a second the entire assembly became supercritical and released heavy doses of neutrons. The reaction died down quickly as the slug fell through the lowest layer. In that instant, the small pile generated nearly twenty million watts of energy and instantly raised the temperature hundreds of degrees. Frisch acknowledged that it was dangerous: "It was as near as we could possibly go towards starting an atomic explosion without actually being blown up, and the results were most satisfactory."[43]

He was reminded one day just how close to edge of disaster he and his team worked. He was standing near Lady Godiva when he unthinkingly leaned in toward the machine with its uranium in place. As he did so, he chanced to look at a neutron detector sitting on a table nearby. What should have been a red blinking light indicating low activity was now an intense, solid red. Frisch immediately backed off and the light returned to blinking. When he leaned toward the machine, his body reflected escaping neutrons back into the uranium, dangerously accelerating the chain reaction.

On another night, Frisch and his twenty-one-year-old assistant, Frederic de Hoffmann, were preparing to perform the experiment again. As a precaution they had parked cars outside their building pointed toward the exit gate just in case they had to evacuate suddenly. In 1945, that was considered sufficient precaution. But this night, just as the uranium slug dropped through the larger ring, the lights in the building went out. In fact, the whole complex went dark. Cars sped away from Omega as fast as they could. This was no nuclear accident, however—the lights went out because the power station in Albuquerque had inexplicably shut down.

There were serious accidents, however. Louis Slotin, another member of Frisch's team, frequently conducted the dragon experiment. During one such episode in February 1945, something went wrong, and the entire apparatus became so radioactively hot that the uranium slug began to blister and melt. Work stopped for several days.[44] Another dangerous episode occurred a few months later, in June. A number of small uranium cubes had been arranged within a polyethylene box six inches square. When the box was lowered slowly into a large tank of water, it suddenly became critical. The tank had been designed with drain valves some fifteen feet apart, and before anyone could lower the water level, a chain reaction began and quickly intensified. No one was hurt or killed, but the room was so radioactively hot that all experiments were temporarily canceled.

The first death in Los Alamos during a fission experiment occurred on August 21, 1945. Harry Daghlian, a young scientist working under Frisch, was assembling small bricks of tungsten carbide, weighing just over six kilograms each, as a reflector around two plutonium hemispheres nicknamed Rufus. He was working alone at night, although the practice was to work only in a team. The experiment called for carefully building a wall, brick by brick, around the plutonium to a height and mass just before it went critical. As a precaution, each brick was slid into place from the outside, not put down one on the top of the other. Sweating in the enclosed room, Daghlian reached over to pick up the last brick from a nearby table, but as he brought the brick over the pile to insert on the other side, it slipped out of his hand and fell into the center. The additional brick provided just enough neutron reflection to make the assembly supercritical, and for an instant an ethereal blue glow burst uniformly in all directions from the center of the pile before dying out. Daghlian quickly pushed the brick off with his hand, stopping the reaction, but it was too late for him—he was effectively a dead man. Second-degree burns covered his hands and abdomen where the radiation had been most intense. The burns festered and his flesh began to dissolve. He ran a high fever and lost his hair. Daghlian lived twenty-eight days, although he was comatose the last week.[45] It was a sobering reminder that the experiments at Los Alamos could be lethal.

Within a year, Louis Slotin, working with the same Rufus hemisphere, would become the second victim of a nuclear accident at Los Alamos. This time, the plutonium was surrounded by a heavy beryllium shell some nine inches in diameter. Slotin was slowly lowering the top half of the beryllium shell to the point where it was prevented from touching the bottom portion by the tip of his screwdriver. Somehow, Slotin let the screwdriver slip and the two tamper halves fell together with the same piercing blue flash and extreme heat that Daghlian had experienced. There were seven other men in the room but fortunately for the others, Slotin's body absorbed most of the radiation, and only he died. Exposed to over nine hundred units of gamma radiation, he lingered only nine days.[46]

In the fall, Bob Christy in the Theoretical Division proposed a simple alternative to the architecture of the implosion bomb. A graduate student under Oppenheimer before the war, he had come to New Mexico from the

Met Lab in Chicago. For over a year, Los Alamos had been working on the assumption that the plutonium core would be hollow, since such a sphere would require far less Pu239. Christy's suggestion was simpler: use a solid core of Pu239. This would eliminate some of the problems associated with creating a uniform explosion, although there were three drawbacks to the design. First, a solid core would be far less efficient. Second, it would require a specially constructed initiator. And third, the core would consume considerably more Pu239.

Christy's idea generated a lot of discussion, but in the end it seemed the best course of action if an implosion device was to be ready by mid-1945. Oppenheimer asked for Groves to weigh in on the matter, and the need for a decision was pressing enough for the general to rearrange his schedule and come to Los Alamos. On February 28, 1945, Groves, Oppenheimer, and others met in the director's second-floor office and settled on the solid-core alternative that now became known as the "Christy Gadget." The choice of a solid core would require quickly overcoming a set of old and new challenges, but if successful, Los Alamos was on schedule to deliver a second type of atomic weapon, perhaps as early as summer 1945.

Chapter Twelve

CONVERGING ROADS: 1945

L eslie Groves's hugely expensive Manhattan Project existed for only one purpose—to deliver a weapon—and the pressure on the general to do so became relentless in 1945. The pressure came not just from within the military—General Marshall and the Military Policy Committee overseeing the Manhattan effort—but also from Bush, who sat on the committee, Conant, Secretary of War Stimson, and even from President Roosevelt. The recent attempt to launch a congressional investigation had been sidelined for the moment, but the demand for accountability was growing.

The urgency of the project was a result not only of the billions of dollars spent but of the progress of the war itself. The unexpected ferocity of the German attack in what was being called the Battle of the Bulge had surprised everyone from General Eisenhower on the ground in Europe to military planners ensconced in comfortable War Department offices in Washington. Despite earlier—and naïve—optimism, the war had *not* ended in 1944. Although it was only a matter of time before German war production collapsed completely and forced a surrender, there could still be months of fighting ahead. In a meeting with Stimson and Groves at the very end of December, Roosevelt asked if the bomb could be used in Germany. Groves, who was shocked by the president's sickly appearance, had to reply that it would be difficult. The bomb was not ready and would not be until the middle of 1945 at the earliest. And German air defenses were far more formidable than those of the Japanese.

In the Pacific, there was no end in sight to the fighting. Japan, like Germany, now had no chance of actually winning the war, but it ferociously clung to the belief that if it made the final Allied drive to the Japanese home islands costly enough, it could negotiate a settlement and perhaps even retain some portion of its empire. The Japanese believed that the Americans would eventually come to terms, leaving in place the emperor and perhaps the military regime.

In reality, however, aerial bombing, blockades, and the loss of territories capable of supplying oil and other critical raw materials had nearly destroyed Japanese war production. Human casualties throughout the shrinking empire were horrific, outnumbering American losses in many cases five to one, sometimes even ten to one or more, as the Allies came closer, island by island and nautical mile by nautical mile.

For America, the question was: What more would be needed to force Japan to surrender? The answer increasingly looked like an invasion of the Japanese home islands. To mount the forces and material necessary to prevail against such an unrelenting, entrenched enemy, the military would need to transfer hundreds of thousands of men, perhaps a million or more, from the European theater to the Pacific, along with supplies, airplanes, tanks, landing vessels, support ships, and all the other components of an unprecedented assault. Above all, it would need more men, and that, by 1945, was becoming a daunting problem.

Not only was recruitment down for all branches of service, but the pool of men eligible for the draft was shrinking. After three years of war, over sixteen million men were already in uniform. Public opinion polls, moreover, revealed a general weariness with the war. Americans badly wanted it to end, although there was still overwhelming support for beating the enemy and demanding nothing less than unconditional surrender. A concern for manpower was to play a growing role in military planning, especially as the war in Europe ended and Japan remained.[1] As an invasion of Japan became more likely, the promise of a bomb so devastating that no enemy could survive its repeated use was therefore enormously attractive.

Such were the circumstances in late 1944 and early 1945 as the unresting Groves drove his team of scientists and soldiers to produce their bomb. He could tell from his own visits to Los Alamos and from his communication with Oppenheimer that the laboratory was struggling with the shift from research and experimentation to production. He accepted that some theoretical issues still needed to be resolved, along with improvements to the detonators and explosive lenses, but he came to believe that the moment had come to "freeze" designs and begin building bombs. Surely, he thought, they were ready to build the uranium Little Boy.

To motivate Oppenheimer, or perhaps to force a decision, Groves formally gave him permission in November 1944 to freeze weapon designs whenever it was expedient to do so. To emphasize the importance of moving ahead, Groves made a trip to Los Alamos for a meeting with Oppenheimer, Parsons, Kistiakowsky, and Bainbridge on December 19. The meeting was sufficiently important for Lauritsen to come from California and Conant from Washington. A full agenda was sidetracked by intense conversations on implosion and an experimental test of the implosion gadget.

At the meeting, Parsons announced that a new Fat Man design— model number 1291—was already in production. It had fewer external parts—two polar caps and five ellipsoids sheets—but still took two days to assemble. A number of dummy units would be used in test drops to give pilots and crews practical experience with dropping large objects.

Called "blockbusters," some dummies would contain nothing but concrete for weight, while others would have conventional explosives. Groves complained that much valuable time was being taken from other, more important programs and diverted to the blockbuster program. The discussion of the projected test of Fat Man also left him unhappy, and again he expressed his concern that too much "time and energy" was being diverted from more urgent priorities. He asked that preparations and resources for such a test be limited, and when Bainbridge asked for housing at the experimental site, Groves denied him on the spot.[2]

Despite his trust in Oppenheimer and Parsons, Groves was impatient with Los Alamos. He believed that the laboratory was losing its focus. At the December 19 meeting, Groves ordered the laboratory to make completion of the gun bomb its highest priority. He said he wanted the weapon completed and available by July 1, 1945. Implosion—the "corpulent competitor" as he called it—was not to jeopardize the delivery of at least one useable weapon. In the past, Groves usually negotiated deadlines with Oppenheimer, but now he gave the laboratory a specific delivery date. It was, in effect, an order.

Oppenheimer and the Technical and Scheduling Conference spent their next few meetings figuring out how to meet Groves's deadline, gathering even on a very cold New Year's Day. Perhaps the greatest unknown at the moment was the precise critical mass of U235 necessary for the gun weapon. Fermi thought determining this number should be their priority. A new gun design, called the "augmented gun gadget," was even proposed. It would employ a different gun barrel and a number of other innovations. But a new weapon for the future did not solve the problems of today. Oppenheimer approved engineering studies but said Los Alamos had to perfect and complete the current gun design.

And there was still the implosion bomb. Oppenheimer undertook another assessment of the implosion program to determine what results could reasonably be expected in the spring and summer of 1945. He found that the laboratory had to decide between multiple alternative designs for almost every important part of the weapon—the Pu239 core, initiator, explosive lenses, and tamper. As with the gun weapon, Groves wanted Los Alamos to chose one implosion weapon design and complete it. As a result, in early 1945, Oppenheimer presided at one of the most important meetings of his tenure at Los Alamos.

On February 28, Groves, Conant, and Tolman came from Washington for a meeting in Oppenheimer's office. Bethe, Kistiakowsky, and Charles Lauritsen from the laboratory attended. Over the course of the day, they made a number of hard decisions. They settled on the Christy solid core and "froze" by selection several other specific components. Fat Man would now incorporate electric bridgewire detonators, lenses made of the explosive materials Composition B ("Comp B") and Baratol, a plutonium core of Delta phase Pu239 alloyed in silver, an initiator, and a large aluminum "pusher"—a thick aluminum layer between the Comp B explosives and the uranium tamper that would "even out" the inward implosive force.[3] This bomb would be tested in southern New Mexico and subsequently dropped on a target in Japan. In one day, Groves had forced decisions that had been languishing for months.

A month earlier, Oppenheimer had informed Groves that his secretary was leaving her post in mid-March. Priscilla Green had married the scientist Duff Duffield and was now expecting her first baby. She was making $250 a month, but Oppenheimer felt that the position deserved three hundred. Groves didn't object and asked if he had anyone in mind. Oppenheimer did—Anne Wilson in the general's office. The suggestion came as a surprise, but it served both men's interests. Oppenheimer would get someone familiar with Groves, his style, and the operation of his Washington office, and the general would have someone in Los Alamos who knew him and what he expected. Two weeks later, Oppenheimer called back and said that Wilson was willing to come to New Mexico. Groves agreed and had O'Leary make sure that someone from the military post at Los Alamos would meet her when she arrived in Lamy on March 5. Wilson was delighted to make the move.

On March 9, 1945, the air force launched Operation Meetinghouse. Taking off from bases in Saipan and Tinian, 334 B-29s conducted a raid on Tokyo. Arriving just after midnight, March 10, the B-29s dropped over 1,700 tons of incendiary bombs from an altitude of only five hundred feet, burning more than sixteen square miles of the city to the ground. Although precise figures are not available, at least 100,000 people died, and perhaps another 125,000 were seriously injured. The Tokyo fire department later estimated that at least 286,000 buildings in that city of wood and paper had been destroyed. The United States lost fourteen planes in the raid, a number deemed acceptable at the time.

As Groves hoped, Parsons continued to make progress on the gun bomb, which was a surprisingly simple mechanism compared with its implosion counterpart. The basic design of Little Boy had been worked out in the first half of 1944, and new information on the critical mass of U235 from Fermi enabled the Metallurgy Division to craft the uranium core. The ballistics were not unusual, but the gun had an odd appearance. It weighed only about 1,100 pounds and was a total of six feet in length. Attached to that was a thicker canister—approximately three feet in length—that screwed into the muzzle of the barrel and contained the uranium target case.[4]

The projectile, housed with the explosive charges in the barrel, consisted of approximately 60 percent of the U235 in the bomb. The target, housed in the heavy metal canister at the other end, consisted of the

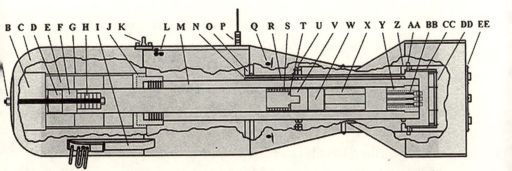

Cross-section drawing of Y-1852 *Little Boy* showing major mechanical component placement. Not shown are the APS-13 radar units, clock box with pullout wires, baro switches and tubing, batteries, and electrical wiring. Numbers in ( ) indicate quantity of identical components. Drawing is shown to scale.

A) Front nose elastic locknut attached to 1.0" diameter cadmium-plated draw bolt
B) 15.0" diameter forged steel nose nut w/14" diameter back end
C) 28.0" diameter forged steel target case
D) Impact absorbing anvil surrounded by cavity ring
E) 13" diameter 3-piece WC tamper liner assembly w/6.5" bore
F) 6.5" diameter WC tamper insert base
G) 18" long K-46 steel WC tamper liner sleeve
H) 4" diameter U-235 target insert discs (6)
I) Yagi antenna assemblies (4)
J) Target-case to gun-tube adapter with four vents slots and 6.5" hole
K) Lift lug
L) Safing/arming plugs (3)
M) 6.5" bore gun tube
N) 0.75" diameter armored tubes containing primer wiring (3)
O) 27.25" diameter bulkhead plate
P) Electrical plugs (3)
Q) Baro ports (8)
R) 1.0" diameter rear alignment rods (3)
S) 6.25" diameter U-235 projectile rings (9)
T) Polonium-Beryllium initiators (4)
U) Tail tube forward plate
V) Projectile WC filler plug
W) Projectile steel back
X) 2-pound WM slotted-tube Cordite powder bags (4)
Y) Gun breech with removable inner breech plug and stationary outer bushing
Z) Tail tube aft plate
AA) 2.25" long 5/8-18 socket-head tail tube bolts (4)
BB) Mark 15 Mod 1 electric gun primers w/AN-3102-20AN receptacles (3)
CC) 15" diameter armored inner tail tube
DD) Inner armor plate bolted to 15" diameter armored tube
EE) Rear plate (w/smoke puff tubes) bolted to 17" diameter tail tube

Reproduced with permission from *Atom Bombs* (2014), by John Coster-Mullen.

remaining U235. The U235 for the projectile was machined into nine washer-shaped rings, 6.25 inches in diameter, which were combined to form a hollow cylinder weighing approximately thirty-eight kilograms (83.7 pounds). The U235 for the target was machined into six discs, four inches in diameter, which were combined to form a solid cylinder weighing approximately twenty-six kilograms (fifty-seven pounds). When the gun fired, the projectile raced down the barrel and slipped over the target; for a millionth of a second, the two pieces combined were seven inches long.[5]

Progress on implosion was slower. The initiators, detonators, and explosive lenses were still plagued with problems. The initiator was a particular challenge. Multiple designs had been proposed and tested. By April 1945, a special Initiator Committee had narrowed the alternative designs to six, and that list was quickly reduced to two. Bethe and Christy favored one, nicknamed the "urchin," while Fermi favored the other. As Bethe later recalled, opposing Fermi was dangerous, since "he was almost always right," but on May 1 the Initiator Committee formally approved the urchin over Fermi's objections.[6]

The configuration of the urchin initiator was intricate. Like the weapon itself, it was a ball within a ball. The outer shell, consisting of two hemispheres, was beryllium, smooth on the outside and nickel-plated. The vertically grooved inside was plated first with gold and then coated with a thirty-curie layer of polonium. Inside this shell was a solid ball of beryllium, also plated in gold and covered with twenty curies of polonium.[7] Because of the radioactive half-life of polonium, the initiator was effective for only 138 days, after which it was necessary to insert a fresh unit.

Experiments demanded more and more polonium, and Groves pressed the Monsanto Company, which produced it, to increase deliveries. Shipments rose from twenty curies in January 1945 to 140 by June.[8] There was more good news: tests with the newly designed initiator were positive. On June 4, Oppenheimer called Groves to report that "the little thing that goes in the middle of FM has been made and looks quite right."

Brode's team was still tinkering with the Archie fusing mechanism, an intricate system that employed radar to close an electrical circuit at a predetermined altitude above the target. Four Archies were used with each fuse, forming a network of relays arranged so that when any two of the units fired, the mechanism sent an electronic firing signal to the next stage, a bank of switches operated by clocks. The switches were to be closed by arming wires mechanically pulled out of the clocks when the bomb was released from the airplane's bomb bay. The clock switches were designed to close fifteen seconds after the bomb had been dropped, protecting the airplane from an accidental detonation. A backup system employed pressure switches designed to close when the bomb fell to an altitude of seven thousand feet. Brode's "philosophy of fusing" called for overlapping systems—every circuit and component of the bomb had a backup. The result of this approach (and of Francis Birch's approach with the gun) was an overbuilt weapon.[9]

Alvarez also announced good news. Dependable detonators at last seemed to be in hand. Not only did the new handlebar-shaped model provide the needed electrical charge, but it also appeared to fire dependably time after time. Experiments showed that they had achieved simultaneity within less than a microsecond.

———————————

Despite engineering progress, there were still voids in what scientists knew about implosion dynamics. What actually went on during an explosion? The men of Bacher's Gadget Group needed more information than they had. They needed to see *inside* the process, to stop time, or at least slow it down. Conventional photography obviously had its limits. No camera could see *into* an explosion, for example. The Gadget men were forced to invent entirely new methods of observation and recording. Bruno Rossi developed a process that used x-rays to follow imploding explosive waves. Later he added flash x-ray photography. X-rays provided extremely useful information but required ingenious preparation beforehand; the biggest challenge was protecting the fragile and sensitive x-ray equipment. If an x-ray machine were placed next to a sphere wrapped in explosives, it would be destroyed by the blast. Rossi solved the problem by building two concrete bunkers placed close to each other with heavily protected portholes in each. The x-ray equipment would be divided between the two bunkers and the combination of sphere and explosives detonated in the space between them at the level of the portholes.[10]

The relative quiet of Los Alamos was shattered repeatedly by the sound of explosions from Anchor Site, some five miles from the Tech Area. In mid-December 1944, a series of experiments using Rossi's techniques confirmed that controlled symmetrical waves could be achieved by using lenses of carefully determined shapes, information that Kistiakowsky put to use in several designs. The "shapes" called for a rectangular block of explosive material—such as the commercially available Comp B—cut or manufactured in the shape of a five- or six-sided pyramid with the tip cut off. These explosives were then assembled into a sphere surrounding the plutonium or uranium, the completed apparatus resembling, as Jim Tuck had put it, a soccer ball. Rossi's group also tested Alvarez's new detonators in January, showing them to be far more dependable than earlier models.

Another technique to study shock waves used radiolanthanum, nicknamed "RaLa," a highly radioactive substance that emits gamma rays, to trace the effects of imploding waves. A small amount of radiolanthanum was placed inside a sphere and then imploded. Gamma waves shooting radially from the center could be picked up by nearby detectors. Radiolanthanum was produced in the reactor at Oak Ridge and shipped in lead containers 1,200 miles to Los Alamos. Working with the material was highly dangerous, especially since Kistiakowsky's men eventually would use a hundred curies at a time, whereas scientists and researchers typically worked with only a fraction of a single curie. The first test with radiolanthanum used the relatively small amount of forty curies, and for protection, Alavarez studied the results on oscilloscopes in a recently obtained army tank. The process was expensive, and Oppenheimer did not approve a substantial investment in RaLa until he obtained Groves's approval.

Still another method of observing implosions used a betatron, a doughnut-shaped accelerator, which could achieve many millions of volts of energy. The laboratory believed that such a device would be extremely helpful to their experiments, but the only betatron available was scheduled to be shipped to the federally operated Rock Island Arsenal in Illinois. Oppenheimer was convinced that the machine was critical to the laboratory's work and sought help from Conant and then from Groves. With the general's assistance, the betatron was diverted to Los Alamos and installed at K Site. The betatron quickly gave a realistic picture of the effects of imploding shock waves, although it could be used to study only small combinations of spheres and explosives—nothing close to the expected size of Fat Man.

Developing and refining the explosive lenses were the greatest difficulties the laboratory faced during the war. In 1943 little was known about the use of high explosives to produce imploding shock waves. Even less was known about shaping and configuring explosives in order to produce controlled, predictable waves. TNT, while stable, was not adaptable for implosion purposes. When Oppenheimer froze weapons designs, several configurations for surrounding the plutonium and the uranium tamper with lenses were still under consideration, including a combination of fast-burning and slow-burning explosives. Critical decisions had to be made quickly, for Oppenheimer, under growing pressure from Groves, wanted full-scale lenses delivered by April 2 and tested by April 15, 1945. Galvanized by the decisions reached on February 28, Oppenheimer set an even more ambitious deadline, calling for final fabrication of high-quality lenses by June 4 for use in the test of Fat Man. The detonation system was to be completed and tested in early June.

By the spring of 1945, Kistiakowsky and his division had spent innumerable hours designing, redesigning, and perfecting explosives at S Site, a canyon below Los Alamos, where 90 percent of the personnel were members of the army's Special Engineering Detachment. In eighteen months, the division crafted almost twenty thousand castings, of various sizes and shapes, acceptable for experimentation—no cracks, bubbles, or flaws. Many more defective castings were produced and rejected. At its busiest, S Site consumed over a ton of explosives every day, or one hundred thousand pounds every month, and generated thousands of high quality charges of between one and 120 pounds. Commercial explosives, such as Composition B, Torpex, Baronal, and Baratol, were tried, but Kistiakowsky finally settled on Comp B and Baratol.

One of the division's major accomplishments was the development of methods for producing high explosives in specific shapes. Raw explosives usually arrived at Los Alamos in the form of a block or cylinder. These were put into kettles, slowly melted to the consistency of molten wax, and poured into molds—the best Kistiakowsky could obtain or construct with the deadlines he faced. The reconfigured explosives were then carefully removed and allowed to cool in ovens at predetermined rates. The production process occasioned the "greatest agony," he later said. There were over sixty explosive lenses in Fat Man, and each had to be poured into molds that would discourage bubbles and imperfections:

> We learned gradually that these large castings, fifty pounds and more each, had to be cooled in just certain ways, otherwise you get air bubbles in the middle or separations of solids and liquids, all of which screwed up the implosion completely. So it was a slow process. The explosive was poured in and then people sat over that damned thing watching it as if it was an egg being hatched, changing the temperature of the water running through the various cooling tubes built into the mold.[11]

The explosives "had to fit together to within a precision of a few thousandths of an inch for a ... total size of five feet and make a sphere. So we had to have very precise molds."[12] After cooling, the explosives were machined with specially designed jigs and blades to remove rough edges or surface defects or adjust the angle or plane. The melting, shaping, and machining of these materials was highly dangerous. While meeting all the other production demands, Kistiakowsky had to develop new methods for handling the materials safely while maintaining high purity. Remarkably, more than fifty thousand explosive lenses were machined without incident.

Aside from the danger, the working conditions at S Site could be extremely unpleasant. Much of the melting and casting was done with steam, and the temperature and humidity quickly became oppressive, especially as summer neared. The technicians also had to endure the distinctive, acrid smell of melting chemicals, which permeated their hair and clothing.

In April 1945, Kistiakowsky reported optimistically, "One can now state with a reasonable degree of assurance that all major research and design gambles involved in the freeze of the programs of X Division have been won."[13] The design gambles might have been won, but the actual production of key equipment was not.

The potential for production delays had emerged two months earlier when scientists working at S Site reported that the capacity for producing lenses was severely strained. There was simply no way they could keep on schedule and meet demands, and it was not possible to order new production equipment and have it installed and working in only a few weeks. Charles Lauritsen argued strongly that Los Alamos needed to decide on one line of lens development if the deadlines set by Groves and Oppenheimer were to be met.

The explosive lenses were essential for implosion. Bacher's men insisted that the best way to achieve a uniform explosion was by surrounding the core and tamper with two layers of explosive lenses, each lens in the shape of a hexagonal or pentagonal pyramid, which were fitted together to form concentric spheres. To achieve a matching fit, the lenses were machined to make the top convex and the bottom concave.

The real breakthrough was in the design of the lenses in the outer layer, which were made by pouring melted Comp B over a cone of Baratol with a parabola-shaped tip. With this combination, the shock wave could be controlled, the initial concave explosive wave being converted into a convex-collapsing wave. Samuel Allison favored limiting development to this model, but Oppenheimer wanted to pursue an alternative design as well, perhaps having Groves's principle of multiple solutions in mind. The problem, Allison argued, was that Los Alamos did not have the resources to continue developing both models.

Oppenheimer deferred making a decision until he could consult with Groves, who arrived a week later and joined a special conference with Oppenheimer and his division leaders. They worked out a compromise: Los Alamos would develop the design favored by Allison, while the team at CAMEL would work on the alternative. Both Groves and Oppenheimer believed this dual approach would provide insurance against failure of one model or the other. Their decision to pursue two alternatives despite the considerable cost reflected their troubling suspicion that notwithstanding the recent breakthroughs, implosion was not yet a certainty. Above all, though, the dual approaches reflected Groves's belief in pursuing multiple solutions to problems.

As spring came and temperatures warmed, the laboratory was still struggling to fill staff vacancies. Oppenheimer ingeniously suggested that the Met Lab pick up some of the more pressing work. In a phone call to Groves's office, he said the work could be done in Chicago without having to move people to Los Alamos and find housing for them.

Oppenheimer requested some thirty thousand man-hours of work, which he calculated would be the equivalent of sixty persons for perhaps three months. Additional army SEDs also arrived, and Colonel Tyler,* the new Los Alamos post commander, received permission from Groves to build two dormitories to house them. The population of the Hill continued to grow, and Groves was forced to authorize an expansion to the hospital as well. The long-sought machinists arrived but put further stress on the already desperate housing situation. Groves partially solved the problem by ejecting army nurses from their quarters and giving them to the machinists. When Parsons asked Groves for an additional thirty staff members, and then 160 more, the general once again called on Admiral Purnell for help. Groves remained unflappable, accepting the unanticipated as normal, except, perhaps, when he broke a tooth on a visit to Los Alamos in late April and was forced to call O'Leary to make a dentist appointment for him as soon as he returned home.

In early 1945, Groves brought his new handpicked deputy, Brigadier General Thomas F. Farrell, to Los Alamos to introduce him. A native New Yorker like Groves and Oppenheimer and a civil engineer, Farrell had worked on the Panama Canal and joined the Corps of Engineers in 1916, in time to serve in Europe during World War I. Groves met him in 1928, remembering him as competent, and General Marshall also knew and respected him. Groves gave Farrell a broad range of responsibilities during the remainder of the war, including representing him at the test of Fat Man and in the Pacific. At Los Alamos, they scrutinized Farrell on that first visit, expecting another general like Groves. Most were

---

*   Gerald Tyler replaced Whitney Ashbridge when the latter unexpectedly suffered a heart attack. Ashbridge survived but was unable to resume his duties at Los Alamos.

surprised. Oppenheimer was impressed and said so—Farrell had not asked one "foolish question."[14]

———————————

In T Building, surrounded by blackboards and energized by the new IBM calculators, Bethe ran further calculations on the expected explosive force, or yield, of Fat Man. In April 1944, using data obtained from his computations and other related studies, he had predicted a yield in the range of five to thirteen kilotons of TNT. Furthermore, he predicted an explosion with multiple effects: shock waves, a radiation "discharge," and air blast. This was critical information for the dozens of young scientists who had to design and build the instruments that would measure the explosion when the gadget was finally tested. Bethe's numbers needed to be as accurate as possible. If the prediction was too high, the instruments would fail to register properly, if at all. If the prediction was too low, the instruments would be destroyed. The margin for error was narrow.

Maurice Shapiro's oddly-named Water Delivery and Exterior Ballistics Group had to determine the altitude from which the bomb should be dropped. If the bomb detonated too high, it would simply waste energy, and if it detonated too low, it would do little more than create a large crater. Shapiro's team worked with John von Neumann on a series of small experiments to investigate the effects of explosions in shallow water. Not far from S Site, scientists poured a two-hundred-foot-wide concrete bowl. Small charges were ignited in this shallow basin with water that varied in depth from a few inches to a few feet. The results, scaled up for explosions of the magnitude expected from fission weapons, established that, contrary to expectations, a surface explosion produced larger gravity waves than an explosion of the same size below the surface. This suggested that the bomb could be used effectively against harbors or ports—information that could be useful in selecting targets in Japan.

The choice of the Christy gadget somewhat eased the strain on the laboratory, and in March Oppenheimer established two new committees and two new divisions to coordinate work. The intricate problems of scheduling the Fat Man program were given to the Cowpuncher Committee, so called because its job was to "ride herd" on implosion. Its members—Bacher, Kistiakowsky, Lauritsen, Parsons, Hartley Rowe, and Allison as chairman—followed the progress of development throughout the laboratory. At their first meeting on March 3, 1945, they developed a coordinated program with priorities that included the initiator, electric detonators, plutonium shipments from Hanford, lens testing, and lens mold procurement. In April they began monitoring and approving concurrent work within divisions and became responsible for the tamper design work in G Division.

April also brought another shipment of Pu239 from the Hanford reactors. It was less than a kilogram, but shipments increased to twice a month in May. The amounts grew as well: the shipments after April brought between one and a half and two kilograms. The plutonium was shipped in stainless steel flasks, typically in a convoy of three trucks with lead and rear escort cars, down the coast to Los Angeles. From there the flasks made their way by train to Lamy. Some plutonium was shipped entirely by one-and-a-half-ton olive-drab trucks from Hanford to New Mexico, with a team from Los Alamos meeting the southbound convoy halfway.[15]

As both gun and implosion weapons moved toward completion, Oppenheimer created an interdivisional Weapons Committee to absorb the work of the Technical and Scheduling Conference. This new committee, with Ramsey as chairman, was responsible directly to Parsons for the delivery of combat-ready weapons. Oppenheimer also created two temporary organizations, the Trinity and Alberta Projects, with the status of divisions. "Trinity" had already been selected as the code name for the test of the Fat Man, and Project Trinity was to oversee test preparations. Project Alberta, directed by Parsons, was to plan for use of the bomb overseas. Oppenheimer later created Z Division to handle future engineering and production needs in adapting airplanes to use the weapons.

Work was now seven days a week. Wives intuitively knew without asking that something big was coming. Groves and Oppenheimer shifted men and resources repeatedly. At last, the multiple lines of research and development that previously appeared to some as random, if not inchoate, were coming together as the completion of one facet of the bomb project enabled the completion of another.

The accelerated pace soon caused overcrowding in G Division's offices, and Oppenheimer was forced to ask Groves for authorization to construct yet another new building in the Technical Area. Groves wasn't happy, but he had little choice—too much was at stake to risk any further delays because of the cost of one building. In fact, G Division needed even more experimental space. As quickly as they could be thrown up, testing and firing sites Alpha, Beta, P, and X were built in nearby canyons.

The hectic work in Washington and Los Alamos stopped suddenly on Thursday, April 12, 1945, when news of Franklin Roosevelt's death reached both Groves and Oppenheimer. One of the general's staff was monitoring a special radio when the news broke and quickly informed Groves, who was preparing for a meeting with Secretary of War Stimson the following day. Groves immediately turned his attention to preparing a report on the Manhattan Project for the new president.

Oppenheimer also received the news by radio. He sent word throughout the laboratory with an invitation to gather at the flagpole in front of the administration building for a memorial service on Sunday morning. The flag was lowered to half-mast. On the morning of the service the mesa was covered in a late, deep snow. Philip Morrison thought it appropriately beautiful: "A night's fall had covered the rude textures of the town, silenced its businesses, and unified the view in a soft whiteness, over which the bright sun shone.... It was no costume for mourning, but it seemed recognition of something we needed, a gesture of consolation."[16]

Oppenheimer spoke briefly but so softly that he could scarcely be heard over the light breeze that fluttered the American flag:

> In the Hindu scripture, in the Bhagavad-Gita, it says, "Man is a creature whose substance is faith. What his faith is, he is." The faith of Roosevelt is one that is shared by millions of men and women in every country of the world. For this reason it is possible to maintain the hope, for this reason it is right that we should dedicate ourselves to the hope, that his good works will not have ended with his death.[17]

Two hundred and twenty miles to the south, the flag was also lowered at Trinity.

————————

Two weeks later, Groves and Stimson met with Harry Truman to brief the new president on the Manhattan Project. They made their way to the White House separately and Groves used a back entrance to prevent the press from making a connection between them. The general was shown into the Oval Office some ten minutes after the secretary of war, and the president gave them an attentive audience. Groves brought with him a twenty-four-page memorandum titled "Atomic Fission Bombs," prepared for the secretary and intended to be shared with the president. In lucid and uncomplicated language, it described the weapons under development, the scientific principles that underlay them, the vast network of plants that had been constructed to produce nuclear materials, and the implications of the work: "The successful development of the Atomic

Fission Bomb will provide the United States with a weapon of tremendous power which should be a decisive factor in winning the present war more quickly with a saving in American lives and treasure. If the United States continues to lead in the development of atomic energy weapons, its future will be much safer and the chances of preserving world peace greatly increased."[18]

Stimson took the lead in the discussion with the president, touching on a number of points, both technical and political. He described the bomb but also wanted to make sure that Truman understood it implications. In his talking points, Stimson had written, "As a result [of the bomb], it is indicated that the future may see a time when such a weapon may be constructed in secret and used suddenly and effectively with devastating power by a willful nation or group against an unsuspecting nation or group of much greater size and material power... although probably the only nation which could enter into production within the next few years is Russia."[19] The president then read Groves's memorandum, gave it back, and asked a number of questions. When it was time to leave, Groves had to ask which door led out of the Oval Office. In a memorandum of the meeting intended for his personal files, Groves noted, "The answers to the remainder of the questions [from the president] were either considerably amplified by General Groves or were answered in their entirety by him."[20]

Neither the president, the secretary of war, nor the general knew that the Russians had been working on a bomb since 1943. Despite the crushing demands of the war against Germany, they had brought together twenty scientists, led by the brilliant physicist Igor Kurchatov, in a small laboratory outside Moscow—known simply as "Laboratory No. 2"—where they conducted experiments and performed calculations on both weapons and reactors. Their work benefited immeasurably from the continuous stream of intelligence fed to them by their spies in America.[21]

April 1945, the laboratory's second anniversary, was the first really good month at Los Alamos since 1943. With some relief, Oppenheimer reviewed the progress in a report for Groves. Frisch and Slotin were close to achieving the first critical assembly of U235 at Omega. With that, the precise weight of the critical mass would be known. Robert Wilson's men were equally close to determining the optimal division of uranium in the gun between the target and the projectile. Barring unforeseen problems, the uranium gun would be ready by August 1, more or less on schedule. At the end of June, Oppenheimer informed Groves that the U235 in Little Boy would receive a cadmium coating to increase safety.[22]

Progress on Fat Man was less encouraging. The extraordinarily complex design produced vexing and persistent challenges for the men trying to assemble the implosion bomb. The actual ratio of fast-burning to slow-burning explosive lenses was still to be determined, and S Site was having trouble manufacturing lenses free of defects. They did not have enough molds to work with, and in spite of all precautions, a high percentage of each batch had to be discarded because of cracks, bubbles, chips, and other defects. Production of explosive lenses, consequently, had fallen seriously behind schedule.

Groves continued to receive reports that alarmed him. His first telephone call of the day on April 28, at 7:40 a.m. Washington time, was to Parsons to ask about the situation at S Site. Parsons did not have good news: The lens molds manufactured in Los Angeles and Detroit were producing unusable castings. They needed between fifty and a hundred new molds, and the delay in acquiring them was seriously holding back the Fat Man bomb. Every day lost pushed delivery farther into the future. Taking matters into his own hands, Groves announced that a meeting would be immediately arranged with the manufacturer in Detroit. Groves hung up with Parsons and called Kistiakowsky to ask whom he would send to the meeting. Kistiakowsky named several persons but volunteered to go himself, telling Groves that he was "grateful for this intercession."

Groves's telephone calls generated conversations throughout the laboratory. At noon, Oppenheimer called Groves to express his reservations. The laboratory wanted to conduct further tests on the molds before arranging a meeting in Detroit. Maybe, with modifications or a change in procedure, the laboratory could use the current models and save valuable time. In any normal course of research and development, this might have been a prudent step to take, but Groves disagreed. O'Leary captured the conversation in the general's telephone log: "General advised he wants to have a good concern lined up to take care of eventualities and not to wait until the last minute." Ten minutes later, Groves called Oppenheimer back to tell him that the meeting in Detroit had been arranged and that Groves himself would attend. Six days later, he reported to Oppenheimer that the Detroit meeting had gone well and that the laboratory should place an order immediately. Groves preferred the manufacturer in Detroit over a competitor because, as he put it, "heat can be placed on them." The problem with defective molds had now cost the laboratory sixteen days.

More time was lost when the Detroit manufacturer fell behind schedule. The new molds did not arrive until May. Production of lenses became an around-the-clock operation the last week of June and the first two weeks of July. With the test of Fat Man just weeks away, three eight-hour shifts kept the molds and furnaces going. Sergeant McAllister Hull, who oversaw the casting, rarely had a chance to return to his barracks. He slept when he could on the floor or on a cot, and fellow SEDs brought him changes of clothes. He kept track of production on large blackboards, typically following six molds at a time, noting their stage of processing and marking the time.

The delay in producing lenses in turn delayed perfection of the timing and detonation systems. And testing of the detonation system was further held back when the contractor developing the firing circuits failed to meet its deadlines. Waiting anxiously at S Site for new molds, men found themselves with tons of raw explosives in brand new buildings erected to handle the increased demands, but without production equipment. With the July and August deadlines closing in with alarming speed, the hopeful spring turned into a problematic summer.

⸻

May found Groves pushing Hanford and Oak Ridge as hard as he could while staying on top of developments at Los Alamos. Monitoring his own military apparatus on the Hill, he told Colonel Tyler that the "military administration at Y was not satisfactory." And what he considered unnecessary or excessive expenditures always caught his attention. Unhappy with the civilian staff's travel habits, he ordered Tyler to "look into the way they are using space on the extra fare trains.... I think there is a tendency to use the closed space [compartments] when they could use the open."

Groves also faced continuing requests from Oppenheimer for more men, particularly machinists to work in the recently authorized shop. The general found some experienced men at the Mare Island Navy Yard, northwest of San Francisco, and then fielded angry objections from yard officials when his organization tried to recruit two hundred and fifty to three hundred men. He accelerated his travel, visiting sites all across the country. His intention was to keep the pressure on every component of the Manhattan Project. Occasionally, circumstances confounded even Groves and threw his frenetic schedule into chaos. At 11:15 on the morning of May 19, for example, he arranged with Conant to travel together to Los Alamos at the end of May. At 3:35 that afternoon, however, he called Oppenheimer and Conant to cancel his trip because he was needed somewhere else.

Groves was anxious to confer with his director in person. However efficient the telephone and teletype, the general learned a lot from his one-on-one meetings with all the senior directors of the Manhattan

Project, especially Oppenheimer. Groves prided himself on being able to "read" men, and while the director of Los Alamos was more guarded than most, Groves always felt more comfortable dealing with him in person. Their discussions in the spring of 1945 centered on progress—or the lack of it—in the implosion program, the projected arrival of uranium and plutonium at the laboratory, and preparations for Trinity. A word or two in the conversation could prompt action or intervention by Groves. Hearing that the dust generated on the roads near Ground Zero at Trinity were causing serious problems, he called Colonel Tyler and told him to "hurry" and get the roads paved.

On May 30, Groves met in his office with Tolman for fifteen minutes, with Oppenheimer for forty-five, and subsequently, for various lengths of time, with Parsons, Szilard, Fermi, and Lawrence, interspersing telephone calls between the meetings. Some meetings, such as those with Oppenheimer and Parsons, dealt with the work at Los Alamos and the many difficulties that remained. Others, such as those with Fermi and Lawrence, involved topics for a high-level meeting planned for the next day. Oppenheimer, Lawrence, and Fermi had been asked to participate as scientific advisors to a special "Interim Committee" established by Secretary of War Stimson to consider a wide range of issues associated with the atomic bomb. Groves was invited as military advisor.

June and July were no less frenzied. The test at Trinity was imminent. If it was successful, the next order of business would be preparations for the use of the bomb in Japan, at which point a new set of challenges would arise.

If Los Alamos was beset by difficulties in May, June revived the atmosphere of promise that had prevailed earlier in the spring. New molds finally arrived from Detroit and were put to use immediately. Lofgren produced a modified detonator with virtually no failures. The production of initiators, each one laboriously crafted by hand, was accomplished despite a mishap when a technician accidentally dropped the first initiator into an open sewer pipe. On June 24, Allison's Cowpuncher Committee reviewed the experiments on critical mass being conducted at Omega Site. Tickling the dragon had paid off—Slotin and Frisch could now specify the precise amount of plutonium needed for Fat Man. The Cowpunchers passed the information to Eric Jette, who then began to cast the sphere.

Working at the edge of the Technical Area, the Chemistry and Metallurgy staff began a frantic around-the-clock race to fabricate the nuclear cores for both weapons. In the Little Boy, it was a series of metal rings; in Fat Man, two hemispheres. The division took the uranium from Oak Ridge in its fluoride state, and the plutonium nitrate solution from Hanford, and reduced both to pure metals. Sam Marshall's team then fabricated the necessary parts for the Little Boy weapon from the uranium metal. With a hydraulic press, they broke blocks of U235, which they called "biscuits," into smaller pieces; this was done inside a box to a prevent loss of material. The pieces were then placed in a crucible, covered, and melted in a furnace at 1,350 degrees. The U235 was then cooled to 1,270 degrees and poured into ring-shaped molds. After two hours, they could be removed and cleaned.

A block away, Charles Garner's Plutonium Group fabricated the purified plutonium. The melted material was first cast into two rough hemispheres, which were pressed in a steel die into their final hemispherical form. These were smoothed and finished to eliminate any gap between the two halves. Garner was actually working on two complete spheres. The first, to be used at Trinity, was alloyed with silver. The second, intended for combat use, was alloyed with nickel. Garner's team had the greater challenge because plutonium is more difficult to handle than uranium. Final testing of the plutonium core was delayed for more than two weeks by manpower shortages in the Chemistry and Metallurgy Division, which could have been foreseen but were not. Oppenheimer fumed and reluctantly sent a telex to Groves explaining the delay.

On June 26, Cyril Smith reported that his division was only a week away from delivering the finished plutonium core destined for Trinity. It weighed 6.2 kilograms, or 13.6 pounds. But as of the 26th, only 7.118 kilograms of useable, finished plutonium was available. Completing the Trinity core left less than one kilogram for a second core, and Smith needed an additional 5.66 kilograms to complete the Fat Man to be used against Japan. Smith was counting on the delivery dates promised by Groves for the additional plutonium.[23]

The Trinity core posed no problems until the last moment when, with the test only days away, small blisters and pinholes were discovered all over its surface. There was no time to recast it: Garner's men polished the metal as best they could. The small, silver ball, Garner said, was "beautiful to gaze upon." Its other bewitching quality was that it was warm to the touch, as though it was alive but sleeping. The core was delivered to Bacher on July 2. Hanford shipped the next batch of Pu239 on time, and the sphere for the second Fat Man was completed and delivered on July 3.

The Trinity core was taken to Omega site and placed in a mockup of the Fat Man and checked for criticality. It was the Fourth of July, the first holiday Los Alamos had celebrated since the laboratory's opening. Most of the staff took the day off or cut their work short. There were festivities and small parties in many neighborhoods. Bacher, Smith, Marshall Holloway, and a handful of others could not celebrate, however. They worked all day to complete the criticality test. It was also the second anniversary of the first implosion experiment in July 1943, and everyone was struck by how far the laboratory had come in only twenty-four months.

Fat Man's design was now effectively fixed for Trinity, and with only minor modifications, the same weapon would be used in Japan. It was

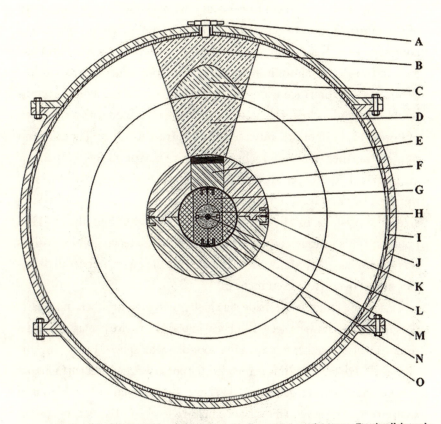

Cross-section drawing of the Y-1561 implosion sphere showing component placement. For simplicity, only one set of the 32 lenses, inner charges, and detonators is depicted. Numbers in ( ) indicate quantity of identical components. Drawing is shown to scale.

A) 1773 EBW detonator inserted into brass chimney sleeve (32)
B) Comp B component of outer polygonal lens (32)
C) Cone-shaped Baratol component of outer polygonal lens (32)
D) Comp B inner polygonal charge (32)
E) Removable aluminum pusher trap-door plug screwed into upper pusher hemisphere
F) 18.5" diameter Aluminum pusher hemispheres (2)
G) 5" diameter Tuballoy two-piece tamper plug
H) 3.62" diameter Pu-239 hemispheres with 2.75" diameter jet ring
I) 0.5" thick Cork lining
J) 7-piece Y-1561 Duralumin sphere
K) Aluminum cup holding pusher hemispheres together (4)
L) 0.8" diameter Polonium-Beryllium Urchin initiator
M) 8.75" diameter Tuballoy tamper sphere
N) 9.0" diameter Boron plastic shell
O) Felt padding layer under lenses and inner charges

Reproduced with permission from *Atom Bombs* (2014), by John Coster-Mullen.

the Christy device, selected in February, with a solid core of Pu239. All of the multiple lines of research and development over two years had coalesced in a deceptively simple configuration. At the center of the 3.6-inch-diameter plutonium sphere was the polonium-beryllium initiator, less than one inch wide. Surrounding the core was a tamper composed of several inches of U238—not U235—and coated with a thin layer of Boron-10 set in plastic intended as a neutron absorber. The core and tamper together were 8.75 inches in diameter. Around the tamper was an 18.5-inch-diameter aluminum "pusher," which in turn was surrounded by two layers of thirty-two high explosive charges of varying sizes—sixty-four in all. Both layers together weighed about 5,300 pounds.* This unique combination of nuclear material and explosives was encompassed by a cork-lined Duralumin shell with an overall diameter of just over fifty-seven inches.[24]

Fat Man's bulky shape made it a challenge to hold together. In an early design, the bomb was protected and held in place by twelve pentagonal metal sections bolted together to form a five-foot-diameter sphere. By the time the outer shell and stabilizing fins were added, the bomb weighed over ten thousand pounds and was held together by 1,500 bolts. A second, simpler Fat Man shell soon emerged, however. This version employed a spherical cover consisting of two polar caps and five equatorial zone sheets and the same ballistic case. This version—which Parsons had formerly code-named the number 1291 model—was relabeled Y-1561 and required only ninety bolts.

On Kistiakowsky's recommendation, Fat Man had a "trap door" that provided access to some of its internal components such as the plutonium core and initiator, even when the device was fully assembled. A specially designed segment in one of the polar caps was removed. Two explosive lenses, one on top of the other, could then be lifted out with a suction

---

* Other configurations were considered, including one design that consisted of twelve pentagon-shaped explosive lenses, each of which was made up of six smaller pentagons, for a total of seventy-two lenses.

cup, revealing the pusher and tamper, which had been cast with a five-inch cylindrical hole in it. The hole allowed the insertion of one of two interchangeable "plugs." The first plug was a matching cylinder of uranium and aluminum with a spherical cavity in the center of the uranium for the Pu239 core and initiator. When this plug was inserted and the explosives replaced and the trap door sealed, the weapon was ready to be attached to its electronics and encased within a ballistic shell. It was now a true weapon. The other plug was a dummy, made of wood and brass. When inserted into the weapon, it rendered a nuclear explosion impossible, even if the explosives lenses accidentally discharged. The dummy plug allowed the preassembled Fat Man to be safely shipped from Los Alamos to the Trinity site or overseas for field use.

In last-minute phone calls to Groves, Oppenheimer reported that two lingering problems still bedeviled Fat Man. The urchin initiator required tweaking, and the explosive lenses needed further refinement. Groves wanted to know what that meant. Oppenheimer explained that while the use of Baratol to reverse the inward explosive wave was a clever innovation, different shapes, ratios, and combinations of lenses were still being considered, and the laboratory did not yet know the optimal mix. Groves told Oppenheimer to make the decision as soon as possible, but that was easier said than done. Teller described the problem:

In the flow of any material, instabilities can develop. In a situation where a material of low density (the high explosives) attempts to push and accelerate material of a higher density (the tamper and plutonium), small deviations from symmetry may grow very rapidly. That raises the possibility that the more easily accelerated lightweight material will make its way through the heavier layers and, instead of a simple spherical implosion, a complex mixing of layers may prevent the assembly of a critical mass of plutonium.[25]

Despite the lack of a definitive design for the explosive lenses, the Ordnance Division had no choice but to proceed with plans for delivery. For the weapons to be transportable by military aircraft, they needed a special casing called the ballistic shell. Developing this shell, testing its aerodynamics in flight, and determining the best methods of release and activation from airplanes were the work of Project Alberta, which also produced detailed plans for shipping the bombs and support equipment overseas. The exterior shells of both bombs had been prepared and tested at Wendover Field in Utah throughout the spring.

Little Boy was a six-foot-long gun barrel with an attached three-foot canister and electronics. It required only a long, conventional tube, or shell, with stabilizing fins on one end. Fat Man was an ellipsoidal shell of armor with fins. The electrical, detonating, and fusing units were mounted in the space between the bomb sphere and the outer shell. Batteries, radar, and diagnostic equipment went on one side of the sphere, and the X-unit on the other.

Running the final lap, Parsons rushed to prepare both Fat Man and Little Boy for delivery. In June, Frisch's Critical Assembly Group concluded tests that suggested the gun would be safe from predetonation. In flight tests in Utah, Little Boy's protective shell appeared stable when dropped from a modified B-29. Fat Man, living up to its name, was wobbly and unwieldy in flight, so a large, box-like set of fins was added to one end. Parsons knew of several other modifications that would make it easier to assemble the bomb and to improve its characteristics in flight, but he had run out of time. He and Los Alamos had to be satisfied with those minor changes or modifications that could be made quickly and easily without affecting the overall architecture of the weapon. Little Boy and, later, Fat Man were scheduled to be shipped to a small island base in the Pacific.

In February, Groves dispatched Commander Frederick Ashworth of the navy, a member of Parsons's team at Los Alamos, to survey two islands in the Pacific as potential sites for the final assembly of the Little Boy and Fat Man. The first was Guam, which Ashworth found in the middle of enormous expansion and construction. A secure area for Los Alamos scientists and the 509th would not be available until August. The second possibility was Tinian, a small island in the Marianas chain. Ashworth found it suitable and immediately reported his findings and recommendation to Washington.[26] Groves chose Tinian and in March sent his deputy engineer, Colonel Kirkpatrick, as his personal representative there. The army agreed to lend Los Alamos part of its air base on the island, where a secure compound would be constructed. Kirkpatrick was to oversee delivery of the various bomb components as well as the construction of buildings for their assembly. Kirkpatrick was well versed on the work of Los Alamos and Wendover, and after spending April and May expediting construction, he returned to Los Alamos for further briefings.[27]

At the same time, laboratory staff began to gather equipment, special tools, and replacement bomb parts for shipment. On June 18, the first contingent of Los Alamos personnel left for Tinian. The various parts of the weapons were crated and would soon follow. The uranium and plutonium cores would be the last components to leave Los Alamos.

Tinian, only twelve miles long and covering thirty-nine square miles, is one of fifteen islands in an archipelago created by a submerged mountain chain. The Japanese had installed a garrison late in the war, but the Americans seized control in a fierce battle that lasted several weeks in July and August 1944. Only 313 of the 8,500 Japanese troops on the island survived. Navy Seabees immediately began to construct what for a time would be the largest airfield in the world, covering virtually the entire island, as well as housing for over forty thousand men. Two main sets of airstrips were built, one west and one north, each with two runways 8,500 feet in length. They were perfect for the hundreds of B-29 Superfortresses that took off and landed throughout the day and night. The special squadron of B-29s and aircrews known as the 509th Composite Group would be situated on the northern part of the island, isolated from the rest of the aircraft. The crews were handpicked for both their flying and navigation skills and their discretion. Led by Colonel Paul Tibbets, they had trained in Utah for nearly a year before flying to Tinian to take up residence. Soon they would share their small patch of heavily guarded island with men and secret weapons from Los Alamos. These men had been selected to drop the first atomic bombs, but with the exception of Tibbets, no member of the crew knew that.

Despite the technological and logistical challenges facing Los Alamos—indeed, all of the Manhattan Project—Groves still found time to point out lapses of military decorum. On April 25, he sent a terse message to Parsons citing two examples. While on a visit to Los Alamos, the general witnessed "laxness" in the appearance of several young naval officers, whose "summer uniform blouses were particularly bad." He also "noted a tendency, on the part of a few, not to leave Fuller Lodge in the morning in time to get to work on time." Groves added that he had similarly chastised Colonel Tyler for similar breeches in the decorum of army officers.[28]

Success on such a broad front gave Oppenheimer a brief respite during which he could review the work at Los Alamos and begin to make tentative plans for the future. He took stock of the fantastic growth of Los Alamos. Once just a handful of structures, the laboratory now occupied two hundred buildings, thirty-seven of which were in the Technical Area and the rest in nearby canyons and mesas. Staff members and their families lived in 620 rooms in more than three hundred apartment buildings and homes as well as in two hundred trailers and fifty-two dormitories.

In the late spring, conversations between Groves and Oppenheimer increasingly touched on what to do when the war ended. Should they continue the laboratory, at least for a while? If so, in what form and under what constraints? What improvements might they make to the existing weapons, and what new weapons, such as Teller's Super, should they pursue?

Oppenheimer summarized the laboratory's progress in a letter to Groves on May 7—the very day that the Germans surrendered unconditionally in a red brick schoolhouse thousands of miles away in Reims, France. All the effort at Site Y, he wrote, was being devoted to completing the first models of the Fat Man and Little Boy by summer. While some work remained to be done on these weapons, it was appropriate to think ahead to late summer and fall. Unless supplies of U235 became suddenly more plentiful—and that was doubtful any time soon—it was clear that the implosion model would be used for the overwhelming majority of bombs to be produced by Los Alamos during the war and stockpiled afterwards. His assessment reflected the general opinion that the implosion process, which could use either uranium or plutonium, was more effective than the gun process. Los Alamos would nevertheless maintain a store of Little Boy components as a protective measure against the ultimate failure of Fat Man or in case the army found the Little Boy tactically superior in field use.[29]

Oppenheimer could find satisfaction in the many achievements of his secret laboratory. At the same time, he now could more clearly see what remained to be done, both in the short run and the long run. Improvements to Fat Man were necessary—its design and engineering, for example, were clumsy and posed problems during release from the airplane. The most important refinement needed was in the configuration of the tamper and active core. Los Alamos scientists now believed that Fat Man could be made perhaps three times more powerful per unit of nuclear material by removing some two-thirds of the uranium tamper and decreasing the amount of plutonium correspondingly. But as Oppenheimer wrote to Groves, there was no possibility of pursuing these alternatives at the present time.

Oppenheimer also reported that the scientists at Los Alamos were still far from knowing how to make a hydrogen bomb. Despite Teller's work and the formation of his own group, the laboratory had no firm ideas about how to assemble a Super. Indeed, it could give no assurance that such nuclear processes could be made to work at all. Because research in Los Alamos had been concentrated for the last two years on fission weapons, its collective knowledge base was at the moment too narrow for the enormous complications of the Super. Oppenheimer could do no more than recommend further study.

Oppenheimer's letter was not premature. Events at Los Alamos were moving with incredible speed. Little Boy was virtually ready, and Fat Man would be available in a month or two. After detonators, the last great challenge was the explosive lenses, and they seemed to be on the verge of resolution. Or so he hoped.

That same month, Oppenheimer shared with his staff a rousing letter from Undersecretary of War Robert Patterson, thanking the scientists for their hard work but reminding them that despite the victory in Europe, the war was not yet over:

> We still have a hard task ahead. Every worker employed on this project is needed! Every man-hour of work will help smash Japan and bring our fighting boys home.
>
> You know the kind of war we are up against in the Pacific. Pearl Harbor—Bataan—Corregidor—Tarawa—Iwo Jima— and other bloody battles will not be forgotten.
>
> We have begun to repay the Japanese for their brutalities and the mass murder of helpless civilians and prisoners of war. We will not quit until they are completely crushed. You have an important part to play in their defeat. [There] must not be a let-up!

In Washington, Groves continued to push production schedules. Los Alamos would need every possible bit of plutonium and uranium for its weapons. And the more weapons the better. Stimson and his close advisors were in the process of assessing the bomb's potential use in Japan and assembling a list of potential targets. The new president was preparing for the Potsdam conference, where, his advisors warned, he would face "tough negotiations" with Stalin and encounter Churchill's volubility and persuasive powers.

Los Alamos was running at full speed. That July, Groves and Oppenheimer could note that the laboratory currently employed 1,300 scientists and technicians, 1,400 members of the Army's Special Engineering Detachment (SED), 1,260 military, two thousand civilian employees, and five hundred construction workers. Almost 6,500 men and women were racing to deliver an atomic bomb. And because of persistent recruitment efforts and intervention by Groves, more men continued to arrive. At one point, Groves called Oppenheimer to tell him that he had persuaded Compton at the Met Lab in Chicago to release forty men for transfer to Los Alamos. Of course Compton wasn't happy with the move. He argued that transferring that many men would endanger or slow down work in key areas. But Groves had the final say. He agreed to write a letter to Compton for the record taking "responsibility" for the transfer.

Groves could take additional pride in the results of his expensive investments in gaseous diffusion and nuclear reactors. Almost 150,000 men and women were working day and night to deliver enough U235 for at least one gun and enough Pu239 for several implosion weapons. He was not a man for celebrations, however.

Oppenheimer, nervous and anxious, was losing weight. Groves was battling his weight as always but remained indomitable and driven. In a rare moment of self-deprecating humor, the general joked with his colleague and senior advisor, James Conant, that the bomb *had* to work. If not, both men would have to buy houses on Capitol Hill because they would spend the rest of their lives testifying before Congress.[30]

Chapter Thirteen

RACE TO THE FINISH

———————————⟨∘⟩———————————

The sense of optimism experienced by Groves and Oppenheimer and his scientists in the spring of 1945, however guarded, was not limited to Los Alamos. America as a whole was beginning to believe that the war was nearing an end, and the events in Europe and the Pacific seemed to confirm that belief.

On March 7, the U.S. Third Army crossed the Rhine into Germany at Remagen. Within a month it was at the Elbe. In the Pacific, Americans landed on a small island most had never heard of before: Iwo Jima. A month later, U.S. Marines invaded Okinawa, establishing air bases that would put American bombers just three hundred miles from Japanese cities.

Groves now knew that the German atomic bomb was a phantom. Among other intelligence, secretly recorded conversations between captured German atomic scientists revealed that poor support and endless quarrels among themselves had prevented a united effort. Their science was flawed as well. Heisenberg himself had grossly overestimated the amount of U235 necessary for a bomb at about two tons.[1] Groves had eagerly supported intelligence efforts since 1942 to garner information on the progress of German nuclear research, establishing a special group, code-named the "Alsos Mission,"* to conduct intelligence activities throughout Europe. Its leaders, Colonel Boris Pash and Samuel Goudsmit, a scientist, had spent nearly two years following Allied troops and collecting scientific information wherever they could in Europe. Pash's appointment had the unintended consequence of redirecting his attention from Oppenheimer to the Germans.

Groves asked Los Alamos scientists to assemble information that would help Alsos agents without a scientific background to recognize nuclear activity in Germany, France, Italy, and Norway.[2] The intelligence they gathered had been scanty at first, but it allowed Alsos to confirm German interest. Agents learned of German activity in a Norwegian heavy water plant, for example, and British commandos destroyed it. When several tons of heavy water that had survived the attack was loaded onto a boat for eventual transport to Germany, local partisans sank the ferry. Groves also worried that the Germans would use radioactive materials to contaminate critical areas, such as the Normandy beaches. Compton, Conant, and Urey quickly made a study of radioactive poisoning, which Groves passed on to General Marshall. "Radioactive materials," they reported, "are extremely effective contaminating agents; are known to the Germans; can be produced by them and could employed as a military weapon."[3] By March 1944, however, the threat seemed to have passed. Groves informed General Dwight D. Eisenhower that although the Germans knew of radioactive materials, it was unlikely that they would use them. This prediction proved correct.

---

* Groves, who did not choose the code name, was horrified when he learned that "alsos" is the Greek word for "grove," but he decided that changing the name would only draw more attention to it.

Hitler, whose imagination had always been captured by the spectacular rather than the strategic, had focused much of Germany's scientific resources on the V-l and V-2 rockets. Failing to understand how fission could produce an explosion, he severely limited financial support to German physicists, whose competition for funds divided them and crippled their efforts. Although it was not known to American intelligence during the war, the Japanese also engaged in a very limited program of fission research. Led by Yoshio Nishina, a small team of scientists developed a crude five-foot cyclotron that could operate only at low power; its production was limited. By the summer of 1944, Nishina's team managed to produce some 170 grams of uranium hexafluoride.[4]

Groves realized in January 1944 that the atomic bomb in all likelihood would be developed too late for Germany. That month he wrote to Field Marshal Sir John Dill of the Combined Chiefs of Staff to report that "the use of the TA [atomic] weapon is unlikely" against Germany.[5]

Roosevelt was ever mindful of the political implications of nuclear weapons. The Quebec Agreement that he and Churchill had signed secretly in August 1943 provided that the United States and the United Kingdom would share information on atomic weapons with each other but with no "third" party. At that time, with Germany in control of most of Western Europe, the only third party with the ability to construct the huge separation plants necessary to manufacture uranium or plutonium, or even to develop bomb technology, was the Soviet Union, but its resources were consumed by the production of conventional arms for its broad front against the Germans. Only a small program was undertaken during the war.

In December 1944, more than a year after the Quebec Agreement, Roosevelt and Stimson decided that the United States could reveal the existence of the atomic bomb at some time in the future to force concessions from the Russians.[6] The Combined Chiefs of Staff of the United States and Great Britain were already planning global policies. Men like Niels Bohr and Leo Szilard hoped to convince Roosevelt to "open up" to the Russians, but that idea met strong resistance came from a coterie of powerful policy advisors to the president as well as from British leaders. Stimson and others urged caution against premature openness. Although Churchill's great distrust of the Soviets was well known to Roosevelt, the president had tentatively suggested to Churchill at Yalta in January 1945 that the two countries might at least brief Stalin on the work of the Manhattan Project. Churchill professed to be shocked and refused adamantly. He feared not only what the Soviets might do with such knowledge but also that information given prematurely would discourage Russian cooperation in settling the war. Moreover, the prime minister feared that sharing information with the Russians would also require a similar revelation to the French.[7]

Although Roosevelt had pursued a policy of cooperation with the Russians, beginning with Lend-Lease and including concessions on military strategy, he shared Churchill's pessimism about Soviet cooperation. The refusal to inform them about the atomic program, however, would make a postwar agreement for the control of atomic energy difficult if not impossible to achieve.

The spirit of cooperation favored by Roosevelt faded quickly as Truman settled into his presidency and witnessed Russia's behavior in its newly occupied territories, especially Poland. The war in Europe was barely over, but the Yalta agreement was unraveling. The president's advisors argued successfully against any further concessions to the Russians and against revealing substantive information about the atomic bomb. Sole possession of such a weapon, they contended, would guarantee the United States a powerful advantage at war's end. Stimson believed that the United States "must find some way of persuading Russia to play ball."[8] The Fat Man and Little Boy bombs were the kind of pressure the Soviets would understand.

It turned out, however, that much of the Truman administration's deliberation about atomic policy regarding the Soviet Union was irrelevant. Stalin already knew a good deal about America's atomic bombs. His spies had been reporting regularly since the earliest days of the Manhattan

Project. From Los Alamos, Klaus Fuchs was particularly helpful. His reports, accompanied by sketches, gave Soviet scientists a detailed portrait of the implosion bomb and its intricately contrived initiator. David Greenglass provided descriptions of the sophisticated molds used to manufacture explosive lenses for Fat Man. And Ted Hall passed along the laboratory's theoretical thinking on a wide range of subjects, including the Super. This was a breech that would haunt Los Alamos for decades.

It was increasingly clear to Oppenheimer and his leaders that when a prototype of the implosion bomb was ready, it would need to be tested before any subsequent models were shipped overseas.

The idea of testing the plutonium gadget was not new. The possibility was first raised in a governing board meeting on January 24, 1944. Groves, however, was not comfortable with the idea of a test. He suspected that a purely experimental gadget would not only consume unnecessary time and resources but also divert scientists away from completing the bomb as a true field weapon. He was certainly unhappy with the prospect of spending what in the summer of 1945 was expected to be a third or even half of the world's supply of Pu239. He pressed Oppenheimer: Were there alternatives to a test? Or could a gadget be tested with less plutonium but still confirm spherical implosion? Oppenheimer responded that it would be difficult to calculate the critical mass for a "limited" test, and more importantly, such a test would not provide all the information scientists hoped to gather. Groves was also concerned that the precious plutonium would be lost, perhaps irretrievably, if the gadget's explosives detonated but a supercritical chain reaction did not occur. Was there a way to recover the precious material in case of a fizzle? Groves insisted that all the options be considered.

Oppenheimer enumerated the challenges of what he called a "proof firing" in a letter of March 10, 1944. For the scientists to collect the information needed, the explosion had to achieve a certain minimum magnitude. In any case, a proof firing would still entail the serious risk of a large nuclear explosion. As he explained to Groves, "The consequences of this are in the first instance that the material involved would be irrecoverably lost, and further that the site for the proof firing would have to be chosen with the possibility of a violent reaction clearly in mind."[9]

The laboratory knew that without a test, it would be impossible to understand the dynamics and effects of a nuclear explosion. The challenge of staging such a test, however, was enormous. No one had ever done anything like testing an atomic bomb, and such an extravagant experiment could not be planned and conducted in a matter of weeks or months. The governing board discussed the prospect again on February 17, 1944, and Oppenheimer asked Ken Bainbridge to plan a separate organizational group within the laboratory with total responsibility for the test.[10] Bainbridge quickly outlined the preliminary scientific requirements. They would need to study blast, earth shock, and neutron and gamma radiation and make a complete photographic record of the explosion and atmospheric phenomena. These basic experimental needs would determine the organization of the test.

The choice of a site for the test was critical. Bainbridge established the criteria and suggested eight locations in the western United States.[11] The prospective site had to be very flat to minimize topographical effects on the explosion. A level, isolated location would also make it easy to truck in supplies and heavy equipment. Ideally, the location would have good weather, with light winds and minimal dust and haze. Towns, ranches and settlements had to be far enough away to avoid the danger of radioactive fallout. The concept of "fallout" was new—less than a year old—and in 1944 no one at Los Alamos thought of it as more than a short-term problem. Interestingly, Groves was among those who most appreciated the danger, and he would not approve an experimental test of an atomic bomb near Los Alamos or any other town or city:

Initially, there was no thought given to the possible dangers of radioactive fallout. The first person to bring this possibility as far as I know was Joseph Hirschfelder.... I was probably much more concerned about this than any of the scientific personnel. I was fully supported in my views by Col. Stafford Warren, our chief medical officer. It was with this background that I placed all of the fallout precautions—collection of data, preparations for evacuations of civilian populations, etc., under the guidance of Warren.[12]

Most of the suggested sites were within driving distance from Los Alamos, but two were not. The military training grounds near Rice, California, and San Nicolas Island off the coast of southern California were rejected because they could not be reached easily. Another suggested site, in the San Luis Valley region near the Great Sand Dunes National Monument in Colorado, could not be used because the valley was occasionally inhabited by Indians, and Secretary of the Interior Harold Ickes had forbidden the seizure of any lands belonging to Native Americans.

Bainbridge, accompanied by either Stevens or de Silva of Los Alamos security, personally inspected all the potential sites and ordered aerial surveys. Oppenheimer, despite the heavy pressures of work, managed to accompany the three men in May for an inspection of the area southwest of Los Alamos. Driving for three days in two three-quarter-ton weapons carriers, the team was stymied by bad weather and poor maps that got them lost several times. Oppenheimer loved it. The excursion was a brief but exhilarating escape from the Hill and his responsibilities.

One of the five remaining sites was in Texas, on the sandbars off the southern coast now known as Padre Island. The others were in New Mexico—the lava region south of Grants, an area southwest of Cuba, the Tularosa Basin, and the Jornada del Muerto in the south. The team ultimately recommended the Jornada, along the old Santa Fe Trail between El Paso and northern New Mexico, because the desert was well suited to their needs and because the land was already under War Department control. Some years before, hundreds of square miles near Alamogordo had been designated the Alamogordo Bombing Range, and by 1945, B-17 and B-29 crews practiced daily bombing runs there before being sent overseas.

On June 29, 1944, at the final meeting of the governing board before its dissolution, Bainbridge reported on his trip to southern New Mexico. The most favorable area was 250 miles south of Los Alamos in a valley approximately fifty miles wide. There were two excellent locations within this rectangular area. A site in the east favored a full test of Fat Man with no expectation of recovering any plutonium. The other, in the west, favored a more limited test with the possibility of recovery. Railroads served both areas. Bainbridge recommended both and pressed for a quick decision, which would allow time to lay down roads and construct buildings for experiments and crews. Oppenheimer deferred the decision until August 1 to allow for better topographical information.

With Bainbridge's organizational recommendations in hand, Oppenheimer asked Kistiakowsky to take the lead in planning for the test, now tentatively scheduled for early to mid-1945. This timeframe was based on projections for those components of implosion that were yet to be completed and for the anticipated delivery of plutonium. Kistiakowsky, then deputy division leader for the implosion program within the Ordnance Division, quickly formed a new High Explosives Group under Bainbridge to oversee completion of a test weapon. By the end of August, Bainbridge had twenty-five men under him, and in another year he would have 250.

Bainbridge was an excellent choice. A Harvard-educated experimental physicist, he had worked with Ernest Rutherford at England's Cavendish Laboratories. When he returned to the United States and joined the faculty of his alma mater, he brought with him the official British MAUD report on the potential for an atomic bomb. At Harvard, Bainbridge designed and built a cyclotron that eventually found its way to Los Alamos in 1943, and he came along with it. A solidly built man with a crew cut, he radiated confidence.

During the early summer months, Bainbridge and Paul Fussell prepared a systematic plan for the test. In their preliminary work, they allowed for a bomb that would deliver a blast equivalent to between two hundred and ten thousand tons of TNT and presumed that some sort of "recovery vehicle" or container would be employed. Several imaginative methods of recovering the plutonium were proposed. One called for constructing a water baffle to contain the plutonium, another for exploding the device in the sand, and a third for detonating the bomb in a large solid container.[13] Kistiakowsky and Neddermeyer favored a large pressure vessel, and Oppenheimer tended to agree. Robert Carlson, who was working under Kistiakowsky, designed a huge metal container that could withstand conventional explosive forces but would vaporize in a nuclear explosion. Groves approved the idea.

The vessel, called Jumbo, was an enormous steel cylinder twenty-five feet long and twelve feet in diameter. The shell itself was six inches thick and laced with steel bands that increased the thickness of the main part of the shell to fourteen inches. The laboratory ordered Jumbo constructed in August 1944 and received it in May 1945 at a railroad siding in Pope, New Mexico, the closest delivery point. The device weighed over 215 tons, and the challenge was how to get it to Trinity and Ground Zero. Bainbridge proposed building a rail line from Pope to Trinity, but Groves balked at the proposed cost of $520,000. Instead, it was transported across the desert on a special sixty-four-wheel trailer that cost only $150,000. Groves was not happy with that expense either, nor with the cost of Jumbo, which was in the millions. When he heard a rumor that an elaborate construction effort would be required to assemble Jumbo once it got to Trinity, he called Parsons and complained. Parsons checked with Major Lex Stevens, who was overseeing work at Trinity, and six hours later a nervous Stevens called Groves to describe what was proposed. Trinity, the general caustically informed the major, was a "field installation;" large buildings and extensive roads were not called for.

Fears of a misfire plagued the scientists. If a nuclear misfire occurred, radioactive material would be scattered. Oppenheimer thought the Clinton Plant at Oak Ridge would be better prepared to undertake plans for plutonium recovery, but he asked the Chemistry and Metallurgy Division to set up facilities in Bayo Canyon, northeast of Los Alamos, to handle contaminated material. Several heated buildings were constructed along with an extraction column for recovery of the plutonium.[14] Groves still urged that as little Pu239 as possible be used and continued to encourage a test that would consume only enough plutonium to set off a chain reaction. Oppenheimer countered that a "small" test would reveal little useful information on nuclear processes but would pose the same level of risk and danger as a full-scale test. Fortunately, by the time of the test, larger than expected quantities of Pu239 were available and confidence in the Fat Man design had increased, so the plans for Jumbo were dropped. The vessel was left upright within a steel frame several hundred yards from Ground Zero. It was a twelve-million-dollar insurance policy that turned out to be unneeded.

Groves finally accepted a full-scale test, but he was quick to remind everyone that Los Alamos, and indeed the Manhattan Project, existed solely to produce workable, deliverable weapons. He still believed that some in Los Alamos were more committed to the "science" of a weapon than to the actual production of one, a suspicion shared by Parsons. The general admonished Oppenheimer, "I feel that you must limit attention to absolute minimum of personnel and effort by that personnel."[15] Oppenheimer, writing back to Groves, rejected the "fallacy of regarding a controlled test as the culmination of the work of this laboratory. The laboratory is operating under a directive to produce weapons; this directive has been and will be rigorously adhered to." But a test was necessary: "The only reason why we contemplate making a test, and why I have in the past advocated this, is because with the present time scales and the present radical assembly design this appears to be a necessary step in the production of a weapon."[16]

In August 1944, Groves officially approved the test site in the Jornada—first by phone, then by telex—and, in September, the site was officially code-named "Trinity." Who actually came up with the name is not known with certainty. One account suggests that Major Stevens chose the name while transporting Jumbo from the rail siding at Pope to Ground Zero. Another explanation was that the name came from an abandoned mine somewhere in the area. But by far the most popular account credits Oppenheimer, who reputedly chose the name Trinity based on the lines of a sonnet by John Donne that he had read the night before:

> Batter my heart, three person'd God, for you
> As yet but knock, breathe, shine, and seek to mend;
> That I may rise and stand, o'erthrow me and bend
> Your force to break, blow, burn, and make me new.[17]

Oppenheimer seemed to confirm the story two decades later in a letter to Groves in which he acknowledged that he had suggested the name and wrote that to the best of his recollection he based it on reading Donne.[18]

In September, Bainbridge, Parsons, Ramsey, and de Silva traveled to Colorado Springs to visit General Uzal Ent, commander of the Second Air Force, whose jurisdiction included the Alamogordo Bombing Range, to formally request permission to use the site. They asked for an area approximately eighteen by twenty-four miles within the northernmost part of the Alamogordo Bombing Range. After four alternative sites were discussed, Ent approved the area 33°28' to 33°50' north latitude by 106°22' to 106°41' west longitude. It was a highly suitable location. The nearest town was twenty-seven miles away. To the north and west, the closest ranches or small settlements were twelve miles away. To the east and south, military lands stretched at least eighteen miles to the east and a greater distance to the south. Much of this land had once belonged to a family of ranchers named McDonald, who had been displaced by the air base at Alamogordo. Colonel William Eareckson, commander of the Alamogordo Bombing Range, provided Bainbridge with extensive aerial photographs of the area. "The Commander and his men flew that area and gave us detailed photos something like six inches to the mile where we could see every fencepost and prairie dog burrow in the place."[19]

With Groves's formal approval, Bainbridge began planning a central camp with scientific and technical buildings and connecting roads. A new team, consisting of himself, Fussell, and army Captain Samuel Davalos, the post engineer at Los Alamos, submitted a set of plans to Oppenheimer and Kistiakowsky. Oppenheimer sent the package to Groves on October 14, 1944, along with a copy of a memo from Kistiakowsky stating that plans for a test "are based on the assumption that a nuclear explosion will take place. The test will provide information on the various effects of the bomb and serve as the basic technical data for planning both tactical use and future development." The information would be useful in two ways:

> First it will tell what is to be expected from a gadget of the same design as that to be tested.... Second, as the design of the gadget is improved and greater TNT equivalent is hoped for from subsequent gadgets, it will be possible ... to predict with good accuracy the destructive effects from these improved models of the gadget.[20]

Groves presumably appreciated the optimism and on October 27 told Oppenheimer to proceed. Contracts for construction of roads and buildings could be issued immediately.

The nerve center for the test would be a small complex of hastily constructed buildings called Base Camp in the south-central part of the site, about ten miles from the point where Fat Man would be detonated. Base Camp initially consisted of a few buildings for scientific work, a mess hall, several dormitories, a meeting room, and a stockroom. More buildings were added as work at Trinity accelerated in the spring. The stockroom, soon nicknamed FUBAR (one of the military's most popular acronyms—"F----d Up Beyond All Recognition"), contained everything from precision instruments to toilet paper, every item trucked down from either Los Alamos or Albuquerque.

As soon as Base Camp was completed in December, Groves ordered a detachment of military police under Lieutenant Harold Bush to guard the area. To assist Bush, the Los Alamos security office assigned John Anderson to represent the intelligence office. Planning the layout and overseeing construction was assigned to John Williams. Anderson took charge of an elaborate badge and pass system, the guards, and communication between Trinity and the outside world. Bush and Anderson came to Trinity knowing only what maps and aerial photographs could tell them. Bush arrived on a frigid New Year's Eve, unprepared for the icy winds that swept through the desert in winter. When Bainbridge made his first visit a few weeks later, snow blocked the road, and he was forced to work his way around by an alternative route. Early arrivals learned quickly that the Jornada was not just cold, it was bleak. The charms of the desert—its vastness and subtle vegetation—were not apparent in subfreezing temperatures. A few months later, though, for a brief moment in the spring, the desert experienced its annual miracle and bloomed. Flowers and a burst of color transformed the land, which after a few days withered back into monochrome.

The pass system was very thorough. Men departing from Los Alamos secured a pass from Bainbridge's office. At the first Trinity guard tower, they exchanged the pass for a badge and wore it at all times. Leaving, they surrendered the badge and retrieved their original pass. The military police kept careful rosters, recording the number of trips each man made to Trinity and the amount of time he spent there. Nevertheless, there were lapses in security. Despite precautions to avoid dual assignments, construction workers who had been in Los Alamos were hired for work at

Trinity, where they recognized some of the scientists preparing for the test.

Bainbridge realized that two-way radios would be invaluable as a means of communicating across the vast site. A request was sent to the government for special radio frequencies for Trinity that could not be monitored. After months of waiting, the assignments came back. Strangely enough, the ground frequency assigned to Trinity was the same one assigned to the railroad freight yard in San Antonio, Texas. The ground-to-air frequency was the one assigned to the Voice of America. Bainbridge suspected that if Trinity could hear the freight yard and the Voice of America, they could hear Trinity as well. There was not time to request different frequencies.

On June 15, Bainbridge gave John Williams, his assistant and the man overseeing construction at Trinity, the specifications for the tower that would hold Fat Man and serve as Ground Zero. It was to be one hundred feet high with a ladder on the northwest corner. As a security precaution, the ladder would not start at the base but begin at the first cross-bracing a dozen or so feet from the ground. Anyone wanting to climb the tower needed a movable ladder to reach the first few rungs. At the top would be an enclosure, which Bainbridge called the "house," with a trap door in the floor. It would be open on the north side with a four-foot balcony that ran along the edge. The other three sides would be corrugated metal sheets.

The base of the tower would be an eighteen-by-eighteen-foot concrete slab overlaid with wide wood planking. Bainbridge originally specified a building—again he called it a "house"—to be constructed around the base with walls at least fourteen feet high and with a wooden garage-style door on the north side large enough to "let a 6 x 6 Mack truck into the house loaded with a Fat Man loaded on a cradle."[21] He changed his mind, however, and opted for a removable canvas tent. Electricity would power lights and equipment.

Williams quickly started construction of the tower and began work on three major equipment shelters, or bunkers. They were originally tagged

A, B, and C but were soon nicknamed North 10,000, West 10,000, and South 10,000 for their locations ten thousand yards each from Ground Zero. These were constructed of concrete and wood and covered with earth. Portholes in the north and west bunkers faced Ground Zero. The main control center would be in the south. Smaller shelters were constructed for experiments, most on the surface but a few dug into the ground. On May 26, Groves ordered the roads leading from Ground Zero to each of the three shelters and to Base Camp blacktopped at a cost of five thousand dollars per mile. The job was to be completed before July 1. The entire Trinity test area, including Base Camp, the trio of bunkers, smaller structures, instrumentation, and observation sites, covered a circle of approximately one hundred square miles with Ground Zero at the center.

Within that circle were gauges to measure blast, geophones and seismographs to measure ground shock, gold foil and fast-ion chambers to capture neutron data, and sentinels to measure gamma-ray emissions. There was also a huge array of photographic equipment, including Fastax cameras at eight hundred yards capable of shooting five thousand frames per second, to record spectrographic data, radiation characteristics, and photometric data and ball-of-fire data.

Williams and his men found their normal ten-hour working day extended to eighteen. They were responsible for the thankless task of providing the necessary wiring, power, transportation, communication, and construction as daytime temperatures were rising. They completed most of Trinity's preparations in early May, along with a complete communications system that included telephone lines, a public address system reaching all buildings including bunkers, and FM radios in most jeeps and trucks assigned to the test.

Groves insisted on measures to disguise Trinity's connection with Los Alamos, and Bainbridge established additional security regulations. Anyone leaving Los Alamos for Trinity had to check in at Major de Silva's office. Everyone at Trinity—military or civilian—was required to sleep and eat at the campsite, not in nearby towns, and to spend all his time at the site. No one was to go to nearby towns for movies or dinner. Further instructions governing the drive from Los Alamos to Trinity were issued:

> The following directions are strictly confidential.... Under no conditions on this trip, when you are south of Albuquerque, are you to disclose that you are in any way connected with Santa Fe. If you are stopped for any reason and you have to give out information, state that you are employed by the Engineers in Albuquerque. Under no circumstances are telephone calls or stops for gasoline to be made between Albuquerque and your destination.[22]

There was one exception. Bainbridge approved a stop at Roy's Cafe in Belen, where it was believed Groves had placed one of his G-2 security men as chef. Weary travelers, reaching San Antonio, New Mexico, in the heat of the late afternoon, occasionally violated these restrictions by stopping illicitly for a beer at Jose Miera's Owl Bar. The rustic establishment had one other asset—the only public telephone within miles, which could be reached by dialing San Antonio 6.

Groves was keenly interested in the expected explosive force, or yield, of the new weapons. The laboratory already had some idea of the potential explosive power of Fat Man. The best guess in mid-1945 was an equivalent of ten kilotons of TNT. But what of the other effects of the explosion? As early as March 1944, Bethe and Christy prepared a memorandum, "Immediate Aftereffects of the Gadget." They predicted that within a radius of thirty feet of the explosion, the temperature would reach about one million degrees Fahrenheit. In less than a hundredth of a second, the central fireball would expand to eight hundred feet in diameter and cool to fifteen thousand degrees. Shortly thereafter, the fireball would rise into the stratosphere and in two or three minutes reach an altitude of over nine miles, with temperatures of about eight thousand degrees.

There were implications for aircraft. Bethe and Christy warned that reconnaissance planes in the area would have to be careful. In the first tenth of a second after detonation a flash of bluish light—as bright as the sun at a distance of about one hundred kilometers—was to be expected. No plane should be any closer than seven miles from Ground Zero at the time of detonation, and no one should look at the explosion until after the first brilliant flash of light. They speculated that the danger from radioactivity was low because of the airplane's distance from the source of radioactivity: "Damage to the plane crew from neutrons is not a danger because the altitude of the plane is about four times the safe distance for neutron effects."[23]

In Los Alamos, Bainbridge continued to plan and schedule events. He now had safety and security personnel, various military attachés and representatives, and scientific consultants involved with his project. He consulted with the group leaders from other units and divisions, as Hugh Richards recalled:

I and 18 other group leaders and/or consultants for the Trinity test attended a weekly meeting chaired by Bainbridge. The meetings lasted one or two hours and served to correlate work and scheduling. Possible new experiments were examined and progress reports given. J. H. Williams, in charge of all services for the test [and Bainbridge's assistant], wisely insisted that all information of general usefulness be circulated to the personnel of the Trinity groups.[24]

Safety was understandably a serious concern. Groves queried Oppenheimer on precautions. What about blast damage? And what if radioactive dust drifted over nearby towns?* Damage to houses and other buildings could lead to legal action. He asked Oppenheimer to make sure that earth shock was measured at various distances from Ground Zero, as such evidence could be useful in lawsuits claiming building damage in nearby communities. Groves also requested that similar measurements be taken of air blast. "It appears to me," he wrote to Oppenheimer, "necessary to have measurements which will demonstrate clearly the limits beyond which air blast damage could not have resulted. Perhaps paper gauges placed at sufficient distances would be helpful for this purpose."[25]

Oppenheimer assured Groves that no one would be endangered by the blast itself: "No over-pressure will exist outside the territory controlled by us which can cause harm to personnel or property." As to radioactive fallout, he was far less certain. The laboratory experience here was "much more meager." What he could tell Groves was that the bomb would be fired "under circumstances that will allow the cloud of active material to rise very high in the atmosphere and this will prevent its spreading at low levels." The test would be conducted when the wind direction would not carry the cloud over any town for at least a hundred miles. It was Oppenheimer's opinion that no community would be exposed to lethal or serious doses of radiation.[26]

Groves's uneasiness reflected his years of experience in large-scale construction projects involving civilian communities as well as his continuing worry that the laboratory was concentrating only on scientific issues and failing to consider all the possibilities in their planning for the test. Oppenheimer, Bainbridge, and the others recognized the dangers of fallout, but none considered the possibility of lawsuits, any one of which could expose the laboratory's secret work to the public.

Bainbridge reported the general's concerns to his staff leaders on May 2.[27] Plans then were made for Major Thomas O. Palmer of the U.S. Army,

---

* The nearest towns to Trinity were San Marcial, San Antonio, Socorro, Carrizozo, Oscuro (now Oscura), Three Rivers, Tularosa, and Alamorgordo.

along with 160 enlisted men on horses and in jeeps, to be stationed north of the test area, the most likely direction of fallout drift judging from previous meteorological records of the area. If necessary, Palmer and his men would evacuate ranches and towns after the blast. Twenty men from Military Intelligence dressed as civilians would be stationed in towns and cities up to a hundred miles away, most of whom would be armed with recording barographs to gather permanent records of blast and earth shocks. Elaborate plans were also drawn up for the evacuation, should it be necessary, of Trinity personnel. The laboratory's medical officer, Dr. Hempelmann, was placed in charge. Each shelter was issued devices for radiation detection and enough vehicles to evacuate everyone assigned to that location. Robert Wilson would lead the evacuation at the North bunker; John Manley at West; and Frank Oppenheimer at South.

Bainbridge was aware that the "best laid plans" might go awry, especially with an atomic bomb. As early as the summer of 1944 some of his staff recommended that a rehearsal shot be conducted with conventional explosives to test procedures and train personnel for the larger experiment. The pretest would also provide a means for calibrating blast and earth shock equipment. Oppenheimer agreed and a tentative date was set for May.

There was little information on the effects of large explosions, but Los Alamos calculated that one hundred tons of Comp B would be an appropriate base amount. A few miles southeast of Ground Zero, workers constructed a twenty-foot tower from railroad ties and lumber and stacked one hundred tons of Comp B that arrived by train from Fort Wingate in wooden boxes marked "high explosives dangerous." The stack added another eighteen feet to the wooden platform. Placed at intervals between the boxes were one thousand curies of radioactive fission by-products from the Hanford Plant. The purpose of the radioactive material was to safely simulate how radioactivity would spread during a nuclear explosion. The material arrived in long, yellow plastic tubes resembling translucent garden hoses, which were snaked among the rows of boxes. Scientists could calculate the effects of the Trinity test and calibrate instruments using scaling techniques. Photographic equipment was placed at distances from the platform that matched the distance from the Trinity tower.

Bainbridge consulted John "Jack" Hubbard, chief meteorologist for the Manhattan District on assignment to Trinity, on the best possible dates. Hubbard, thirty-nine years old, had studied meteorology at the University of Washington and Caltech before working for Pan American–Grace Airways in Buenos Aires, where he gained first-hand experience with unstable air masses. He then spent some years as a civilian meteorologist working for the Air Force Research Center and Northwest Airlines doing studies on coastal cities in Asia. He joined the Manhattan Project in early 1945 and was sent to Los Alamos.

Drawing on the little historical weather information that was available for the Jornada and what he could glean from meteorological equipment set up at Trinity, Hubbard determined that the weather would be ideal for the test at 4:00 a.m. on May 7. Bainbridge went along with the date and put the plan in motion. Men began to gather after midnight in the cold desert air. The weather was perfect, just as predicted. The countdown began, everyone was ready at his assigned position, and recording instruments were running, when the test was suddenly shut down. A call had come over the radio that the observation plane was not yet in place. There was a thirty-minute delay. Finally, at 4:38 a.m., the Comp B was ignited from multiple locations within the stack. In an instant, an enormous, highly luminous orange sphere appeared, the light from which could be seen in Alamogordo, sixty miles away. It faded within seconds and passed through an oval configuration before assuming the shape of a mushroom and rising to fifteen thousand feet.[28]

The pretest was extremely successful, confirming that plans for the test of the implosion bomb were realistic. Scientists now had a set of baseline data to use in calibrating instruments. Mishaps were minor but reinforced the need for careful planning and execution. Cameramen forgot to start two cameras at the North and South shelters, and another man forgot to release several flash bombs. Two other men were stranded in the desert when their jeep broke down and weren't rescued until the next day. But Los Alamos now had vital experience in large explosions in desert conditions.

Everyone was pleased with the results except the construction crew who had built the massive wooden tower. They were stunned to drive by and see nothing but a blackened scar on the ground. One man told a scientist, "We put our heart into that thing."[29]

Most took the successful rehearsal as a good omen. But it did not solve other problems, such as personnel shortages, the heat and lack of humidity, the exhausting sixteen- and eighteen-hour days, and finding the necessary equipment and supplies. Some items were impossible to find at first. Seismographs were needed to record earth shock waves, but the only instruments available had been sold to the Argentine government the week before the laboratory's order was placed. Only the direct intervention of Groves and his office enabled Los Alamos to reverse the sale and have the seismographs sent to Trinity instead. Ordinary garden hose was urgently needed to protect sensitive wires between instruments and control points. Ten thousand feet of garden hose that had been ordered was lost during a shipping strike, and commercial hose had to be found as a substitute.

Twice in one week in May, airplanes from the nearby Alamogordo Army Air Base strayed over Trinity airspace. Although air traffic had been banned over the area by the base commander, several planes nevertheless wandered from their nighttime course and mistook the lights of Base Camp for illuminated targets. They dropped bombs that hit the carpentry shop and the stables and started a number of small fires. These were so-called practice bombs that weighed a hundred pounds but contained only three pounds of explosives. Fortunately, the camp suffered little damage and no one was hurt.

Bainbridge made important personnel assignments in June. Fermi and Victor Weisskopf became chief consultants for physics experiments, Bob Carlson and Joe Hirschfelder took on bomb damage experiments, Norris Bradbury was made responsible for the final assembly of Fat Man at Trinity, John Williams provided support services for the test, John Manley was asked to design and run air blast and shock experiments, and Julian Mack was asked to gather spectrographic and photographic records. The population of Trinity ballooned—250 scientists and technicians were now working side by side with military personnel.

In May, Frank Oppenheimer left his job at Oak Ridge and arrived in Los Alamos as an assistant to his brother; his wife Jackie came with him. Groves personally approved the transfer. For months, the general had watched his director closely. The increased stress was obvious. To provide emotional support, Frank was asked to come to Los Alamos to be close to his brother. For Groves, it was simply a matter of protecting his greatest asset at Los Alamos. Frank quickly took an active role at Trinity as special assistant to Bainbridge, and for most of June and early July he made the rounds at Trinity in the oppressive heat, checking and re-checking the elaborate experiments and filling in wherever another set of hands was needed.

———————

A number of dates for the full test were set and subsequently canceled because of technical difficulties. In March, the test was scheduled for July 4, but that date soon proved unrealistic because of delays in the delivery of lens molds from Detroit. Confusion and rumors proliferated as more dates were set and canceled, and Oppenheimer eventually found it necessary to clarify the situation. In a June 14 memorandum to group leaders, he acknowledged that adhering to the July 4 date was now impossible. Besides the delay of the lens molds, there were what Oppenheimer called "metallurgical difficulties" with the plutonium sphere.[30] A frustrated Groves could do little but wonder if better planning might have prevented the shifting of dates.

Bainbridge and Oppenheimer asked the Cowpuncher Committee, which exercised overall command of scheduling, to match outside deliveries with priorities within the organization and establish a date for the test. By the middle of June, the Cowpunchers had determined that July 13 was the earliest possible date for a test but that July 23 was more likely.

The Cowpunchers kept the meteorologist Hubbard busy with their jostling of dates and times. Bainbridge had already listed for Hubbard the weather conditions he wanted—forty-five-mile visibility, clear skies, less than 75 percent humidity, and no rain for at least twelve hours *after* the test. After surveying every unit within the laboratory and consulting the U.S. Army Air Force's Weather Division, Hubbard recommended July 18–19, with July 20–21 and July 12–14 as his second choices. July 16, his third choice, was risky at best, he warned. The decision, however, was driven more by the availability of explosive lenses and detonators and by pressure from Groves than by the weather forecast. With Hubbard's recommendations in hand, the Cowpuncher Committee met on June 20 and changed the likely test date from July 13 to 16, although they were prepared to change it again if necessary.

As the pace of events accelerated all across the Manhattan Project, Groves needed to get to New Mexico as soon as he could, though to avoid arousing unwanted interest he would not go there directly from Washington. On June 30, he told Conant that he would leave Sunday or Monday, July 8 or 9, for the West Coast, and Conant agreed to meet him in California. Groves then called Oppenheimer to inform him of the schedule and that he would bring Conant and Bush with him to Albuquerque. Oppenheimer replied that at the moment, the "trip" looked okay for the 14th and somewhat better for the 18th. He would keep Groves informed.

The fluctuating test dates resulted in a tense telephone exchange between Groves and Oppenheimer on July 2. Anxious for Los Alamos to fix a date and not succumb to what he suspected was another round of unnecessary refinements to the gadget, Groves asked when was the earliest the test could take place? Oppenheimer replied that the Cowpunchers now had moved the test to the 17th. The 14th was still a possibility, but the laboratory was not sure it could meet that deadline. The 17th, said Oppenheimer, was a sure thing, and everyone ought to be able to "go fishing" on the 18th.

Groves objected. The 17th was unacceptable because—he was speaking in code—of the "various things" that were going on. He meant the president's meetings at Potsdam. Exasperated, Groves asked to be transferred to Parsons. After a brief conversation regarding shipment of weapons to Tinian, he was transferred back to Oppenheimer, who continued to press for a July 17 test date. Groves finally told him it *had* to be earlier, and Oppenheimer reluctantly agreed. Jean O'Leary noted in Groves's diary, "Dr. O said they would meet the earlier date but it went against his feeling but if the Gen wanted it that way they would do it."

Groves hung up, unsettled by Oppenheimer's uncertainty. He called Conant, who reassured him that he was right to insist on the earlier date and offered to telephone Tolman, who by chance was consulting in Los Alamos, and urge him to reinforce the importance of the earlier date with Oppenheimer. Within a few hours, Tolman telephoned. Groves asked him to explain to Oppenheimer and the "upper crust" at the laboratory that the general was not "needling them but that there was nothing he could do about it"—July 17 was not acceptable. The test had to be earlier, preferably by the 14th.

Tolman then handed the phone to Oppenheimer, who for the third time that day spoke with Groves. It was a familiar scene. O'Leary watched as Groves adjusted his headset and shifted continuously in the chair that he had occupied for most of the day. Parsons and others watched Oppenheimer light one cigarette after another, gesticulating with it as he spoke. Groves reported Conant's support, reminding him that Conant was the alternate to Bush as chairman of the Military Policy Committee, which had the final say. The problem, Oppenheimer replied in a tired voice, was that the plutonium from Colonel Nichols was slow in arriving and of poor quality. Completion of the bomb's core was a hostage to that reality. Groves said they had no choice but to try to comply with a test date of the 14th. Exhausted, they hung up.

The matter was hardly settled. Two days later, Oppenheimer called Groves and anxiously reported that there were continuing difficulties that affected the July 14 date. He wanted three more days. The problems were now predominantly in Kistiakowsky's shop, where they were having trouble producing defect-free explosive lenses, and it appeared that the gadget wouldn't be ready until July 17 after all. Oppenheimer explained that some of the outer ring of lenses didn't fit "dimensional tolerances," and there were difficulties with the electrical wiring. It wasn't worth the risk to push for an earlier date, he told Groves, but everyone was working around the clock to fix the problems.

Kistiakowsky, who was not present for Groves's and Oppenheimer's conversation, believed that the lens problems were not the only reason that Oppenheimer wanted a delay:

> Part of the difficulty was that Oppenheimer insisted that we assemble two identical explosive facsimile bombs. One with the real core would go to Trinity, the other with a dummy core would be exploded twenty-four hours earlier at Los Alamos in a very sophisticated rig which was to tell us finally if we had the spherically symmetrical wave. It made more work at a time of crisis and I didn't think it was necessary. It was the beginning of problems [over the Trinity test] between Oppie and me.[31]

Groves cut off the discussion and once again cited the importance of the Potsdam Conference. The test was fixed for July 16.

As construction at Trinity was completed, attention shifted to preparations for the many experiments to be conducted during the test. This new
phase brought dozens of additional scientists down from Los Alamos for
the first time. Some made short visits, and others stayed for weeks at a time.

The most important experiments were designed to determine the
nature of the implosion process. Seeking a better understanding of simultaneity, scientists were especially keen to learn the intervals between the
firing of the first and the last of thirty-two detonators. Other experiments
would try to determine the time between the firings of the detonators and
the emission of gamma rays. Bruno Rossi for example, would study the
fission rate by running a three-inch copper pipe from the top of the tower
to a small tent one thousand yards away known as North 1,000. Inside the
pipe was a thin copper wire surrounded by small cylinders of copper of
decreasing radius. Oscilloscopes at the north shelter would be just far
enough from the blast and survive just long enough to take a reading. A
crude trestle supported the pipe. Other experiments would study the
release of nuclear energy by measuring gamma rays in the fission products
released or by studying delayed neutrons.

There was a daring proposal for Herb Anderson and Fermi to enter
Ground Zero shortly after the explosion, when it would be highly radioactive, and take soil samples to determine the ratio of fission products to
unconverted plutonium. A number of precautionary schemes were proposed. Someone suggested a semi-rigid blimp with a scoop that would
descend as soon as possible after the blast to collect a soil sample. The idea
was scrapped because it was feared that desert temperatures would make
the blimp unwieldy. Helicopters were also considered but rejected because
in 1945 they were incapable of flying at five thousand feet, the average
altitude of the Jornada. Finally, two army tanks with sealed lead linings
were modified to serve as recovery vehicles and shipped to Trinity.

Groves and Oppenheimer wanted a detailed photographic record. Julian Mack was designated to preside over a variety of optical and photographic experiments that would measure and record visual effects, such as the fireball. Mack would use both color and black-and-white films in movie cameras that ran from below normal speed to thousands of frames per second. Photographs would also be taken from airplanes flown by Parsons and Alvarez.

———————————

Work at Base Camp intensified. The weather was hot, with daytime temperatures often soaring over one hundred degrees. Everyone had to deal with the dust kicked up by the endless stream of trucks and jeeps and other vehicles that roamed the extensive network of roads linking bunkers, Base Camp, and the dozens of experiment sites. Groves had approved paving a few of these roads, but most of them were simply rough paths that had been bulldozed and graded. Some roads weren't even graded; they were just trails. The surface of these roads was caliche, a common desert soil that was ground finer and finer with every car or truck that passed over it. Manley remembers long dust trails, some a half-mile high, following vehicles as they lumbered over the desert. When lit from behind by the rising or setting sun, they looked like a transparent khaki curtain pulled over the horizon by a truck or jeep.

Daily life at Trinity was a challenge. Sanitary conditions were difficult to maintain at Base Camp, particularly in the mess hall. The hard water from nearby wells quickly clogged pipes. Special hard-water soap was issued. As the rains came in late June and July, a sunbaked reservoir filled up with water and the nights echoed with the croaking of thousands of frogs. Scorpions, snakes, and other desert creatures were a constant menace. It was Standard Operating Procedure each morning to shake out shoes and clothing carefully before dressing. One scientist driving a jeep stopped to inspect a roadside shelter. When he returned to the jeep he was startled to see a sidewinder furiously biting into a tire.

There were a few amusements. The McDonald ranch house had a man-high concrete reservoir filled with water used for swimming. A well at the house supported several trees, the only oasis of green for miles. Passing herds of antelope, hunted down with the security patrol's submachine guns, contributed to the camp's menu, as did the occasional wandering cow. Nearby towns were off limits, so the staff set up a beer fund as protection against dehydration. The low-alcohol swill came in a plain white steel can labeled with the single word "BEER." The joke was that the army owned only five movies and showed one of them every night for nearly six months. Workers at Trinity rose at 5:00 a.m. and breakfasted before six. Dinner was at 6:00 p.m., and evening hours, particularly for scientific and technical personnel, were spent primarily in late work, group meetings, or informal briefings.

At Trinity, the same nagging, troublesome fear that had haunted the laboratory for two years lingered beneath the exhaustion and anticipation—would the gadget work? Doubt expressed itself in many forms: checking and rechecking installations, electrical lines or equipment, or black humor, like the doggerel that circulated throughout the laboratory in July:

> From this crude lab that spawned a dud
> Their necks to Truman's axe uncurled
> Lo, the embattled savants stood
> And fired the flop heard round the world.

Late in the day on July 7, Groves called Oppenheimer and informed him that he would arrive in Albuquerque by airplane on Sunday, July 15, and drive down to Trinity with Conant, Tolman, and Bush. He stressed that he would be in touch continuously with his office, and if anything changed he was prepared to alter his schedule by one or two days. O'Leary would know how to reach him. Oppenheimer replied simply that arriving on Sunday would give them an opportunity to "discuss the things that will happen the following month." He meant Japan, but both men knew that any discussion ultimately depended on Fat Man.

On July 11, Groves flew with Vannevar Bush and an aide to the Hanford plant in Pasco, Washington. From there they would make their way down to Berkeley, pick up Tolman, and proceed to Los Angeles. Groves's "official" schedule called for the four of them to return to Washington, D.C., but their real destination was Albuquerque. From there, Trinity was a three-hours car ride south.

Five years later, Oppenheimer recalled the atmosphere at Los Alamos as the day of the test approached:

> Very shortly before the test of the first atomic bomb, people at Los Alamos were naturally in a state of some tension. I remember one morning when almost the whole project was out of doors staring at a bright object in the sky.... Our director of personnel was an astronomer and a man of some human wisdom; and he finally came to my office and asked whether we would stop trying to shoot down Venus. I tell this story only to indicate that even a group of scientists is not proof against the errors of suggestion and hysteria.[32]

The work grew more exacting and demanding, the urgency for completion and perfection more intense. Everybody knew that *the* day was drawing near. Oppenheimer himself was restless and apprehensive. He lost even more weight, and his clothes drooped from his frame. His smoking never ceased. Just weeks before the test he developed a case of chicken pox that kept him home for several frustrating days. When he returned to work, barely recovered, he was more anxious than ever. Rabi arrived in Los Alamos a few days before the test and stayed close to Oppenheimer in an effort to inject a calculated calm into the tense atmosphere.

Summertime thermals could make flying over the mountains anything but pleasant, and Groves's secret flight to Albuquerque on the afternoon of July 15 was turbulent. When his party landed—relieved, and some still nauseated—they were immediately driven to the Base Camp, arriving around five o'clock. Compton and a few others were scheduled to arrive later in the day. In Germany, President Truman prepared for his first meeting with Joseph Stalin.

Now it was only a matter of waiting for the dark sphere in the tower to work.

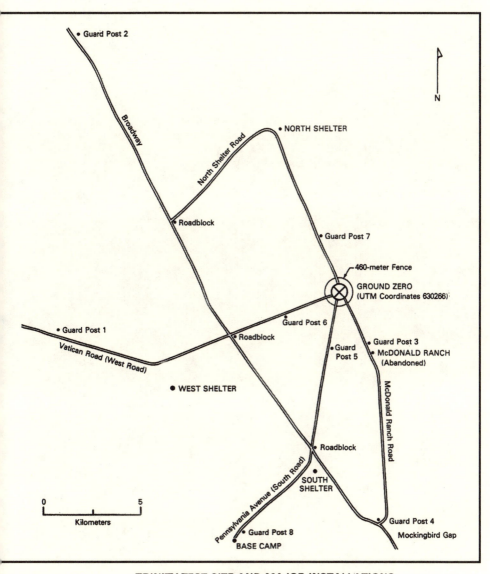

TRINITY TEST SITE AND MAJOR INSTALLATIONS

**Map of Trinity Site
July 1945**

Chapter Fourteen

MEN WILL SEE WHAT WE SAW

———————◆———————

Everyone knew that the test was just days away, and the tension pervaded every office and laboratory at Los Alamos. Whether behind the high fences of the Tech Area or in the canyons below Pajarito, it was impossible to escape the realization that two years and three months of intense, frustrating, yet often exhilarating work would soon bear fruit in a desert two hundred and twenty miles to the south. Even without details, wives knew something big was about to happen. Bradbury certainly felt the strain. He had begun his own countdown in early July. High on his list was determining the safest method of loading and shipping the explosive lenses to Trinity and then to the Pacific. A slight flaw or crack caused by a bump in the road or turbulence in an airplane might affect or even prevent simultaneity. Could a gadget be successfully transported? As a test, Bradbury shipped a bomb with explosives but a dummy core by truck to Trinity on July 3. The dummy, covered by a tarpaulin, lay at the base of the tower for twenty-four hours. When it returned to Los Alamos the next day, it was disassembled and thoroughly checked. It had survived the trip with no damage.

To find out how the weapon would fare if hit in transit by antiaircraft fire, Bradbury conducted a second test, this time in Pajarito Canyon, using a similar full-scale bomb with a dummy core. Twenty-millimeter cannon shells comparable to those used by Japanese antiaircraft guns were fired at the bomb from a distance. Fat Man did not explode, but smoke poured from some of the shell holes. After several anxious hours and no explosion, Bradbury and Bainbridge concluded that unless a detonator was hit directly, the bomb had a fair chance of surviving enemy fire.

On Tuesday, July 10, the crews at S Site began nearly two days of around-the-clock work to prepare the lenses for incorporation into the Trinity Fat Man. Both Kistiakowsky and Bradbury personally examined each lens, which was brown in color because of a varnish used to seal the explosive. On Wednesday, the two men checked for cracks, chipped corners, and other imperfections that might affect the explosion. Each lens was then x-rayed, verified, and assigned a serial number. Imperfections revealed by x-rays had to be repaired or the lens replaced. Repairs, Kistiakowsky knew, could be fatal: "In some desperation, I got hold of a dental drill and, not wishing to ask others to do an untried job, spent most of one night, the week before the Trinity test, drilling holes in some faulty castings so as to reach the air cavities indicated in our x-ray inspection film. That done, I filled the cavities by pouring molten explosive slurry into them, and thus made the castings acceptable."[1]

When all lenses had passed inspection, the best ones were assembled in building TA-22-1 at S Site and encased in the bomb's Duralumin shell. The cylindrical plug and a set of two explosive lenses were left out of the Trinity Fat Man. Using the bomb's "trap door," a dummy brass and wood plug and inert plastic lenses were inserted. The bomb was then wrapped in Butvar plastic, boxed and braced inside a pine shipping crate, securely strapped to the bed of a truck, and covered by a tarpaulin for the eight-hour journey to the base of the tower at Trinity. Meanwhile, Edward Creutz was waiting in Pajarito Canyon with a dummy Fat Man, which he would use in a test of the symmetry of the spherical explosive wave—the test Kistiakowsky thought was an unnecessary complication. The best lenses remaining after the assembly of the Trinity Fat Man were sent to Creutz.

A cavalcade of cars and trucks now began to leave Los Alamos for Trinity—not all at once but departing gradually. Philip Morrison carried the plutonium core and the tiny initiator in the back seat of a car that left on July 12. The core was snugly fitted inside a magnesium box, which had holes for ventilation and was covered with rubber shock absorbers for the drive. When the plutonium arrived at Trinity, the young officer responsible for delivery, Lieutenant Vaughn Richardson, found Bainbridge at the base of the tower and asked for a receipt in exchange for his unusual cargo. Bainbridge instead directed him to the McDonald ranch house, which was being used as a makeshift laboratory for the final assembly of the bomb's core. There General Farrell signed the receipt and turned the core and initiator over to Louis Slotin, who then co-signed.

The same day, Kenneth Greisen, part of the team that developed the detonators for Fat Man, drove them down to Trinity in his Oldsmobile for final insertion in the bomb. Along the way, he was pulled over by the New Mexico Highway Patrol for speeding. He worried that the officer would want to check his trunk and Greisen would be forced to say that he couldn't answer any questions about the contents. To his relief, Greisen was simply issued a speeding ticket and sent on his way.

As Oppenheimer prepared to leave Los Alamos, he told his wife in confidence that if the event in the desert was successful, he would send her the message "You can change the sheets." In turn, Kitty gave him a four-leaf clover she had found in their garden.

At a little past one o'clock a.m. on July 13, under cover of night and accompanied by a convoy of army trucks, the pre-assembled Fat Man itself began the journey to Trinity. Kistiakowsky, riding in the lead car, fell asleep somewhere between Los Alamos and Santa Fe. Suddenly he was awakened by sirens and flashing lights. The MPs, anxious to protect their cargo, had decided to warn the few cars on the road to let them pass. Kistiakowsky told them not to do the same thing when they drove through Albuquerque.

The convoy drove south through Albuquerque on U.S. Highway 85, passing through the small towns of Belen, Lemitar, Socorro, and San Antonio. Turning east in San Antonio onto U.S. 380 toward Carrizozo, they entered the shadowed valley of the Jornada just as light appeared on the horizon. Twelve miles down the road, at a sign that read "Stallion Gate," the tired drivers turned south onto the unmarked road to Trinity. The darkened form of the Oscura Mountains in the east broke the monotonous landscape. After a few miles, they reached the first checkpoint.

The convoy threw up clouds of dirt as it bounced along the rutted, unpaved road across the valley floor. Drivers could see little in front of them or behind. They passed a security tower and MPs in army jeeps with long FM antennas. At last, after stopping at a road block, the convoy turned right, passed another guard post, and in the distance caught its first view of the tall metal tower at Ground Zero.

The plutonium core was ready for final assembly at the McDonald ranch house. Two of the rooms had been thoroughly cleaned and the windows sealed. To minimize the chance of dirt getting into the weapon, the walls and floor had been scrubbed and the entire room sealed by covering every corner with six-inch-wide tape.

Marshall Holloway was responsible for the pit assembly, the final merging of the fissionable material and tamper. He was assisted by Bacher, Slotin, Daghlian, and several others. They gathered on Friday morning, July 13, in one of the sterile rooms, where a horizontal steel beam had been placed within inches of the ceiling and braced by vertical metal supports. The beam allowed the men to employ a standard, one-half ton Yale chain hoist to lift and maneuver the heavy uranium pieces.

Holloway's men, wearing white gowns and gloves, gently laid the plutonium hemispheres on a table covered with ordinary brown wrapping paper and inspected them carefully, then they did the same with the initiator. Both the plutonium and the initiator were slightly warm from internal radioactivity. They then inspected a U238 cylinder with rounded ends, which was part of the bomb's tamper. It had been cut in half lengthwise and hollowed in the middle to accept the double balls of Pu239 and initiator. When originally cast, the uranium was silver colored, but it quickly oxidized, first turning blue, then the color of eggplant. The core was inserted and the two uranium pieces mated to one another and attached on each end. It was as if a tennis ball had been placed midway in a large beer can. To make sure there were no gaps between the two halves, sheets of gold foil were inserted to act as a gasket. The men worked slowly and cautiously, and it wasn't until mid-afternoon that they were ready to drive the fully assembled plug, protected in a wooden box punctured with air holes, to Ground Zero.

While Holloway worked on the plug, Bacher and his team prepared to lift Fat Man from the truck. A twenty-thousand-dollar heavy-duty electrical hoist had been installed on an L-shaped rig above the cabin at the top of the tower—what Bainbridge called the "house"—which could be rotated 360 degrees. This flexibility permitted the hoist to lift equipment to the cabin from the side or up the middle of the tower through a trap door in the cabin floor.

At one o'clock, a second team of men gathered at the tower. Kistiakowsky had chosen this time—the thirteenth hour of the thirteenth day—because he considered it auspicious, though few men caught his historical allusion to the eleventh hour of the eleventh day of the eleventh month, when the guns of World War I had fallen silent. The truck from Los Alamos carrying Fat Man pulled up to the tower and backed in, directly under the "house." The pine box was disassembled and the plastic wrapping removed. A heavy U-shaped steel bracket, six feet wide, was attached to opposite sides of the sphere and connected to the hoist. The gadget was carefully lifted from the bed of the truck and suspended as the vehicle was moved out of the way, then it was lowered to the floor. A white tent in the shape of a peaked box was erected around the bomb to shield it from prying eyes and dust. Meanwhile, the plug was driven to the tower from the ranch house.

Norris Bradbury now stepped in with Kistiakowsky and the rest of his assembly team. The Fat Man sphere, still attached to the U-shaped bracket, had been positioned directly below the cabin ten stories up and pivoted so that the polar cap faced up. In that position, the men had easy access to the trap door in the casing and the dummy plug and lenses. When the cap and a temporary aluminum plug were removed, the first of two plastic mock lenses, one on top of the other—the shape and size of the real explosives stored in nearby boxes—was visible. The dummy lenses were slowly removed one at a time with a portable job hoist and a suction cup to avoid damaging the real explosives already in position. Finally, the wooden dummy plug with the brass top was withdrawn.

It was now almost three o'clock, and the heat from the afternoon sun was intense. Bradbury and Kistiakowsky waited fifteen minutes for a general inspection to be performed and then turned the bomb over to the Holloway for insertion of the plug. Hovering in the background was a nervous Oppenheimer, his blue denim sleeves rolled above his elbows and his white Trinity security badge hanging from a button on his shirt.

It was stifling in the small tent, which, to minimize dust, had no ventilation. Temperatures soared. In this claustrophobic space, which smelled of sweat and heated canvas, a few men removed their shirts and undershirts. For both documentary and instructional purposes, a movie cameraman captured the operation on sixteen-millimeter film. One still photograph from a single frame of that film would in the years to come symbolize Oppie and the bomb: a darkened profile of his head and pork-pie hat against the lighter background of the canvas tent.

The most difficult part of the final assembly now began. Holloway and members of his G Team prepared to insert the uranium capsule. The dummy plug used during transport was removed using a large metal hook screwed into the brass top. The real plug was far heavier, and an extension rod and job hoist were required to lift it above the opening in the trap door.* The electric hoist was controlled by a hand-held metal box with "up" and "down" buttons. A member of Holloway's team reversed the direction of the motor and, as carefully as he could, lowered the plug into the opening in the bomb, another team member guiding it with a pair of tongs. The plug descended part way then stuck against the wall of the tamper. No gentle shaking with the tongs could dislodge it. Assembly stopped abruptly. This was a potential disaster. To maximize the effect of the uranium tamper, every piece of the bomb's core had been exactingly machined in Los Alamos to fit within a few thousandths of an inch. Oppenheimer lurched forward to take a look. Holloway and Bacher immediately suspected that the desert heat had temporarily affected the plug; something similar had happened in Los Alamos a week earlier. Holloway checked with Roy Thompson, who stood nearby. They agreed to wait a few minutes to see whether it would settle on its own. When Holloway looked again, he saw that the cylinder had dropped neatly into place. With relief, the men realized that the plug had expanded during its two days in the desert. As it rested against the tamper, the temperature of the two parts equalized, permitting one to slip into the other.

Just after six o'clock, Bradbury's High Explosives Group took over again in order to insert the final two explosive lenses. The larger of the two lenses weighed over a hundred pounds, requiring use of the hoist. Small pieces of blotter paper were stuffed between lenses where the fit was not precise. Although it proved unnecessary, there was also a grease gun with a small tip handy to ease together parts that were too tight.

Shortly before the circular metal shield was reattached and the bomb sealed, Boyce McDaniel inserted a long manganese wire into a

---

* The plug was eight and three-quarters inches long and five inches thick and weighed approximately 105 pounds.

hypodermic tube that had been pre-inserted into the center of the bomb. The wire would be withdrawn at regular intervals, checked with a Geiger counter for any abnormal rise in radioactivity, and replaced with a fresh one. McDaniel was originally scheduled to be with Raemer Schreiber as part of the laboratory team at Tinian. At the last minute, however, it was decided that one of them needed to stay and work on the Fat Man test. They flipped a coin: Schreiber went to Tinian and McDaniel to Trinity.

The assembly complete, Fat Man was turned upright and left under the tent, guarded by MPs until Saturday morning. Oppenheimer relaxed and left the tent to light a cigarette.

At eight o'clock on the morning of July 14, the canvas tent was disassembled and the bomb in its bracket was slowly lifted to the top of the tower through the trapdoor in the cabin floor. When the bomb was four or five feet off the ground, the hoist paused so that Bradbury's men could place a stack of mattresses underneath it. Each mattress was folded over twice and wrapped in black plastic, resembling a dark bale of hay. Bradbury hoped the mattresses would serve as insurance in case the winch failed: "We were scared to death we would drop it, because we didn't trust the hoist.... It wasn't that we were afraid of setting it off, but that we might damage it in some way."[2] As it rose, most of the men there had their last look at the Fat Man sphere. The broad strips of white tape covering the thirty-two detonator holes made it look bandaged as if wounded. When the bomb reached the cabin, the opening in the floor was replaced with three panels of wood planking, and the bomb was rested in a special metal cradle. The corrugated metal walls and ceiling would be put in place later.

At nine o'clock, a team headed by Greisen climbed the tower to attach the detonators, X-unit, electrical cables, and other equipment, procedures that took half a day. After various tests were performed, all five pairs of electrical leads and one coaxial lead to the bomb were disconnected. Bradbury had given Greisen precise instructions:

Before the detonators are mounted on the sphere all electrical leads to the x-unit will be broken by removing the double female- or double male-ended extension leads which are required to connect this unit to any source of power—signal or anything else. It is understood that this involved a total of 5 pairs plus one co-axial lead.... These leads will be removed from the tower and locked up by the parties concerned with their re-insertion.[3]

Another series of leads was taken from a black box—known as the informer because of its function of giving electrical instructions—and similarly stored. Both Bradbury and Kistiakowsky climbed the tower to verify that the leads were disconnected. Once these cables were removed, no further tests of the detonators or the electrical system were possible. At the same time, the bomb could not be detonated by accident or by the electrical system. Thirteen and a half pounds of plutonium and five thousand pounds of high explosives were effectively dormant. Bradbury's thorough "hot run" schedule concluded with two items:

Sunday the 15th: Look for rabbit's feet and four leaf clovers.
Monday the 16th: BANG!

For the moment, the men of Trinity had an unexpected respite. It was a strange feeling after weeks of exhausting eighteen-hour workdays to find that on Saturday afternoon there was little to do. Scientists tweaked their experiments. They conducted tests of electrical circuits in the bunkers and shelters and completed last-minute positioning of equipment. Now it was a matter of waiting for the test itself. Then potentially calamitous news arrived from Los Alamos.

Creutz had detonated the dummy Fat Man in a magnetic field in Pajarito Canyon in a test of explosive simultaneity, and there was bad news. He immediately telexed a coded message to Oppenheimer warning him that the real bomb, the one on the tower, was not likely to work properly. The explosives would go off all right, but the symmetrical series of shock waves would not converge as required. A dark cloud descended on everyone, especially Oppenheimer. The Trinity test would go on as scheduled because too much had been invested to simply pack up and return to the Hill. But now more than two years of work seemed destined to fail.

Oppenheimer bore the news as bravely as he could, but the façade was thin. Those around him could see that the lack of sleep, the endless cigarettes of the last few days, and now this terrible news had brought him to edge of collapse. And tomorrow, he would have to explain all this to General Groves. Anger turned against Kistiakowsky who, more than anyone, was responsible for the lens configuration:

> Everybody ... became terribly upset and focused on my presumed guilt. Oppenheimer, General Groves, Vannevar Bush— all had much to say about that incompetent wretch who forever after would be known to the world as the cause of the tragic failure of the Manhattan Project. Jim Conant, a close personal friend, had me on the carpet it seemed for hours, coldly quizzing me about the causes of the impending failure.... Sometime later that day [Saturday] Bacher and I were walking in the desert and as I timidly questioned the results of the magnetic test. Bob accused me of challenging no less than Maxwell's equations* themselves![4]

---

* Maxwell's equations are a set of partial differential equations that, together with the Lorentz force law, form the foundation of classical electrodynamics, classical optics, and electric circuits.

But Kistiakowsky's question was a good one: Were the analysis and calculations wrong? Still working late at night in his Los Alamos office, Bethe wondered the same thing and undertook a closer examination of the results.

Oppenheimer's day was made worse by having to drive late Saturday afternoon to Albuquerque to greet visiting dignitaries and army representatives, who were beginning to gather at the Hilton Hotel for the trip to Trinity on Sunday. He had no choice but to share the dark news. Joseph Hirschfelder from Los Alamos was there, and as soon as he saw his director's long face he knew something was terribly wrong.

For two years, the work of the laboratory had seemed to lurch back and forth between failure and success. On Sunday morning, July 16, the gloom of the previous day disappeared as suddenly as it had set in. In a coded message from the Hill, Bethe reported that he had reanalyzed the results of Creutz's experiment on the basis of electromagnetic theory. His reappraisal suggested that the implosion *was* symmetrical. Now the only concern was the one great unpredictable—the weather.

Oppenheimer was relieved but remained tired, fretting and moving nervously from one place to another. The tension occasionally made him snappish. Bob Krohn overheard a brief exchange between Oppenheimer and Frederick Reines, who mentioned that he was glad the test was near because he had been working hard. Oppenheimer looked at him and curtly replied, "What? Working on your face?"[5]

A few months earlier, Bainbridge had been asked by Richard Tolman and General Farrell, perhaps under urging from Groves, to keep Oppenheimer away from the final assembly of Fat Man and the tower at Ground Zero. They feared that Oppenheimer's state of mind might be affected adversely by the tension preceding the test. Bainbridge balked. Fat Man belonged to Oppenheimer as much as to anyone, and under no circumstances would he forbid his director's presence during any phase of the test: "No way. The bomb was Robert's baby and he would and did follow every detail of its development until the very end."[6]

Joe McKibben had the complex job of supplying the timing and remote operating signals that not only detonated the bomb, but controlled experiments spread over the desert. Hundreds of miles of wire had been laid, and every scientist whose equipment required a control wire wanted McKibben personally to inspect *his* circuit. McKibben and a colleague had built the timing device: "Charles Tuner and I designed a timing drum. The drum was to make one revolution per second starting at minus 45 seconds. Two rows of pins were placed on the drum to activate a pair of micro switches. These operated the stick-polar relay that reversed the current in the twisted pair lines to the four stations."[7] The "stations" were the North, West, and South bunkers, where observational and control equipment was located, as well as a smaller bunker at West 800 yards, which would activate the equipment near Ground Zero and Fat Man in the tower.

The fate of the test depended on McKibben's equipment, a burden that weighed heavily on him. He conducted numerous dry runs, even before Fat Man was lifted into the tower's cabin. Everything worked, but there were some scary moments. "On one of these dry runs there was a lightning storm between S 10,000 and the tower. A consequence of this storm was that ... the detonator circuit ignited prematurely. The early ignition was observed as a voltage drop on a meter connected to the detonator voltage supply." McKibben fixed the problem by connecting a twisted-pair line in series with the line between W 800 and the arming relays.[8]

More visitors from Los Alamos arrived and were driven by bus to view the test from Compañia Hill, some twenty miles northwest of Ground Zero, from which they would have an unobstructed view. Oppenheimer had prepared a memorandum for the observers, instructing them about the departure time, what to wear (it would be cold at night), the use of goggles and welder's glass, and the danger of rattlesnakes, but it did not warn them about rain. Before leaving Los Alamos, Teller bumped into

Robert Serber and asked him what he planned to do about rattlesnakes. "I'll take along a bottle of whiskey," Serber replied. Teller then remembered that Serber had been at Oppenheimer's summer conference in 1942 when the possibility of igniting the atmosphere had first been raised. What would Serber do if *that* happened? He thought a moment and replied, "Take a second bottle of whiskey."[9]

Cars were dispatched to Santa Fe and Albuquerque to pick up the last of the notables. Among them were Charles Thomas, the Manhattan District's coordinator for chemical research, Ernest Lawrence, Sir James Chadwick, and William L. Laurence of the *New York Times*, the only newsman allowed to cover the test. Others, including Tolman, Lauritsen, Rabi, Sir Geoffrey Taylor, and von Neumann, were expected later in the day. By the time everyone arrived, there would be over 425 scientists and observers in addition to the military contingent.

On Sunday afternoon before Groves arrived, Oppenheimer made the climb to the top of the tower. He wanted to see Fat Man one last time. Exercising great care, he took almost fifteen minutes to reach the top, the metal bars of the ladder, which had baked in the desert sun for hours, burning his hands. The cabin was small and dominated by the dark object in the center, with little space to maneuver around it. He was alone. The smell was a mixture of heated canvas and corrugated metal. Connected to all its cables, Fat Man looked like a hospital patient. Two and a half years of success and failure, dead ends and false starts, were embodied in that large sphere. The gadget was both beautiful and ugly.

Oppenheimer reached over and touched the device at a place where the surface was clear of cables. It was mildly warm, but from the sun and not radioactivity. It was time to go. The cabin was one place where he could not smoke.

Groves, Bush, and Conant arrived around five in the afternoon. After a quick bite to eat at the mess hall, Groves found Oppenheimer in the middle of a group of excited scientists, all animatedly urging that the test be postponed. The general was alarmed: "There was an air of excitement at the camp that I did not like, for this was a time when calm deliberation was most essential. Oppenheimer was getting advice from all sides as to what should and should not be done."[10]

Storm clouds were gathering in the distance, and the rain and lightning that Hubbard had warned about were now predicted to arrive around midnight. Hubbard himself was in the group around Oppenheimer, arguing that the weather was unstable and repeating over and over that he had *never* liked July 16 as a test date. With the best meteorological equipment at his disposal, he knew the weather was going to be bad, although it would clear eventually—maybe by three a.m., maybe by four. He couldn't be certain at this stage. Hubbard talked at length about cloud layers, variable winds, and other factors. For Groves and Oppenheimer, the questions were simple—would the weather clear or not? And if so, when?

Groves, who later remembered Hubbard as "frantic and incoherent," wrote off his advice. "I had completely abandoned Hubbard.... Oppenheimer may have talked to him over the telephone but I would have paid no attention to any advice given by Hubbard at this time. He had failed and in my opinion at the time had failed miserably."[11] Groves then turned to a second meteorologist, air force Colonel Ben Holzman, whom he had personally recruited for the test, for a second opinion. Unfortunately, Holzman agreed with Hubbard. Groves was irritated. "Many of Oppenheimer's advisors at the base camp (and by six p.m. these included not only the senior scientists, but many in secondary positions) were urging that the test be postponed for at least twenty-four hours."[12]

As quickly as he could, Groves pulled Oppenheimer aside for a private, calmer discussion about the weather. Groves thought the test should go on as planned, although they could make a final decision about the precise time later in the evening. The general had support for his position. Oppenheimer's colleague and confidant Robert Bacher made it plain that delaying the test by one day would actually delay it for two or three days. His team of scientists, who knew Fat Man as well as anyone did, were exhausted, and he wasn't sure they could bounce back in twenty-four hours. A delay, he warned, "would be dangerous."[13] Kenneth Bainbridge was equally adamant: a postponement beyond the 16th would mean "holding things up for many days before we could get back to the peak we had achieved at that point."[14]

In the end, it was Groves who made the final decision. "There was only one dissenting vote that could have called off the test," he recalled. "And that was my own. The operation was not run like a faculty meeting. Advice was sought and carefully considered but then decisions were made by those responsible. There was no one but myself to carry this responsibility."[15]

Groves, Oppenheimer, and the other leaders of the project met again at eleven o'clock that night, but the sky was a dull gray-black. Not a star could be seen through the overcast. The decision was again postponed until one a.m.

Fermi tried to relieve the tension with humor, which Groves did not at first appreciate:

> I had become a bit annoyed with Fermi ... when he suddenly offered to take wagers from his fellow scientists on whether or not the bomb would ignite the atmosphere, and if so, whether it would merely destroy New Mexico or destroy the world.... Afterwards, I realized that his talk had served to smooth down the frayed nerves and ease the tensions of the people at base camp.[16]

The general urged Oppenheimer to get some sleep, and he himself retired to a tent at Base Camp that he shared with Bush and Conant—a number of green tents with white roofs had been set up for special visitors—and slept for an hour. Oppenheimer couldn't sleep. He spent the time pacing around, lighting cigarettes, and discussing the situation with others at the camp—discussions that only agitated him further.

At a little past one, Groves and Oppenheimer drove to the command bunker at South 10,000. It was small and congested, and tension was high. General Farrell, who was assigned to witness the test from the bunker, watched Groves do everything he could to calm Oppenheimer:

> The scene inside the shelter was dramatic beyond words. In and around the shelter were some twenty-odd people concerned with last-minute arrangements prior to firing the shot.... For some hectic two hours preceding the blast, General Groves stayed with the Director, walking with him and steadying his tense excitement. Every time the Director would be about to explode because of some untoward happening, General Groves would take him off and walk with him in the rain, counseling with him and reassuring him that everything would be all right.[17]

At the same time, Bainbridge gathered his arming party together at Base Camp and drove to the tower. He was relieved to see that there was no lightning in the immediate area. With him were Captain Bush, Lieutenant Lloyd, Sergeants Alderson and Stewart, Hubbard, McKibben, and Kistiakowsky. "We drove to point zero in 3 cars and then we stayed there while Jack Hubbard, Alderson and Stewart continued their weather measurements as we wanted the best and latest information at all levels in that area."[18] On the way to the tower, Bainbridge stopped at South 10,000 and locked the main arming switches.

Instructions for watching the test had been issued earlier to observers. At Base Camp, a short siren would sound five minutes before the test. At that time everyone was to face south, away from Ground Zero. Three minutes later a long siren would sound, and people were then to sit on the ground, preferably in a shallow depression, with their faces and eyes directed away from the expected explosion. Everyone was to remain in this position until the blast wave passed over, about fifty seconds after the explosion. Two short blasts would signal that it was safe to rise. Observers could then turn and look at Ground Zero through welder's goggles and a two-inch-by-four-inch piece of special glass. The glass had been issued in an envelope with a statement certifying that it met federal specifications for use in arc welding helmets. Similar instructions were given to the men on Compañia Hill.

Interest in the test was also high in Los Alamos. Many men who were not assigned to Trinity or Compañia Hill decided to try for a view of the shot from the roads around Trinity or from one of several mountains near Los Alamos. The laboratory's Intelligence Office heard of these plans and tried to discourage them. Security precautions were intensified just before the test. All telephone conversations were secretly monitored, and agents in Santa Fe and other small towns were alerted to catch infractions. One scientist told a companion at the La Fonda Hotel in Santa Fe that a drive to Socorro in the early morning would bring a sight that the man would never see again. Unknown to the scientist, his companion was a confidential informant, who turned the scientist's name in to the Security Office.[19] The scientist eventually resigned.

On Sunday at five o'clock p.m., MPs at each gate to Los Alamos began to record mileage readings from all automobiles leaving the Hill. These records were compared against the mileage upon return, and at least ten men were suspected of having traveled far enough to view the explosion. Three other Los Alamos men were apprehended on Sunday on Highway 380 near Carthage and were taken to a security checkpoint sixty miles away. Others, including a few wives, were more surreptitious. They drove or hiked only a few miles away from Los Alamos to mountain tops where they had relatively unobstructed views of southern New Mexico. There were not enough security men to monitor the movement of every man and woman in Los Alamos on the eve of Trinity. Some of them inevitably made it to a high point where they hoped to catch sight of the explosion, even 220 miles away.

At Trinity, tension and excitement mounted. Bainbridge continued his rounds, checking and rechecking everything he could. Groves asked Bainbridge, Kistiakowsky, and Lieutenant Bush to spend the night at the tower. In addition, he asked for someone to sit with the bomb until shortly before final arming, just to be sure that there were no intruders and nothing unforeseen happened to Fat Man. Hornig was chosen for the last shift at midnight. He spent the evening alone in the tower except for occasional visits from someone checking a circuit or taking a reading. He planned to read a book titled, *Desert Island Decameron*. Hornig sat in the cabin on a folding chair, the only light coming from a single sixty-watt bulb hanging from the ceiling. He could see the bomb's thirty-two detonators connected by a web of cables to the five-hundred-pound electronic X-unit, which he had designed. A signal sent from South 10,000 would activate it and shoot high-voltage electrical charges to each of the detonators.

It was a long, lonely evening for Hornig: "All I had was a telephone. I wasn't equipped to defend myself, I don't know what I was supposed to do. There were no instructions! The possibility of lightning striking the tower was very much on my mind."[20] The tower was grounded, but if it that failed and lightning caused the explosives to go off, Hornig would never know it. He tried to read his book but eventually gave up. The rising wind whipped the metal walls and shook the canvas flap so violently that it threatened to come undone and drench both him and the bomb. The light swung back and forth like a pendulum and flickered throughout the evening. When lightning flashed in the distance, the canvas wall turned beige-white as if lit by a thousand flash bulbs going off at once. His last visitor, Boyce McDaniel, climbed the tower at two o'clock to pull the manganese wire and take one last reading. The bomb was still stable. Presently, Hornig got the call to come down. He disconnected the firing circuit from the dummy control unit used during equipment checks and reconnected it to the live control circuit, made a final check of the connections that ran to the bomb, and then left. He was very likely the last person to see Fat Man.

Gripping each wet rung as tightly as he could, Hornig descended the ladder and left for Base Camp. "It was pouring, and I went back to the canteen, had some coffee, and sat around waiting to see what was going to happen next because nobody knew whether we could fire. Trucks were sliding off the road into ditches everywhere.... The whole desert was under water, and the roads, which were bad under any circumstance, were muck. It was very, very depressing."[21] Finally, at 4:30 he drove to the South Shelter, where he would be responsible for flipping a switch that could stop the test in an emergency. He called it the "chicken switch." If anything went awry with the automatic firing devices or with some critical part of the system, he could close down the firing circuit to prevent an explosion. Hornig had been up seventy-two hours straight.

Groves and Oppenheimer met with the meteorologists as planned at two a.m., just as a drizzle and occasional flashes of lightning turned to rain and wind. Hubbard said four o'clock was no longer possible because the thunderstorm would not have passed through by then. At 3:30 Groves set Zero Hour for 5:30 a.m. Only a catastrophe would stop the test now. Groves was unhappy with the fluid situation, once again blaming the meteorologists, and took matters into his own hands.

> The decision to fire the bomb at 5:30 was made by me after thorough discussion with Oppenheimer. I believed at the time it was a decision he would have taken too, but whether he would have done so without my presence I do not know. At any rate the decision was made not by reference to any high altitude winds or anything else except looking up at the sky and trying to guess how much cloud cover there was.[22]

If all went according to plan, Fat Man would now explode just before dawn. Oppenheimer was not the only one to catch the significance of the timing: a new sun rising just before the old. Groves captured these last tense hours in a report later sent to Stimson, suggesting somewhat disingenuously that Oppenheimer had participated in the decision-making:

> After about an hour of sleep I got up at 0100 and from that time on until about five I was with Dr. Oppenheimer constantly. Naturally he was nervous, although his mind was working at its usual extraordinary efficiency. I devoted my entire attention to shielding him from the excited and generally faulty advice of his assistants who were more than disturbed by their excitement and the uncertain weather conditions. By 0330 we decided that we could probably fire by 0530. By 0400 the rain had stopped but the sky was heavily overcast. Our decision became firmer as time went on. During most of these hours the two of us journeyed from the control house out into the darkness to look at the stars and to assure each other that the one or two visible stars were becoming brighter.[23]

On the ground, spectators and scientists moved into shelters or into the buildings of Base Camp to get out of the rain, although some hardier souls remained outside. Those on Compañia Hill took cover as best they could, whether in cars and buses or under tarpaulins, and shivered in the cold night air as the temperature dropped.

Hubbard and Bainbridge issued a final weather report forty-five minutes after the rain stopped: "Winds aloft very light, variable to 40,000, surface calm. Inversion about 17,000 feet. Conditions holding for next two hours. Sky now broken, becoming scattered."[24] When Hubbard told him that the winds now favored a test, Bainbridge was relieved: "This looked good as far as the safety of the people in the observation post and in the main camp. There were a few clouds but this was going improve with time. So...we decided to go ahead with the test."[25]

Shortly after four o'clock, Groves returned to Base Camp in a jeep, leaving Farrell at the bunker to watch over Oppenheimer.

Zero Hour was now firmly set for 5:30 a.m.

Bainbridge gathered his arming party and drove to the tower shortly before five o'clock. They had barely thirty minutes to complete their work. At the base of the tower, he opened the locked box containing four master switches and closed each of them. The party quickly drove to the small W 800 bunker, where McKibben threw another set of switches. Using an ohmmeter, he "determined that all the outgoing lines were still continuous [working] except the line that closed the arming relays, which was open inside a locked box at S 10,000."[26] McKibben threw the main bank of timing and sequence switches as Bainbridge called them out from the checklist he read by flashlight. From W 800, they rushed back to the tower, where Bainbridge threw the special arming switch and connected the arming, power, firing, and informer leads. Every step he took was called by FM radio to South bunker, where Williams, working with a copy of the checklist, could catch any step that was out of order or missed. A bank of searchlights bathed the tower in a harsh light, giving B-29 reconnaissance planes a view of the target. Kistiakowsky climbed halfway up the tower to adjust a searchlight that illuminated the cupola for experiments at West 10,000.

As he left the tower, Bainbridge broadcast the weather report by radio to outlying shelters and to the teams on Compañia Hill. Coordinating the activities on the hill was David Dow, who kept in contact with the main bunker by shortwave radio.

At the North bunker, the photographer Berlyn Brixner pulled the tarp off of the cameras on the roof. Sixteen-millimeter and thirty-five-millimeter movie cameras, specially designed to run between one and 650 frames per second, were ready to capture the explosion on both color and black-and-white film. Brixner also positioned a Mitchell thirty-five-millimeter studio camera and four Kodak black-and-white cameras to shoot a "panorama" of the explosion and follow the expected fireball as it rose into the sky. More than fifty motion picture cameras were scattered over the desert. All were electronically connected to the command bunker and would begin filming thirty seconds before detonation.

The North bunker was jammed not only with photographic equipment but with several racks of electronics that controlled, among other things, a number of John Manley's experiments. Data came into the bunker over cables or from FM transmitters attached to poles. To the right of the twelve-foot doorway was a periscope that would safely project an image of the explosion onto a screen on the wall.

At South 10,000, Bainbridge unlocked the primary firing switches shortly after five o'clock. McKibben started the automatic timers at 5:09. In twenty minutes, a more precise timer would automatically take over, and, just seconds before making the final connection, it would alert a second bank of switches to activate instruments arrayed across the desert floor.

An urgent call from Kirtland Air Base in Albuquerque brought word from Parsons that the weather there was so bad that the base commander would not let the observation airplanes take off. The test could not be postponed any further, so Parsons was told he would have to arrive whenever he could. After considerable argument, the planes were released, but the pilots became disoriented in the overcast skies and arrived at Trinity too late to drop their special gauges. Parsons, Alvarez, and others from Los Alamos remained observers from a distance.

Everyone moved into place. At the South shelter, Oppenheimer, Farrell, Bainbridge, and Kistiakowsky gathered inside the cramped bunker. Hornig sat at the master control panel to the right of the entrance and Allison at a small desk to the left with his clock, a microphone, and the controls to Trinity's public address system. SED Val Fitch and his boss, Ernest Titterton, were responsible for making timing measurements on the bomb as well as providing time markers for other experiments, but the most important function of the bank of electronics they commanded was to send the signal to detonate the gadget. Only Hornig, with his "chicken switch," could stop the test if something went wrong. Standing behind him was Oppenheimer. Joe McKibben quickly positioned a small movie camera in front of a panel of four meters that monitored the test's elaborate timing system. Then he flipped on a set of small floodlights that illuminated the panel and its meters.

Wilson and his team were at the North bunker. Manley and others waited at West. At Base Camp, Fermi, Rabi, Holloway, and Lieutenant Bush took their places on the ground in a shallow depression. A few men made last-minute adjustments to their equipment. Robert Krohn made light conversation with Fermi and asked him whether the goggles and welder's glass were really necessary. Fermi said he didn't know, but what was going to happen was too important to miss.[27] Groves lay down on a tarpaulin laid over the sand, Compton on one side of him, Conant and Bush on the other. Compton whispered that he never imagined that a few seconds could take so long.

On Compañia Hill, Teller reminded everyone that the blast could produce a burn comparable to a bad sunburn and passed around army-issue sun ointment. He put on a pair of dark glasses and a pair of welder's glasses. Nearby, Richard Feynmann, Klaus Fuchs, James Chadwick, and Geoffrey Taylor made themselves as comfortable as possible on the chilly hill.

As Allison continued the countdown on the project's radio channel, a California station briefly crossed frequencies with Trinity, and the "Star-Spangled Banner" interrupted the countdown. Forty miles away in Carrizozo, Alvin and Elizabeth Graves waited in a motel room with a barograph to record shock waves. In nearby San Antonio, army MPs broke the rules and woke the Owl Bar's owner, Jose Miera, telling him that if he came outside he would see something never seen before. Campers from Los Alamos in the Chupadera Mountains near Socorro and a few Hill wives in the mountains above Los Alamos waited in hopes of seeing the flash of light.

At Potsdam, President Truman was preparing to take a tour of war-ravaged Berlin and Hitler's bunker.

Last-minute wagers of a dollar were made on the size of Fat Man's explosion. Norman Ramsey bet his dollar on a small explosion, just one ton. Teller bet on forty-five thousand tons, Oppenheimer on three thousand, and Rabi on twenty thousand.

From his various meteorological instruments, Hubbard noted that the temperature was 71.2 degrees and the surface winds calm. At ten thousand feet, the winds were at fourteen knots.

Over Trinity's radio, Allison's calm voice gave the countdown at five-minute intervals. Oppenheimer grew so shaky that he clung to a post to steady himself and stared straight ahead. At minus forty-five seconds the precision timer took over and a small bell began to chime every second. Now only Hornig could stop the process. Williams, Bainbridge, and Kistiakowsky rushed outside the shelter. All were silent except for Allison, who seated at his desk, counted down to zero and then shouted, "Now!" It was 5:29:45 a.m.

———————

As soon as the automated firing circuit closed at the command bunker, the electronic X-unit on the side of the bomb discharged, sending five thousand volts to thirty-two detonators, which in turn simultaneously ignited the outer row of fast-burning explosive lenses. The initial explosive wave was reformed by the slower-burning inserts of Baratol and became concave. The imploding wave ignited the inner layer of Comp B explosives and accelerated, slamming into the aluminum pusher and tamper, liquefying them, and ultimately compressing the Pu239 core and its initiator. At that instant, the beryllium and polonium combined to generate a flood of neutrons that took the core from subcritical to supercritical. Only eighty generations of neutrons hitting atoms and freeing other neutrons were needed to release an incomprehensible amount of energy. All this took place in a millionth of a second.

The tower's cupola disappeared in a ball of light and heat thirty feet in diameter, which reached a temperature of one million degrees Fahrenheit. A hundredth of a second later, it expanded to a diameter of eight hundred feet and cooled to eight thousand degrees.

What first struck witnesses was light—a stupendous burst of extreme light more brilliant than a dozen mid-day suns—followed by warmth. The surrounding desert and mountains were instantly washed in white brilliance. Even those with their eyes closed and their backs to the tower were able to sense the explosion of light and feel the heat on their bodies. All over Trinity, observers instinctively turned toward the light, forgetting their instructions to wait until the blast wave passed over before turning toward Ground Zero. Almost everyone was momentarily blinded and dazed. Those recovering first saw through their welder's glasses a huge ball of fire, like the sun, rising majestically from the desert floor in a swirling inferno of reds and oranges and yellows. It was an intense, terrible beauty.

At North 10,000, the Fastax camera screamed as its motor burned through hundreds of feet of film in a few seconds capturing the fireball as it rose in slow motion. Brixner jumped from behind the bunker to the roof and grabbed the aiming controls of the five movie cameras designed to capture a panorama view of the fireball. He stayed at it for several minutes.

At North 10,000 Manley and the others caught their first glimpse of the explosion through the projection periscope as light flooded in from the open door at the rear of the bunker. Everyone ran out the door to see the luminous cloud rising.

The fireball rose from a darker stem, becoming less intense, though it still lit the mountains behind, taking on a bluish haze at its perimeter. Everyone stood mute and transfixed by the play of lights. Forty-five seconds later, the shock wave hit. Two men standing outside at South 10,000 were knocked down. Then came a loud crack, followed by a tremendous roar that thundered across the desert in a wave of sound, jolting everyone who was standing, shaking small blades of grass, and spilling into the burrows of small animals before echoing against the distant mountains. Five minutes later the valley still rumbled.

Groves was dazzled more by the light and fireball than the shock wave, which he thought was rather gentle. To him, the fireball was shaped like a derby hat. "But the light had been so much greater than any human had previously experienced or even than we had anticipated that we did not shake off the experience quickly."[28] Groves turned silently to shake hands with Bush and Conant.

General Farrell, who was with Oppenheimer at South 10,000, said the explosion was "unprecedented and terrifying. The fireball lit every peak and crevasse with a beauty and clarity that no one could describe."[29]

Fermi's first impression was that of an intense flash of light followed by a sensation of heat on his body. When he rose to look toward Ground Zero, he saw the mushroom rise quickly to over thirty thousand feet. As he waited calmly for the shock wave, he tore a sheet of paper into small pieces that he dropped one by one as the air blast hit him. By watching the distance they traveled, he was able roughly to calculate the force of the explosion. Fermi's experiment would have looked like madness except that people were too awestruck by what they saw in the distance to notice such a small thing close at hand.

On Compañia Hill, dazed observers felt the heat on their arms and faces as their eyes struggled to adjust to the brilliant light. As soon as Victor Weisskopf, at Base Camp, saw the smoke ball surrounded by its blue glow, he guessed it was caused by gamma rays and wondered how much radiation was being emitted: a thousand billion curies? Inside South 10,000, light poured in from behind the shelter, obliterating any details on the bank of four meters that McKibben was filming. Before he remembered that the shock wave had not yet hit, he ducked outside, thinking that "this thing had really gone big."

Bainbridge was overwhelmed. It was oddly satisfying, and his first response was relief that he would not have to climb the tower and examine Fat Man to determine what had gone wrong. On Compañia Hill, the hushed silence gave way to light applause and finally, after many long minutes, to great relief and loud congratulations.

For some there was hesitation and a sense of foreboding. Oppenheimer later said that he recalled the words of the Bhagavad Gita:

> I am become death,
> The shatterer of worlds.

Bainbridge turned to Oppenheimer as the light faded and softly said that they were now all sons of bitches. William Laurence, who watched the blast from Compañia Hill, saw it as the "grand finale of a mighty symphony of the elements, fascinating and terrifying, uplifting and crushing, ominous, devastating, full of great promise and great foreboding."[30]

The light continued to dim, and as it did, morning rose gently from behind the dissipating cloud. The mighty roar softened to a murmur in the mountains and then died out completely. The sense of relief spread. For many, the tension of previous weeks lifted in a feeling of euphoria. Kistiakowsky rushed up to Oppenheimer, put his arm around his shoulders, and reminded him of the bet they had made: his salary for a month against ten dollars from Oppenheimer that the bomb would work. It occurred to him later, in a more reflective moment, "that at the end of the world—in the last millisecond of the earth's existence—the last men will see what we saw."[31]

Oppenheimer drove with Farrell in a jeep back to Base Camp just as the sun moved above the horizon. Along the way, Farrell recounted a story from the First World War of how, as a young lieutenant, he waited for the order to lead his men out of the trench and into combat. "That was nothing like what we have just been through," he told Oppenheimer. The end of the war was near, perhaps the end of all wars, he added. When the two men ran into Groves, Farrell repeated that the war was over. "Yes," replied Groves, "after we drop two bombs on Japan." He then turned to Oppenheimer and congratulated him. "I am proud of you all." Oppenheimer, still dazed by the bomb's success, could only mumble, "Thank you."[32]

The day before the test, bombing runs had been canceled at Alamogordo, angering pilots and crews. For many, the air base was their final training stop before being sent overseas, and most crews needed as many flight hours as they could get. The ban had been scheduled to lift shortly after the test, and Groves learned later that many crews, who knew nothing of what was happening, were already on the airstrips when the blast occurred. Startled by the light, they supposed that something had exploded or, worse, a plane had gone down.

The explosion had been seen elsewhere as well. The first flash of light was witnessed in Albuquerque, Santa Fe, Silver City, Gallup, and El Paso. Windows were broken in Alamogordo, San Antonio, and even Belen and were rattled in Silver City and Gallup. A rancher sleeping near Alamogordo awakened suddenly thinking a plane had crashed in his yard. Wives in the mountains near Los Alamos who were still awake and looking in the right direction saw a great flash of light that lit up the trees and heard—or thought they heard—a long, low rumble. A forest ranger in Silver City reported an earthquake to the Associated Press, and newspapers in Texas and New Mexico received reports of meteors and crashing B-29 bombers. Mary Lapaca of Socorro reported a rocket bomb over her house.

The Associated Press office in Albuquerque soon had a number of queries and reports on a strange explosion in southern New Mexico. Groves had stationed Philip Belcher, an army intelligence officer, at the wire service's office to prevent the release of alarming stories, but by late morning the AP representative felt he had to release some kind of story. If the army had no official story, he told Belcher, the service would issue its own. Groves had prepared for this situation weeks earlier. When Lieutenant Belcher reported the AP's ultimatum, Colonel Eareckson issued one of the prepared news releases from the Alamogordo Bombing Range at noon, Mountain War Time:

Alamogordo, July 16—The Commanding Officer of the Alamogordo Army Air Base made the following statement today: "Several inquiries have been received concerning a heavy explosion which occurred on the Alamogordo Base reservation this morning. A remotely located ammunition magazine containing a considerable amount of high explosives and pyrotechnics exploded. There was no loss of life or injury to anyone, and the property damage outside of the explosives magazine itself was negligible. Weather conditions affecting the content of gas shells exploded by the blast may make it desirable for the Army to evacuate temporarily a few civilians from their homes."[33]

It was a cannily crafted press release, explaining the explosion and setting the stage for a possible evacuation. New Mexico newspapers ran the story in different versions, and it was picked up by a number of radio shows. No follow-up was issued by Alamogordo.

The concern about evacuation was real. It momentarily seemed necessary at Trinity when Dr. Henry Barnett's monitoring crew suddenly at the North bunker noticed their radioactivity counters clicking wildly. Barnett gave the order to evacuate, and soon trucks and jeeps roared down the road to Base Camp. Later it was determined to be a false alarm. The men's film badges showed that no radioactivity had reached the shelter. When a real radioactive cloud passed over another location, the men put on masks. That danger, too, passed, and by 9:30 a.m., Bainbridge gave the order for men at all observation sites to return to Base Camp.

Groves had hoped to consult with Oppenheimer after the test about the next steps for the laboratory, but he had not counted on the stupefying effect of the explosion: "These plans [to hold discussions] proved utterly impracticable, for no one who had witnessed the test was in a frame of mind to discuss anything. The reaction to success was simply too great."[34] At just before seven a.m. Groves used the telephone and scrambler at Base Camp to call Jean O'Leary, who was waiting in their offices. Using a prearranged code, he passed on the news that the bomb had worked. She was now to call Harrison in the War Department and tell him he could send another prearranged message to Potsdam. Harrison sent the news as soon as he got off the phone: "Operated on this morning. Diagnosis not yet complete but results seem satisfactory and already exceed expectations. Local press release necessary as interest extends a great distance. Dr. Groves pleased. He returns tomorrow. I will keep you posted."[35]

When he got the message, Stimson turned to a colleague and remarked, "I have been responsible for spending two billion dollars on this atomic adventure. Now that it is successful I shall not be sent to prison in Fort Leavenworth."[36]

In the mix of fading euphoria and exhaustion that followed the test, Groves managed to have Oppenheimer help him draft a longer, more detailed summary of the technical results for Stimson in Potsdam. He remained at Trinity until Bainbridge concluded that all danger of radioactive fallout had passed. If radioactivity had posed a danger, the general was prepared to act, even to the point of asking the governor to declare martial law.

Seismographs collected valuable information for Groves. A tremor was picked up at a small station nine thousand yards away. At San Antonio, twenty-eight miles away, it was not enough to crack a wall. Other seismographs located farther away detected nothing.[37]

Around three o'clock p.m., Groves joined Vannevar Bush and Conant in the procession of cars back to Albuquerque and his waiting plane. They spent the night in Nashville then flew directly into National Airport in Washington. Groves was back in his office by two o'clock on the afternoon of the 17th, tired but elated at the events of the last two days.

At a little after three o'clock on the day of the test, Bainbridge returned to Base Camp from South 10,000 for something to eat and for some sleep. He would spend one more night in the desert before returning to the Hill. Kistiakowsky and Hornig drove back to Los Alamos. They traded off driving, but they were so tired that they both repeatedly fell asleep at the wheel, driving off the road a half-dozen times. Oppenheimer got into a car with a renewed energy that amazed those who saw him. He seemed to strut, one person observed.

Although it would be weeks before a thorough assessment of the Fat Man could be made, the preliminary assessments showed that the explosive results had been greater than expected. Groves arranged for Stimson and Truman to receive even better news on Tuesday: "Doctor has just returned most enthusiastic and confident that the little boy is as husky as his big brother. The light in his eyes discernable from here to Highhold and I could hear his screams from here to my farm."[38]

Stimson was elated at the news. But he did not yet know that Fat Man more than exceeded the original prediction of ten kilotons of TNT, producing an explosive force well over seventeen kilotons and perhaps as much as twenty. Groves expected the Little Boy uranium gun to be every bit as powerful as Fat Man. These were truly the weapons with which to crush Japan and barter with Stalin, he told Farrell.

From Trinity and Compañia Hill, men began to return to Los Alamos, tired and quiet. Jim Tuck was surprised that no one said a word on the long bus ride back to Los Alamos. His companions were either asleep or lost in their own thoughts. Several hours after the explosion, Fermi and Herbert Anderson, in their lead-lined tanks, were the first to enter Ground Zero, where they took samples of the radioactive earth. The scene was startling—a crater 1,200 feet wide in which all vegetation had vanished. In the center was a shallow bowl nearly 130 feet wide and some nine feet deep. The desert sand had been pulverized and fused into a dull, green glass, which was quickly nicknamed "Trinitite." Five miles away scientists could see Ground Zero shimmering like a giant emerald in the sun. The steel tower had completely disappeared, and a half-mile away Jumbo had been torn from its sturdy metal tower and sat forlornly, right side up, with the tower flattened around it.

Men positioned around Trinity monitored their locations for radioactive fallout. The top of the giant mushroom cloud hovered over the northeast corner of the site for several hours, allowing most of the heavier particles to fall out, while the middle portion drifted to the west and northwest, and the lower section moved eastward. Monitors reported unusually high intensity in a canyon twenty miles northeast of Ground Zero. One mile east of the canyon lived a family with a child, whose presence so close to a hot spot briefly raised the question whether someone should visit them to see how they were "feeling."[39] Late in the day, Farrell called O'Leary to report that it had not been necessary to evacuate anyone, although as O'Leary noted in her log, it "came awfully close in 3 or 4 places but now doesn't appear that they will have to do anything."

Three small teams were sent to inspect the crater and the surrounding area. The first was Fermi and Anderson, but around eleven a.m. two more men in protective clothing and respirators spent an hour photographing Jumbo. At 2:30 p.m., six men with similar protective garb drove in to retrieve neutron detectors. They alit from their jeeps only once and got no closer than five hundred yards. The radioactivity was still so high they were allowed only ten minutes in the test area.

Scientists quickly began to analyze the data collected from the various instruments around Ground Zero. Some experiments were successful, but others were not. Fat Man's yield was twice as great as anticipated, and a number of instruments had been calibrated too low to record the effect they were designed to measure. That was the problem with the piezoelectric blast gauges, for example, and the unexpectedly intense radiation generated by the explosion fogged photographic film.

On Tuesday afternoon, back in his office in Los Alamos, Oppenheimer called O'Leary with messages for Groves. The general had asked Oppenheimer to instruct laboratory personnel to not discuss the test, but that request, Oppenheimer reported to O'Leary, "had been defeated." Everyone was talking about it. He also wanted Groves to know that the bomb was more powerful than the previous day's preliminary assessments had suggested.

The following day, July 18, with Farrell's help, Groves prepared a thirteen-page memorandum titled "The Test." He attached sketches, photographs, copies of news releases, and a statement by Ernest Lawrence. After the barest description of the place and time of the Trinity test, he came to the obvious point: "The test was successful beyond the most optimistic expectations of anyone. Based on the data which it has been possible to work up to date, I estimate the energy generated to be in excess of the equivalent of 15,000 to 20,000 tons of TNT; and this is a conservative estimate."

He went on to describe the light and heat from the fireball and the rising mushroom-shaped cloud, noting that the "huge concentrations of highly radioactive materials resulted from the fission and were contained in this cloud." The blast was so powerful that he no longer considered the Pentagon a "safe shelter" from an atomic bomb. To get his point across, Groves referred to the attached sketch of the Jumbo tower before the explosion and a photograph of it afterwards. He also recounted the last few hours with Oppenheimer before the test. "I devoted my entire attention to shielding him from the excited and generally faulty advice of his assistants who were more than disturbed by their excitement and the uncertain weather conditions."[40]

When the report was finished, Harrison rushed it to the airport, where a special courier plane was waiting to fly it directly to the secretary of war at Potsdam.

The next day, Groves sent an effusive letter to Oppenheimer congratulating him and the laboratory on its success.

Since I returned to Washington I have done little else but think about and talk about the truly magnificent results of the test conducted at Trinity. General Farrell and I have discussed the project in all its many phases and have reviewed it from every

possible angle. We both feel that the job is a high water mark
of scientific and engineering performance. Your leadership and
skill and the loyal and able performance of all your subordinates made it possible.[41]

Later that afternoon, even before Groves's congratulatory letter
arrived, Oppenheimer called him with a provocative suggestion. He proposed "murdering" the Little Boy bomb and using its U235 in an implosion weapon. Doing so, he argued, would increase the number of bombs
that could be made in the next month or so. Oppenheimer would send a
follow-up telex with the details. Groves thought that canceling Little Boy
would be a terrible mistake and that proceeding with the current gun
design was the safer course. Still, the idea intrigued him, and as he had
done in similar situations, he called Conant, described Oppenheimer's
proposal, and said that he thought they should continue with Little Boy.
O'Leary recorded Conant's response: "JB [Conant] stated most emphati-
cally 'SO DO I'. I AGREE WITH YOU 100%." Groves relayed his decision
to Oppenheimer by telex:

> Dear Dr. Oppenheimer: I have received your teletype dated
> July 19, 1945, and have discussed its contents with some of our
> Washington associates. Factors beyond our control prevent us
> from considering any decision other than to proceed according
> to schedules for the time being. It is necessary to drop the first
> Little Boy and the first Fat Man and probably a second one in
> accordance with our original plan. It may be that as many as
> three of the latter in their best present condition may have to
> be dropped to conform with planned strategic operations.[42]

Groves followed his telex with a phone call to Los Alamos. Oppenheimer argued again that using the U235 in a Fat Man would increase the
number of weapons and improve the reliability of the current Fat Man.

No harm would come from the change, which could be accomplished in a week to ten days. The strength of Oppenheimer's argument persuaded Groves to defer a final decision until both men met in Chicago a few days later. There they discussed Oppenheimer's proposal with Tolman, and Groves decided to proceed with Little Boy as designed.

In Chicago, Oppenheimer shared with Groves the latest results of the Trinity test. At ten miles the brilliance of the explosion had been equivalent to that of ten thousand suns, and enough gamma radiation had been emitted to kill every living thing within two-thirds of a mile. Fermi's earlier warning that there was one chance in thirty of Fat Man's destroying New Mexico and one chance in a thousand of destroying the world now seemed amusing, but everyone was quietly relieved that it had proved inaccurate.[43] There was talk of using the bombs in Japan, and Groves had little doubt that the bomb would be used regardless of the consequences.

On July 30, Groves wrote to Stimson with a description of the likely effects of the bomb if used directly on ground troops. "If dropped on the enemy lines, the expected effect on the enemy would be to wipe out his resistance over an area 2000 feet in diameter; to paralyze it over an area of a mile in diameter; and to impede it seriously over an area five miles in diameter."[44]

The same day, Groves submitted a detailed description of the Trinity test to the army chief of staff, General Marshall, along with an update on weapons production. He repeated Oppenheimer's findings on the lethal effects of the blast and heat but explained that tanks could drive safely through Ground Zero after thirty minutes or so. And there was more good news: A complete Little Boy was already at Tinian, and a Fat Man would arrive within twenty-four hours. Groves also updated his delivery schedule for further Little Boy and Fat Man weapons:

> In September, we should have three or four bombs. One of these will be made from [Uranium] 235 material and will have a smaller effectiveness, about two-thirds that of the [plutonium]

test type.... There should be either four or three bombs in
October, one of the lesser type [Little Boy]. In November there
should be at least five bombs and the rate will rise to seven in
December and increase decidedly in early 1946.[45]

President Truman waited eight days before mentioning the success at
Trinity to Stalin. Churchill had been given news of the test on July 16, and
Groves's lengthy report had been shared with the British as soon as it
arrived. To Truman's casual mention of the bomb, Stalin merely replied,
"Good," and expressed the hope that it would be used against Japan. The
Americans and the British were still unaware of the espionage that Klaus
Fuchs, David Greenglass, and Ted Hall had been carrying on for two years.

Los Alamos now turned its attention to the Pacific. Scientists would
work with both Fat Man and Little Boy at Tinian, and they would accompany and arm the weapons in flight, but there was a growing realization
that their role in the war was diminishing. General Farrell had signaled
the change when he signed a receipt for the nuclear core at Trinity, and the
shift in control would be complete as soon as the first B-29 lifted off from
Tinian with a bomb. A few men were uncomfortable with this. It was one
thing to make a bomb, some thought; it was another to use it. But most of
Oppenheimer's men believed they had done their job, and the briefest
glance at a newspaper reminded everyone of the costly ongoing fight in
the Pacific.

Arthur Compton was struck by what a young Los Alamos physicist
told him in the days after Trinity and before Hiroshima: "I have buddies
who have fought through the battle of Iwo Jima. Some of them have been
killed, others wounded. We've got to give these men the best weapons we

can produce. If one of these men should be killed because we didn't let them use the [atomic] bombs, I would have failed them. I just could not make myself feel that I had done my part."[46]

Later, many would share the view expressed by Lieutenant Fred Olivi, the co-pilot on the B-29 *Bockscar*, who witnessed the drop on Nagasaki: "Those poor Japs. But they asked for it."[47]

Chapter Fifteen

PRIMARY TARGETS

The airplane that would deliver Little Boy and Fat Man to Japan was America's biggest and newest aircraft, the B-29. Almost one hundred feet long with 141-foot wings, it weighed seventy thousand pounds unloaded and unfueled. It was left unpainted to reduce weight and increase its range. It was as pure an aircraft as America could make—sleek, powerful, and shining like polished silver in the sun.

Groves had selected the airplane in 1944 when the only other craft capable of carrying atomic weapons was the British Lancaster. The B-29 theoretically could carry twenty thousand pounds, although the practical weight was more like twelve thousand, comfortably over the projected weight of Little Boy or Fat Man. It was also fast for the time. The B-29 could fly at 350 miles per hour and cruise at 220. Pressurized and capable of reaching thirty-two thousand feet, it could soar above antiaircraft fire and most fighter planes. Working with the air force, Groves ordered fifteen B-29s specially designed for dropping unusually large bombs, and Parsons assigned a small team to work with the manufacturer, Martin Aircraft in Nebraska. The first of the special B-29s was completed in October 1944 and flown to a new bomb group stationed at Wendover Army Air Base in Utah, codenamed Kingman or, more simply, W-47. Wendover was 125 miles west of Salt Lake City, near the Nevada border and in the midst of vast salt flats. The remote setting was perfect for bombing practice with unusually shaped bomb casings.

The tests of this first set of B-29s were unsatisfactory, however, especially in bombing accuracy, and Groves ordered a second lot of fifteen aircraft, which arrived in the spring of 1945. These planes incorporated new features, including fuel injection and electrically controlled propellers. The bomb bay had been further modified for releasing the new weapons, and all the armor stripped from the plane except for the tail turret. Bombing accuracy improved tremendously.

Colonel Paul Tibbets was made commanding officer of the new 509th Composite Group in September 1944. His father had wanted him to be a doctor, and for a while he pursued pre-medical studies in college. But at some point Tibbets realized that he really wanted to fly. There was a row with his father, but his mother, Enola Gay Haggard Tibbets, supported him. It was a good decision: Tibbets was a natural pilot. He joined the Army Air Force in 1937, and after Pearl Harbor he flew antisubmarine patrols in the Atlantic. He took over the 340th Bombardment Wing in England in February 1942, and six months later he led a hundred planes in the first American daylight bombing raid over occupied Europe. He was chosen over many others to lead the 509th because he was competent, cool under fire, and had been one of the early test pilots for the B-29.

While Tibbets led his men and airplanes in rigorous training exercises at Wendover, the group's forward base was being constructed in the Pacific on Tinian—known in the laboratory as "Destination"—a small island in the Marianas Chain. Parsons and his Project Alberta team would occupy a part of the island near the ocean that belonged to the First Squadron of the 509th Group. Construction of a secure complex was the responsibility of the same Colonel Fitzpatrick who inspected Tinian as a prospective base months earlier. Four Quonset huts were constructed as laboratories, with air conditioning to protect bomb components and delicate instruments from the heat and humidity. The huts were enclosed within a special high-security, heavily guarded fence. There were also storage buildings, a shop, and an administrative building. A mile away were three air-conditioned assembly buildings in which Fat Man and Little Boy would be prepared before each drop.

An isolated assembly building was obviously necessary for secrecy and because of the explosives employed. As always, Groves was intensely interested in the details. At the very end of 1944, Parsons wrote to Groves that working with Fat Man in the field was more dangerous and complex than working with Little Boy:

> It is believed fair to compare the assembly of the gun gadget to the normal field assembly of a torpedo.... The case of the implosion gadget is very different, and is believed comparable in complexity to rebuilding an airplane in the field. Even this does not fully express the difficulty, since much of the assembly involves bare blocks of high explosives and, in all probability, will end with the securing in position of at least thirty-two boosters and detonators, and then connecting these to firing circuits, special coaxial cables, and [a] high voltage condenser circuit.[1]

Both weapons would be loaded into a B-29 from a six-foot pit dug into an isolated airstrip and lined with concrete. Two heavy metal removable ramps laid across the rectangular opening would allow the trailer carrying a weapon to be precisely maneuvered over a hydraulic lift built into the base of the pit. When in position, the lift would be raised and the weapon transferred to it, the ramps removed, and the bomb slowly lowered again, still resting on its trailer. There was enough room in the pit for members of the team to move around and make final adjustments. Little Boy would be just below the surface, while the top of Fat Man would be partially visible. The airplane would then approach, pivot, and be maneuvered backwards till its bomb bay was directly over the bomb. The same lift would slowly elevate the weapon into the bay of the B-29, where it would be detached from its dolly and connected to the airplane's internal hitching mechanism.

———————

In mid-May, Oppenheimer prepared a memo for Groves and Farrell on the anticipated radiological effects of a nuclear explosion. Farrell, who would represent Groves in the Pacific and have overall field responsibility for the weapons, understandably wanted to be able to prepare flight crews. Oppenheimer offered the unvarnished facts. The active material in the bomb was toxic, perhaps a billion times the lethal dose. At detonation, the radiation produced was injurious within "a radius of a mile and lethal within a radius of about six-tenths of a mile." Three precautions, he said, were necessary:

1. Aircraft must maintain a minimum distance from the detonation in order to avoid radiation. Taking into account the dilution of the atmosphere, this minimum distance is about two and one-half miles. Operations should be conducted so that this distance is exceeded if the operations proceed as planned.

2. Following aircraft must avoid coming close to the cloud of active material, and monitoring to determine the extent and disposition of the activity will be necessary if aircraft are to enter the area within hours of the primary detonation.

3. Certainly if there has been rain, and conceivably without this, some activity may reach the ground in the neighborhood

of the target area. Monitoring will be necessary if this area is to be entered within some weeks of the primary detonation. The probable results of monitoring will be that it is quite safe to enter.[2]

Victor Weisskopf supplemented Oppenheimer's memo with one of his own on the hazards of flying through a radiological cloud and the types of eye protection needed by spectators, either from the air, or from the ground, as at Trinity.[3]

Groves realized as early as the spring of 1944 that Los Alamos would have to send some of its scientific and technical staff into a war zone, and he asked Oppenheimer to begin to prepare for that eventuality. In June, Oppenheimer told Groves that he would solicit volunteers for the work rather than appoint them because of the location and danger. He informed his division leaders on June 13 that men would be needed for assembly, fusing, loading, and checking circuits and test equipment. Volunteers needed to understand the danger in traveling to a war zone and the likelihood that it would mean transfer to military status. Oppenheimer urged his division leaders not to apply pressure but to seek volunteers with certain characteristics. "[A]daptability, high morale, ability to do work under unusual and difficult conditions, stamina, tact, and willingness to accept necessary military discipline should all be given weight in the selection." And volunteers needed to know that there were dangers and restrictions involved:

The men concerned should be fully warned that participation in combat field parties will involve duty on advanced bases away from the United States for lengths of time that cannot be accurately scheduled and for which no termination date can be fixed in advance, may very well require transferring to military status, and is likely to involve extensive inoculations.[4]

The recruiting effort began slowly but gained momentum toward the end of 1944, particularly as the fighting in the Pacific looked as if it would last longer than the European war. Oppenheimer eventually reported to Groves that the response had been "by no means unanimously favorable, but a considerable number of men have signified their willingness to go."[5] Oppenheimer thought that the Los Alamos field force should be a mixture of military men, such as Parsons, but also civilian scientists, such as Alvarez. Civilians would go under the University of California's contract but with insurance and provision made for families during the period of overseas duty. If scientists could go only as members of the military, however, then they should be given a suitable military rank. Kistiakowsky volunteered, as did Hornig, Hempelmann, Alvarez, Ramsey, and Agnew.[6] Ultimately, each civilian was temporarily assigned military status.

A full field team was not assembled until December, and the schedule as of that month called for the ship and aircrews to leave for Tinian by May 1, 1945. Specific crew appointments were made in April and May, including Parsons as officer in charge, Ramsey as scientific and technical deputy, Ashworth as operations officer, and thirty-four others, mostly enlisted men, and General Farrell representing Groves. They would not go all at once. Parsons and Alvarez, for example, would not fly overseas until after the Trinity test.

Although all scientists remained on the Los Alamos payroll, they were given per diem pay, uniform allowances, and additional insurance policies. Each man was given a uniform and a rank presumably consistent with his civilian salary, and with the exception of Parsons, none was permitted to carry firearms.

The trip was not an easy one. Harlow Russ, one of the first engineers from Los Alamos to arrive at Tinian in April, had no idea that the complicated and tedious journey would involve several long days of flying with many stops. The first leg of the trip was by bus from Los Alamos to Kirt-land Field in Albuquerque. From Kirtland he and his companions flew by C-54 cargo plane to Wendover Field, Utah, then to Mather Field near Sacramento, and finally to nearby Hamilton Field, a major departure point for the Pacific. The next series of flights took them to Hickam Field in Honolulu, Johnson Island, Kwajalein Atoll, and finally to Tinian. Kwajalein was part of the Marshall Islands, and several of the islands in the cluster were still occupied by the Japanese.[7]

Members of the First Technical Attachment had to adjust to a climate vastly different from that of New Mexico. The heat and humidity were relentless, with temperatures hovering at ninety degrees. Daily rain and high humidity soaked clothing, paper, food—virtually everything exposed to it. Clouds of mosquitoes and packs of rats compounded their misery. The only consolation was that formal uniforms were not required. The men of Los Alamos were only now discovering what thousands of Marines had experienced on Peleliu, Guadalcanal, Iwo Jima, and hundreds of other tropical islands.

Groves arrived in Los Alamos for a meeting with Oppenheimer and Parsons on June 27, 1945. High on the agenda was a discussion of shipments to Tinian. He wanted to know what was ready to be shipped and when it would leave New Mexico. Two days later, Oppenheimer and Parsons gave him a detailed schedule for shipment of bomb components to Tinian. Oppenheimer made a point of responding to Groves's order that he "ship as much as he can as soon as he can." As a precaution, Groves was asked to inform Fleet Admiral Nimitz of the shipments so that the vessel carrying Fat Man and Little Boy would not be mistakenly diverted. Their concerns proved unfounded, and the first shipment of supplies and bomb components arrived at Tinian in May, including multiple outer casings for both Little Boy and Fat Man. The uranium and plutonium cores, code-named BRONX, were sent overseas under special, highly secret arrangements. Oppenheimer and Parsons arranged for half of the uranium core and the plutonium sphere to be sent separately. The plutonium and the target portion of U235 went by airplane and the U235 projectile went by ship. The plutonium was part of a "package" comprising the active core, high-explosive lenses, electrical firing unit, and detonators. This bundle did not leave the continental United States until after the Trinity test.[8]

Duplicate initiators were also sent to Tinian. Forty were shipped for Little Boy, allowing for final inspection and selection on site. After examination of the original batch of forty, sixteen were selected for testing, and four were ultimately chosen for insertion into the gun bomb.

Fabrication of the U235 core continued until the last minute in Los Alamos. The uranium projectile was finally completed on June 15 and the target on July 24, and both were given a final examination before shipment overseas. The U235 projectile made its way across the Pacific on the USS *Indianapolis* in a metal canister welded to the deck and attended by a twenty-four-hour guard. Not listed on the passenger manifest were two men from Los Alamos, James Nolan and Robert Furman. The ship docked, unloaded its secret cargo, then departed for the United States. On the return voyage, the *Indianapolis*, sailing under strict radio silence, was torpedoed by a Japanese submarine. The heavy cruiser suffered a slow, tragic death, as did many of her crew. As the ship sank, most of the men dived into the ocean to await rescue, but because of poor communications, help did not arrive for three days, and hundreds of men drowned or were eaten by sharks.

Unaware of the tragedy, the men at Tinian used the last days of July and the first few days of August to run tests and to examine and reexamine each component of the bombs. To gain field experience flying over the enemy with a single large weapon, Tibbets's men flew training missions in which they dropped a dummy bomb or a bomb filled with ordinary explosives, flying as far as Iwo Jima and even Japan.

A few men from Los Alamos brought along American-made goods to use as barter. Luis Alvarez, for example, brought along a case of American bourbon, Harold Agnew a case of soap. To Alvarez's dismay, American liquor was cheap and available everywhere. Soap, however, was greatly in demand, and Agnew was able to acquire a number of highly prized Pacific conch shells that were particular favorites of GIs.

During the first days of August, the Los Alamos and 509th teams anxiously awaited the go-ahead for the weapon. Bad weather was predicted for Japan for early-to-mid-August, and the 509th was ready now. Parsons and Ramsey cabled Groves for permission to drop.

Trinity had enlarged the thinking at Los Alamos about the use and delivery of the bomb. Parsons received a memorandum from Bainbridge and Kistiakowsky the day after Trinity with suggestions. Parsons was informed that the immediate flash of light had been greater than expected. This discovery suggested that considerably more damage might be accomplished if enemy troops could be drawn into visual range of the bomb. They speculated that "no one within a radius of five miles could look directly at the gadget and retain his eyesight."[9] Accidental blinding had occurred at Trinity, in fact. A man at Base Camp who had been asleep in the open, was suddenly awakened by the first flash of light. Instinctively he looked in its direction and was blinded for several hours. He missed the most intense light but the effect nevertheless stunned him. Another suggestion was to use a device such as a siren or flashing beacon dropped from a plane in advance of the bomb in order to encourage the enemy to look in that direction. The memo concluded with a wry note that the trick might not work indefinitely.

A few days after Trinity, Oppenheimer had new information for Groves and Parsons. Fat Man or Little Boy could be expected to produce a blast equal to between eight and fifteen kilotons of TNT. Based on the Trinity test, the weapons were now set to detonate at 1,850 feet, with an additional 180 feet added to compensate for any lag in the instruments. A precise setting was impossible, but 1,850 feet was considered optimal, and radioactive contamination was not expected to reach the ground. With a blast of this magnitude at this altitude, aircrews should take care not to look in the direction of the blast for some time; the ball of fire would persist longer than at Trinity because there would be little dust. Oppenheimer thought Little Boy had a good chance of "optimal performance." He gave it a 12 percent chance of a less than optimal blast, a 6 percent chance of an explosion equal to less than five kilotons of TNT, and a 2 percent chance of an explosion under one kiloton.[10] Oppenheimer did not mention the likely effects of radiation on human beings.

———————

In Washington, military planners continued to update their assessment of the war in the Pacific. On July 6, the Combined Chiefs of Staff issued another of their "Estimate of the Enemy Situation" reports, painting a picture of a shrinking, dying empire but one that still retained lethal assets. Most notably, the Japanese army had 110 infantry and four armored divisions, totaling 4.6 million men, and the armored divisions were expected to increase by thirty by the end of 1945. Supplying these armies was difficult, however. Aircraft production, for example, had dropped from 2,300 planes in late 1944 to between 1,200 and 1,500 in June 1945. Aviation fuel was in critically short supply, as were basic materials for armaments. Food shortages were endemic and growing worse.

Allied intelligence believed that the Japanese High Command was now focused on the defense of the home islands, particularly Kyushu and Honshu. It was thought likely that by the end of 1945 the Japanese would have assembled more than thirty-five active divisions, fourteen depot divisions, and some two million troops in order to repel an Allied invasion. All available aircraft would be employed, mostly in suicide attacks. "Their air effort might amount initially to 400–500 sorties of combat type aircraft and 200–300 sorties of trainer type aircraft during any 24 hour period; this effort will, however, decline rapidly." And what of surrender?

Since the Japanese Army is the principal repository of the Japanese military tradition it follows that the Army leaders must, with a sufficient degree of unanimity, acknowledge defeat before Japan can be induced to surrender. This might be brought about either by the defeat of the main Japanese Armies in the Inner Zone [home islands] or through a desire on the part of the Army leaders to salvage something from the wreck with a view to maintaining military tradition. For a surrender to be acceptable ... it would be necessary for the military leaders to believe that it would not entail discrediting warrior tradition and that it would permit the ultimate resurgence of a military Japan."[11]

For Groves, there was no question that the bomb would be used if the war lasted long enough and Los Alamos was able to deliver a practical weapon in time. It was unthinkable to him that, when American lives were being lost every hour of every day, the nation would fail to use the new weapon that could end the war immediately. And he saw little difference between the destruction and loss of life caused by a hundred airplanes with thousands of bombs and that caused by one airplane with a single, unusually powerful weapon. Groves believed that the decision to use the bomb actually had been made in 1942 when President Roosevelt authorized an all-out effort that would cost hundreds of millions of dollars: "From that time on it was impossible for anybody to back out. It was like having to lean on a toboggan going downhill."[12]

Groves had many reasons for wanting the bomb to be used. Of course, the most important were to end the war and to justify the two billion dollars spent to manufacture the weapons. But deployment of the bomb would also send a powerful signal to the Russians and punish the Japanese at the same time. He had a deeply personal reason as well: demonstrating the sheer power of the new weapon would bring him the recognition usually accorded only to a general who wins a great battle.

In March 1945, Undersecretary of War Robert Patterson telephoned Groves and during the discussion asked him if there were men within the Manhattan Project who were "flinching" at the use of the atomic bomb. Groves replied that he hoped not. Hesitation would "make a mess" of the Manhattan Project and the reputations of those who had labored for almost three years to make the one weapon that could end World War II.[13]

Groves was aware that some scientists objected to the use of the bomb, but he believed most of those were at the Met Lab in Chicago. Still, the conversation with Patterson confirmed Groves's opinion that it would be politically useful to involve scientists at some level in planning for the use of the bomb, particularly in the selection of potential targets. He established what he called the Target Committee, which would operate on the assumption that the United States would drop at least two bombs on two different targets. After a conversation with Rear Admiral William Purnell, Groves had come to believe that the first bomb would demonstrate its sheer destructive power, and the second would convince Japan that the United States could make as many atomic bombs as it wanted.[14] In early July, Groves sent a message to Oppenheimer explaining the necessity for dropping multiple bombs on Japan.[15]

The Target committee met for the first time on May 2 in Washington with General Lauris Norstad presiding and Groves and Farrell attending from the central Manhattan District office. Norstad, who had movie-star good looks, was the deputy chief of air staff at Army Air Headquarters at the time. Oppenheimer was not able to attend but sent John von Neumann, Robert Wilson, William Penney, and Joyce Stearns from Los Alamos. Groves opened the meeting with a briefing on the importance of selecting targets and strongly emphasized the need for secrecy. With that, he left to attend another conference. Early in the discussions it was clear to everyone that visual bombing was a necessity because radar equipment was not yet sophisticated enough to pinpoint targets. Weather, then, was a major consideration. The best available meteorological information suggested that July was less favorable for precision bombing over Japan than August, which would provide perhaps six or seven days of clear weather. September was generally unfavorable. Early August was the obvious window of opportunity.

The aerial war in Japan was the responsibility of the Twentieth Air Force. For months its bombers had systematically pummeled the major Japanese cities, but the few that had not yet been hit made attractive targets for the atomic bomb. Penney was given the task of calculating the prospective bomb damage in each city, and Stearns was asked to compile further target data from the Joint Army-Navy Target Group.

The involvement of civilian scientists in military matters was something of a novelty in 1945.[16] Perhaps the discussion that day was too lengthy or convoluted. Whatever the reason, it rattled at least one Twentieth Air Force colonel, William P. Fisher, who felt compelled to remind the committee of its directive, at least as far as the military was concerned:

> It should be remembered that in our selection of any target, the 20th Air Force is operating primarily to laying waste all the main Japanese cities, and that they do not propose to save some important primary target for us if it interferes with the operation of the war from their point of view. Their existing procedure has been to bomb the hell out of Tokyo, bomb the aircraft, manufacturing and assembly plants, engine plants and in general paralyze the aircraft industry so as to eliminate opposition to the 20th Air Force operations. The 20th Air Force is systematically bombing out the following cities with the prime purpose in mind of not leaving one stone lying on another: Tokyo, Yokohama, Nagoya, Osaka, Kyoto, Kobe, Yawata & Nagasaki.[17]

At the end of the meeting, the committee adopted the following criteria for selection: targets should be large urban areas not less than three miles in diameter, they should lie between Tokyo and Nagasaki, and they should have high strategic value. A second meeting was planned for Oppenheimer's office in Los Alamos on May 10 and 11.

Participants in the two-day meeting at the laboratory briefly reviewed the Washington discussions and again took up technical questions and target selection. Besides the Fat Man intended for Trinity, one Little Boy and one Fat Man were being prepared for Japan. Another Fat Man would be available in late August, and additional implosion bombs would be available later in the fall, depending on delivery of plutonium from Hanford.

The committee discussed the optimal altitude for detonation of both weapons and the procedures a crew should follow if unable to make a clear drop on its target. If a bomber had to return to Tinian with its payload, the first priority would be to land with the greatest caution and keep the bomb intact. If a "normal" return landing could not be made, Fat Man should be jettisoned into shallow water from a low altitude. Little Boy could not be dropped into the ocean, because water leaking into the nuclear core would set off a chain reaction, and an explosion could severely damage the American installation on Tinian. For Little Boy, the best emergency procedure would be to remove the explosive powder from the gun and crash land the airplane. The committee members agreed that some sort of instruction book might be helpful to the pilot in case of an emergency landing.

The air force provided a list of five cities it was prepared to hold for "special use." The first was Kyoto, a large industrial center with over a million residents. This city made a particularly attractive target because it was an intellectual and religious center whose residents might more fully appreciate the significance of an atomic weapon. Groves also favored Kyoto because aerial surveys had identified over twenty-six million square feet of industrial plants, and another twenty million square feet were thought to be dedicated to war production of some kind.[18]

The second target city was Hiroshima, an important army depot and port of embarkation in the middle of an urban industrialized area. It was thought that the large hills surrounding the city might reflect the blast and shock waves and thus intensify the destruction.

The third city was Yokohama, the home of aircraft and electrical equipment factories and oil refineries. Industries damaged in the bombing of Tokyo were being relocated to Yokohama as quickly as they could be disassembled or salvaged. It was also one of the most heavily defended cities in Japan.

The Kokura Arsenal, one of the largest arsenals in Japan, was the fourth proposed target. Its destruction would take out a substantial quantity of light ordnance, antiaircraft, and beachhead defense materials.

The fifth target was Niigata, an important port of embarkation on the northwest coast of Honshu. The committee briefly considered adding the emperor's palace at Tokyo to the list but concluded that it should be spared for the sake of future relations with Japan. Kyoto and Hiroshima both received the committee's highest "AA" rating, while Yokohama and Kokura received only an "A;" Niigata was assigned a "B."

The possibility of demonstrating the weapon was also raised and rejected. Philip Morrison, who attended the meeting as a technical advisor to the committee, suggested at one point that if the United States was not going to stage a public demonstration of the bomb before dropping it on a city, then perhaps it should at least warn the Japanese that a uniquely destructive weapon was about to be used against them. Even a leaflet dropped from an airplane, he said, might allow for civilians to be evacuated. Morrison did not know that General Marshall was also considering the possibility of warning the Japanese before striking an urban target. One of the military representatives at the meeting quickly rejected Morrison's suggestion on the grounds that a warning would give the Japanese an opportunity to shoot down American planes. Morrison received no support from Oppenheimer or, in fact, from anyone else in the room.

There was broad agreement that it was important to use the weapon to gain psychological as well as military advantage. The bomb must be deployed so as to maximize its terror, forcing the capitulation of Japan and warning the rest of the world. The committee also discussed the possibility of following the atomic attack with a heavy incendiary mission, which would catch the enemy with its fire-fighting ability destroyed or paralyzed. So little was known about the phenomena associated with atomic weapons—fireball, radioactive cloud, and weather—that it was decided that an incendiary mission should take place no earlier than the day after the nuclear attack. The meeting concluded with Parsons and Ramsey agreeing to meet with Groves to pursue the matter.

A third and final Target Committee meeting was held in Washington on May 28. Groves and Norstad did not attend but sent General Farrell and Colonel Fisher as their representatives. Little had changed from the previous meeting, although William Penney and John von Neumann reported on the conventional hundred-ton test at Trinity. Lingering radiation proved negligible, and it was now believed that aircraft would be safe while flying near bombed targets in Japan. Colonel Fisher reported that the Twentieth Air Force was beginning to deploy "Tallboy" and "Grand Slam" bombs in Japan, weapons that the British had developed for hardened targets. Tallboy was a twelve-thousand-pound bomb and Grand Slam twenty-two thousand. Their thicker casings gave them deeper penetration of their targets. Fisher also reported that at the current rate of activity in Japan, all strategic bombing would be complete by January 1, 1946. Thereafter, finding intact targets would be difficult.[19]

Groves and Farrell undertook their own planning and with representatives from the air force identified three cities as their priority choices: Kyoto, Hiroshima, and Niigata. They would not aim at specific industrial targets but at the center of the city.

A tense meeting between Groves and Stimson on May 30 revealed how divided they were over use of the weapon. Stimson asked if Groves had prepared a list of targets. Groves responded yes and added that he planned to take the list to General Marshall the next day. Stimson asked to see it first, but Groves demurred. It was back in his office, across the river, and would take some time to fetch. The secretary of war then pointed to a phone on his desk and said, "I have all day and I know how fast your office operates. Here's a phone ... you pick it up and call your office and have them bring that report over."[20] Twenty minutes later the list of targets arrived. Stimson reviewed it and immediately objected to Kyoto as a target. He had traveled to Japan earlier in his career and knew the cultural value of the ancient city. He refused to allow it to be a target. Groves didn't share Stimson's concern, but when he submitted a revised list of targets to General Marshall, Kokura had replaced Kyoto. He didn't give up trying to change Stimson's mind, however. "[U]ntil he left for Potsdam ... I must have seen him a half dozen times to a dozen times," Groves recounted. "On each occasion I asked him to reconsider on Kyoto and on each occasion he told me no."[21]

As the Target Committee met, American military leaders were planning an invasion of Japan. Among the many proposals, at least one estimated that 1.5 million men in thirty-six divisions would be needed for an attack on Kyushu in November 1945.[22] Casualties would be heavy. Against this backdrop, the use of a new weapon, however terrible, to end the war before an invasion was unquestionably attractive.

Still, Stimson thought that discussions about dropping the atomic bomb should go beyond the selection of targets. In early May, he established what he called the Interim Committee, a seven-member group whose charge was to assess not only the use of the bomb but its postwar implications. The committee consisted of Stimson himself as chairman; James Byrnes, Truman's representative, who would become secretary of state in July; Ralph A. Bard, an undersecretary in the Navy Department; William L. Clayton from the State Department; Bush; Conant; Karl Compton; and George Harrison, as assistant to Stimson. In addition, on a recommendation from Conant, Stimson set up a Scientific Panel and invited Oppenheimer, Lawrence, Arthur Compton, and Fermi to serve as members.

The Interim Committee's assumptions were, first, that America had needed to develop an atomic bomb because the Germans had been working on one and, second, that the bomb could now help end the war with Japan. But it was also clear to the committee that use of the bomb would justify the two-billion-dollar investment in the Manhattan Project and increase America's diplomatic muscle in the postwar world.

Stimson called a fourth and final meeting of the Interim Committee for May 31, hoping to incorporate non-military views into the discussions. The carefully structured agenda excluded any debate about whether the bomb should be used, and the committee's Scientific Panel was invited to participate for the first time in the deliberations. The agenda called for discussion of topics like temporary control of the bomb, postwar research and controls, and future nonmilitary uses. In his meticulous wartime diaries, Stimson wrote that the meeting was intended to reinforce the idea that "we were looking at this [the use of the bomb] like statesmen and not like merely soldiers anxious to win the war at any cost."[23]

From Groves's perspective as a military officer, not a statesman, the purpose of the Interim Committee appeared not to be to solicit advice but to make it clear to the outside world that more than the military were involved in making decisions. In fact, the committee consisted entirely of civilians. Groves was asked to attend only as a consultant, as was General Marshall.[24]

On May 30, the day before the final meeting of the Interim Committee, Stimson and his assistant secretary of war, John J. McCloy, went to see General Marshall, who suggested that the atomic bomb might be used first against a large military objective, such as a naval installation, and if such a strike did not induce the Japanese to surrender, then the next step would be attacks on large manufacturing centers where civilians could be warned to evacuate. To protect American aircraft, a specific target would not be disclosed, but a list of cities would be provided. Marshall wanted every effort made to establish a record of the warning.

Marshall was fully aware of Japan's "fanatical but hopeless defense methods," especially as American forces closed in. He understood that new tactics and new weapons were needed. Marshall also revealed, to Stimson's surprise, that he and his war planners were seriously considering gas—not the newest and most potent, but something that would sicken the enemy sufficiently to "take the fight out of them." It might be a form of mustard gas, which he saw as no less humane than phosphorous and flame throwers. Marshall added that such a gas would not be used against civilians or dense populations but merely against those "last pockets of resistance which had to be wiped out but had no other military significance."[25]

———

All the members were present for the Interim Committee's final meeting, along with Stimson's aide Arthur Page, Generals Marshall and Groves, and Harvey H. Bundy as guests. Stimson began by noting that the bomb had implications beyond the war against Japan. Arthur Compton and Oppenheimer then outlined the next several generations of weapons. Oppenheimer stressed that development of these improved devices was merely a question of time. Beyond the Trinity bomb, for example, was a second generation with explosive forces equivalent to between fifty and one hundred kilotons of TNT. These fission devices could theoretically serve as ignition mechanisms for "super" weapons with explosive forces between ten and one hundred megatons of TNT.[26] He also added that such weapons were beyond the capability of the laboratory at the moment; they were weapons for the future.

Stimson and the others agreed that the Manhattan District could not be disbanded immediately after the end of hostilities. It should continue research and development and provide a stockpile of weapons. When the subject of Russia was raised, Oppenheimer repeated Niels Bohr's belief that

Soviet Union must be told eventually about the atomic bomb, although without details. There was modest agreement on this matter until Byrnes, who joined the meeting late, learned of the discussion and objected strenuously. After some lively conversation, the consensus was reached that while the United States must retain world leadership in atomic matters, the matter of informing Russia would be deferred.

The meeting broke for lunch in another room set out with four tables. Oppenheimer sat with Lawrence, Compton, Byrnes, Groves, and Stimson. A conversation between Byrnes and Lawrence prompted the question of the bomb's use. Lawrence suggested that the bomb be deployed in some "innocuous way" before being used against a city and taking a massive civilian toll. There were immediate objections. Such a demonstration *might* be successful in moving the Japanese government to capitulate, particularly if the display were dramatic enough, but Oppenheimer was forced to remind everyone that a display, however dramatic, could not surpass seeing the havoc wreaked by the bomb on physical structures like buildings. A surprise drop was essential to prevent counteraction by the Japanese, and an explosion on an island might not convince Japanese leaders that the explosion was caused by a single weapon. Subsequent arguments against use of the bomb on a Japanese city were batted down one by one.

Stimson adjusted the agenda when the meeting resumed. As the afternoon wore on, a consensus emerged that the bomb should be deployed against the Japanese *without* warning and against a target that would impress as many of the enemy as possible. Oppenheimer told the committee that the explosion would be a "brilliant luminescence that would rise to a height of 10,000 or 20,000 feet."[27] Deployment of the bomb was now policy. Moreover, the committee recommended that Little Boy and Fat Man be dropped on different targets. Notes taken by an aide described the decision: "The Secretary [Stimson] expressed the conclusion, on which there was general agreement, that we could not give the Japanese any warning; that we could not concentrate on a civilian area; but that we should seek to make a profound psychological impression on as many of the inhabitants as possible."[28] The decision to make a "profound psychological impression" doomed one or more Japanese cities, because only in a large urban setting would there be enough buildings and homes and factories to destroy and large populations to witness the destruction firsthand. This grim truth underlay the committee's conclusion.

Groves was able to bring up what he called "undesirable scientists." The program to develop weapons, he said, had been plagued from the beginning by "the presence of certain scientists of doubtful discretion and uncertain loyalty." No doubt he was thinking of Leo Szilard. At various times in the past two years, Groves and Compton had tried to get Szilard to resign. When that failed, Groves studied the possibility of having Szilard declared an enemy alien and incarcerated. The committee agreed that nothing could be done until the bomb had been used or at least until the Trinity test. Once the public knew about the atomic bomb, it would be appropriate to "sever" the offenders from their laboratories.[29] This is not the decision Groves sought, but at least he had succeeded in putting the issue on the record. In the future, he would belittle Szilard wherever he could and excise him from the history of the project.

Although the Interim Committee had concluded its work, Stimson had asked the Scientific Panel for written recommendations, so it met once more on June 16, this time in Los Alamos. Earlier, James Franck of the Met Lab had delivered to Stimson and others a sixteen-page memorandum, written by him and his colleagues, urging a "demonstration of the new weapon" on a deserted island or some other location where the bomb's power could be witnessed by a world audience. The memo also urged international control of the new weapon. Stimson had not yet responded, but he wanted the panel's opinion. Lawrence again advocated a demonstration to which Japanese observers would be invited. Fermi apparently sided with Lawrence, but Compton spoke out forcefully against the idea. Oppenheimer repeated his arguments against a demonstration, and a majority of the panel ultimately supported him. In the panel's report to Stimson,

Oppenheimer acknowledged that the recommendation was not unanimous but wrote, "We find ourselves closer to these latter views [actual use of the bomb against the Japanese]; we can propose no technical demonstration likely to bring an end to the war; we see no acceptable alternative to direct military use."[30]

The members of the Interim Committee, as well as the Scientific Panel, were certainly aware that all the targets under consideration were cities inhabited overwhelmingly by civilians. In counterpoint, it was also known that a considerable amount of Japanese war production was scattered throughout neighborhoods as a foil against bombing. There was no way to target one and not the other. If the bomb were to be used, it would have to be used against a city. General Curtis LeMay understood this and was unapologetic:

> It was their [Japanese] system of dispersal of industry. All you had to do was visit one of those targets after we'd roasted it, and see the ruins of a multitude of small houses, with a drill press sticking up through the wreckage of every home. The entire population got into the act and worked to make those airplanes and munitions of war... men, women, children. We knew we were going to kill a lot of women and kids when we burned [a] town. Had to be done.[31]

A few days after the meeting, Oppenheimer was confronted in Chicago by Szilard, who aggressively argued that it was a bad idea to use the bomb against Japan. He believed just as strongly that the United States needed to tell the Russians about the bomb. Szilard, like everyone else, knew nothing of the three Soviet spies working at Los Alamos. "The weapon is shit," he told Oppenheimer, who asked Szilard what he meant. "Well," he replied, "this is a weapon which has no military significance. It will make a big bang—a very big bang—but it is not a weapon which is useful in war."[32] Oppenheimer and most others disagreed.

Despite these debates, target selection continued until the end of July. On July 24, the target list was narrowed to four cities: Hiroshima, Kokura, Niigata, and Nagasaki, a new addition. This decision was reached after much discussion among Stimson, General Henry H. Arnold, and others in Washington. Stimson was relieved to learn that Truman also favored sparing Kyoto because of its historical and cultural value.[33]

From Washington, Groves phoned Oppenheimer in Los Alamos to ask when the bombs' nuclear components would be ready for shipment. Oppenheimer reported to Groves that a Little Boy core would be ready after August 1 and a Fat Man after August 5. A second Fat Man core would be available sooner than expected because of recent shipments from Hanford. Oppenheimer also gave Groves an updated report on the weapons' destructive power. New calculations from the Trinity test confirmed preliminary calculations that these bombs would deliver a force equivalent to between eight and fifteen kilotons of TNT, and the fireball would be more brilliant than the one at Trinity.

The next day, July 25, in a memo to Secretary of War Stimson, Marshall outlined the "directive" he proposed for the atomic bombing of Japan:

> The 509th Composite Group, 20th Air Force will deliver its first special bomb as soon as weather will permit visual bombing after about 3 August 1945 on one of the targets: Hiroshima, Kokura, Niigata and Nagasaki.... Additional bombs will be delivered on the above targets as soon as made ready by the project staff. Further instructions will be issued concerning targets other than those listed above.... The foregoing is issued to you by direction and with the approval of the Secretary of War and the Chief of Staff, USA.[34]

The draft was approved and the directive issued.

At the end of July Oppenheimer met in Los Alamos with General Farrell and his aide, Lieutenant Colonel Moynahan, both of whom were leaving shortly for Tinian and would oversee the bombing of Japanese targets. Oppenheimer, tense and chain-smoking, stressed the importance of a visual drop. Moynahan found Oppenheimer almost frantic. "Don't let them bomb through clouds or through an overcast.... [They've] got to see the target. No radar bombing; it must be dropped visually.... [D]on't let them detonate it too high. The figure fixed on is just right. Don't let it go up or the target won't get as much damage."[35]

At Destination, Parsons and Ramsey received permission from Washington to drop the bombs as soon after August 3 as weather permitted. Little Boy was fully assembled and ready on the 3rd, but aircrews were forced to wait three more days until the weather cleared. Parsons had perfected a timetable much like Bainbridge's Trinity schedule: unpack Little Boy and assemble with U235, conduct electrical tests, and connect the weapon to a standby power source for monitoring. The batteries would not be connected until shortly before loading Little Boy into the airplane. The Little Boy assembly team was led by Francis Birch.

When assembled and encased in its ballistic shell, Little Boy was 120 inches in length and twenty-eight inches in diameter and weighed approximately 9,700 pounds. Within its hardened armor steel shell was the bomb mechanism itself, the forward half of which contained the U235 target rings, tamper, and initiators. These items alone accounted for half of the weight of the weapon. The U235 target's final weight was 25.6 kilograms (56.5 pounds), while the projectile, located in the second half of the weapon, was 38.5 kilos (eighty-five pounds). Together, the U235 core weighed just over sixty-four kilos (141 pounds). Also located within the shell was Little Boy's version of the X-unit, the arming and fusing systems consisting of clock and barometric switches, the "Archie" tail warning radar devices and external Yagi antennae, and a series of replaceable safety plugs that either armed or disarmed the weapon.[36]

Entrance to the laboratory's high-security Technical Area. (Los Alamos National Laboratory)

The fully assembled gadget. Donald Hornig (in hat) was the last man to see Fat Man before the test. (LANL)

The unpacked gadget being hoisted to the top of the Ground Zero tower at Trinity. (LANL)

The tower at Ground Zero, Trinity, near one of the three paved roads at Trinity authorized by General Groves. (LANL)

Oppenheimer watches as the 105-pound plug is lowered into the bomb. (LANL)

Implosion gadget at the base of the Trinity tower inside the tent that shielded it from dust and prying eyes. The white "bandages" cover detonator holes. The dark horizontal cylinder on the lower right is the uranium plug containing the plutonium core and initiator. Louis Slotin, in dark glasses, stands by. (LANL)

The 215-ton steel cylinder nicknamed "Jumbo." Built to contain the scarce plutonium in case the bomb fizzled and only the high explosives detonated, it ultimately wasn't used. (LANL)

Jumbo after the explosion. The unused vessel was left several hundred yards from Ground Zero. The explosion flattened the frame but left Jumbo standing upright. (LANL)

The McDonald ranch house at Trinity. Scientists assembled the gadget's plutonium core and initiator and housed sensitive equipment in the abandoned structure. (LANL)

South 10,000 bunker, the command center at Trinity, seen from the rear. (LANL)

The Trinity explosion at 5:30:52 a.m., July 16, 1945, seven seconds after detonation. (LANL)

Aerial view of Ground Zero after the Trinity test. The dark area is scorched earth and the green glass (called "Trinitite") produced when the explosion melted the desert sand. The lighter circle directly below is from the 100-ton test on May 7. (LANL)

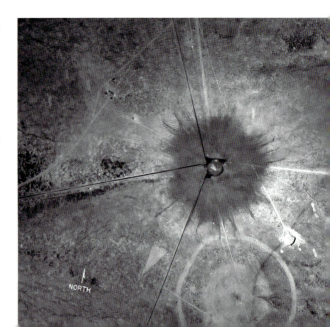

NORTH

Final assembly of Little Boy at Tinian. The exposed section reveals the electronics package that will detonate the bomb. (LANL)

Little Boy. The ballistic shell of the 9,700-pound gun bomb was 120 inches long and twenty-eight inches in diameter. (LANL)

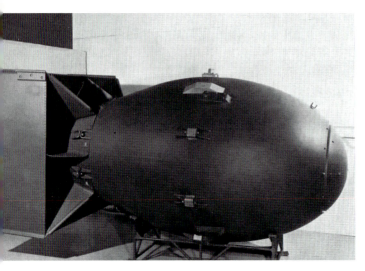

Fat Man. The ballistic shell for the five-ton implosion bomb was 128 inches long, including fins, and sixty inches in diameter. (LANL)

Groves and Oppenheimer, in his signature porkpie hat, at Ground Zero, Trinity, in September 1945. Visitors to Trinity were required to wear protective "booties" because of residual radiation. The ridge in the background hints at the depth of the crater formed by the explosion. (LANL)

Little Boy could be disarmed with three green-handled plugs that broke electrical circuits. Called "safing devices" by bomb designers, these five-pin metal plugs had wood handles and were a little more than three inches long and one and a quarter inches wide. These were inserted on the ground as the weapon was being prepared for use and replaced in flight with three red plugs, which would connect all circuits and thereby arm the bomb. They were inserted into the weapon through one-and-a-half-inch holes mid-way in the bomb's steel casing, just below the metal bracket that could accommodate a hook and winch. The bomb was officially known as Unit L-11.

There was an additional safety system built into the weapon at Los Alamos. Birch, who led the Gun Group, became concerned that a crash on takeoff could possibly trigger the ignition of the high explosives and set off a nuclear explosion. Word had already reached Los Alamos of catastrophic takeoffs at Tinian. He therefore instructed his men to modify Little Boy with a two-piece breech plug. The plug was accessed by first removing a seventeen-inch circular outer plate and then a smaller, inner plate. Removal of the inner plate and the breech plug allowed the insertion of small bags of explosives. As they waited for the weather to clear, Parsons and Jeppson practiced loading the explosive powder bags. When the plane was safely in the air and en route to its target, Parsons would insert the bags of powder through the opening in the breech block. The bomb bay of the B-29, which Tibbets would pilot, was quickly modified with a small platform for Parsons to stand on while working in flight. Final arming would occur when the three green plugs were pulled from the body of the bomb and replaced with red plugs. Parsons hoped to come back and present at least one plug to General Groves as a trophy.

The B-29s of the 509th were extraordinarily well-tuned machines. Each of the four Wright R-3350 eighteen-cylinder engines was assigned two mechanics. Each bolt in the fuselage was regularly examined for wear or defect. And although stripped of excessive armament, each machine gun was fitted with one thousand rounds of ammunition. Each plane held

7,400 gallons of high-octane aviation fuel distributed between two tanks. Armed MP's guarded the planes day and night.

On August 5, word came that the weather the next day would be good over Hiroshima, the primary target. There were two secondary targets, including Kokura. U.S. Army Intelligence suspected that an Allied prisoner of war camp was in or near the city, although its exact location and the number of prisoners were not known. Because of its terrain, Kokura was a better target for bomb damage than Hiroshima, but the army hesitated to bomb an area with Allied prisoners of war. It was widely believed that the Japanese purposely moved prisoners into camps in major target cities to discourage Allied bombing. The War Department nonetheless ruled that the presence of Allied prisoners was not to be a factor in selecting targets.[37] As soon as favorable weather was predicted, General Curtis LeMay ordered the crew to proceed on or after August 6.

A preliminary briefing for the crews took place Saturday afternoon, August 4, and everyone, including those flying observation and weather planes, attended. When Tibbets took the stage, conversation in the audience of at least eighty men stopped instantly. Everyone sensed the importance of the moment. Behind him were two large blackboards, both draped with cloths. Tibbets reminded everyone that they would be dropping a single bomb of inordinate destructive power. To illustrate, he asked Parsons to show a movie of the Trinity shot. Unfortunately, the projector jammed and began to chew up the film, so Parsons did his best to describe the fierce light and fireball and the mushroom cloud that formed and rose to over thirty thousand feet. Photographs from Trinity were passed around. He did not tell the audience the source of the bomb's destructive power.

Tibbets took over again and called up two intelligence officers. The drapes were pulled from the blackboards, revealing maps of Hiroshima, Kokura, and Nagasaki. These were the targets, in order. Weather would determine the departure time as well as the target. Tibbets reminded everybody that whatever his previous service in the war, it was "small potatoes" compared with tomorrow's work. They were special men, and if all went well, they would shorten the war by six months. Where Tibbets picked up the "six months" figure is not known, but most of the men acquainted with the new weapon hoped it would end the war in a matter of days. The briefing lasted less than an hour, and everyone was told to say nothing of what he had just heard or seen. The mission would take off as soon as weather permitted.

At two o'clock on Sunday afternoon, the gun-metal colored Little Boy was placed in its special trailer in Assembly Building 2, and everyone present was invited to write a message or a name on the exterior ballistic case. It was then wheeled to the loading pit and lifted into the *Enola Gay*, named after Tibbets's mother. The entire operation, from transportation to loading, was supervised by Los Alamos teams and guarded by a heavy contingent of military police. As extra protection against prying eyes, the bomb was draped with a tarpaulin until in the pit. Loading Little Boy into the *Enola Gay* took less than twenty-five minutes. The final briefing, held at midnight, was followed by an early breakfast of ham and eggs. Crews were driven to the airfield and photographed in front of their airplane. In the *Enola Gay*, Paul Tibbets was commander, Major Thomas Ferebee bombardier, and Captain Ted van Kirk navigator. Parsons, although a commander in the navy, represented Los Alamos as bomb commander. He was assisted by Lieutenant Morris Jeppson.

At 2:45 a.m. on August 6 (11:45 a.m. on August 5 in Washington), the *Enola Gay* took off from Tinian with an escort of fighters and reconnaissance planes. A crowd of 350, including Admiral Purnell and General Farrell, waved to the crew from the side of the runway. The airplane's radio call signal was "Dimples 82." The heavily laden plane took almost the entire runway for lift-off. Fifteen minutes later, Parsons, assisted by Jeppson, began the eleven-step process of arming the bomb. Step one called for Parsons to make sure the green plugs were installed and the electrical circuits of the bomb disconnected. The next four steps involved removing the rear plates and breech plug. Step six was inserting four two-pound bags of Cordite powder. The final steps involved reinserting the breech plug, connecting the firing line, reinstalling the armor plates, and, last, removing all tools and securing the platform. Arming was now complete. All that remained was to replace the green plugs with the red.

At 6:05 a.m., the *Enola Gay* flew over Iwo Jima and headed toward Japan. An hour and a half later, Jeppson reentered the bomb bay to exchange the green plugs with red: all circuits were now live and the bomb fully armed. Jeppson would spend most of the remaining flight in the forward compartment, monitoring an electrical console with meters, switches, and warning lights. This was a big moment for the twenty-three-year-old from Logan, Utah. Shortly after nine o'clock, Hiroshima was in sight.

At 9:14:30 a.m., August 6, 1945, Ferebee released the bomb from an altitude of 31,600 feet. Suddenly relieved of five tons of weight, the airplane lurched up several dozen feet, and Tibbets quickly banked right 155 degrees in a steep turn. A few minutes later a brilliant flash lit the interior of the *Enola Gay*. The bomb had detonated at 1,950 feet. Seconds later the airplane was severely jolted twice by shock waves. The large ball of fire, at first seeming to churn within itself, quickly changed to swirling purple clouds and boiling flames that surged upward. Temperatures reached 5,400 degrees, and on the ground the heat ignited flammable objects like wood and cloth as far away as four thousand yards. Roofing tiles bubbled at 1,300 yards, and objects like granite were chipped or grated at seven hundred yards. Birds in flight simply disappeared. Every exposed human being or animal within half a mile was reduced to black char in less than a second. One of three young boys at a swimming pool had dived below the surface to see how long he could hold his breath, and when he surfaced a few moments later he was startled to find that his two friends had disappeared and the buildings around him were rubble.

The heat and blast were the obvious effects. But there was radiation as well—gamma rays, x-rays, neutrons, and over two hundred radioactive isotopes. Later, some of these would cause further deaths and illness.

From one of the nearby instrument planes, *The Great Artiste*, Harold Agnew took the only motion pictures of the Hiroshima bombing with a sixteen-millimeter home movie camera. The mushrooming cloud reached a height of thirty thousand feet in less than three minutes and rose another ten thousand feet before flattening out on top. The crew of a combat plane 360 miles away at an altitude of twenty-five thousand feet clearly saw the cloud.

The devastation of Hiroshima, a city with a population of three hundred thousand, was unprecedented. The center of the city was leveled, with more than sixty thousand buildings destroyed. In fact, over 90 percent of the buildings in the city were either damaged or demolished. A few modern concrete buildings survived as shells. The force of the explosion was so great that handrails on bridges between the central city and suburbs were stripped loose. Shortly after the blast, great waves of fire swept across the city, and thirty or forty minutes later it inexplicably began to rain. But the water that fell had absorbed the residue of fires on the ground and dangerous radiation still floating in the sky. Parched, many survivors drank the sticky, dark liquid; others ingested it later by eating contaminated food. "Black rain," as it came to be known, had not fallen at Trinity.

How many people died instantly or over the next hours and days is impossible to determine accurately, in part because of a lack of accurate census data. Various studies over the years suggest that at least sixty-five thousand died instantly, and the number of dead reached one hundred thousand within twenty-four hours. Total deaths by the end of 1945 are estimated at 140,000.[38] Despite the extensive destruction, Little Boy's yield was disappointing: only sixteen kilotons, compared with Trinity's 17.5 kilotons. Moreover, only seven hundred grams (twenty-five ounces) of U235 actually fissioned, giving the bomb an efficiency of a mere 1.2 percent.[39]

The *Enola Gay* returned to a crowd of well-wishers at Tinian. Tibbets hardly had time to work his way out of his plane before he was awarded the Distinguished Service Cross. Cameramen recorded the landing and subsequent events for posterity. No one on that tarmac could imagine the war's lasting more than a few days or weeks.

Parsons immediately sent a coded message to Groves, who had spent the night in his office in Washington waiting for news. Jean O'Leary and a few other staff members had joined him Sunday morning: "Results clearcut, successful in all respects. Visible effects greater than New Mexico test." A smiling Groves shared the news with everyone in the office then telephoned Harrison at the War Department, who in turn cabled Stimson in Potsdam and called General Marshall. It was just before 11:30 in the morning, Washington time. Oppenheimer was telexed the same two lines from Parsons but Groves added a personal, explanatory note: "Flashed from the plane by Parsons one five minutes after release."[40]

Groves followed up with a telephone call to Oppenheimer at two o'clock that afternoon:

> GROVES: I'm proud of you and all of your people.
>
> OPPENHEIMER: It went all right?
>
> GROVES: Apparently it went with a tremendous bang.
>
> OPPENHEIMER: When was this, was it after sundown?
>
> GROVES: No, unfortunately, it had to be in the daytime on account of security of the plane.
>
> OPPENHEIMER: Right. Everyone is feeling reasonably good about it and I extend my heartiest congratulations. It's been a long road.
>
> GROVES: Yes, it has been a long road and I think one of the wisest things I ever did was when I selected the director of Los Alamos.
>
> OPPENHEIMER: Well, I have my doubts, General Groves.
>
> GROVES: Well, you know I've never concurred with those doubts at any time.[41]

The transcript of the conversation suggests that Los Alamos expected the bomb to be set off in the dark, as at Trinity, when perhaps the psychological effect would be strongest. And Oppenheimer relates that his colleagues are feeling "reasonably good" about the bombing. Were there those who were feeling bad?

And there was something else. Though neither man articulated it, they both sensed, if only as a whisper, that with Hiroshima their unique relationship had turned a corner. They would still need each other, but not as much, and they would need each other less and less in the weeks and months to come.

Oppenheimer hung up to share the news with his staff, while Groves dashed off a three-page report to General Marshall and sent it by courier. The report briefly summarized the circumstances under which the "vital plane"—the *Enola Gay*—had prepared for the strike, the weather it encountered, and descriptions of the explosion. Groves pointed out that "the target was Hiroshima, the one reserved target where there was no indication of any POW camp." The results were stunning:

> Entire city except outer-most ends of dock areas was covered with a dark grey dust layer which joined the cloud column. It was extremely turbulent with flashes of fire visible in the dust.... One observer stated it looked as though whole town was being torn apart with columns of dust rising out of valleys approaching the town.[42]

The rest of the general's day was taken up with more than forty telephone calls, made or received. He sat at his desk talking into his headset well into the night. Harrison, Compton, Lawrence, and Conant, among others, called with congratulations. Groves called and congratulated the directors of his plants in Oak Ridge, Hanford, and a number of other locations. Oppenheimer called back in the afternoon and asked when the news from Japan would be made public. Groves replied it was up to the president, but he would send copies of Parsons's messages from Tinian for Oppenheimer and his "top-flight" people to read. There were almost as many calls in and out of Groves's office the following day.

The day after Hiroshima, General Farrell received instructions from the War Department to begin a propaganda campaign against the Japanese. Following a plan made in advance, Farrell and his assistant, Colonel Moynahan, ordered sixteen million leaflets dropped on heavily populated Japanese cities. The leaflets described the new and powerful Allied weapon that destroyed Hiroshima. They were supplemented by Japanese-language newspapers that contained photographs and details of the explosion. Over Radio Saipan, the army began broadcasting brief descriptions of the bombing every fifteen minutes. The campaign continued until the Japanese government began negotiations.[43]

The leaflets dropped on forty-seven cities read in part, "We [the United States] are in possession of the most powerful destructive explosive ever devised by man. A single one of our newly developed atomic bombs is actually the equivalent in explosive power to what 2,000 of our giant B-29's are carrying on a single mission." The leaflets were not all dropped on the same day, and because of poor coordination, they were dropped on Nagasaki only after the city was bombed.[44]

Tinian now turned its attention to preparations for dropping Fat Man.

Los Alamos was jubilant. Following his conversation with Groves, Oppenheimer called the laboratory staff together in the auditorium in T Building. He jauntily walked down the aisle to the stage, looking to one scientist like a prizefighter who had just won his big match. Some who were there also remembered that he clasped his hands together above his

head in a gesture of victory and read the message flashed by Parsons—
"Clear-cut results, exceeding TR test in visible effects."[45]

Shortly after confirming the news, President Truman made his own public announcement of both Hiroshima and the atomic bomb. The news electrified every town and city throughout America, but it had a special meaning for the residents of Santa Fe. The banner headline in the *Santa Fe New Mexican* for August 8 said it all:

> Los Alamos Secret Disclosed by Truman
> ATOMIC BOMBS DROP ON JAPAN

Twenty-four hours after news of the bombing reached Moscow, Stalin called into his office his leading nuclear scientists and ordered them to develop Soviet atomic weapons "in the minimum of time, regardless of cost." A week later, the head of military intelligence cabled one of the leaders of a Soviet spy ring: "Take measures to organize acquisition of documentary materials on the atomic bomb! The technical process, drawings, calculations." Uranium mining in central Asia was quickly accelerated.[46]

At least three complete Fat Man weapons without cores were sent to Tinian from Los Alamos. Each was fully assembled, with dummy plugs in place of the plutonium and uranium capsule, and stored in Building 3. Before use in the field, the weapon had to be disassembled, inspected, and reassembled, the nuclear capsule had to be inserted, and the weapon had to be placed inside its Duralumin shell. Backup explosive lenses were available in case one was damaged in shipment.

The assembly teams at Tinian found that the assembly of Fat Man was far more complicated and taxing than that of Little Boy. On August 7, beginning with the assembly of the explosive lenses, engineers followed a precisely scripted procedure—similar to the one followed at Trinity. After the uranium and plutonium cylinder had been inserted, completing the three-hundred-pound pusher, tamper, and core, the remaining explosive lenses were laid down and the top polar plate attached.[47] All cables and electronics were then attached and tested. The outer shell was attached and given a coating of light yellow paint and left to dry.

It was necessary to seal the weapon where segments of the ballistic case were joined together to protect the elaborate barometric system. Los Alamos had devised three coatings. The first was an adhesive, the second was fibrous tape to bridge the gaps and add strength, and the third was a layer of shinny enamel known as Red Enamel Number 1201, made by the Glyptal Company.[48] The completed F-31 Fat Man was a massive device. The outer case with its fins was a little over 128 inches long and sixty inches in diameter at its widest point. The weapon weighed over five tons. Everyone present, including those from Los Alamos and members of the security team, was invited to sign his name or add a brief message, just as the team had done with Little Boy. Perhaps the most haunting of the fifty or so messages honored the dead of the USS *Indianapolis*, news of which had finally reached Tinian. The fully assembled bomb was then covered with a tarp.

On the afternoon of August 8, Fat Man was slowly driven to the loading pit on the isolated part of the airfield. It remained covered by a tarp until the last minute. By eight o'clock p.m., the weapon was sitting inside a B-29 named *Bockscar*, fully connected and ready for takeoff.

The final briefing for the flight crew took place just after midnight on August 9. It was short. There were only two targets, Kokura and Nagasaki. Everyone in the briefing room knew that this mission was different from the last in one important way—the Japanese were likely to be expecting them. As in the Hiroshima mission, the fighter escorts would drop out before Iwo Jima. Lightning flashed outside, and thunder rattled the briefing room. At one a.m., the crews boarded their airplanes and began preflight checks. Major Charles Sweeney was in command of the flight. He had joined the Army Air Corps in April 1941 and in May 1944 was assigned to the Grand Island Army Airfield in Nebraska as a B-29 pilot instructor. He transferred to the 509th in January 1945 and in May became commander of the 393rd Bombardment Squadron, the combat wing of the 509th. He was personally chosen by Tibbets to lead the second strike. Sweeney's own plane, the *Great Artiste*, was fitted with special photographic gear and too heavy to accommodate Fat Man. Instead, *Bockscar* was loaded with 7,250 gallons of fuel, but during the preflight check it was discovered that fuel from two 320-gallon self-sealing reserve tanks in the rear bomb bay was unavailable because of a malfunctioning pump. Six hundred and forty gallons of fuel would not be accessible during the long flight, but Sweeney decided to risk it.[49] Assisting him were Captain Kermit Beahan as bombardier and Colonel Frederick Ashworth taking Parsons's place as bomb commander.

Bockscar took off at 3:48 a.m. into stormy weather that buffeted the plane for hours. Shortly after takeoff, Ashworth began the arming, a much simpler process than the one Parsons had faced on the *Enola Gay*. Ashworth pulled out two green safing plugs from the nose of the bomb and replaced them with two red arming plugs. Fat Man was now live. The B-29 rendezvoused with one escort plane over Yakashima but had to wait for another one, burning up forty-five minutes of fuel in the process. Finally, Sweeney headed for Kokura, his primary target. Advance reports predicted good weather there with low clouds, whereas the forecast was for increasing cloudiness over the secondary target, Nagasaki. But when *Bockscar* arrived at Kokura, the city was covered by heavy fog and smoke. Sweeney made three runs, but Beahan found it impossible to locate the aiming point. After circling and wasting more fuel, the aircraft was forced to proceed to Nagasaki. At 11:30 a.m., *Bockscar* made contact with the city by radar. Twenty minutes later, Beaham located his target in a visual bombing run and at 11:50:20 a.m. released Fat Man from 28,900 feet. Sweeney forced the B-29 into a steep turn.

Nagasaki suffered the same swift death as Hiroshima. The bomb went off at 1,650 feet. A great blaze of light followed by shock waves hit *Bockscar* as it made its turn. The aircraft slowly circled the dying city as the ball of fire grew and changed colors. At five minutes past noon, the plane left the city to refuel on Okinawa. En route, Ashworth sent word to Farrell on Tinian that Fat Man had been successfully dropped on Nagasaki, and he sent a coded radio message to Tinian to be relayed to Jean O'Leary in Washington, with copies to General Spaatz and Admiral Nimitz: "Bombed Nagasaki 090158Z virtually with no fighter opposition and no flak. Results 'technically successful.... Visible effects about equal to Hiroshima. Trouble in airplane following delivery requires us to proceed to Okinawa. Fuel only to get to Okinawa.'"[50] While accurate results were impossible to determine at this early stage, it seemed to Ashworth and other members of the crew that while the visible effects were comparable to those at Hiroshima, the flash of light from Fat Man was brighter, the shock wave was stronger, and the cloud was larger and rose more swiftly.[51]

Photographs taken the next day revealed that while the explosion had indeed been more spectacular and powerful than the one at Hiroshima, only 44 percent of Nagasaki had been destroyed. The difference in the level of destruction was apparently due to the differences in geography, but a preliminary analysis suggested that the energy blast at Nagasaki had been nearly twice that at Hiroshima, some twenty-one kilotons, greater than at Trinity. And compared with the gun, the implosion bomb was far more efficient. It fissioned some 1.3 kilograms (2.8 pounds) of Pu239, or 21 percent, 17.5 times better than Little Boy.[52] Many reinforced concrete buildings and metal structures were demolished. The blast followed the steep hills and ravines that surround the city and dispersed. The exact extent of the explosive burst was later determined by noting the effects of charring on remaining telephone poles. Fat Man was actually several miles off target, but it exploded, fittingly enough, over the Mitsubishi armament plant that had made the torpedoes used in the attack on Pearl Harbor. Unbeknownst to the Americans, the Japanese had placed a prisoner of war camp near Nagasaki, and a few men—two of them Americans—became the only Allied victims of the atomic bomb.[53]

Again, it is impossible to determine accurately the number of deaths at Nagasaki, but studies estimate that forty thousand persons were killed instantly, and another thirty to thirty-five thousand died by the end of the year.

Bockscar, with less than fifty gallons of fuel, was forced to make an emergency landing in Okinawa. When the plane finally returned to Tinian at 8:45 p.m., it was met by a crowd of well-wishers but no cameras. Sweeney was later to come under considerable criticism for taking off without the use of his reserve tanks, wasting fuel over Yakashima waiting for a second observer plane, and making three runs over Kokura with low fuel. Paul Tibbets was especially harsh, but Sweeney brushed aside the criticism. Despite the difficulties, the mission had been successful. After the war, he eventually attained the rank of brigadier general.

On the day the United States bombed Nagasaki, the Soviet Union invaded Japanese-occupied territory in China at a little past midnight Moscow time. The heavy assault was launched against Manchuckuo on three fronts simultaneously. This followed a late-night meeting between the Soviet foreign minister, Vyacheslav Molotov, and the Japanese ambassador, Naotake Sato, in which Molotov informed his counterpart that the Soviet Union was terminating all treaties with Japan and was now at war with his nation.

Accelerated plutonium production schedules allowed Los Alamos to prepare the world's third Fat Man plutonium core for shipment to Tinian. On August 10, Groves wrote to General Marshall that this additional weapon would be ready for use on a target in Japan after August 24. He then added:

> The second implosion bomb should be ready 24 August.... Additional bombs will be ready for delivery at an accelerated rate, increasing from about three in September to possibly seven in December, with a sharp increase in production expected early in 1946.

Marshall returned the letter the same day with a hand-written note penciled on the bottom:

> It is *not* [Marshall's emphasis] to be released over Japan with-out express authority from the President.
> G. C. Marshall[54]

Groves held back the shipment. The production projections he sent to Marshall included the surprising news that enough U235 for a second gun bomb would be available by October, and there would be enough for a third one by December.

The next day, Groves placed a call to Oppenheimer and confirmed that there would be no further shipments to Tinian. Whatever nuclear material was already in the Pacific would be brought back, and nothing was to leave Los Alamos. Groves also wanted to assemble three provisional parties to inspect Hiroshima and Nagasaki as soon as they were accessible. Who from Los Alamos should go? Oppenheimer recommended Nolan, who was already at Tinian, and Charles Baker, Philip Morrison, Bill Penney, and Robert Serber for the laboratory's scientific team. Groves admitted his distress that there were few reports on Nagasaki, but Oppenheimer reassured him that the laboratory's preliminary assessment from aerial photographs was that the bombing was "materially greater in striking power." Groves also asked Oppenheimer if there was any reason not to release movie footage from Trinity. There was no objection, although the footage was very poor in quality. Concerned about security as always, the general asked how many prints of the movie existed? There were two: one in Los Alamos and the one that had been shredded by the projector at Tinian.

The bombings of Hiroshima and Nagasaki made it clear to the Japanese that no city in their country was safe from the new terror. With the Soviet invasion, there was no hope of a mediator or go-between to help Japan negotiate an end to the war. Japan surrendered unconditionally on August 14th.

When word of the surrender reached Los Alamos, all work stopped. The Tech Area siren sounded and cars honked. Kistiakowsky, inspired by a lively and well-lubricated party at Bob Bacher's house, set off twenty-one fifty-pound boxes of old explosives in an open field. Scientists ran from their laboratories into the streets, shaking hands and slapping one another on the back. In the residential neighborhoods women screamed and cried when they heard the news on the radio and ran next door to make sure their neighbors knew. As evening fell, informal parties convened across the mesa. Bottles of scotch and bourbon found their way out of cabinets, and a few couples retrieved a treasured pre-war bottle of champagne from its hiding place. And more than one family lifted a photograph of a loved one who had perished in America's long, terrible war.

———————————

One young scientist at Los Alamos had more than the surrender of Japan to celebrate. Bob Krohn, who had been one of the first arrivals on the Hill in 1943, had been given a special assignment the day after Nagasaki by Ken Bainbridge. He was told that a drop was expected on a third Japanese city within a week or so, and that the laboratory wanted to fly a B-29 through the mushroom cloud to collect radioactive samples. Krohn was told to design and build as soon as possible a filter mechanism that could be attached to the airplane. "I had one week to get the filter built and then I would take it to Tinian on a military plane and install it on a B-29.... I could put a hole in the side of the plane if necessary.... I got the shop started the next day, then got a call from Bainbridge that ... it appeared that Japan was ready to surrender." Fortunately for Krohn, who was expected to accompany his detector through the radioactive cloud, the experiment was canceled. He could stay on the Hill and celebrate with everyone else.[55]

Emotions ran high in Los Alamos for a few days and then settled down to a mixture of relief and regret—what now? There was a growing realization that their work was done and that they would be returning to their old neighborhoods and jobs. The men at Los Alamos also knew that the bombs inevitably had inflicted enormous civilian casualties. In the days immediately after Hiroshima and Nagasaki, however, there were no casualty reports, no photographs of the devastated cities. They would come later.

But most of the people on the Hill realized that a unique experience was coming to an end, a wild ride like nothing they would know again. They would be leaving friends and comrades—the new families they had assembled on the Hill. Most would miss the mesa as well, because Topeka, San Antonio, Chicago, New York, Madison, Los Angeles, and a hundred other hometowns did not offer the mountains and canyons, the crisp spring mornings, and the magnificent sunsets of their secret city in New Mexico. They would miss Oppie's splendid isolation.

The Interim Committee's Scientific Panel had one last duty to perform: a final report on nuclear weapons and postwar planning for the secretary of war. Oppenheimer took the lead in preparing the final draft. Ernest Lawrence came from California and spent a weekend discussing the report and its recommendations with Oppenheimer, whom he found tired and less than optimistic about the future control of weapons. Oppenheimer finally submitted the report and a cover letter in mid-August. The committee, he told Stimson, was convinced that weapons "quantitatively and qualitatively far more effective than now available" could be made. At the same time, the committee was unable to "devise or propose effective military countermeasures for atomic weapons." They could not suggest a program that would assure "to this nation for the next decades hegemony in the field of atomic weapons [and] we are equally unable to insure that such hegemony, if achieved, could protect us from the most terrible destruction."

Oppenheimer then made a particularly trenchant point:

> The development, in the years to come, of more effective atomic weapons, would appear to be a most natural element in any national policy of maintaining our military forces at great strength; nevertheless we have grave doubts that this further development can contribute essentially or permanently to the prevention of war. We believe that the safety of this nation—as opposed to its ability to inflict damage on an enemy power—cannot lie wholly or even primarily in its scientific or technical prowess. It can be based only on making future wars impossible. It is our unanimous and urgent recommendation to you that, despite the present incomplete exploitation of technical possibilities in this field, all steps be taken, all necessary international agreements be made to this end.[56]

Oppenheimer succinctly captured the essential issues that America—and the world—now faced with the atomic bomb.

On Tinian, Los Alamos scientists waited to hear if a third bomb was to be dropped. When it became clear that the war was over and there was nothing more for them to do but pack up, these men found themselves marooned. No orders arrived to return them to New Mexico or anywhere else. Norman Ramsey, who had flown on an observer plane on the Nagasaki drop, hand-wrote a long letter to Oppenheimer begging for his help in securing the necessary paperwork to return. He also expressed a deep concern over the possibility of a nuclear explosion being detonated by fire in the aircraft during takeoff, especially in the case of Fat Man. Ramsey suggested that future implosion bombs might be a "trap door model with a cylindrical plug through the HE [high explosives] so that the active material can be inserted in flight...."[57]

The "demobilization" of the nation's first atomic strike force took place in stages. Ramsey and his fellow scientists and technicians didn't leave until September 17, just in case the Japanese reneged on their unconditional surrender and hostilities resumed. Finally, key components of the additional Fat Man weapons were boxed up and shipped home along with valuable or useable equipment and electronics. Any items that could "reveal" the nature of the new weapon and were not needed back in the States were dumped into the sea. The island commander was asked to leave the isolated compound of huts and buildings used by Los Alamos and the 509th intact and protected for at least six months. But within weeks, the jungle began to creep back between buildings and over the isolated runway. Inch by inch it hid the evidence of the laboratory's brief occupation.

On August 7, the day after Hiroshima, Groves met in person with George Marshall; General Henry "Hap" Arnold, the commander of the Army Air Force; and George Harrison to brief them on the bombing. As always, Groves prepared a three-page report for the chief of staff, who looked at it and read several parts aloud to Arnold and Harrison.[58] In the discussion that followed, Groves apparently displayed an unseemly enthusiasm about the destruction. Marshall gently chided him with the reminder that American success came at the price of many Japanese lives. Groves responded that he wasn't thinking of Japanese casualties so much as the American GIs who made the Bataan Death March. On the way out, Arnold slapped Groves on the back and told him that he felt the same way.[59]

Most Americans in the fall of 1945 more or less shared that feeling. It was less the pleasure of revenge than satisfaction that justice had been exacted. And the many millions who had suffered under the Japanese Greater East Asia Co-Prosperity Sphere in China and Indochina, in the Philippines, Korea, Borneo, and numerous other islands and exotic lands, shared the belief that justice had been served.

Now America would begin the process of transforming its former enemies into allies but with the explicit understanding of who had won the war. For Japan, the process would start with occupation and a photograph—a tall general standing next to a short emperor and former god.

Chapter Sixteen

THE EXTRAORDINARY WORKING RELATIONSHIP

S uddenly, it was gone—the nearly impenetrable veil of secrecy was torn away. Overnight, America learned that it had atomic bombs and the huge industrial plants and secret mountain laboratory that made them. It learned about the determined general and the cerebral, conflicted scientist who led the team that designed the bomb and about the hundreds of thousands of ordinary men and women who helped along the way. The public didn't know the details of course. Ceramic barriers, polonium and beryllium initiators, explosive lenses, tampers and trap-doors, Pu239 and U235 cores—this information remained classified. President Truman, however, penciled a note in his diary that the bomb at Trinity contained "thirteen pounds" of a special "explosive," an act that would have apppalled Groves had he known.

But as intriguing as the vast, mysterious enterprise that culminated in the destruction of Hiroshima and Nagasaki was, to most Americans, including those at Los Alamos, it meant only one thing—an end to the war. Within a week the long, costly conflict that had laid waste to nations and consumed so many lives was at last over. The longer-term consequences were far more complex and uncertain. Could there be another world war if atomic bombs were now part of the arsenals of nations? What did it mean for the United States and Great Britain to have the bomb and no one else? And what of the victims of Hiroshima and Nagasaki? These and a thousand other questions had few answers in September 1945.

For Groves and Oppenheimer, the end of the war brought enormous relief, sweetened by success, as well as a new set of challenges. The issues Groves faced were far more daunting, at least in the short term. What was to become of the extraordinary network of industrial plants, laboratories, and communities he had so energetically built and then artfully managed? Almost 150,000 men and women were employed in thirty-three Manhattan Project installations on 550,000 acres with an annual payroll of two hundred million dollars. Both Oak Ridge and Hanover were still operating around the clock to generate U235 and Pu239. Should he cut back production or perhaps shut down some operations entirely? There was every incentive to reduce the civilian payroll, especially as the Manhattan Engineer District's total spending approached two billion dollars. But how long would the MED continue to exist and in what form? For the moment, he was still in charge of the Manhattan Project, and he expected to continue in that role until Congress acted.

Groves and Oppenheimer also became the focus of intense public interest. Groves was heavily quoted and featured in newspaper and magazine articles, and his testimony before congressional committees was closely watched and reported. He turned public relations over to Lieutenant Colonel Bill Consodine, a former reporter who quickly produced and distributed a series of news releases and staged publicity photographs—the general at his desk with a telephone, the general at a table with stern-looking men in business suits, and most effective of all, the upper-body shot that revealed the distinguished face. A press release also went out shortly after Hiroshima describing the general:

> A soft-spoken Major-General with a flair for the "Impossible" emerged today from the shadows of Army-imposed anonymity to be revealed as the driving force behind a $2,000,000,000 "calculated risk" which he directed to successful completion in three years as one of the world's greatest scientific and engineering achievements, the large-scale tapping of the energy within atoms to produce a new weapon of war.[1]

In the flush of victory, the adjectives flowed—intelligent, hard-driving, no-nonsense, masterly. Secretary of War Stimson, however, cut through all the rhetoric in his summary of the man's true legacy: "The case was rare indeed where a single individual had the fortune to be as effective as Groves had in the winding up of a great war."[2]

The press was delighted with the general as a military hero, but it was more intrigued with Oppenheimer. With his lean, pensive face, he looked like the quintessential intellectual scientist. The ubiquitous cigarette or pipe and the porkpie hat played well—he was an egghead, but he dressed and smoked like everyone else. And his articulate yet sometimes hesitant responses to questions from the press and Congress impressed and captivated everyone, at least in the beginning. The press inevitably focused more on his intelligence and style than his substance. One War Department press release embarrassingly quoted an unnamed associate as saying, "Oppie is so smart no one can fool him for a second—he knows more about most of our specialties that we know ourselves—in fact he's the smartest of the lot in everything."[3]

Oppenheimer had to consider the short-term future of the laboratory, but he also had to decide what to do next. Return to teaching? Play a role in the future development and control of nuclear weapons? Or could he do both? The Berkeley classroom seemed a small stage after Los Alamos. Now he was on magazine covers and featured in newsreels across the country. Friends couldn't help but tell him how well he photographed. It was a new life that he found both unnerving and thrilling.

Once the shock of America's powerful new bombs began to fade and Groves and Oppenheimer moved off the front pages, journalists turned their curiosity to the effects of an atomic bombing, particularly radiation. They began just days after Hiroshima. On August 8, a chemist and science writer, Harold Jacobson, announced in an interview with the *Washington Post* that Hiroshima would be uninhabitable for at least seventy-five years. Jacobson had no connection with Los Alamos or the Manhattan Project, but his dire pronouncement received wide coverage in the press. Unfortunately, the interview was also picked up by the Japanese and extensively quoted. The article sent Groves scurrying to prepare a reply. He called Oppenheimer and read him Jacobson's statement. Oppenheimer called it "lunacy." Based on what Los Alamos had learned at Trinity, "there would be no appreciable activity on the ground and what little there was would decay very rapidly." Groves was given permission to quote him.

On August 9, the Paris edition of *Stars and Stripes*, the newspaper of the armed forces in Europe, ran two front-page articles on Hiroshima. One of them, headlined "Text of Jap Broadcast to U.S. Detailing Horror of Hiroshima," included the line, "Medical relief agencies ... were unable to distinguish much less identify the dead from the injured." At the end of the story was a photograph of Groves eyeing a map of the Japanese home islands.

A month later, an Australian reporter named Wilfred Burchett was able to make his way to Hiroshima. He found the city flattened, a sea of rubble. In interviews with hospitalized survivors, he was told of an "atomic plague" that had gripped the city and was killing patients long after the explosion itself. His story was published in London's *Daily Express* in early September.

Stories like these and a host of newspaper and magazine articles that Groves deemed inaccurate or misleading led to one of the hottest press events of the fall. Shortly after the public had learned of the Manhattan Project, a reporter asked Groves if newsmen could visit the Trinity site. Groves was initially opposed, but he began to change his mind when news stories continued to dwell on the effects of radioactivity in Hiroshima and Nagasaki. On August 25, he asked Dr. Hempelmann for the latest report on residual radioactivity at Trinity. Hempelmann told him that there was still a fair amount near the crater at Ground Zero—some ten REMs* per hour—and some intensity for another hundred feet or so. Groves then asked if it would be possible to take reporters into the crater. Hempelmann was concerned that such a visit would be unsafe. Radioactivity had fallen off quite rapidly in the first few days after the explosion, but the decline had slowed in the following weeks. Still, he did not have the most recent figures and agreed to collect them and call back. As it turned out, more recent data suggested that a brief visit to Ground Zero would not entail inordinate risk. Three days later, Groves called Tolman and asked him what he thought of the press junket. "It's a good idea," Tolman replied.

Groves instructed Consodine to organize the press visit to Ground Zero. He wanted the best coverage he could get to offset the growing number of stories about radioactivity as the press gained access to the survivors of Hiroshima and Nagasaki. Groves would personally lead the tour and wanted Oppenheimer to join him. He called Oppenheimer on September 7 with the plan. Some twenty journalists had been cleared for the visit. They would fly into the Alamogordo Airbase and be driven north into Trinity. Groves would fly into Albuquerque the night before; would Oppenheimer pick him up? Hempelmann was ordered to bring along a

---

* REM stands for Roentgen Equivalent Man, an early unit for reporting radiation. The term is no longer used.

number of "gadgets"—Geiger counters and film badges for everyone. Despite reassurances that the radioactive levels were safe, everyone visiting Trinity in mid-September wore white, disposable "booties" over his shoes. Groves wanted to allay fears of lingering radioactivity, and he believed that the American public deserved to see the power of the weapon their tax dollars had purchased. The press tour of Trinity produced one of the most emblematic photographs of the era: the general and the scientist, in their white booties, standing next to the melted remnants of one leg of the tower.

Groves's battle with the press over radioactivity continued for months. American newspapers continued to pass along stories from Japanese radio broadcasts, including a report that servicemen helping to clear the rubble in Hiroshima and Nagasaki displayed "burns" and lower white and red blood corpuscle counts. Others reported that surviving victims of the bombings would not live. Groves placed a call on August 25 to Colonel Charles Rea, director of the army hospital at Oak Ridge, and read to him from one newspaper account: "So painful are these injuries [caused by the atomic bomb] that the suffering plead: 'please kill me,' the broadcast said. No one can ever completely recover." Groves wanted to know how to respond to inquiries from American reporters. Rea, who had read the same account in his local newspaper, responded that many victims suffered thermal burns, the effects of which would manifest themselves over days and weeks, not overnight. Moreover, Rea thought a lot of the information was "hokum" and that Americans were getting a "good dose of propaganda." Groves agreed but wanted more information. Rea promised to prepare additional background on the matter.[4]

General Farrell wrote a long memorandum to Groves at the end of September summarizing the use and effects of atomic weapons in Japan. He confirmed Groves's suspicion that misinformation was being disseminated by the Japanese themselves:

> The Japanese officials and press gave out misleading statements concerning the lasting effects of radio-activity. A leading

Japanese scientist said that he thought it possible that poison gases were released at the time of the explosion.... Japanese and American news stories stated that personnel who came into the [bombed] areas to assist in evacuation were injured. The true story was that the evacuation personnel were in Hiroshima to carry out an evacuation previously ordered and were caught by explosion of the bomb suffering many casualties.[5]

Whatever misinformation was floating around in the fall of 1945, it was nonetheless true that doctors in Hiroshima and Nagasaki were discovering radiation sickness, or what they soon called the "atomic bomb illness." Many survivors began to report a combination of symptoms—diarrhea, loss of appetite, nausea and vomiting, and blood in their stools, among others. Some of these symptoms would disappear then reappear. Purple spots began to develop on the skin, mouths and gums bled, and hair began to fall out. As one doctor wrote in his diary, "People who appeared to be recovering developed other symptoms that caused them to die. So many patients died without our understanding the cause of death that we were all in despair.... As time passed, anorexia and diarrhea proved to be the most persistent symptoms in patients who failed to recover."[6]

In the rush to construct a deliverable atomic bomb, little attention had been given to the slowly growing evidence within the Manhattan Project itself that ionizing radiation could produce illness and even death. Postwar studies have suggested that such evidence was available, although not complete, as early as 1940.[7] Louis Hempelmann sent a memorandum to Oppenheimer in February 1944 warning that some ailments caused by radiation would not appear for many years.[8] Not one person got sick after Trinity because no one was close enough to the explosion to be subject to radiation. That was not the case at Hiroshima and Nagasaki. Truman, Stimson, and other policy makers received casualty figures from the bombings

of Hiroshima and Nagasaki, but possible radiological effects do not seem
to have been mentioned.

On August 12, 1945, Groves released to the public a long, dense report
on the Manhattan Project. The year before, he had approved Vannevar
Bush's suggestion that Henry DeWolf Smyth, the chairman of the physics
department at Princeton and an associate director of the Met Lab in Chicago, write an official history of the atomic bomb project that could be
published at some appropriate time in the future. Groves provided Smyth
access to Hanford, Oak Ridge, Los Alamos and other sites and to a mass
of documents. The windows and doors in Smyth's offices in Princeton's
Palmer Laboratory were locked and barred, and Groves posted armed
guards. Groves and Conant reviewed the first full draft, and the final was
submitted to Tolman. When the report was finally issued, it bore the
ponderous title *Atomic Energy for Military Purposes: The Official Report
on the Development of the Atomic Bomb under the Auspices of the U. S.
Government, 1940–1945.* The "Smyth Report," as it became known, stayed
on the *New York Times* best seller list for three months. Some scientists
and policy makers criticized it as too revealing and others as too shallow.
Still others felt the history emphasized physics at the expense of engineering. These criticisms did not seem to diminish the public's appetite for any
information on these new weapons, and 127,000 copies were sold.

Oppenheimer called Groves on September 6 to ask when Parsons and
the others at Tinian would be permitted to return to the States, and Groves
told him that orders had been issued to bring the team back. There followed an unusually extended conversation between the two men, touching on a wide range of issues and lasting over an hour. Oppenheimer

wanted to know if certain operations currently under way at Los Alamos could be transferred to private industries such as the DuPont or the Hercules Companies. Groves thought that likely, but any transfer needed to be considered in the larger context of the laboratory's future. Oppenheimer also felt that "the situation at Y needs a lot of work if it is to be made permanent." Kistiakowsky would be in Washington in the next few days and would give details of the challenges facing the laboratory. Groves knew that retaining staff was a growing challenge, and he asked that everyone working at the laboratory be reassured that he need not fear losing his job. It wasn't that people were in a hurry to leave, Oppenheimer responded, but "that they are not putting very much heart into the job anymore." Groves called Conant the next day to report the conversation. "Everything is uncertain out there," he told Conant, suggesting that the two of them visit Los Alamos as soon as possible to exert, as he put it, "soothing influences."

Kistiakowsky delivered more discouraging news a few days later. Attitudes were bad and morale was down. Groves called Conant and told him that "things have drifted at Y and drifted badly particularly as Oppie has been ill and away from work for a while.... No one seems to take hold when Oppie was gone." They discussed his resignation. Groves thought Oppenheimer's departure was inevitable and in fact desirable. But who would replace him? Groves preferred to see Bob Bacher take over but was willing to consider Bradbury. Conant agreed that Bacher was the first choice, but he was not sure about Bradbury. Would Norris even consider the position?

On September 14, Groves and Oppenheimer once again conducted a marathon telephone conversation. To combat the malaise at the laboratory, Groves planned a visit for Tuesday, September 19. He wanted three meetings arranged, one after the other: the first with division heads, the second with civilian staff, and the third with SED and military personnel. He would thank them and brief them on legislation now being discussed in Congress. Oppenheimer asked about a new director. Groves hoped it might be someone like a university president—Conant was mentioned as an example. If such a man were not available, then in Groves's view

Bacher was the strongest candidate. Why didn't Oppenheimer discuss the possibility directly with Bacher, although with no one else? Oppenheimer asked if the laboratory might be relocated, perhaps closer to a major city, which might help retention. No decision could be made yet, Groves said, and the laboratory would stay on the mesa for the foreseeable future.

Groves made his visit, and then he and Oppenheimer flew back to Washington together the following day on the general's personal plane. By the time they landed, the field of candidates to replace Oppenheimer had narrowed to one—Norris Bradbury. Bacher could not be talked into taking the helm of a mountain laboratory with an uncertain future, and even Bradbury was going to need persuasion.

───────────────

For those working at Los Alamos, the fall of Japan meant not only the end of the war but a new reality. Work at the laboratory was ending, and despite Groves's reassurances, the staff faced the prospect of unemployment. Each day brought the conclusion of one task or another, and the words "winding down" were on everyone's lips. Senior men—Fermi, Bethe, Allison, Bacher, and others—would soon return to their posts at prestigious universities. Other men would return to complete graduate degrees. Military men like Parsons could look forward to illustrious service careers. But most others, particularly those whose scientific careers began at Los Alamos, felt some anxiety over the future of the organization and their employment. Concern was equally strong in the army's Special Engineering Detachment.

Oppenheimer's future was uncertain as well, although for him it was not a matter of employment. He could return to Berkeley, but he also had offers from Harvard, Princeton, Colombia, and Caltech. As much as a return to teaching in California appealed to him, he knew that his influence, which extended beyond the Hill, was the fruit of his central role in weapons development. He now believed that he needed to participate in the emerging political debates in Washington over the control of nuclear weapons.

Groves was more than willing to let Oppenheimer resign. Any achievements by Los Alamos after the war would be anticlimactic for Oppenheimer, and Groves was eager for anyone who raised security concerns, particularly someone with a questionable political past, to be out of the picture. He knew that with the war over, there would be closer scrutiny of his emergency wartime decisions.

In an earlier letter to Groves in May 1945, Oppenheimer tried to establish what he called "cognizance" of the laboratory's future. Los Alamos would continue the production of Fat Man bombs while seeking to perfect the uranium bomb. It was important, Oppenheimer urged, to shift major parts of the laboratory's work to private contractors. His recommendation that components such as the polonium initiator, the plutonium cores, and explosive lenses be manufactured by commercial firms reflected his belief that such manufacturing had never been part of the laboratory's "true" function, even though the exigencies of war and pressure from Groves had made it part of the work at Los Alamos. Resolution of the laboratory's future, Oppenheimer argued, could be made more easily by eliminating these activities. "I also know," he added, "that the whole organization, temper, and structure of Site Y Laboratories is singularly unsuited for peacetime perpetuation." His letter ended with a declaration of intent to leave:

> In particular, the Director himself would very much like to know when he will be able to escape from these duties for which he is so ill qualified and which he has accepted only in an effort to serve the country during the war.[9]

Oppenheimer could leave Los Alamos, but could he escape his role as father of the atomic bomb?

Oppenheimer was not alone in sensing a new social responsibility. Demand for a voice in shaping America's nuclear policy was growing among the scientists of the Manhattan District. The farsighted saw the need for postwar international controls. Although discussions on the use and import of the bomb occurred in all Manhattan projects, they were most clamorous at the University of Chicago's Metallurgical Laboratory. The men there had spent the war contributing to the development of the bomb but not building it. As the "uncle" and not the "father," perhaps they could more easily separate themselves from Fat Man and Little Boy and objectively evaluate the nature of the weapon and its future.

However much Groves discouraged it, Bush and Compton found themselves increasingly engaged in conversations with concerned scientists. Both men were aware that military and diplomatic concerns, not scientific ones, were now dominating political discussions, but Compton in particular wanted to know what his colleagues were thinking. He went a step further in June 1945 by asking leaders at the Met Lab to submit their ideas on the use of nuclear weapons and postwar controls. Their reply, a memorandum titled "Political and Social Problems," reflected their mounting anxiety. They pointed out that other nations would inevitably possess atomic weapons and that if the United States were the first to use them, it "would sacrifice public support throughout the world, precipitate the race of armaments, and prejudice the possibility of reaching an international agreement on the future control of such weapons." They concluded by urging "that the use of nuclear bombs in this war be considered as a problem of long-range national policy rather than military expediency, and that this policy be directed primarily to the achievement of an agreement permitting an effective international control of the means of nuclear warfare." Compton promptly sent the report to Stimson, noting, however, that the authors of the report had omitted two important considerations:

(1) that failure to make a military demonstration of the new bomb may make the war longer and more expensive of human lives, and

(2) that without a military demonstration it may be impossible to impress the world with the need for national sacrifices in order to gain lasting security.[10]

The Met Lab memorandum represented the deeply-felt views of many who had undertaken their work in response to a threat—a German atomic bomb—that no longer existed. Both Niels Bohr and Leo Szilard had supported work on the weapon throughout the war as a safeguard against the Germans, but as the war neared its end, they urged that the atomic bomb be used only as a threat and that all the secrecy surrounding it end as soon as possible.

Szilard, the man responsible for persuading Einstein to write to Roosevelt in 1939, was quite concerned over the fate of the weapon. In July 1945, in response to Compton's invitation to submit ideas, he circulated a petition at the Met Lab calling for the bomb not to be used. To use the bomb, the petition read, "was to bear the responsibility of opening the door to an era of devastation on an unimaginable scale."[11]

Szilard attempted to galvanize support from scientists in other Manhattan laboratories. He wrote to Edward Teller in Los Alamos asking him to sign the petition. Teller consulted Oppenheimer, who, according to Teller, replied that it was inappropriate for scientists to use their prestige as a basis for political statements. In an unusually conflicted letter to Szilard, Teller wrote, "The things we are working on are so terrible that no amount of protesting or fiddling with politics will save our souls." Then he added, "But I am not really convinced of your objections [to the use of the bomb]. I do not feel that there is any chance to outlaw any one weapon. If we have a slim chance of survival, it lies in the possibility to get rid of war. The more decisive the weapon is, the more severely it will be used in any real conflict and no agreements will help."[12]

Groves was furious when he heard of Szilard's efforts. He considered it more than meddling—it was disloyalty. Szilard's petition was part of a pattern, in Groves's view, going back to 1942. The scientist was "a pain the neck," and while Szilard had shown determination at the beginning of the war, "as soon as we got going, so far as I was concerned he might just as well have walked the plank."[13] Groves was determined finally to silence the man. Szilard, he knew, had met in May 1943 with Lord Cherwell (Frederick Lindermann), Winston Churchill's scientific advisor and the head of Oxford University's Clarendon Laboratory. If by chance Szilard had passed along secret information during the meeting, he could be charged with violating the Espionage Act. Groves wrote to Cherwell on July 4, 1945, asking if he could recall that conversation. "Frankly, Dr. Szilard has not, in our opinion, evidenced wholehearted cooperation in the maintenance of security," Groves wrote. Cherwell responded a week later, saying that Szilard "always had rather a bee in his bonnet about the awful implications of these [atomic bomb] matters." Unfortunately, Cherwell could add little else to help Groves. "My impression is that his security was good to the point of brusqueness. He did, I believe, complain that compartmentalization was carried to undue lengths in America."[14]

In the end, the discussions and petitions didn't matter. The decision to use the atomic bomb was made by a combination of statesmen and military leaders and, finally, by the president of the United States. Some argue that the decision was simply the result of momentum. So much money and effort had been expended that the technological imperative had taken over: America had the bomb and therefore would use it. Hiroshima and Nagasaki revealed the futility of the protests. The scientists who were responsible for the weapon's existence had little influence over its use as the war neared its end. This was an uncomfortable reality for some. Stimson, in a press conference following the Hiroshima and Nagasaki drops, revealed a deep emotion: The bomb, he said, "is so terrific that the responsibility of its possession and its use must weigh heavier on our minds and our hearts."[15]

Truman was not without his own concerns. He called for legislation that would put atomic energy into the hands of a permanent civilian authority. Congressional hearings on what became known as the May-Johnson Bill exposed the public to the acrimonious division between scientists. Groves, Bush, and Oppenheimer, among others, supported the legislation in the hearings. Oppenheimer was even persuaded to recruit endorsements from Fermi and Lawrence. Groves himself was a superb witness—confident, authoritative, and comfortable looking each of his congressional inquisitors directly in the eye.

In November, Oppenheimer joined 191 of his colleagues in a petition sent to both the president and to members of Congress arguing for national and international control of atomic energy. At the same time, he belittled the concerns of some of his colleagues in the scientific community over military influence. In an appearance before Congressman Andrew J. May, chairman of the House Military Affairs Committee, he said he did not think it likely the military would dominate the proposed civilian agency.

———

With Groves's attention increasingly focused on the debate over nuclear weapons in Washington, Oppenheimer was forced to deal with the reality of a postwar Los Alamos. The Japanese surrender eliminated many of the pressures on the laboratory. One scientist described the situation like a whistling teapot suddenly pulled from the stove. New issues arose: job placement, work continuity, and the return of employees to civilian life. The demands on his time were growing daily, and repeated command appearances in Washington interfered with his effective administration of the laboratory.

Parsons, Kistiakowsky, and others agreed among themselves that the present Fat Man was prototypic at best, an assessment confirmed by data from Trinity and observations in Japan. The uranium tamper was too large, too wasteful, and inefficient, and the explosive lenses were fragile.

Research had already suggested several new designs, including a "levitated bomb" in which empty space between the plutonium and the initiator would allow the inward compressive forces to accelerate. The bomb's electronic system was crude, and the X-unit was heavy and bulky. With Groves's approval, Oppenheimer put his men to work refining the implosion bomb. Word was passed to group and division leaders to keep their men as busy they could, even if it meant pursuing activities of little value. Kistiakowsky issued a lengthy memorandum to his group and section leaders titled "What to Do Now." He was careful to add that the memo's indications might well be changed "on instructions from Washington."

At the same time, Kistiakowsky and other leaders found themselves discouraging men from leaving the laboratory immediately. Several months would be needed for Los Alamos to be, as Kistiakowsky put it, "liquidated or reorganized." At that time, staff members could leave without harm to the project. To the group and section leaders of his diverse division he wrote, "Probably with the end of the war, the emphasis should be changed from short range practical developments to a better study of the fundamentals. I feel ... that our work will not be complete until we have looked over our past activities, filled gaps in our knowledge of the basic phenomena underlying the implosion process and have written up our present knowledge."[16]

Ongoing conversations with Groves, Bush, Conant, and others fortified Oppenheimer's belief that the laboratory would survive in one form or another. In late August, Oppenheimer sent a memo to all of his division and group leaders announcing the "principles" under which Los Alamos would be operated for the next few months. It was important, he said, that no activity should lead to the "abandonment of work on adequate weapons." Present personnel were not to be retained unless necessary for the work at hand or that foreseen for the next several months, but at the same time, "separations" should allow for men to find suitable employment elsewhere.

Oppenheimer also thought it important that "key people" not leave until their functions and responsibilities were transferred to others.[17]

Knowing how eager his senior leaders were to resume their academic careers, he organized a Los Alamos "encyclopedia"—a history and a documentation of the laboratory's work—partly as insurance against the sudden departure of these key men. Hans Bethe was put in charge. Bethe, in turn, asked Robert Wilson, Kennedy, Cyril Smith, Darol Froman, and others to prepare major volumes in their respective scientific or technical areas. Each volume would be written by staff members. The encyclopedia, as Bethe saw it, had two purposes: to make available to scientists the results achieved and the methods developed at Los Alamos and to put on record the techniques of making an atomic bomb. He added drolly that it might be "useful to our prospective successors."[18]

Good news came unexpectedly in the fall. The revelation to the public of Los Alamos brought job offers for the men who worked there from institutions across America. Senior men had their pick of positions, but even junior scientists and technicians received invitations from industry and universities. Because the war had drawn most young men into active service, many of those headed for a university education before the war had been forced to postpone their college entry. Those with deferments at Los Alamos, or the few lucky service men with college degrees who were stationed on the Hill, possessed skills and experience critically needed by laboratories and industry. Oppenheimer found himself repeating his work of 1943—wooing and cajoling men—but this time asking them not to come to Los Alamos but to stay.

General Groves faced a different reality. The huge production facilities at Oak Ridge and Hanford were still necessary suppliers of U235 and Pu239, but Groves felt it prudent to trim their operations by releasing extra staff and shutting down production facilities that had been built when urgent delivery deadlines justified the expenditure of huge sums of money. The liquid-thermal diffusion plant at Oak Ridge was closed, and a few weeks later another plant shut down. Hanford technicians set themselves to perfecting operational procedures and to exploring ways to store plutonium nitrates.

Both Hanford and Oak Ridge had a single purpose—the production of critical material. Los Alamos, on the other hand, served both research and production needs. Oppenheimer had recommended that his staff continue research into more efficient bomb designs while production was shifted to private industry. But with the political fluctuations in Washington, Groves could not be sure what sort of government agency would eventually emerge. From his perspective, it seemed best to keep Los Alamos operating as it was with certain adjustments. Work on the Super could continue, but not as a priority. He allowed the laboratory to take over Sandia Field, a little-used airbase in Albuquerque, for centralizing the assembly of atomic weapons, and he transferred the facilities at Wendover Field in Utah to Albuquerque. Above all, no new major programs would be undertaken until Congress took action.

Norris Bradbury was an excellent choice to replace Oppenheimer. He was a lieutenant commander in the naval reserves and had had an outstanding career at Pomona College, the University of California, the Massachusetts Institute of Technology, and Stanford University. He had come to Los Alamos in 1944 as a physicist as well as one of the laboratory's few weapons experts. He had played major roles at Trinity and in Project Alberta. Groves appreciated his impressive scientific resume at Los Alamos as well as his leadership and proved ability to work closely with the military. The only question in Groves's mind was whether the laboratory needed one director or two co-directors?

Oppenheimer insisted that Los Alamos should have one director. He had learned enough about management from studying Groves to believe that while consensus was important, an organization like the laboratory needed a single leader. When Groves suggested to Oppenheimer that perhaps selecting both Bradbury and a coordinator might be the best solution, Oppenheimer placed an urgent call to Washington to protest. Groves was out of the office, so Oppenheimer left a terse message with Jean O'Leary—there was only one job and that was as interim director and coordinator. The staff at Los Alamos agreed with him, he added. He went on to tell O'Leary that when he and Bradbury came to Washington to meet with Groves the following week, they would come on the assumption that there was but one job and if Bradbury was selected, he would be selected "for the one job." O'Leary noted on the call sheet that she had never heard Dr. O "feel so strongly" about any matter.[19] With the laboratory's future uncertain, Groves and Oppenheimer reached a compromise. Bradbury would be asked to serve as interim director for six months. To assure cooperation from remaining staff members, Groves announced that he expected Oppenheimer and the division leaders to choose a permanent director from their own ranks. In the end, Bradbury kept his post until his retirement twenty-five years later.

———————————

Groves retained his deep bond with Los Alamos even after Oppenheimer's departure. His relations with other parts of the Manhattan effort were detached and businesslike, but his connection to the laboratory was personal, almost fatherly. Only *he* managed the laboratory, working first with Oppenheimer and now Bradbury, intervening, making decisions, and serving to some extent as de facto co-director. As soon as Bradbury was selected, Groves called and asked what he could do to help. Bradbury, desperate to retain as many of the talented men drawn to Los Alamos during the war as he could, told the general that he needed good housing, and lots of it, if he was going to succeed in retaining and attracting staff. In a complete turn-around, Groves agreed immediately. And when the matter of mail censorship came up, he quickly instructed the new post commander, Colonel Lyle Seeman, to ease up and apologize for mistakes of the past.[20]

Oppenheimer's departure left Bradbury with the challenging task of holding together what staff he could, negotiating the organization's future, and maintaining America's domination of atomic weapons. It would not be easy. Wartime fervor had inspired men to accept hardship and isolation, but the communal sense of service was evaporating in peacetime. The harsh realities of life in Los Alamos remained. Top leaders had departed or were preparing to depart, leaving Bradbury with what James Tuck called the "second team."[21] Scientists disagreed about what to do beyond improving wartime weapon designs. Should they pursue the Super? Should they diversify their work into other areas of nuclear research, including those not related to weapons, such as health and manufacturing? Oppenheimer was increasingly remote as the weeks passed, and it was clear to those closest to him that he was pulling away. Groves was busy in Washington defending Manhattan District expenditures and battling Congress over legislation. And Truman was under considerable pressure to regard the new weapon as leverage against a Soviet Union increasingly perceived as hostile.

At Groves's urging, Bradbury called his senior staff together to evaluate the state of the laboratory and to sound out what each of them saw as its future. None doubted that the government would continue to support weapons research, and all were comfortable with the organization's reporting to a new government agency or commission. Bradbury was concerned that overcautious security restrictions in proposed legislation could reduce the number of good men attracted to work at Los Alamos. It was also quite possible that the political appointees who would run the new agency would be insensitive to research needs. Bradbury and his staff had little choice but to plan for work considered ideal by Los Alamos standards—that is, activities favoring scientific interests yet not inconsistent with postwar needs for stockpiling nuclear weapons. Bradbury, with Oppenheimer present, let an anxious staff know his assessment of the situation on October 1. He emphasized that the weapons to be stockpiled were not necessarily intended for use but for ensuring that the nation had the bargaining strength it needed to bring about world agreement. "To weaken the nation's bargaining power during the Administration's attempt to bring about international cooperation would be suicidal," he said. Bradbury hoped that the emphasis on weapons would decrease over the years and added, almost as if to reassure himself, that "we are not a warring nation; the mere possession of weapons does not bring about war."[22]

Bradbury's philosophy was simple—he wanted to "leave the best possible project for our successors; continue weaponeering until it is clear that we can taper off; [and] decrease the size of the project consistent with the housing facilities on the mesa."[23] He asked that at least fifteen Fat Man weapons be stockpiled. Groves agreed, with the understanding that these bombs would be modified with composite cores and new methods of fusing, detonation, and packaging. The laboratory would begin a program to develop more efficient and more powerful weapons with improved implosion techniques. Some of this work was already underway and would not be stopped. Bradbury speculated that it would be about three years before production of weapons could be halted. Until that time, however, the goal was weapons that would "insure peace."

Bradbury called for more tests like Trinity, in which scientists could learn more about the forces unleashed in a nuclear explosion. Perhaps the occasional demonstration of an atomic bomb would have a psychological impact on the world, an impact strong enough to secure cooperation in controlling the weapon. And another Trinity might even be fun.

And there was the Super. It gripped the imaginations of both scientists and military leaders. Was building one feasible? Bradbury, Oppenheimer, and Groves agreed that the question presented many intriguing scientific challenges, however terrifying such a weapon might be. Bradbury considered construction of the Super improbable at the moment, but the possibility would no doubt need to be explored in the months and years to come.

Teller, seeing an opening in Oppenheimer's departure, pressed hard for work on the Super to be accelerated. He approached Bradbury but was unable to get a commitment from the new director, so he tried to enlist Oppenheimer. The departing director, however, was also unwilling to use his influence to promote thermonuclear research, at least not at the moment.[24] Teller would have to seek support elsewhere, most likely from the military itself.

As Oppenheimer sat in the audience listening to Bradbury, his satisfaction in a job well done was tempered by an uneasiness for the future. He was leaving Los Alamos, a place he first roamed on horseback decades before, and the men he had brought to the mesa only recently. The work of the laboratory was now in other hands. It had been exciting, perhaps the highpoint of his life. Later, when he was asked why scientists, including himself, had been attracted to weapons of such terrible destruction, he replied simply that they were "technically sweet." He also found time to write to Groves: "[T]here is no need for me to add words of appreciation for what you did during the war.... The United States knows that it is in your debt, and will forever remain so."[25]

Festivities were planned for Oppenheimer's departure. Groves came with a group of important officials to present to the Los Alamos Laboratory a certificate of appreciation from the secretary of war. On October 16, 1945, Los Alamos was bright and cool. Fuller Lodge was decorated with flags and colorful bunting. Groves wore his brown Army Service uniform and matching side cap. Oppenheimer was in a gray suit and blue shirt and his famous porkpie hat. From a low platform, Groves presented the certificate to Oppenheimer and made a brief speech acknowledging the important work of the men and women of Los Alamos. The general was in a reflective mood that day, and he said nothing of his own role in the success of the laboratory. There was a genuine sentiment of gratitude for the work done and the circumstances under which it had been performed. Many in the audience were surprised and moved.

Accepting the citation from Groves, Oppenheimer spoke as always in a low, measured voice. He thanked Groves on behalf of the laboratory's men and women, expressing the hope that everyone could look at the scroll in the future with pride. Pausing, he said that "if atomic bombs are to be added to the arsenals of a warring world, or to the arsenals of nations preparing for war, then the time will come when mankind will curse the names of Los Alamos and Hiroshima." Oppenheimer paused again and finished on a note of hope.

The peoples of this world must unite, or they will perish. This war, that has ravaged so much of the earth, has written these words. The atomic bomb has spelled them out for all men to understand. Other men have spoken them, in other times, of other wars, or other weapons. They have not prevailed. There are some, misled by a false sense of human history, who hold that they will not prevail today. It is not for us to believe that. By our works we are committed, committed to a world united, before this common peril, in law, and in humanity.[26]

⸻

What had begun with Hiroshima was now completed with Oppenheimer's departure from Los Alamos: the extraordinary working relationship between him and Groves came quietly to an end. Both had served each other and the nation well. They would not lose contact with one another altogether, but the electrifying meetings, the intimate, daily contact—the deferential, often eloquent, sometimes terse letters, telexes, and phone calls—would dwindle to an occasional exchange, and the subject was never about construction, or recruitment, or delivery dates, or the intricate, often complex details of atomic weapons. Continuing to address one another by the respectful but affectionate "General Groves" and "Dr. Oppenheimer," each man wished the other's wife and family well.

Would the program to develop an atomic bomb have been as successful without Groves and Oppenheimer? Yes—in time. There were other capable military officers to build industrial plants and scientific laboratories and oversee the monumental effort. Thomas Farrell and Kenneth Nichols were two. And there were competent scientists to lead what became Los Alamos as well, among them Ernest Lawrence and Robert Bacher. But it is unlikely that without Groves and Oppenheimer the program would have succeeded as quickly and magnificently as it did. Almost certainly, there would have been no weapons in 1945, and perhaps not even in the first half of 1946. And by then, assuming the Japanese had not surrendered, the United States would have invaded Japan with terrible casualties on both sides. Groves was unique in his combination of experience, ruthless drive, intelligence, and ability to make tough decisions. Oppenheimer's keen mind, his matchless ability to synthesize problems and solutions, and his power to gather talented men around him and inspire them were incomparable. And both had good luck on their side.

They were very different in personality and background, but what made their collaboration so fruitful was an acceptance of who they were and the times in which they lived. They rose to the occasion as professionals, as human beings, and as Americans. The war brought them together, and with their shared strengths and weaknesses—intelligence, ambition, arrogance, trust, mutual appreciation, the willingness to use the other to gain what he wanted, a readiness to occasionally break the rules, and, not least, a deep patriotism—they forged success.

It was not their differences that shaped history but their similarities.

Chapter Seventeen

RETROSPECTION: 2015

S even decades have passed since Leslie Groves and Robert Oppenheimer surveyed the Los Alamos Ranch School as a possible location
for the secret laboratory that ultimately would produce the atomic
explosions at Trinity and Hiroshima and Nagasaki. The world is very different today, and the legacies of the Manhattan Project and Los Alamos,
of atomic bombs, and of the two men most responsible for the development of those fearsome weapons continue to be debated. Controversy
remains, but perhaps there is agreement on at least one point. The two
most extraordinary men associated with the development of atomic weapons during World War II were Leslie Groves and Robert Oppenheimer.

Groves remained as head of the Manhattan Project until December
31, 1946, when the Manhattan Engineer District, with all of its production

plants, laboratories, and stores of uranium and plutonium, was turned over to the new civilian-run Atomic Energy Commission. The road from the fall of 1945 to the end of 1946 was not smooth. There were bitter, protracted debates over the fate and control of weapons not only in Congress but among scientists and the military as well. Groves testified frequently before Congress, and while he never opposed civilian control of atomic energy in principle, he did see a need for a strong executive and a role for the military. He was increasingly at odds with elements in Congress and in the scientific community and erroneously became identified with those advocating total military control. The talents he displayed during the war—leadership, organization, and drive—did not serve him as well in the political and cultural battles that followed Hiroshima and Nagasaki.

Although the existence of his secret world was revealed, its details were not. While he was still in command of the Manhattan enterprise, Groves struggled to maintain control, but some of his decisions made enemies and cost him support. During a critical debate in 1946 on legislation, he flatly refused to provide technical information to Senator Brien McMahon, the chairman of the powerful special committee on atomic energy, on the grounds that McMahon was not cleared to know. Groves and McMahon became bitter enemies. Ed Condon, who had come to Los Alamos in 1943 but left after a few weeks because of what he perceived to be unrealistic security imposed by Groves, returned to make life difficult for the general when he was named scientific advisor to Senator McMahon and his committee.

There were also incidents involving awards and promotions that further angered army colleagues and his vocal opponents in Congress. In August 1945, Secretary of War Stimson wrote to George Marshall recommending that Groves be awarded the Distinguished Service Cross. Marshall agreed that Groves deserved it, but pointed out that conferring this award would possibly inflame public opinion at a time when Americans were coming to grips with the atomic bomb. And, he asked, should the award be given without also honoring the scientists who played such a vital role in the Manhattan Project? The decision was put off for a few weeks, but Groves received the DSC on September 12, a move that particularly rankled many in the army. Independently, Truman thought Groves deserved to be promoted to the permanent grade of major general—the temporary wartime rank to which he was appointed in 1944. Marshall took exception, citing the rules for promotion in the postwar army, but under pressure promoted Groves to assistant chief of engineers, a position that carried the rank of major general. Groves's enemies resented what they saw as blatant careerism.

Other events generated additional bad press. Several prewar cyclotrons discovered in Japan were destroyed instead of being returned to universities for research purposes. Most did not work, but scientists nonetheless protested angrily. A cable ordering their destruction originated in Groves's office but was apparently not carefully vetted at several critical stages. The general took much of the blame.

At the same time, old friends and supporters from the war began to step down, among them Stimson and Generals Marshall and Styer. The circle of friends and associates who could—and would—rise to his defense grew smaller.

With the end of the Manhattan Project in sight, Groves faced the question of his next assignment. The new secretary of war, Robert Patterson, along with the secretary of the navy, James Forrestal, established the Armed Forces Special Weapons Project to assemble, maintain, and store atomic weapons and to establish radiological safety and weapons security standards for the United States. Groves, who had already taken an early step in this direction when he established Sandia Base at Albuquerque for the assembly and storage of bombs, was placed in charge. It was an important job, but he was restrained in his ability to make decisions and had a far less compliant set of masters with whom to contend. More importantly, the job was only a shadow of his previous position at the head of the Manhattan Project. Like Oppenheimer, he would never again have the power and influence that he had had during the war.

In late 1947, President Truman sent a list of presidential army promotions to Congress. Groves's name was not on it, and a surprising number of senators objected to the omission. Congress refused to act on the presidential list until Groves's name was added. Edward Royall, Patterson's successor, proposed to Truman that Groves be promoted to lieutenant general. Royall asked Groves to help win congressional support for the entire promotion list. He did so, and the list was approved. As a special act of recognition, the Senate made his appointment as lieutenant general retroactive to July 16, 1945, the date of the Trinity test.

Groves hoped that he might be promoted to chief of engineers, a post he thought appropriate for a man of his accomplishments. But when he met with General Dwight Eisenhower, now the chief of staff of the U.S. Army, for a performance evaluation on January 30, 1948, he received a hostile reception. Eisenhower flatly told him that he would never be named chief of engineers, and furthermore, there would be no job comparable to what he had enjoyed during the war. Groves was confronted with a long list of complaints that included rudeness to fellow officers and egregious self-promotion. At the end of the meeting, Groves felt he had no choice but to resign. He submitted his letter of resignation the next day, effective the end of February. The Department of the Army issued a terse press release quoting only one line from the general's letter: "I have applied for retirement from the Army effective February 29."[1] He had served in the Regular Army for twenty-nine years and four months.

Groves quickly received multiple job offers and accepted a position with the Rand Corporation—subsequently Remington-Rand—as vice president for research. Honors came, including seven honorary degrees from universities over the years. In the early 1960s, Groves began to write his memoirs. Commandeering a private office in the National Archives building, Groves kept researchers and secretaries busy with his orders. His book, *Now It Can Be Told*, was a best seller. The copy he sent to Oppenheimer was inscribed, "Could anyone else have run Los Alamos as well?"[2]

For the rest of his life, Groves carefully followed what newspapers, magazines, and historians wrote about him and his Manhattan Project. He was scrupulous about writing to editors to point out errors of fact or misstatements. When that wasn't possible, Groves clipped articles from magazines and made notes of offending content in the margins or on attached sheets of papers. Congressional testimony didn't escape his attention either. After Robert Bacher, testifying before a joint committee in July 1949, inaccurately reported the origins of the novel concept of using a composite core of U235 and Pu239 in a Fat Man bomb, an irritated Groves wrote to his former subordinate Kenneth Nichols that Bacher "apparently has forgotten entirely Oppenheimer's urgent recommendation to me soon after July 16th, 1945," that a composite core replace the solid-plutonium core in the bomb that was dropped on Nagasaki.[3] Groves's papers, now in the National Archives and Records Administration, contain many such examples of a man dutifully attending to his legacy.

Leslie Richard Groves died of a heart attack on July 13, 1970.

Robert and Kitty Oppenheimer left Los Alamos in November 1945 and returned to California, where he resumed his teaching career at Caltech. But like Groves, Oppenheimer found himself in the middle of the great debate over control of atomic weapons. He was frequently asked to testify before Congress and was appointed to a number of special committees. Soon after the war, President Truman appointed him to a board of consultants, from which he was able to influence a report prepared by Dean Acheson and David Lilienthal that recommended international control of atomic energy. The report provided the basis for Bernard Baruch's proposal to the United Nations, an effort that was ultimately vetoed by a suspicious Soviet Union. As a result of the many requests for his time, Oppenheimer continuously traveled back and forth between the West and East Coasts.

In 1947, Oppenheimer accepted an offer from Lewis Strauss to become the director of the Institute for Advanced Study in Princeton, New Jersey. A rear admiral in the naval reserves and a former assistant to the secretary of navy during the war, Strauss would soon become one of the first commissioners of the new U.S. Atomic Energy Commission (AEC) and later, in 1953, its chairman. The directorship not only brought Oppenheimer closer to Washington, but provided him with a house on 285 acres of wooded land, a cook, and a gardener. Although neither man foresaw it at the time, Strauss would be instrumental in ending Oppenheimer's consulting career with the government.

With the establishment of the AEC in 1947, Oppenheimer was asked to serve as chairman of its General Advisory Committee, an important position, especially during the first few years, and Oppenheimer's influence on atomic matters was never higher than during this period. The committee's members were not all scientists but included representatives from business and industry. Oppenheimer tried to leverage his personal prestige to temper what he perceived as an all-out arms race with the Soviets. Edward Teller, Ernest Lawrence, and other scientists, as well as leaders of the newly established U.S. Air Force, were pushing hard for the hydrogen bomb (the "Super"), although there was no clear path to building it. Oppenheimer, who was not convinced by the technical proposals of the time, instead argued for the development of larger, more efficient fission bombs. Whether he sought the distinction or not, Oppenheimer came to be seen as the leading opponent of thermonuclear weapons.

The revelation of the Russian atomic bomb in 1949 ended that debate. President Truman ordered the AEC to start work immediately on the hydrogen bomb using all resources necessary. It was to be another Manhattan Project. Oppenheimer's influence declined while that of Strauss, an avowed anti-communist, grew. Strauss had grown to dislike Oppenheimer, whom he blamed for delaying work on the Super, and a caustic remark by Oppenheimer further damaged their relationship. In testimony before a congressional committee, Strauss had made an impassioned case for strict controls of isotopes. A few days later, Oppenheimer testified before the same committee and sarcastically dismissed Strauss's concerns: "My own rating of the importance of isotopes ... is that they are far less important than electronic devices, but far more important than, let us say, vitamins, somewhere in between."[4] His comment provoked laughter but made an enemy of the chairman of the AEC, who sat embarrassed in the audience.

Strauss now asked the FBI not only to undertake another investigation of Oppenheimer's past but to put him under round-the-clock surveillance, much like what he had been subjected to during the war. His home and office were illegally bugged, his telephones tapped, and agents followed him wherever he went. His political past, with its complicated roster of communist associates, including his wife, brother, and sister-in-law, was combed for evidence of disloyalty. Strauss dropped Oppenheimer from the General Advisory Committee in 1952 and began to close off his connection as a consultant. Throughout 1953, Strauss continued to compile the strongest case he could against the scientist, and in December he and Senator McMahon persuaded President Eisenhower to revoke Oppenheimer's security clearance. Oppenheimer was asked to Strauss's office, where he was told that his clearance had been revoked because of suspected disloyalty. He was given a choice: resign and let the matter drop, or face a review board. Oppenheimer chose to appear before a board. Several days later, Kenneth Nichols, now the general manager of the AEC, presented Oppenheimer with a list of charges.

There were multiple accusations, but at the heart of the AEC's case were Oppenheimer's actions during the late 1940s, when he recommended delaying development of the Super until all avenues for achieving international control had been explored. Strauss and others saw Oppenheimer's position as a deliberate stalling tactic intended to benefit the Soviets. A few saw it as the work of a dedicated communist working inside the system.

Although by 1954 both the United States and the Soviet Union possessed hydrogen weapons, Oppenheimer was held partially responsible for the loss of America's domination of weapons technology.

The AEC's month-long hearing, held in a dilapidated wartime building near the Washington Monument, began on April 12, 1954. When Oppenheimer and his wife entered the room, they were startled to see the three board members sitting behind a table filled with black binders containing all the evidence compiled by the FBI, none of which had been shared with Oppenheimer or his lawyers. What was only an administrative hearing was conducted as a criminal case, with one of the AEC's lawyers, Roger Robb, acting as prosecutor. Oppenheimer's lead attorney, Lloyd Garrison, was respected but inexperienced with administrative hearings, and in Oppenheimer's case he was further handicapped by the fact that government lawyers possessed security clearances and access to classified information and he did not. Neither Oppenheimer nor Garrison knew that the FBI had bugged Garrison's office and telephone and that all conversations between attorney and client were recorded and transcripts given overnight to Strauss and Robb.

The hearing was supposed to be secret, but the news leaked out after two days, and the case became front-page news across America. On April 14, the headline in the *New York Times* announced, "DR. OPPENHEIMER SUSPENDED BY A.E.C. IN SECURITY REVIEW."

Oppenheimer defended himself as best he could, spending twenty-seven hours in the witness chair. For the most part, he handled the prosecution's questions well, but at times he responded hesitantly, even awkwardly, such as when he tried to explain the 1943 incident in his kitchen with Haakon Chevalier. Witnesses were called by both sides. Some, such as Rabi and Bacher, were unreservedly supportive of Oppenheimer, and others were not. Teller acknowledged his former director's able leadership at Los Alamos but then delivered a damaging blow: "I feel that I would like to see the vital interests of this country in other hands which I understand better and therefore trust more."[5]

Groves also testified. While strongly defending his choice of Oppenheimer as director of Los Alamos during the war, he said he could not approve a clearance for the man under current regulations. There was little else he could have said. The rules had changed since 1943, and the Oppenheimer hearings were a reminder to Groves that in the present political climate, he too could be called to account for his actions a decade before. He was supportive where he could be, however. Asked if the revocation of Oppenheimer's clearance and his consequent ineligibility to serve as a consultant would be in the "public interest," Groves answered no:

> The revocation under such extreme publicity as has occurred I think would be most unfortunate, not because of the effect on Dr. Oppenheimer—that I leave to one side—but because of what might be a very disastrous effect upon the attitude of the academic scientists of this country toward Government research of any kind, and particularly when there was not a war on.[6]

The AEC found Oppenheimer loyal but nonetheless a security risk and revoked his clearance. Atomic secrets, many of which he had helped to discover, were now closed to him. Oppenheimer became a villain to some and a hero to others.

In April 1963, President John Kennedy announced that Oppenheimer would receive the recently established Fermi Award for scientific achievement and contributions to humanity. Kennedy was assassinated before he could present the award to Oppenheimer, but President Lyndon Johnson saw to it that the honor was conferred at the White House in December. Oppenheimer was deeply moved by the gesture: "I think it just possible, Mr. President," Oppenheimer said at the ceremony, "that it had taken some charity and some courage for you to make this award today."[7]

A few months later, Norris Bradbury invited the Oppenheimers to visit the laboratory, in June. They declined the offer to stay on the hill and instead lodged with their old friend Dorothy McKibbin in Santa Fe. On June 16, Oppenheimer spoke to an overflow audience in the laboratory's largest auditorium. A decade had passed since the security hearing, but the memory of it lingered on the Hill, and the audience included many men who had willingly worked on the thermonuclear bomb. Oppenheimer didn't speak of the past or personal tragedy but about Niels Bohr. Many of his listeners were shocked at his appearance, and his voice, always low, was now little more than a loud whisper. It was clear that he was ill. When he finished, he was stunned when the audience rose to their feet and applauded for ten minutes. Oppenheimer was forced to return to podium and beg them to leave. But they had sent their message—he was still one of them.

Robert Oppenheimer died of throat cancer on February 18, 1967. In a memorial service in Princeton three weeks later, the Juilliard String Quartet played one of his favorite works, Beethoven's C-Sharp Minor Quartet, Opus No. 14. Sitting in the audience, silver-haired and distinguished, was Lieutenant General Leslie Groves.

And what of the other senior men of Los Alamos?

Soon after the success of the Hiroshima mission, Deak Parsons was awarded the Navy Distinguished Service Cross and promoted to the wartime rank of commodore. In November 1945, he was named deputy chief of naval operations for special weapons and a few months later, in January 1946, promoted to rear admiral without ever having commanded a ship. He stayed involved with atomic weapon developments and was an assistant to the naval deputy commander who oversaw the first postwar experimental tests of atomic bombs in the Pacific in July 1946, almost a year to the day after Trinity. In fact, the bombs tested were both implosion weapons, incorporating the improvements that Parsons and Oppenheimer had suggested in the summer of 1945. There were two tests—an airdrop that missed its target by several thousand feet and an underwater detonation of about the same yield but with a far more impressive dome of rising water.

With the creation of the Atomic Energy Commission, Parsons was appointed a deputy to Leslie Groves, who commanded the Armed Forces Special Weapons Project. In 1952, Parsons was named deputy chief of the Bureau of Standards. He and his wife stayed in touch with Robert and Kitty Oppenheimer throughout the late 1940s and early 1950s. The rise of McCarthyism alarmed Parsons, and in late 1953 he wrote a supportive letter to Oppenheimer. He was upset on December 4, 1953, when he read in the newspaper that President Eisenhower had ordered that Oppenheimer be separated from the U.S. nuclear program by a "blank wall." That night he developed severe chest pains and was taken to the Bethesda Naval Hospital, where he died the next day. He was fifty-two years old.

Robert Bacher returned to Cornell after the war to lead the Laboratory for Nuclear Studies. He was named a member of the Scientific and Technical Subcommittee of the United Nations Atomic Energy Commission and in 1946 was tapped to be one of the first commissioners of the AEC. He resigned in 1949 and became chairman of the Division of Physics, Mathematics, and Astronomy at Caltech. In 1962 he became the institute's vice president and provost. He died in 2004.

Edward Teller, the "father of the hydrogen bomb," experienced a meteoric rise after the war. Like Oppenheimer, he woke up one morning to find his face on the cover of *Time* magazine. When the war ended, Teller stayed in Los Alamos for nearly a year, preoccupied with pushing ahead on development of the Super. Sensing the division among his colleagues on further development, Teller quickly became the major proponent of thermonuclear weapons. He cultivated a growing circle of friends among the military and political leaders in Washington who similarly favored expansion of America's atomic arsenal.

After a brief return to the University of Chicago, Teller, with the support of Ernest Lawrence and the military, pushed for a new weapons laboratory to pursue alternative hydrogen bomb designs. The Lawrence

Radiation Laboratory was established in 1952 at Livermore, in northern California, and in 1971 its name officially became the Lawrence Livermore Laboratory. Although Teller was its director only briefly—from 1958 to 1961—the new scientific center was a useful base for his work on weapons and his political activity. Teller was instrumental in preventing the inclusion of underground testing in the 1963 Nuclear Test Ban Treaty, and in the 1980s he championed the Strategic Defense Initiative (popularly known as "Star Wars") to construct a complex missile shield against enemy missiles bearing nuclear warheads. Teller died quietly in 2003 at age ninety-five.

Enrico Fermi left Los Alamos at the end of the war and returned to the University of Chicago. Although initially opposed to the development of the Super, he ceased arguing against it after President Truman's decision to proceed. He served as a consultant to Los Alamos and to the Lawrence Livermore Laboratory and died of cancer in 1954.

Hans Bethe returned to his post as professor of physics at Cornell University. Although he too initially opposed development of the Super, he changed his mind after the Russian atomic bomb and Truman's decision to move forward. He served as a consultant to Los Alamos until his death in 2005. Bethe served on numerous official committees and acted as a consultant to Presidents Kennedy and Eisenhower. In 1967 he received the Nobel Prize for his youthful work on the thermonuclear properties of stars.

Norris Bradbury, who became the "interim director" of Los Alamos in 1945, remained as its leader through the difficult postwar years until his retirement in 1970. During his twenty-five-year tenure, he oversaw programs to improve fission weapons by making them smaller, safer, and more powerful, as well as the intensive program to develop the Super. He was awarded the Department of Defense Medal for Distinguished Public Service in 1966 and the Enrico Fermi Award in 1970. Throughout his years as director, Bradbury walked the difficult line between promoting further weapons development and arguing for a realistic arms control policy. He died in Los Alamos in 1997.

Harold Agnew, whose early career took him from witnessing Fermi's reactor success in Chicago to filming the bombing of Hiroshima with his own sixteen-millimeter movie camera, left Los Alamos to complete his doctorate under Fermi at the University of Chicago. He returned to the laboratory as part of the team working on the thermonuclear bomb, leaving in 1961 to serve as scientific advisor to NATO and the U.S. Air Force. He returned one last time to Los Alamos to become its director following Bradbury's retirement in 1970. He stepped down in 1979 and died at home in 2013.

Three alumni of Los Alamos have special historical legacies. Both Klaus Fuchs and David Greenglass were eventually arrested and convicted for their wartime activities. In 1950, the British Government arrested Fuchs and tried him, not for high treason, for which the penalty was death, but for violation of the Official Secrets Act. Because Fuchs had passed secret information to a wartime ally instead of an enemy, he received only a fourteen-year sentence. After his release, Fuchs moved to East Germany and again took up physics research. He died unrepentant for his wartime spying in 1988.

Acting on information from the British, the U.S. Federal Bureau of Investigation was able to uncover the work of David Greenglass and his brother-in-law and sister, Julius and Ethel Rosenberg. The Rosenbergs were found guilty of espionage in a 1951 trial that lasted three weeks and were executed in 1953. Greenglass, whose collaboration as a state's witness won him leniency, was sentenced to fifteen years in a federal prison. He died in late 2014. Some years before his death, he admitted to a reporter that he had lied on the witness stand. To save his wife from prosecution and perhaps execution, he told the court that his sister, Ethel, had typed all the secret information that was subsequently passed to the Soviets.

Ted Hall, the youngest scientist to work in Los Alamos during the war and its youngest spy, was never caught. Although he was questioned by the FBI in 1951 he was not charged with espionage. He went on to work at the

University of Chicago and later at Cambridge University in England, where he died in 1999 of renal failure.

———

Seven decades have brought changes to the Hill. Los Alamos is no longer a collection of wooden army buildings but a permanent city of twelve thousand residents. The principal actors—Groves, Oppenheimer, Fermi, Parsons, Bethe, Teller, Bacher, Kistiakowsky, and other senior leaders—are dead, and the few survivors from the Manhattan Project days are old. Second and third and fourth generations now live on the mesa. The world is different, too. The stockpiles that Oppenheimer warned against have become a reality, and the size and power of these weapons dwarf Trinity and surpass even the most fanciful thinking of the early days.

The thermonuclear Super so avidly pursued by Edward Teller became a reality only seven years after Trinity, although it was not an easy road for either Teller or Los Alamos. Many of the approaches devised by Teller and his team simply wouldn't work. Bearing names like Classical Super, Box-in-a-Box, and Alarm Clock, these schemes failed to bring about a fusion reaction. The breakthrough occurred in early 1952 when Stan Ulam, a member of the Theoretical Division at Los Alamos, realized that x-rays generated during a conventional fission explosion could create the necessary "trigger." He took his idea to Teller, who quickly produced an improved concept that led to the first successful thermonuclear bomb. The concept came to be known as radiation implosion.

A device based on the Ulam-Teller concept was tested later in the year at America's South Pacific testing ground on Eniwetok Atoll in the Marshall Islands. Code-named "Mike," the apparatus used a fission bomb to ignite liquid deuterium cryogenically chilled to a temperature of 423 degrees below zero Fahrenheit. This was not a weapon in any conventional sense but a purely experimental gadget. The deuterium and refrigeration plant weighed sixty-five tons and occupied a building eighty-eight feet wide, forty-six feet deep, and sixty-one feet high. At 7:15 a.m., local time, on November 1, 1952, the world's first thermonuclear explosion produced a burst of light and heat that dwarfed the artificial sunrise in the Jornada seven years before. Within a few seconds, the fireball had reached a diameter of three and a half miles and created a crater 164 feet deep and over a mile in diameter. The yield was 10.4 megatons, or over ten million tons of TNT, roughly five hundred times the yield of the first Fat Man.

The world's first "deliverable" thermonuclear weapon, the MK-14, entered the U.S. stockpile two years later. Though it fit into a B-36 or B-47 airplane, it was nevertheless a behemoth—over eighteen feet long and five feet in diameter, weighing twenty-nine thousand pounds. It was only a matter of time however, before the size of the weapons shrank and their power increased. By the 1960s there were thermonuclear weapons small enough to be clustered in the nosecone of a rocket. Fission weapons greatly improved as well, both in size and versatility. Some were designed to demolish huge structures such as dams and power plants, others to carve deep canyons and canals in the ground. A few weapons were designed as artillery shells six and eight inches in diameter.

The Soviets quickly developed their own implosion weapon and detonated it in 1948. Since it was built using the information provided by Fuchs and others, it was, unsurprisingly, almost an exact duplicate of Fat Man. It was followed by a succession of increasingly sophisticated fission weapons and finally fusion devices. The largest thermonuclear weapon ever designed and tested was Russian. Nicknamed the "Tsar Bomba," the device weighed twenty-seven tons, and when it was detonated on October 30, 1961, it produced a yield of between fifty and fifty-eight megatons. Shortly thereafter, Soviet Premier Nikita Khrushchev announced that his country possessed an even more powerful weapon, one capable of yielding one hundred megatons. Fortunately, it was never tested.

Today, nine countries are known or suspected to have nuclear weapons: the United States, the United Kingdom, Russia, France, China, India, Pakistan, North Korea, and Israel. Others, like Iran, are no doubt hoping to join the list.

The legacy of Groves and Oppenheimer and the laboratory they built is mixed. They will always be remembered for Fat Man and Little Boy, the ancestors of today's storehouse of devastating weapons. Some see Los Alamos as the tragedy of the age, for when science achieved undreamt of powers, it turned them to destruction.

And yet there is another way to read the story. During the war, Los Alamos was a unique and exhilarating place. The atmosphere permitted by Leslie Groves and fostered by men like Robert Oppenheimer was in many ways an extension of the university—a community in which professors acted as friends, surrogate fathers, and mentors. It was also the beginning of "Big Science"—projects heavily if not exclusively funded by the government that in the decades to come would include the race to the moon and the Star Wars missile shield. The laboratory's methods—simultaneously exploring multiple solutions to a problem, entrusting administration to long- and short-term committees, dependence on brilliant theory and clever engineering—worked and provided a roadmap for others to follow. However uneven its administration or its use of resources, Los Alamos set the standards for the great scientific undertakings of the future. Many of those who worked at the laboratory during the war moved on to help shape the discoveries of the second half of the twentieth century.

Perhaps Oppenheimer summed up the experience best. A decade after the war, he wrote:

> The story of Los Alamos is long and complex. Part of it is public history. For me it was a time so filled with work, with the need for decision and action and consultation, that there was room for little else. I lived with my family in the community which was Los Alamos. It was a remarkable community, inspired by a high sense of mission, of duty and destiny, coherent, dedicated, and remarkably selfless. There was plenty in the life of Los Alamos to cause irritation: the security restrictions, many of my own devising, the inadequacies and inevitable

fumbles of a military post unlike any that had ever existed before, shortages, inequities, and in the laboratory itself the shifting emphasis on different aspects of the technical work as the program moved forward; but I have never known a group more understanding and more devoted to a common purpose, more willing to lay aside personal convenience and prestige, more understanding of the role that they were playing in their country's history. Time and again, we had in the technical work almost paralyzing crises. Time and again the laboratory drew itself together and faced the new problems and got on with the work. We worked by night and by day; and in the end the many jobs were done.[8]

Oppenheimer might have added that he and his colleagues owed much to the talents and indefatigable industry of Leslie Groves.

The bomb appears to have been a moral burden for very few of those who worked on it. Although little can be said of something as personal as guilt, there was little sense of collective anguish. "It was war," one young graduate of the Hill said afterward. "Someone else would have made it," argued another. Robert Christy wrote long after the war, "So war is a very bloody thing. I didn't see the blood, but at least I was aware of it. And therefore you have to view it in that context. I felt then that although this [the bombing of Japan] was a terrible event, it probably saved many, many more Japanese lives."[9]

The special feeling shared by Los Alamos alumni extends beyond their having worked together in war and isolation. Close to the heart of many is what Alice Kimball Smith describes as the "dilemma of intellectuals caught in a sudden shift of values which they themselves helped to produce."[10] Others felt a heavier burden. Oppenheimer himself was ambivalent.

He was proud of his leadership of the laboratory and relieved that its creations helped to end the war. His vanity and ambition were certainly well served by the experience. To the extent that he sought fame, he received it beyond any expectation. Yet the prospect of further devastating wars waged with the creations of Los Alamos appalled and frightened him. He could not escape some responsibility for that possibility, and he was to say, "In some sort of crude sense which no vulgarity, no humor, no overstatement can quite extinguish, the physicists have known sin; and this is a knowledge which they cannot lose."[11]

In his last speech to the laboratory as director, on November 2, 1945, Oppenheimer tried to put the work of Los Alamos into perspective:

> But when you come right down to it the reason that we did this job is because it was an organic necessity. If you are a scientist you cannot stop such a thing. If you are a scientist you believe that it is good to find out how the world works; that it is good to find out what the realities are; that it is good to turn over to mankind at large the greatest possible power to control the world and to deal with it according to its lights and its values.

Yet he concluded on a humanistic note:

> But there is another thing: we are not only scientists; we are men, too. We cannot forget our dependence on our fellow men. I mean not only our material dependence, without which no science could be possible, and without which we could not work; I mean also our deep moral dependence, in that the value of science must lie in the world of men, that all our roots lie there. These are the strongest bonds in the world, stronger than those even that bind us to one another, these are the deepest bonds—that bind us to our fellow men.[12]

Groves experienced no regrets over the development of the atomic bombs. Nor did he doubt that the bombings of Hiroshima and Nagasaki helped end the war. He wrote to his former secretary, Jean O'Leary, "I wish the people who complain so loudly about the Japanese who were killed [by the atomic bomb], could take a trip to the war cemetery in Honolulu and see the graves of the thousands of American boys who were killed by the Japanese."[13]

Historians and demagogues now debate the legacy of Los Alamos. Was the bomb really necessary? Would the war have ended without Hiroshima and Nagasaki? Was it not just a matter of weeks until Japan surrendered? Like all great historical questions, this one will never have a clear resolution. Choices were made at the end of a long war characterized by much brutality and suffering. Decisions were made with the best information available at the time. Truman, Groves, Oppenheimer—all acted in the context of their strengths and weaknesses, their beliefs and prejudices.

When asked about the scientist's role in developing the atomic bomb during the war, Richard Feynmann responded this way:

> Once in Hawaii I was taken to see a Buddhist temple. In the temple a man said, "I am going to tell you something that you will never forget." And then he said, "To every man is given the key to the gates of heaven. That same key opens the gates of hell."[14]

═══════════════

Los Alamos today is an open city. The security gates and barbed wire fences were removed in 1957, and in 1962 President Kennedy signed legislation that returned most of the land on Pajarito Plateau to private hands. For the first several decades after the war, veterans from the early days occupied most of the organization's management posts. But one by one they retired or passed away, and younger generations took over. Today, only a handful of those bright young men and women who came to the Hill during the war survive in retirement.

The Los Alamos laboratory of today employs over 9,300 persons. Its annual budget of $2.1 billion is split between work on weapons; proliferation, safeguards, and security; and environmental management. Most of the mesa's original laboratory buildings have been torn down and replaced with modern construction. The World War II Technical Area was razed to make room for a motel, restaurants, businesses, and a new community center. A dozen buildings or areas from the war years survive, but almost all of them sit on other mesas or in the surrounding canyons. The building where Fat Man was assembled in 1945 has been preserved, as has the small cabin where Emilio Segrè performed his experiments on spontaneous fission. Even the clapboard building where Louis Slotin had his accident is still standing.

Ashley Pond survives along with some of its ducks because of the indignation of residents who fought to protect something of the past and to combat the modern penchant for covering everything flat with concrete and asphalt. A surprising number of the original Los Alamos Ranch School buildings still exist. The homes of Bathtub Row are there, all but one still occupied by families. The exception is the home now converted to a small but excellent county museum, each room of which is a window into a bygone era on the mesa: the Anasazi, the settlers, the boys' school, the laboratory. The current owner of the home once occupied by Robert and Kitty Oppenheimer has promised eventually to donate it to the community. And Fuller Lodge is still open, a witness to eighty years of history and a gathering place for the community. It is said that there are moments at dawn or dusk when the Lodge echoes with the sounds of schoolboys and scientists. A few blocks away, visitors can visit a new science museum named after Norris Bradbury. The exhibits tell the story of the laboratory in all its complexity, including Hiroshima and Nagasaki.

Residential development has extended onto nearby mesas and the valleys below. Occasionally, residents are reminded of the pioneering 1940s. Builders of a new motel in 1976 dug a foundation and discovered the area highly contaminated by plutonium residue from the old Technical Area's laundry.

The offices at 109 East Palace Avenue in Santa Fe were permanently closed in June 1963, when Dorothy McKibbin retired. A bronze plaque on the exterior reads:

> 109 East Palace
> 1943 Santa Fe Office 1963
> Los Alamos Scientific Laboratory
> University of California
> All the men and women who made the first atomic bomb
> passed through this portal to their secret mission at Los Ala-
> mos. Their creation in 27 months of the weapons that ended
> World War II was one of the greatest scientific achievements
> of all time.

Two hundred and twenty miles away at Trinity there is silence. The crater at Ground Zero is little more than a shallow saucer in the vast floor of the Jornada del Muerto. The last bits of Trinitite—the fused green sand produced by the blast—have been removed by the carloads of tourists who make the journey to see the birthplace of the atomic age when the Trinity site is opened to the public once a year. Base Camp is gone except for a few sagging wooden buildings and the foundations of others. The McDonald ranch house has been restored as part of a larger but incomplete effort by the U.S. Park Service to preserve America's atomic legacy. The control bunker at South 10,000, where Oppenheimer once clung to a post, was torn down in the 1970s, and many other structures have either collapsed or show signs of retreating into history with each sandstorm. Long strands of black wire that ran from instruments straight to Ground Zero lie undisturbed on the desert floor, but weathered away are the footprints of all the young men who worked and sweated that long-ago July morning and witnessed two suns rise.

NOTES

ABBREVIATIONS:

GRO: General Leslie R. Groves Papers, Formerly Collection RG200, National Archives and Records Administration (NARA), College Park, MD.

JRO: J. Robert Oppenheimer Papers, Manuscript Division, Library of Congress, Washington, DC.

LANL: Los Alamos National Laboratory, Los Alamos, New Mexico. Before 1981, the organization was known as LASL, Los Alamos Scientific Laboratory.

MED: Record Group 77, "Records of the Office of the Chief of Engineers: Records of the Manhattan Engineer District," Modern Military Branch, NARA.

CHAPTER ONE: JULY 16, 1945—EARLY MORNING

1.   "Journey of Death" is the most frequently used translation of the Spanish phrase, Jornada del Muerto. According to the noted New Mexico historian Fray Angelico Chavez, it is more correctly translated as, "Dead Man's Route." Fray

Angelico Chavez, *My Penitente Land* (Albuquerque: University of New Mexico Press, 1974).

2.   K. D. Nichols, *The Road to Trinity* (New York: William Morrow and Company, 1987), 195.

3.   "Fat Man" was the nickname given to the plutonium implosion weapon, "Little Boy" the nickname given to the uranium gun bomb. Recent historical research conducted by the Los Alamos National Laboratory has shown that these names were given to the World War II atomic bombs by the U.S. Army Air Force as a means of distinguishing between the two. Until mid-to-late 1944, scientists at Los Alamos generally referred to both weapons as "gadgets" or some other common term, such as "device."

4.   Henry L. Stimson, Memorandum of Conference with the President, June 6, 1945, Yale University Archives, Henry L. Stimson Papers, Library of Congress microfilm.

CHAPTER TWO: REVOLUTIONARY DEVELOPMENTS

1.   Edward Teller with Judith Shoolery, *Memoirs: A Twentieth-Century Journey in Science and Politics* (Cambridge: Perseus Publishing, 2001), 145–46.

2.   Ibid., 145.

3.   Westinghouse Electric & Manufacturing Company, *The Book of Record of the Time Capsule of Cupaloy* (New York: Westinghouse Electric & Manufacturing Company, 1938), 46.

4.   Richard Hewlett and Oscar E. Anderson Jr., *A History of the United States Atomic Energy Commission*, vol. 1, *The New World, 1939–1946* (University Park, PA: Pennsylvania State University Press, 1962), 17. Hewlett's and Anderson's thorough study of the origins and activities of the Manhattan Engineering District is a basic research tool for historians, especially those without access to classified materials. Volume 2 covers the period 1946–1948 and the creation of the Atomic Energy Commission.

5.   James Hershberg, *James B. Conant: Harvard to Hiroshima and the Making of the Nuclear Age* (New York: Alfred A. Knopf, 1993), 147.

6.   Richard Rhodes, *The Making of the Atom Bomb* (New York: Simon & Schuster, 1986), 416.

7.   Hewlett et al., *A History of the United States Atomic Energy Commission*, 34.

8.   Ibid, 38.

9.   Ibid., 42.

10. Hewlett et al., *A History of the United States Atomic Energy Commission*, 49.

11. Ibid., 54–55.

12. Ibid., 71.

13. Ibid., 73.

14. Leslie R. Groves, *Now It Can Be Told: The Story of the Manhattan Project* (New York: Harper, 1962), 17.

CHAPTER THREE: GENERAL AND PHYSICIST

1.   William Lawren, *The General and the Bomb: A Biography of General Leslie R. Groves, Director of the Manhattan Project* (New York: Dodd, Mead & Company, 1988), 44.

2.   Ibid., 52.

3.   Leslie R. Groves and J. J. Ermenc, *The Career of General Leslie R. Groves, Director of the American Atomic Bomb Project*, Transcript of tape-recorded interview, November 7, 1967. GRO.

4.   Lawren, *The General and the Bomb*, 62.

5.   Ibid., 61–62.

6.   K. D. Nichols, *The Road to Trinity* (New York: William Morrow and Company, 1987),102–8.

7.   Lawren, *The General and the Bomb*, 63.

8.   Ibid., 111.

9.   Leslie Groves, comments on Hewlett and Anderson's *New World*, GRO.

10. Groves and Ermenc, *The Career of General Leslie R. Groves*, 16.

11. Leslie R. Groves, *Now It Can Be Told: The Story of the Manhattan Project* (New York: Harper, 1962), 3–4.

12. Ibid., 19.

13. Ibid., 20.

14. Leslie R. Groves Correspondence Files, GRO.

15. Groves, *Now It Can Be Told*, 5.

16. Groves and Ermenc, *The Career of General Leslie R. Groves*, 64.

17. Groves, *Now It Can Be Told*, 40.

18. Brian VanDemark, *Pandora's Keepers: Nine Men and the Atomic Bomb* (New York: Little Brown and Company, 2003), 78.

19. Robert S. Norris, *Racing for the Bomb: General Leslie R. Groves, The Manhattan Project's Indispensible Man* (South Royalton, VT: Steerforth Press, 2002), 195.

20. Shirley Streshinsky and Patricia Klaus, *An Atomic Love Story: The Extraordinary Women in Robert Oppenheimer's Life* (New York: Turner Publishing Company, 2013), 14.

21. Alice Kimball Smith and Charles Weiner, *Robert Oppenheimer: Letters and Recollections* (Cambridge: Harvard University Press, 1980), 159.

22. U.S. Atomic Energy Commission (USAEC), *In the Matter of Robert Oppenheimer* (Washington, DC: Government Printing Office, 1954), 8. Hereafter referred to as AEC.

23. Some of those men who received their Ph.D. under Oppenheimer, or did postdoctoral work with him, include: Melba Phillips, Harvey Hall, Leo Nedelsky, Frank Carlson, Wendell Furry, Milton Plesset, Arnold Nordsieck, Robert Serber, Fritz Kalckar, Glenn Camp, Stanley Frankel, George Volkoff, Julian Schwinger, Hartland Snyder, Bertrand Peters, Leonard Schiff, Sidney Dancoff, Philip Morrison, David Bohm, Willis Lamb, Edwin Uehling, Robert Christy, Joseph Keller, William Rarita, and Chaim Richman.

24. Richard Rhodes, *The Making of the Atom Bomb* (New York: Simon & Schuster, 1986), 447.

25. Gregg Herken, *Brotherhood of the Bomb: The Tangled Lives and Loyalties of Robert Oppenheimer, Ernest Lawrence, and Edward Teller* (New York: Henry Holt and Company, 2002), 12.

26. Haakon Chevalier, *Oppenheimer: The Story of a Friendship* (New York: George Braziller, 1965), 19–20.

27. Ibid., 21 and 19–20.

28. Herken, *Brotherhood of the Bomb*, 15.

29. AEC, 8.

30. Kai Bird and Martin J. Sherwin, *American Prometheus: The Triumph and Tragedy of J. Robert Oppenheimer* (New York: Knopf, 2005), 114.

31. AEC, 8.

32. Peter Goodchild, *J. Robert Oppenheimer: Shatterer of Worlds* (Boston: Houghton Mifflin Company, 1981), 32.

33. Ibid., 34.

34. Ibid., 39.

35. Bird and Sherwin, *American Prometheus*, 154.

36. AEC, 10.

37. Rhodes, *The Making of the Atomic Bomb*, 382.

CHAPTER FOUR: THE EXTRAORDINARY PARTNERSHIP

1. Alice Kimball Smith and Charles Weiner, *Robert Oppenheimer: Letters and Recollections* (Cambridge: Harvard University Press, 1980), 207.

2. Gregg Herken, *Brotherhood of the Bomb: The Tangled Lives and Loyalties of Robert Oppenheimer, Ernest Lawrence, and Edward Teller* (New York: Henry Holt and Company, 2002), 43.

3. Richard Rhodes, *The Making of the Atom Bomb* (New York: Simon & Schuster, 1986), 381.

4. Lillian Hoddeson and others, *Critical Assembly: A Technical History of Los Alamos During the Oppenheimer Years, 1943–1945* (New York: Cambridge University Press, 1993), 42.

5. Herken, *Brotherhood of the Bomb*, 51.

6. Smith et al., *Robert Oppenheimer: Letters and Recollections*, 215.

7. Interview with John Manley by author.

8. Herken, *Brotherhood of the Bomb*, 66.

9. Hoddeson et al., *Critical Assembly*, 43.

10. S. S. Schweber, *In the Shadow of the Bomb: Oppenheimer, Bethe, and the Moral Responsibility of the Scientist* (Princeton: Princeton University Press 2000), 370.

11. Robert Serber, "Theoretical Studies at Berkeley," *Behind Tall Fences* (Los Alamos, NM: Los Alamos Historical Society, 1996), 45.

12. Ibid., 56.

13. Hoddeson et al., *Critical Assembly*, 55.

14. Arthur H. Compton, *Atomic Quest: A Personal Narrative* (Princeton: Princeton University Press, 1956), 127.

15. Jennet Conant, *109 East Palace: Robert Oppenheimer and the Secret City of Los Alamos* (New York: Simon & Schuster, 2005), 30–31.

16. Herken, *Brotherhood of the Bomb*, 68.

17. Leslie R. Groves, *Now It Can Be Told: The Story of the Manhattan Project* (New York: Harper, 1962), 61–62.

18. K. D. Nichols, *The Road to Trinity* (New York: William Morrow and Company, 1987), 73.

19. AEC, 37.

20. Nuel Pharr Davis, *Lawrence & Oppenheimer* (New York: Simon & Schuster, 1968), 141–45.

21. Groves, *Now It Can Be Told*, 62.

22. Brian VanDemark, *Pandora's Keepers: Nine Men and the Atomic Bomb* (New York: Little Brown and Company, 2003), 110.

23. Rhodes, *The Making of the Atom Bomb*, 448–49.

24. Conant, *109 East Palace*, 53–54.

25. Robert Oppenheimer's prewar political activities are discussed in the AEC hearings, and by Nuel Pharr Davis and Bird and Sherwin.

26. Conant, *109 East Palace*, 39.

27. Herken, *Brotherhood of the Bomb*, 58.

28. Davis, *Lawrence & Oppenheimer*, 187–90.

29. AEC, 170.

30. Ibid., 167–68.

31. Peter Goodchild, *J. Robert Oppenheimer: Shatterer of Worlds* (Boston: Houghton Mifflin Company, 1981), 128.

32. U.S. Atomic Energy Commission, *The First Reactor* (Washington, DC: Government Printing Office, n.d.), 21–22.

33. Robert Oppenheimer and others, "The Use of Materials in a Fission bomb," November 26, 1942, LANL.

34. Richard Hewlett and Oscar E. Anderson Jr., *A History of the United States Atomic Energy Commission*, vol. 1, *The New World, 1939–1946* (University Park, PA: Pennsylvania State University Press, 1962), 115.

35. James Conant to Leslie Groves, December 9, 1942, MED.

36. AEC, 164.

37. Nichols, *The Road to Trinity*, 104.

38. Robert S. Norris, *Racing for the Bomb: General Leslie R. Groves, The Manhattan Project's Indispensible Man* (South Royalton, VT: Steerforth Press, 2002), 245.

39. VanDemark, *Pandora's Keepers*, 111.

CHAPTER FIVE: A MILITARY NECESSITY

1. An excellent history of the Los Alamos Ranch School is: John D. Wirth and Linda Harvey Aldrich, *Los Alamos: The Ranch School Years 1917–1943* (Albuquerque: University of New Mexico Press, 2003).

2. Alice Kimball Smith and Charles Weiner, *Robert Oppenheimer: Letters and Recollections* (Cambridge: Harvard University Press, 1980), 236.

3. Richard Rhodes, *The Making of the Atom Bomb* (New York: Simon & Schuster, 1986), 450.

4. In response to a letter from William Dudley in 1970, Groves claimed that he had never heard of Los Alamos until Oppenheimer suggested it during the November 16 visit to Jemez Springs. However, his memory is contradicted not only by Dudley's recollections, but by a letter sent by Oppenheimer to Manley just a week before on November 6, 1942 reporting a conversation with both Groves and Dudley in Berkeley about Los Alamos as a potential site.

5. Leslie R. Groves, *Now It Can Be Told: The Story of the Manhattan Project* (New York: Harper, 1962), 66.

6. Early negotiations concerning acquisition of the Los Alamos area are covered in Volume 1 of the Manhattan District, now partially declassified, in the collections of both LANL and MED. LANL published Volume 1 as *Manhattan*

District History, Nonscientific Aspects of Los Alamos Project Y, 1942 through 1946, Publication LA-5200, March 1973.

7.   Peggy Pond Church, *The House at Otowi Bridge: The Story of Edith Warner and Los Alamos* (Albuquerque: University of New Mexico Press, 1960), 83.

8.   Jennet Conant, *109 East Palace: Robert Oppenheimer and the Secret City of Los Alamos* (New York: Simon & Schuster, 2005), 62.

CHAPTER SIX: LARGE-SCALE EXPERIMENTS

1.   Interview with John Manley by author.

2.   John Manley, "Remarks by John Manley on the Passing of Robert Oppenheimer," LANL.

3.   Robert Wilson, "A Recruit for Los Alamos," *All In Our Time* (Chicago: Bulletin of the Atomic Scientists, 1974), 153–54.

4.   Contract Between the United States of America and the University of California, April 20, 1943, LANL.

5.   AEC, 12.

6.   Lillian Hoddeson and others, *Critical Assembly: A Technical History of Los Alamos During the Oppenheimer Years, 1943–1945* (New York: Cambridge University Press, 1993), 58.

7.   Alice Kimball Smith and Charles Weiner, *Robert Oppenheimer: Letters and Recollections* (Cambridge: Harvard University Press, 1980), 231.

8.   William Lawren, *The General and the Bomb: A Biography of General Leslie R. Groves, Director of the Manhattan Project* (New York: Dodd, Mead & Company, 1988), 102.

9.   Robert S. Norris, *Racing for the Bomb: General Leslie R. Groves, The Manhattan Project's Indispensible Man* (South Royalton, VT: Steerforth Press, 2002), 629.

10.   Smith et al., *Robert Oppenheimer: Letters and Recollections*, 247.

11.   Alan B. Carr, *The Forgotten Physicist: Robert Bacher, 1905–2004*, Monograph 6 (Los Alamos, NM: Los Alamos Historical Society, 2008), 14.

12.   Los Alamos Laboratory, "Second Memorandum on the Los Alamos Project," August 9, 1943, LANL.

13. Contract Between the United States of America and the University of California, LANL.

14. AEC, 12.

15. Nuel Pharr Davis, *Lawrence & Oppenheimer* (New York: Simon & Schuster, 1968), 163.

16. Edward Teller with Judith Shoolery, *Memoirs: A Twentieth-Century Journey in Science and Politics* (Cambridge: Perseus Publishing, 2001), 167.

17. AEC, 12.

18. Smith et al., *Robert Oppenheimer: Letters and Recollections*, 250.

19. Ibid., 245.

20. Carr, *The Forgotten Physicist*, 12.

21. Smith et al., *Robert Oppenheimer: Letters and Recollections*, 254.

22. AEC, 12.

23. Los Alamos Laboratory, "Third Memorandum on the Los Alamos Project," no date, LANL.

24. Jennet Conant, *109 East Palace: Robert Oppenheimer and the Secret City of Los Alamos* (New York: Simon & Schuster, 2005), 37.

25. Interview with Priscilla Green Duffield by author.

26. Public Lecture by Priscilla Green Duffield, Los Alamos, NM, April 19, 2006, LANL.

27. Dorothy McKibbin, "109 East Palace Avenue," LASL News, June 28, 1963.

28. Vincent C. Jones, *United States Army in World War II, Special Studies, Manhattan: The Army and the Atomic Bomb* (Washington, DC: Center of Military Studies, 1985), 468.

29. Leslie R. Groves, *Now It Can Be Told: The Story of the Manhattan Project* (New York: Harper, 1962), 162.

30. Letter, Major Stanley Stewart to Brigadier General Leslie Groves, March 13, 1943, GRO, National Archives.

31. Leslie R. Groves and J. J. Ermenc, *The Career of General Leslie R. Groves, Director of the American Atomic Bomb Project*, Transcript of tape-recorded interview, November 7, 1967, GRO, 65.

32. Letter, Richard Tolman to General Groves, March 20, 1943, LANL.

33.   Los Alamos Laboratory, "Memorandum on the Los Alamos Project as of March 1943," March 14, 1943, LANL.

34.   Letter, Robert Oppenheimer to General Groves, May 27, 1943, LANL.

35.   Robert Oppenheimer, "Restricted Memo to Staff," May 5, 1943, LANL.

36.   Jean O'Leary kept a daily log of General Groves' activities while in Washington. The log contains a record of meetings and all telephone calls to and from Groves, often with brief descriptions of the conversations. References to phone calls by Groves in this book are taken from this record, part of the GRO collection at the National Archives, and not individually cited hereafter.

CHAPTER SEVEN: THE LOS ALAMOS PRIMER

1.   Notes on Serber's lectures appear as *The Los Alamos Primer*, LA-1 (Los Alamos, NM: Los Alamos Scientific Laboratory, n.d.). This document was given to all new arrivals in Los Alamos in 1943.

2.   Nuel Pharr Davis, *Lawrence & Oppenheimer* (New York: Simon & Schuster, 1968), 171.

3.   Among the lighter elements, the typical energy-producing, or exoergic, reaction is the building up of heavy nuclei from light ones. The energy that is liberated in the process goes into kinetic energy and radiation. Such a reaction in a mass of deuterium will spread when the atoms are heated to very high temperatures; hence, the process is called thermonuclear.

4.   Among those attending were: Robert Bacher, Kenneth Bainbridge, Hans Bethe, Felix Bloch, Owen Chamberlain, Robert Christy, Edward Condon, Enrico Fermi, Richard Feynmann, Stanley Frankel, Al Graves, Joseph Kennedy, John Manley, Joseph McKibbin, Edwin McMillan, Seth Neddermeyer, Eldred Nelson, Isidor Rabi, Emilio Segre, Robert Serber, Cyril Smith, Hans Staub, Edward Teller, Richard Tolman, Arthur Wahl, Victor Weisskopf, John Williams, and Robert Wilson. Lillian Hoddeson and others, *Critical Assembly: A Technical History of Los Alamos During the Oppenheimer Years, 1943–1945* (New York: Cambridge University Press, 1993), 435.

5. Lillian Hoddeson and Allison Kerr, "Interview With Robert Krohn," January 7, 1981, LANL.

6. Jennet Conant, *109 East Palace: Robert Oppenheimer and the Secret City of Los Alamos* (New York: Simon & Schuster, 2005), 63.

7. Kai Bird and Martin J. Sherwin, *American Prometheus: The Triumph and Tragedy of J. Robert Oppenheimer* (New York: Knopf, 2005), 215.

8. Hoddeson et al., *Critical Assembly*, 75.

9. AEC, 12.

10. Leslie R. Groves, *Now It Can Be Told: The Story of the Manhattan Project* (New York: Harper, 1962), 154.

11. Bird and Sherwin, *American Prometheus*, 224.

12. Minutes of the Governing Board, May 31, 1943, LANL.

13. K. D. Nichols, *The Road to Trinity* (New York: William Morrow and Company, 1987), 114.

14. Alice Kimball Smith and Charles Weiner, *Robert Oppenheimer: Letters and Recollections* (Cambridge: Harvard University Press, 1980), 264.

15. Minutes of the Governing Board, August 5, 1943, LANL.

16. Richard Hewlett and Oscar E. Anderson Jr., *A History of the United States Atomic Energy Commission*, vol. 1, *The New World, 1939–1946* (University Park, PA: Pennsylvania State University Press, 1962), 238–39.

17. Bird and Sherwin, *American Prometheus*, 226.

18. Memorandum, Robert Oppenheimer to General Groves, June 7, 1943, LANL.

19. Letter from Leslie Groves to Robert Oppenheimer, June 17, 1943, LANL.

20. Hewlett et al., *A History of the United States Atomic Energy Commission*, 239.

21. Nichols, *The Road to Trinity*, 115.

22. Letter, General Leslie Groves to Commanding General, Services of Supply, February 27, 1943, MED.

23. Letter, General Groves to Robert Oppenheimer, June 18, 1945, LANL.

24. Robert Oppenheimer, "First Memorandum on Los Alamos," n.d., LANL.

25. Smith et al., *Robert Oppenheimer: Letters and Recollections*, 266.

CHAPTER EIGHT: FORTUNATE CHOICES

1. AEC, 171.

2. Robert S. Norris, *Racing for the Bomb: General Leslie R. Groves, The Manhattan Project's Indispensible Man* (South Royalton, VT: Steerforth Press, 2002), 197–98.

3. Leslie R. Groves and J. J. Ermenc, *The Career of General Leslie R. Groves, Director of the American Atomic Bomb Project*, Transcript of tape-recorded interview, November 7, 1967, GRO, 62.

4. William Lawren, *The General and the Bomb: A Biography of General Leslie R. Groves, Director of the Manhattan Project* (New York: Dodd, Mead & Company, 1988), 164.

5. Ibid., 145.

6. Robert Bacher, "Robert Oppenheimer (1904–1967)," *Proceedings of the American Philosophical Society* 116, no. 4, (August 1972): 281.

7. K. D. Nichols, *The Road to Trinity* (New York: William Morrow and Company, 1987), 103.

8. AEC, 165.

9. Charles L. Critchfield, "The First Implosion at Los Alamos," *Behind Tall Fences* (Los Alamos: Los Alamos Historical society, 1996), 171.

10. James W. Kunetka, *Oppenheimer: The Years of Risk* (New Jersey: Prentice-Hall, 1982), 61.

11. Interview with Norris Bradbury by author.

12. Richard Rhodes, *The Making of the Atom Bomb* (New York: Simon & Schuster, 1986), 570.

13. Jennet Conant, *109 East Palace: Robert Oppenheimer and the Secret City of Los Alamos* (New York: Simon & Schuster, 2005), 119.

14. Bacher, "Robert Oppenheimer (1904–1967)," 283.

15. Conant, *109 East Palace*, 180.

16. Kai Bird and Martin J. Sherwin, *American Prometheus: The Triumph and Tragedy of J. Robert Oppenheimer* (New York: Knopf, 2005), 261.

17. Peter Goodchild, *J. Robert Oppenheimer: Shatterer of Worlds* (Boston: Houghton Mifflin Company, 1981), 127–28.

18. Letter, Robert Oppenheimer to General Groves, November 20, 1942, LANL and MED.

19. Lillian Hoddeson and others, *Critical Assembly: A Technical History of Los Alamos During the Oppenheimer Years, 1943–1945* (New York: Cambridge University Press, 1993), 59.

20. Alice Kimball Smith and Charles Weiner, *Robert Oppenheimer: Letters and Recollections* (Cambridge: Harvard University Press, 1980), 270.

21. AEC, 166.

22. Leslie R. Groves, *Now It Can Be Told: The Story of the Manhattan Project* (New York: Harper, 1962), 160.

23. Robert Oppenheimer, "Memorandum to Dr. Peierls," November 1, 1942. LANL.

24. Otto Frisch, *What Little I Remember* (Cambridge: Cambridge University Press, 1979), 150.

25. Norris, *Racing for the Bomb*, 647, cited in footnote 22.

26. Bird and Sherwin, *American Prometheus*, 286.

27. Groves, *Now It Can Be Told*, 144.

28. E. B. Held, *A Spy's Guide to Santa Fe and Albuquerque* (Albuquerque: University of New Mexico Press, 2011), xxv–xxvi.

29. Donald F. Hornig, Oral History Interview I by David F. McComb, December 4, 1968,(Lyndon B. Johnson Library, Austin, Texas).

30. Smith et al., *Robert Oppenheimer: Letters and Recollections*, 269.

31. Interview with Robert Krohn by author.

32. Val L. Fitch, "Soldiers in the Ranks," *All in Our Time* (Chicago: Bulletin of the Atomic Scientists, 1974), 191–92. After the war, Fitch won the Nobel Prize in Physics in 1980 for his work in K mesons.

33. Iris Bell, *Los Alamos WAACs/WACs: World War II 1943–1946* (Florida: Coastal Printing Incorporated, 1993), 9.

34. Ibid., 47.

CHAPTER NINE: ALL POSSIBLE PRIORITY

1.   Edward Teller with Judith Shoolery, *Memoirs: A Twentieth-Century Journey in Science and Politics* (Cambridge: Perseus Publishing, 2001), 188.

2.   Charles L. Critchfield, "The First Implosion at Los Alamos," *Behind Tall Fences* (Los Alamos: Los Alamos Historical society, 1996), 101.

3.   Richard Rhodes, *The Making of the Atom Bomb* (New York: Simon & Schuster, 1986), 477.

4.   Lillian Hoddeson and others, *Critical Assembly: A Technical History of Los Alamos During the Oppenheimer Years, 1943–1945* (New York: Cambridge University Press, 1993), 80.

5.   Arthur Wahl, "Los Alamos 1943," *Behind Tall Fences* (Los Alamos: Los Alamos Historical Society, 1996), 88.

6.   Hoddeson et al., *Critical Assembly*, 120–21.

7.   Rhodes, *The Making of the Atom Bomb*, 512.

8.   Letter, Leslie Groves to Robert Oppenheimer, June 20, 1944, LANL.

9.   Hugh T. Richards, *Through Los Alamos, 1945: Memoirs of a Physicist* (Madison, WI: Arlington Place Press, 1993), 61.

10. Rhodes, *The Making of the Atom Bomb*, 524.

11. Edward F. Hammel, "Recollections of Plutonium Metallurgy Work in D-Building," *Behind Tall Fences* (Los Alamos: Los Alamos Historical Society, 1996), 106.

12. Minutes of the Advisory Board, August 17, 1944, LANL.

13. Hoddeson et al., *Critical Assembly*, 105.

14. Ibid., 117.

15. Ibid., 116.

16. Leslie R. Groves and J. J. Ermenc, *The Career of General Leslie R. Groves, Director of the American Atomic Bomb Project*, Transcript of tape-recorded interview, November 7, 1967, GRO, 60.

17. John Raper, "Forbidden City," *The Cleveland Press*, March 13, 1944. This article was first reported in The Nuclear Secrecy Blog, by Alex Wellerstein,

September 20, 2013. This thoughtful and highly informative blog is at: http://blog.nuclearsecrecy.com.

18. Letter, Captain William Parsons to General Leslie Groves, May 19, 1944, LANL.

19. Hoddeson et al., *Critical Assembly*, 35.

20. Nuel Pharr Davis, *Lawrence & Oppenheimer* (New York: Simon & Schuster, 1968), 216.

21. Hoddeson et al., *Critical Assembly*, 131–32.

22. Minutes of the Governing Board, October 28, 1943, LANL.

23. Hoddeson et al., *Critical Assembly*, 135–36.

24. Minutes of the Governing Board, June 17, 1943, LANL.

25. Rhodes, *The Making of the Atom Bomb*, 540.

26. Minutes of the Governing Board, November 4 1943, LANL.

27. Minutes of the Governing Board, September 23, 1944, LANL.

28. William Lawren, *The General and the Bomb*: *A Biography of General Leslie R. Groves, Director of the Manhattan Project* (New York: Dodd, Mead & Company, 1988), 101.

29. Peter Goodchild, *J. Robert Oppenheimer*: *Shatterer of Worlds* (Boston: Houghton Mifflin Company, 1981), 112–13.

30. Memorandum, George Kistiakowsky to Robert Oppenheimer and William Parsons, June 13, 1944, LANL.

31. Letter, Robert Oppenheimer to Seth Neddermeyer, June 15, 1944, Oppenheimer Papers, Library of Congress, Washington, DC.

32. Goodchild, *J. Robert Oppenheimer*, 230.

33. Telex, Robert Oppenheimer to Leslie Groves, July 14, 1944, LANL.

34. Kai Bird and Martin J. Sherwin, *American Prometheus: The Triumph and Tragedy of J. Robert Oppenheimer* (New York: Knopf, 2005), 279.

35. K. D. Nichols, *The Road to Trinity* (New York: William Morrow and Company, 1987), 139.

36. AEC, 167.

37. Minutes of the Advisory Board, July 20, 1944, LANL.

CHAPTER TEN: SPLENDID ISOLATION

1. Fern Lyon and Jacob Evans, eds., *Los Alamos: The First Forty Years* (Los Alamos, NM: Los Alamos Historical Society, 1984), 21.

2. Los Alamos Laboratory, "Second Memorandum on the Los Alamos Project," August 9, 1943, LANL.

3. Bernice Brode, "Tales of Los Alamos," *LASL Community News* (June 1960).

4. Phyllis K. Fisher, *Los Alamos Experience* (New York: Japan Publications, 1985), 32.

5. Letter, J. Robert Oppenheimer to General Leslie Groves, June 21, 1943, LANL

6. Kathleen Mark, "A Roof Over Our Heads," *Standing By and Making Do: Women of Wartime Los Alamos* (Los Alamos: Los Alamos Historical Society, 1988), 32.

7. Eleanor Stone Roensch, *Life Within Limits* (Los Alamos: Los Alamos Historical Society, 1993), 21–23.

8. Memorandum, Robert Oppenheimer to General Groves, June 21, 1943, LANL.

9. Fern Lyon and Jacob Evans, eds., *Los Alamos: The First Forty Years* (Los Alamos, Los Alamos Historical Society, 1984), 50.

10. *Los Alamos Daily Bulletin*, April 17, 1944, LANL.

11. Los Alamos Scientific Laboratory, "Second Memorandum on the Los Alamos Project," August 9, 1943, LANL.

12. Minutes of the Governing Board, October 28, 1943, LANL.

13. Los Alamos Laboratory, "Memorandum on Censorship Regulations," July 1, 1943, LANL.

14. Alice Kimball Smith and Charles Weiner, *Robert Oppenheimer: Letters and Recollections* (Cambridge: Harvard University Press, 1980), 256.

15. Ruth Marhsak, "Secret City," *Standing By and Making Do: Women of Wartime Los Alamos* (Los Alamos, NM: Los Alamos Historical Society, 1988), 2.

16. Edward Hammel, "Reflections of Plutonium Metallurgy Work in D-Building," *Behind Tall Fences* (Los Alamos, NM: Los Alamos Historical Soceity,1996), 103.

17. Letter, General Groves to Robert Oppenheimer, July 29, 1943, LANL.

18. For the Lansdale quotes on Kitty, see Goodchild, 89–90. For his quotes on Robert and Kitty, see Rhodes, 626, fn 45.

19. Charlotte Serber, "Labor Pains," *Standing By and Making Do* (Los Alamos, NM: Los Alamos Historical Society, 1988), 57.

20. *Behind Tall Fences*, no author, 168.

21. Phyllis K. Fisher, *Los Alamos Experience* (New York: Japan Publications, 1985), 58.

CHAPTER ELEVEN: A NECESSARY REORGANIZATION

1. Memorandum, Robert Oppenheimer to Robert Bacher, "Organization of Gadget Division," August 14, 1944, LANL.

2. Peter Goodchild, *J. Robert Oppenheimer: Shatterer of Worlds* (Boston: Houghton Mifflin Company, 1981), 119.

3. Kai Bird and Martin J. Sherwin, *American Prometheus: The Triumph and Tragedy of J. Robert Oppenheimer* (New York: Knopf, 2005), 280.

4. Memorandum, Robert Oppenheimer to George Kistiakowsky, "Organization of Explosive Division," August 14, 1944, LANL.

5. Goodchild, *J. Robert Oppenheimer*, 119.

6. Minutes of the Governing Board, June 29, 1944, LANL.

7. Minutes of the Advisory Board, July 20, 1944, LANL.

8. Minutes of the Advisory Board, August 3, 1944, LANL.

9. AEC, 165.

10. Robert S. Norris, *Racing for the Bomb: General Leslie R. Groves, The Manhattan Project's Indispensible Man* (South Royalton, VT: Steerforth Press, 2002), 652, fn 29.

11. Minutes of the Governing Board, June 17, 1944, LANL.

12. Minutes of the Advisory Board, August 17, 1944, LANL.

13. Richard Hewlett and Oscar E. Anderson Jr., *A History of the United States Atomic Energy Commission*, vol. 1, *The New World, 1939–1946* (University Park, PA: Pennsylvania State University Press, 1962), 252.

14. Norris, *Racing for the Bomb*, 651, fn 8.

15. Ibid., 363–64.

16. Robert F. Christy, oral interview by Sara Lippincott, June 15, 17, 21 and 11, 1994 (Archives, California Institute of Technology, Pasadena, CA), 41.

17. Hugh T. Richards, "The Making of the Bomb: A Personal Perspective," *Behind Tall Fences* (Los Alamos, NM: Los Alamos Historical Society 1996), 128.

18. Lillian Hoddeson and others, *Critical Assembly: A Technical History of Los Alamos During the Oppenheimer Years, 1943–1945* (New York: Cambridge University Press, 1993), 160.

19. Christy, 48.

20. Edward Teller with Judith Shoolery, *Memoirs: A Twentieth-Century Journey in Science and Politics* (Cambridge: Perseus Publishing, 2001), 169.

21. Richard Rhodes, *The Making of the Atom Bomb* (New York: Simon & Schuster, 1986), 453.

22. Brian VanDemark, *Pandora's Keepers: Nine Men and the Atomic Bomb* (New York: Little Brown and Company, 2003), 124.

23. Rhodes, *The Making of the Atom Bomb*, 543.

24. Teller, *Memoirs*, 176–77.

25. Memorandum, Robert Oppenheimer to Leslie Groves, May 1, 1944, LANL.

26. Stan M. Ulam, *Adventures of a Mathematician* (New York: Charles Scribner's Sons, 1976), 141.

27. Rhodes, *The Making of the Atom Bomb*, 539.

28. Teller, *Memoirs*, 177.

29. Hewlett et al., *A History of the United States Atomic Energy Commission*, 240.

30. Memorandum, George Kistiakowsky to William Parsons, "Program and Requirements of the Research and Development Phase of the HE Project," November 24, 1943, LANL.

31. Hoddeson et al., *Critical Assembly*, 302.

32. Ibid., 167

33. Ibid., 169.

34. Memorandum, Captain William Parsons to Robert Oppenheimer, "Home Stretch Measures," February 19, 1945, LANL.

35. Letter, Robert Oppenheimer to General Groves, October 8, 1944, LANL.

36. Memorandum, Captain William Parson to General Leslie Groves, May 19, 1944, LANL.

37. Ibid.

38. Los Alamos Laboratory. Minutes of the Administrative Board, September 28, 1944, LANL.

39. Minutes of the Administrative Board, November 24, 1944, LANL.

40. Letter, James Byrnes to President Roosevelt, March 3, 1945, MED.

41. Hoddeson et al., *Critical Assembly*, 293.

42. Hewlett et al., *A History of the United States Atomic Energy Commission*, 374.

43. Otto Frisch, *What Little I Remember* (Boston: Cambridge University Press, 1979), 159–60.

44. William R. Stratton, *A Review of Criticality Accidents*, LA-3611 (Los Alamos, NM: Los Alamos Scientific Laboratory, September 1967), 25.

45. Memorandum, Louis Hempelmann to David Dow, September 19, 1945, LANL.

46. Darol K. Froman, "Preliminary Report on the Accident in Pajarito Laboratory," May 21, 1946, LANL.

CHAPTER TWELVE: CONVERGING ROADS: 1945

1. An excellent discussion of manpower during WWII can be found in D. M. Giangreco's book, *Hell to Pay: Operation Downfall and the Invasion of Japan, 1945–1947*.

2. Captain John Derry to General Groves, "Notes on Conference in Dr. Oppenheimer's Office on 19 December, 1944, January 9, 1945, LANL.

3. Lillian Hoddeson and others, *Critical Assembly: A Technical History of Los Alamos During the Oppenheimer Years, 1943–1945* (New York: Cambridge University Press, 1993), 293–94.

4. Los Alamos Laboratory. "Status on the Gun Gadget Development," May 7, 1945, LANL.

5. John Coster-Mullen, *Atom Bombs: The Top Secret Inside Story of Little Boy and Fat Man* (Self-published: J. Coster-Mullen, 2001), 27. Coster-Mullen's book is the most thoroughly-research technical examination of both Fat Man and

Little Boy utilizing personal inspections and declassified sources. The exact weights for the U235 projectile and target are still formally classified, but Coster-Mullen's numbers are highly realistic working numbers.

6.   Hoddeson et al., *Critical Assembly*, 318.

7.   Coster-Mullen, *Atom Bombs*, 48.

8.   Hoddeson et al., *Critical Assembly*, 309.

9.   Ibid., 260.

10. Ibid., 269.

11. Richard Rhodes, *The Making of the Atom Bomb* (New York: Simon & Schuster, 1986), 577.

12. Ibid.

13. Hoddeson et al., *Critical Assembly*, 299.

14. Robert S. Norris, *Racing for the Bomb: General Leslie R. Groves, The Manhattan Project's Indispensible Man* (South Royalton, VT: Steerforth Press, 2002), 382.

15. Ibid., 371.

16. Alice Kimball Smith and Charles Weiner, *Robert Oppenheimer: Letters and Recollections* (Cambridge: Harvard University Press, 1980), 287.

17. "Remarks by Robert Oppenheimer on the Death of President Roosevelt," April 15, 1945, LANL.

18. Leslie R. Groves, "Memorandum for Secretary of War Stimson," 23 April 1945, LANL.

19. Henry Stimson, "Memorandum Discussed with the President," April 25, 1945. GRO.

20. Leslie R. Groves, Memo for the files, April 25, 1945, GRO.

21. Rhodes, *The Making of the Atom Bomb*, 502.

22. Letter, Robert Oppenheimer to General Groves, June 30, 1945, LANL.

23. Cyril Smith to G. S. Garner and S. K. Allison, June 26, 1945, LANL.

24. Coster-Mullen, *Atom Bombs*, 41. The precise details of the implosion weapon are still classified. These descriptions and measurements are informed guesses based on the available documentation and, where possible, physical examination of existing components.

25. Edward Teller with Judith Shoolery, *Memoirs: A Twentieth-Century Journey in Science and Politics* (Cambridge: Perseus Publishing, 2001), 202.

26. Letter, Col. Frederick Ashworth to General Leslie Groves, "The Base of Operations of the 509th Composite Group," February 24, 1945, MED.

27. Vincent C. Jones, *Manhattan: The Army and the Atomic Bomb* (Washington, DC: Center of Military History, 1985), 526–27.

28. Letter, L. R. Groves to Captain Parsons, April 25, 1945, LANL.

29. Letter, Robert Oppenheimer to General Groves, May 7, 1945, LANL and MED.

30. James Hershberg, *James B. Conant: Harvard to Hiroshima and the Making of the Nuclear Age* (New York: Alfred A. Knopf, 1993), 170.

CHAPTER THIRTEEN: RACE TO THE FINISH

1. Letter, Sherrod East to Leslie Groves, December 5, 1961, GRO.

2. Minutes of the Governing Board, September 16, 1943, LANL.

3. Leslie R. Groves, *Now It Can Be Told: The Story of the Manhattan Project* (New York: Harper, 1962), 201.

4. Richard Rhodes, *The Making of the Atom Bomb* (New York: Simon & Schuster, 1986), 581.

5. Letter, General Leslie Groves to General Dwight Eisenhower, March 22, 1944. MED.

6. Martin J. Sherwin, *A World Destroyed: The Atomic Bomb and the Grand Alliance* (New York: Knopf, 1975), 5.

7. Ibid., 136.

8. Ibid., 198.

9. Letter, Robert Oppenheimer to Leslie Groves, March 12, 1944, LANL.

10. Kenneth T. Bainbridge, "Oral History File," n.d., LANL.

11. Kenneth T. Bainbridge, "Trinity," LA-1012, 4, LANL.

12. Notes on a meeting with Dr. Kenneth Bainbridge on Trinity, dictated May 13 1963, GRO.

13. Memorandum, James Tuck to Robert Oppenheimer et al., June 30, 1944, LANL.

14. Minutes of the Advisory Board, December 7, 1944, LANL.

15. Letter, Leslie Groves to Robert Oppenheimer, November 1, 1944, LANL.

16. Alice Kimball Smith and Charles Weiner, *Robert Oppenheimer: Letters and Recollections* (Cambridge: Harvard University Press, 1980), 286.

17. Ferenc Morton Szasz, *The Day the Sun Rose Twice* (Albuquerque: University of New Mexico Press, 1984), 40–41.

18. Robert S. Norris, *Racing for the Bomb: General Leslie R. Groves, The Manhattan Project's Indispensible Man* (South Royalton, VT: Steerforth Press, 2002), 397.

19. Bainbridge, "Oral History File," LANL.

20. George Kistiakowsky to Robert Oppenheimer, October 13, 1944, LANL.

21. Kenneth Bainbridge, "Regarding the Arrangements Made on Details of Schedules and Tower Construction," June 15, 1945, LANL.

22. Bainbridge to all members of the Trinity Project, March 21, 1945, LANL.

23. Hans Bethe and Robert Christy, "Memorandum on the Immediate Aftereffects of the Gadget," March 30, 1944, LANL files.

24. Hugh T. Richards, "The Making of the Bomb: A Personal Perspective," *Behind Tall Fences* (Los Alamos, NM: Los Alamos Historical Society 1996),131.

25. Letter, General Leslie R. Groves to Robert Oppenheimer, April 27, 1945, LANL.

26. Letter, Robert Oppenheimer to Leslie Groves, June 27, 1944, LANL.

27. Memorandum, Kenneth Bainbridge to Thomas Jones, May 2, 1945, LANL.

28. Richard Tolman to General Groves, "Report on the First Trinity Test," May 13, 1945, LANL.

29. Interview with Robert D. Krohn by author.

30. J. R. Oppenheimer to All Group Leaders Concerned, "Trinity Test," June 14, 1945, LANL.

31. Peter Goodchild, *J. Robert Oppenheimer: Shatterer of Worlds* (Boston: Houghton Mifflin Company, 1981), 159.

32. Rhodes, *The Making of the Atom Bomb*, 657.

CHAPTER FOURTEEN: MEN WILL SEE WHAT WE SAW

1. George Kistiakowsky, "Trinity—A Reminiscence," *Bulletin of the Atomic Scientists*, June 1980, 20.

2. Ken Johnson, "A Quarter Century of Fun," *The Atom*, Los Alamos Scientific Laboratory, April 1970, 11.

3. Norris Bradbury to Personnel Concerned on the Trinity Assembly," n.d., LANL.

4. Kistiakowsky, "Trinity—A Reminiscence," 20.

5. Interview with Robert Krohn by author.

6. Kenneth Bainbridge, "A Foul and Awesome Display," *Bulletin of the Atomic Scientists,* May 1975, 43. Also "Orchestrating the Test," *All In Our Time: The Reminiscences of Twelve Nuclear Pioneers* (Chicago: Atomic Scientists of Chicago, 1974), 222.

7. Joseph L. McKibben, "Timing on the Trinity Bomb Explosion," *Behind Tall Fences* (Los Alamos, NM: Los Alamos Historical Society), 113.

8. Ibid., 114.

9. Edward Teller with Judith Shoolery, *Memoirs: A Twentieth-Century Journey in Science and Politics* (Cambridge: Perseus Publishing, 2001), 211.

10. Groves, 291.

11. Robert Cahn, "Behind the First A-Bomb," *Saturday Evening Post,* July 16, 1960.

12. Leslie R. Groves, *Now It Can Be Told: The Story of the Manhattan Project* (New York: Harper, 1962), 292.

13. Alan B. Carr, *The Forgotten Physicist: Robert Bacher, 1905–2004*, Monograph 6 (Los Alamos, NM: Los Alamos Historical Society, 2008), 28.

14. Allison Kerr, Interview with Kenneth Bainbridge, January 5, 1965, LANL.

15. Leslie Groves, Notes on "Reach to the Unknown," by John Savage and Barbara Storms, *Atom* 2, no. 8 (Los Alamos Scientific Laboratory: 1965).

16. Groves, *Now It Can Be Told*, 296–97.

17. K. D. Nichols, *The Road to Trinity* (New York: William Morrow and Company, 1987), 195.

18. Kerr, Interview with Kenneth Bainbridge, n.d., LANL.

19. T. C. Jones to Claude C. Pierce, "Security and Intelligence Operations in Connection with Trinity," July 30, 1945. MED.

20. Donald Hornig, "Babysitting the Bomb," *The Manhattan Project: The Birth of the Atomic Bomb in the Words of Its Creators, Eyewitnesses and Historians* (New York: Black Dog & Leventhal Publishers, 2007), 298.

21. Ibid., 6.

22. Leslie Groves. Personal notes on July 16, 1960, article, "Behind the First A-Bomb," *Saturday Evening Post*, GRO.

23. Leslie Groves, "Memorandum for the Secretary of War, The Test," July 18, 1945, LANL.

24. Los Alamos Scientific Laboratory, *Los Alamos: Beginning of an Era,* 49. A more complete report on the Trinity test can be found in K. T. Bainbridge, "Trinity." This work has been published by LASL as publication LA-6300-H.

25. Kerr, "Interview with Kenneth Bainbridge."

26. McKibben, "Timing on the Trinity Bomb Explosion," 115.

27. Interview with Robert D. Krohn by author.

28. Groves, *Now It Can Be Told*, 296.

29. David Hawkins, *Manhattan District History: Project Y, The Los Alamos Project*, vol. 1, LAMS-2532 (Los Alamos: Los Alamos Scientific Laboratory, 1961), 275–76.

30. William L. Laurence, *Dawn Over Zero: The Story of the Atomic Bomb* (New York: Alfred A. Knop, 1946).

31. James Hershberg, *James B. Conant: Harvard to Hiroshima and the Making of the Nuclear Age* (New York: Alfred A. Knopf, 1993), 234.

32. Groves, *Now It Can Be Told*, 298.

33. *Los Alamos: Beginning of an Era*, 56.

34. Groves, *Now It Can Be Told*, 297.

35. Los Alamos Scientific Laboratory, *Los Alamos: Beginning of an Era*, 57.

36. Richard Rhodes, *The Making of the Atom Bomb* (New York: Simon & Schuster, 1986), 686.

37. Lillian Hoddeson and others, *Critical Assembly: A Technical History of Los Alamos During the Oppenheimer Years, 1943–1945* (New York: Cambridge University Press, 1993), 375.

38. *Los Alamos: Beginning of an Era*, 57.

39. Stafford Warren, "Report on Test II at Trinity," 16 July 1945, Records Group 77, MED.

40. Leslie R. Groves, "Memorandum for the Secretary of War, The Test," July 18, 1945, LANL.

41. Letter, Leslie Groves to Robert Oppenheimer, July 19, 1945, LANL.

42. Telex, Leslie Groves to Robert Oppenheimer, July 19, 1945, LANL.

43. Notes taken by General Groves at a meeting, Chicago, July 24, 1945, MED.

44. Letter, Leslie Groves to Secretary of War Henry Stimson, July 30, 1945, GRO.

45. Leslie R. Groves. "Memorandum to the Chief of Staff," July 30, 1945, LANL.

46. Arthur H. Compton, *Atomic Quest: A Personal Narrative* (Princeton: Princeton University Press, 1956), 243.

47. John Coster-Mullen, *Atom Bombs: The Top Secret Inside Story of Little Boy and Fat Man* (Self-published: J. Coster-Mullen, 2001), 69.

CHAPTER FIFTEEN: PRIMARY TARGETS

1. Letter, William Parsons to General Groves, December 26, 1944, Box 51, MED.

2. Memorandum, Robert Oppenheimer to General Farrell, May 11, 1945, LANL.

3. Memorandum, Victor Weisskopf to Robert Oppenheimer, June 18, 1945. LANL.

4. Robert Oppenheimer, interoffice memorandum, June 13, 1944, LANL.

5. Letter, Robert Oppenheimer to General Groves, September 20, 1944, LANL and MED.

6. Letter, Robert Oppenheimer to General Groves, December 15, 1944, LANL.

7. Harlow W. Russ, *Project Alberta: The Preparation of Atomic Bombs for Use in World War II* (Los Alamos, NM: Exceptional Books, 1990), 35.

8. Letter, Robert Oppenheimer and Williams Parsons to General Groves, "Bronx Shipments," June 29, 1945, LANL.

9. Kenneth Bainbridge and George Kistiakowsky to William Parsons, July 17, 1945, LANL.

10. Memorandum, Robert Oppenheimer to General Groves and William Parsons, July 23, 1945, LANL.

11. Combined Chiefs of Staff, "Estimate of the Enemy Situation," July 6, 1945, Record Group 218, CCS 381, NARA.

12. James Carroll, Interview of Leslie Groves, June 15, 1949, GRO.

13. William Lawren, *The General and the Bomb: A Biography of General Leslie R. Groves, Director of the Manhattan Project* (New York: Dodd, Mead & Company, 1988), 238.

14. Robert S. Norris, *Racing for the Bomb: General Leslie R. Groves, The Manhattan Project's Indispensible Man* (South Royalton, VT: Steerforth Press, 2002), 381.

15. Letter, Leslie Groves to Robert Oppenheimer, July, 1945, LANL.

16. Notes on Interim Meeting of Target Committee, May 2, 1945, MED.

17. "Initial Meeting of the Target Committee," May 2, 1945, LANL.

18. Leslie R. Groves, *Now It Can Be Told: The Story of the Manhattan Project* (New York: Harper, 1962), 274.

19. "Minutes of the Third Target Committee Meeting," May 2, 1945, LANL.

20. Richard Rhodes, *The Making of the Atom Bomb* (New York: Simon & Schuster, 1986), 640.

21. Fred Reed, Interview of Leslie R. Groves, n.d., GRO.

22. Groves, *Now It Can Be Told*, 264.

23. Martin J. Sherwin, *A World Destroyed: The Atomic Bomb and the Grand Alliance* (New York: Knopf, 1975), 204.

24. Norris, *Racing for the Bomb*, 389.

25. Henry Stimson. "Memorandum of conversation with General Marshall, 'Objectives toward Japan and methods of concluding war with minimum casualties.'" Office of Secretary of War, July 1940–September 1945, S-1 Records, NARA.

26. Sherwin, *A World Destroyed*, 205.

27. "Notes of the Interim Committee Meeting," May 31, 1945, LANL.

28. Sherwin, *A World Destroyed*, 302.

29. "Notes of the Interim Committee Meeting," May 31, 1945.

30. Gregg Herken, *Brotherhood of the Bomb: The Tangled Lives and Loyalties of Robert Oppenheimer, Ernest Lawrence, and Edward Teller* (New York: Henry Holt and Company, 2002), 134.

31. Curtis E. LeMay with MacKinlay Kantor, *Mission With LeMay* (New York: Doubleday, 1965), 384.

32. Spencer R. Weart and Gertrud Weiss Szilard, *Leo Szilard: His Version of the Facts* (Cambridge: MIT Press, 1978), 185.

33. Richard Hewlett and Oscar E. Anderson Jr., *A History of the United States Atomic Energy Commission*, vol. 1, *The New World, 1939–1946* (University Park, PA: Pennsylvania State University Press, 1962), 365, 394.

34. Vincent C. Jones, *Manhattan: The Army and the Atomic Bomb* (Washington, DC: Center of Military History, 1985), 534.

35. Kai Bird and Martin J. Sherwin, *American Prometheus: The Triumph and Tragedy of J. Robert Oppenheimer* (New York: Knopf, 2005), 314.

36. John Coster-Mullen, *Atom Bombs: The Top Secret Inside Story of Little Boy and Fat Man* (Self-published: J. Coster-Mullen, 2001), 18–23.

37. General Farrell to General Groves, September 27, 1945, MED.

38. Rhodes, *The Making of the Atom Bomb*, 734.

39. Chuck Hansen, *U.S. Nuclear Weapons: The Secret Story* (Arlington, TX: Aerofax, 1988), 21.

40. Telex, Leslie Groves to Robert Oppenheimer, August 6, 1945, LANL.

41. Transcript of telephone conversation between General Groves and Robert Oppenheimer, August 6, 1945, MED.

42. Memorandum, Leslie Groves to Chief of Staff George Marshall, August 6, 1945, MED, NARA.

43. Memorandum, General Farrell to General Groves, September 27, 1945, MED.

44. Norris, *Racing for the Bomb*, 420.

45. Memorandum, General Farrell to General Groves.

46.   Ronald Takaki, *Hiroshima: Why America Dropped the Atomic Bomb* (New York: Back Bay Books, 1996), 68.

47.   Coster-Mullen, *Atom Bombs*, 52–57.

48.   Russ, *Project Alberta*, 56.

49.   Gordon Thomas and Max Morgan Witts, *Enola Gay* (New York: Stein & Day, 1977), 276.

50.   War Department Classified Message Center, August 9, 1945, MED, NARA.

51.   Jones, *Manhattan: The Army and the Atomic Bomb*, 541.

52.   Hansen, *U.S. Nuclear Weapons*, 21.

53.   Memorandum, General Farrell to General Groves, September 27, 1945, LANL.

54.   Letter, Groves to George Marshall, August 10, 1945, MED.

55.   Robert Krohn, "Biographical Statement," made available to the author.

56.   Letter, Robert Oppenheimer to the Secretary of War, August 17, 1945, J. Robert Oppenheimer Papers, Library of Congress.

57.   Letter, Norman Ramsey to Robert Oppenheimer, n.d., LANL.

58.   Leslie Groves, "Memorandum to the Chief of Staff," August 6, 1945, GRO.

59.   Groves, *Now It Can Be Told*, 324.

CHAPTER SIXTEEN: THE EXTRAORDINARY WORKING RELATIONSHIP

1.   Robert S. Norris, *Racing for the Bomb: General Leslie R. Groves, The Manhattan Project's Indispensible Man* (South Royalton, VT: Steerforth Press, 2002), 434.

2.   William Lawren, *The General and the Bomb: A Biography of General Leslie R. Groves, Director of the Manhattan Project* (New York: Dodd, Mead & Company, 1988), 256.

3.   Leslie Groves Correspondence Files, n.d., GRO.

4.   "Transcript of Telephone Conversation Between General Groves and Lt. Col. Charles Rea, Oak Ridge Hospital, 9:00 a.m., August 25, 1945," GRO.

5.   Thomas Farrell to Leslie Groves, "Report of Overseas Operations—Atomic Bomb," 27 September 1945, GRO.

6. Michihiko Hachiya, *Hiroshima Diary* (Chapel Hill: University of North Carolina Press, 1955), 97.

7. Memorandum, Louis Hempelmann to Robert Oppenheimer, February 1944, LANL.

8. Sean L. Malloy, "'A Very Pleasant Way to Die': Radiation Effects and the Decision to Use the Atomic Bomb against Japan," *Diplomatic History* 36, no. 3 (April 2012).

9. Letter, Robert Oppenheimer to Leslie Groves, May 7, 1944, LANL and MED.

10. Memorandum, Arthur Compton to Secretary of War Henry Stimson, "Memorandum on Political and Social Problems from Members of the Metallurgical Laboratory and the University of Chicago," June 12, 1945, MED, Harrison-Bundy Files, NARA.

11. Richard Hewlett and Oscar E. Anderson Jr., *A History of the United States Atomic Energy Commission*, vol. 1, *The New World, 1939–1946* (University Park, PA: Pennsylvania State University Press, 1962), 299.

12. Edward Teller to Leo Szilard, July 2, 1945, MED.

13. Brian VanDemark, *Pandora's Keepers: Nine Men and the Atomic Bomb* (New York: Little Brown and Company, 2003), 79.

14. Letters from Leslie Groves to Lord Cherwell, July 4, 1945 and Lord Cherwell to Leslie Groves, July 12, 1945, GRO.

15. Hewlett et al., *A History of the United States Atomic Energy Commission*, 416.

16. George Kistiakowsky, "Memo to Group and Section Leaders of X Division, What to Do Now," November 13, 1945, LANL.

17. Robert Oppenheimer to Division and Group Leaders, August 20, 1945, LANL.

18. Hans Bethe to Division and Group Leaders, "Los Alamos Encyclopedia," August 26, 1945, LANL.

19. Transcript of telephone conversation between Robert Oppenheimer and Jean O'Leary, September 15, 1945, MED.

20. Lawren, *The General and the Bomb*, 276.

21. Nuel Pharr Davis, *Lawrence & Oppenheimer* (New York: Simon & Schuster, 1968), 250.

22.   Norris Bradbury, "Notes on Talk Given by N. E. Bradbury at Coordinating Council," October 1, 1945, LANL files.

23.   "Notes of a Talk Given by Commander N. E. Bradbury at Coordinating Council," October 8, 1945, LANL

24.   Stanley A. Blumberg, and Gwinn Owens, *Energy and Conflict: The Life and Times of Edward Teller* (New York: G. P. Putnam's Sons, 1976), 186–87.

25.   Lawren, *The General and the Bomb*, 277.

26.   Remarks by Robert Oppenheimer, October 16, 1945, LANL.

CHAPTER SEVENTEEN: RETROSPECTION: 2015

1.   Press Release, February 29, 1948, GRO

2.   Robert S. Norris, *Racing for the Bomb: General Leslie R. Groves, The Manhattan Project's Indispensible Man* (South Royalton, VT: Steerforth Press, 2002), 524.

3.   Letter, Leslie Groves to K.D. Nichols, July 13, 1949, GRO.

4.   James Kunetka, *Oppenheimer: The Years of Risk* (New Jersey: Prentice Hall, 1982), 144.

5.   AEC, 710.

6.   Ibid., 178.

7.   Kunetka, *Oppenheimer*, 269.

8.   Hearing, 14.

9.   Robert F. Christy, Oral Interview by Sara Lippincott, June 15, 17, 21 and 11, 1994 (Archives, California Institute of Technology, Pasadena, CA), 55–56.

10.   Alice Kimball Smith and Charles Weiner, *Robert Oppenheimer: Letters and Recollections* (Cambridge: Harvard University Press, 1980), 9.

11.   Richard Lewis and Jane Wilson, eds., *Alamogordo Plus Twenty-Five Years* (New York: Viking Press, 1971), 46.

12.   Smith et al., *Robert Oppenheimer: Letters and Recollections*, 317–25.

13.   William Lawren, *The General and the Bomb: A Biography of General Leslie R. Groves, Director of the Manhattan Project* (New York: Dodd, Mead & Company, 1988), 288.

14.   S. S. Schweber, *In the Shadow of the Bomb: Oppenheimer, Bethe, and the Moral Responsibility of the Scientist* (Princeton: Princeton University Press 2000), 19.

REFERENCES

I n recreating both the story of the relationship between Leslie Groves and Robert Oppenheimer and the development of the atomic bombs at Los Alamos, I relied heavily on government documents and records, historical collections, and published histories and biographies.

The National Archives and Records Administration (NARA) in College Park, Maryland, contains three major collections of interest to the early history of atomic weapons development and to the extensive communication and correspondence between Groves and Oppenheimer. The first is the files of the "Office of Scientific Research and Development, S-1," in the Industrial and Social Branch of the Archives. This collection contains the files and records of ORSD under the direction of Vannevar Bush and his assistant, James B. Conant. The more relevant collection, however, is the extensive holdings of the Modern Military Branch, Record Group 77, "Records of the Office of the Chief of Engineers: Records of the Manhattan Engineer District." This collection has three major divisions: the general records of the Manhattan Engineering District; special material, "Top Secret-Special Interest to General Groves," gathered for use by Groves in preparing his biography; and the files of Secretary of War Henry Stimson, the Harrison-Bundy collection. Each of these divisions of the materials contains documents explaining the role of Los Alamos during the war.

The third collection is the papers of Lt. General Leslie R. Groves, now grouped as Collection GRO (formerly RG 200). This collection contains, among other materials, his voluminous correspondence, both before and after the war, and his daily telephone log. Copies of his letters, memoranda, and telexes to and from Robert Oppenheimer appear both in this collection and also in the records of the Manhattan Engineer District.

The richest sources of information on the wartime Laboratory are the files of the present Los Alamos National Laboratory in Los Alamos, New Mexico. A great percentage of the correspondence between Groves and Oppenheimer is duplicated here, along with transcripts of telephone conversations between the two men. Unfortunately for historians, the majority of these records are not openly available. Some documents of historical note have been put online by LANL or incorporated into publications, and others, such as some utilized in this book, are the result of Freedom of Information Act requests. The major categories follow.

- The Laboratory's "Technical Report Series" includes much information about administrative detail among the technical information. Unfortunately, many of the early documents are still classified.
- The minutes of the Laboratory's Governing and Administrative boards, which operated from 1943 to 1944, contain information on the day-to-day decision-making and operations of the Laboratory.
- The minutes of various ad hoc Laboratory committees created for special purposes, e.g., the Cowpuncher Committee and Project Trinity.

- The correspondence of Oppenheimer and other major Manhattan Project figures, including Groves, Bush, Conant, and Tolman.
- Internal Laboratory memoranda between individuals and administrative groups.
- The "Manhattan District History," a multivolume series, which is still in part classified. It is duplicated in the Manhattan District collection of the National Archives.

Two other collections provide useful information. The Department of Energy, formerly the Energy Research and Development Administration (ERDA), and before that, the Atomic Energy Commission, keeps historical documents, many of which are duplicates of those in the National Archives. At present these materials are under the control of DOE's Division of Classification. The Library of Congress now holds the private papers of J. Robert Oppenheimer as part of their Manuscript Division.

Two published books rigorously document important aspects of the early Los Alamos Laboratory. Under the aegis of the Laboratory, David Hawkins wrote the "Manhattan District History: Project Y, the Los Alamos Project" in 1946. A declassified version has been made public as David Hawkins, *Manhattan District History: Project Y, The Los Alamos Project,* vol. 1, LAMS-2532 (Los Alamos: Los Alamos Scientific Laboratory, 1961). Although it is largely a technical history, it does give interesting insights into the many scientific developments that necessitated administrative action. For the historian, the more useful work is Richard Hewlett and Oscar E. Anderson Jr., *A History of the United States Atomic Energy Commission,* vol. 1, *The New World, 1939–1946* (University Park: Pennsylvania State University Press, 1962). For this work, commissioned by the AEC, the authors were permitted full access to all records in multiple sources. Thorough documentation permits the interested reader to identify major documents and their location.

Three other books are of particular value in the history of the relationship between Groves and Oppenheimer and the role of Los Alamos in the development of early weapons. The first is Richard Rhodes's magisterial history, *The Making of the Atomic Bomb*, in which the work of Los Alamos is cast against the larger wartime effort to develop atomic weapons. It is without doubt the most comprehensive and readable history of the Manhattan Project. The second book is *Critical Assembly: A Technical History of Los Alamos During the Oppenheimer Years, 1943–1945*, by Lillian Hoddeson and others. As the title suggests, the book concentrates heavily on technical details that are often veiled in terminology that protects still classified information. And the third book is John Coster-Mullen's *Atomic Bombs: The Top Secret Inside Story of Little Boy and Fat Man*. The author has spent over two decades personally examining WWII weapon casings and studying declassified publications and sources to construct the most accurate descriptions of Fat Man and Little Boy.

Two biographies are exceptional. The first is Kai Bird and Martin J. Sherwin's biography of Robert Oppenheimer, *American Prometheus: The Triumph and Tragedy of J. Robert Oppenheimer*, and the second is Robert S. Norris's excellent biography of Leslie R. Groves, *Racing for the Bomb: General Leslie R. Groves, The Manhattan Project's Indispensible Man*.

Two online sources are useful to those interested in early atomic history: Restricted Data: The Nuclear History Blog (http://blog.nuclearsecrecy.com) and The Atomic Heritage Foundation (http://www.atomicheritage.org).

The following are published works which are relevant to Leslie Groves, Robert Oppenheimer, their relationship, and the early years of the Los Alamos Scientific Laboratory:

Bacher, Robert. "Robert Oppenheimer (1904–1967)." *Proceedings of the American Philosophical Society* 116, no. 4 (August 1972).

Barnett, Erin, and Philomena Mariani, editors. *Hiroshima: Ground Zero 1945*. New York: International Center of Photography, 2011.

Bell, Iris. *Los Alamos WAACs/WACs: World War II 1943–1946.* Sarasota, FL: Coastal Printing Incorporated, 1993.

Bernstein, Jeremy. *Hans Bethe: Prophet of Energy.* New York: Basic Books, 1980.

Bird, Kai, and Martin J. Sherwin. *American Prometheus: The Triumph and Tragedy of J. Robert Oppenheimer.* New York: Knopf, 2005.

Blumberg, Stanley A., and Owens, Gwinn. *Energy and Conflict: The Life and Times of Edward Teller.* New York: G. P. Putnam's Sons, 1976.

Brode, Bernice. "Tales of Los Alamos." *Los Alamos Scientific Laboratory Community News* (June through August 1960).

Brown, Anthony Cave, and MacDonald, Charles B. *The Secret History of the Atomic Bomb.* New York: The Dial Press, 1977.

Burns, Patrick, editor. *In the Shadow of Los Alamos: Selected Writings of Edith Warner.* Albuquerque: University of New Mexico Press, 2001.

Bush, Vannevar. *Modern Arms and Free Men.* New York: Simon & Schuster, 1949.

———. *Pieces of the Action.* New York: William Morrow & Company, 1970.

Byrnes, James F. *Speaking Frankly.* New York: Harper & Brothers, 1947.

Carr, Alan B. *The Forgotten Physicist: Robert Bacher, 1905–2004.* Monograph 6. Los Alamos, NM: Los Alamos Historical Society, 2008.

———. *The University of California Contract to Operate the Los Alamos Laboratory, 1942–1947: A Documentary History.* LA-UR-04-7896. Los Alamos, NM: Los Alamos National Laboratory, 2004.

Carroll, James. Interview of Leslie Groves, June 15, 1949. RG200. NARA.

Chavez, Fray Angelico. *My Penitente Land.* Albuquerque: University of New Mexico Press, 1974.

Chevalier, Haakon. *Oppenheimer: The Story of a Friendship*. New York: George Braziller, 1965.

Christy, Robert F. Oral Interview by Sara Lippincott. June 15, 17, 21 and 11, 1994. Archives, California Institute of Technology, Pasadena, California.

Church, Peggy Pond. *The House at Otowi Bridge: The Story of Edith Warner and Los Alamos*. Albuquerque: University of New Mexico Press, 1960.

Committee for the Compilation of Materials on Damage Caused by the Atomic Bombs in Hiroshima and Nagasaki. *Hiroshima and Nagasaki: The Physical, Medical, and Social Effects of the Atomic Bombings*. New York: Basic Books, 1981.

Compton, Arthur H. *Atomic Quest: A Personal Narrative*. Princeton, NJ: Princeton University Press, 1956.

Conant, Jennet. *109 East Palace: Robert Oppenheimer and the Secret City of Los Alamos*. New York: Simon & Schuster, 2005.

Coster-Mullen, John. *Atom Bombs: The Top Secret Inside Story of Little Boy and Fat Man*. Self-published: J. Coster-Mullen, 2014.

Davis, Nuel Pharr. *Lawrence and Oppenheimer*. New York: Simon & Schuster, 1968.

DeGroot, Gerard. *The Bomb: A Life*. London: Jonathon Cape, 2004.

Fergusson, Erna. *Our Southwest*. New York: Alfred A. Knopf, 1941.

Fermi, Laura. *Atoms in the Family*. Chicago: University of Chicago Press, 1954.

Fermi, Rachel, and Esther Samra. *Picturing the Bomb: Photographs from the Secret World of the Manhattan Project*. New York: Henry Abrams, 1995.

Fisher, Phyllis K. *Los Alamos Experience*. New York: Japan Publications, 1985.

Frisch, Otto. *What Little I Remember.* Boston: Cambridge University Press, 1979.

Giangreco, D. M. *Hell to Pay: Operation Downfall and the Invasion of Japan. 1945–1947.* Annapolis, MD: Naval Institute Press, 2009.

Gibson, James N. *Nuclear Weapons of the United States: An Illustrated History.* Atglen, PA: Schiffer Books, 1996.

Goodchild, Peter. *J. Robert Oppenheimer: Shatterer of Worlds.* Boston: Houghton Mifflin Company, 1981.

Gowing, Margaret. *Britain and Atomic Energy, 1939–1945.* New York: Macmillan Co., 1964.

Groueff, Stephane. *Manhattan District.* New York: Little, Brown & Co., 1967.

Groves, Leslie R. *Now It Can Be Told.* New York: Harper & Row, 1962.

Groves, Leslie R., and J. J. Ermenc. *The Career of General Leslie R. Groves, Director of the American Atomic Bomb Project.* Tape recorded interview, November 7, 1967. GRO, NA.

Hachiya, Michihiko. *Hiroshima Diary.* Chapel Hill: University of North Carolina Press, 1955.

Hacker, Barton C. *The Dragon's Tail: Radiation Safety in the Manhattan Project, 1942–1946.* Berkeley: University of California Press., 1987.

Hansen, Chuck. *U.S. Nuclear Weapons: The Secret Story.* New York: Orion Books, 1988.

Hargittai, Istvan. *Judging Edward Teller.* Amherst, NY: Prometheus Books, 2010.

Held, E. B. *A Spy's Guide to Santa Fe and Albuquerque.* Albuquerque: University of New Mexico Press, 2011.

Herken, Gregg. *Brotherhood of the Bomb: The Tangled Lives and Loyalties of Robert Oppenheimer, Ernest Lawrence, and Edward Teller.* New York: Henry Holt and Company, 2002.

Hershberg, James. *James B. Conant: Harvard to Hiroshima and the Making of the Atomic Age.* New York: Alfred A. Knopf, 1993.

Hewlett, Richard G., and Oscar E. Anderson Jr. *The New World, 1939–1946.* University Park: Pennsylvania State University Press, 1962.

Hoddeson, Lillian, Paul W. Henriksen, Roger A. Meade, and Catherine Westfall. *Critical Assembly: A Technical History of Los Alamos during the Oppenheimer Years, 1943–1945.* New York: Cambridge University Press, 1993.

Holloway, David. *Stalin & the Bomb.* New Haven: Yale University Press, 1994.

Hornig, Donald F. Oral History Interview I by David F. McComb. December 4, 1968. Lyndon B. Johnson Library, Austin, TX.

Hunner, Jon. *Inventing Los Alamos: The Growth of an Atomic Community.* Norman, OK: University of Oklahoma Press, 2007.

Irving, David. *The German Atomic Bomb.* New York: Simon & Schuster, 1967.

Jenkins, Rupert, editor. *Nagasaki Journey: The Photographs of Yosuke Yamahata, August 10, 1945.* San Francisco: Pomegranate Artbooks, 1995.

Jette, Eleanor. *Inside Box 1663.* Los Alamos, NM: Los Alamos Historical Society, 1977.

Johnson, Ken. "A Quarter Century of Fun." *The Atom.* Los Alamos Scientific Laboratory, April 1970.

Jones, Vincent C. *United States Army in World War II, Special Studies, Manhattan: The Army and the Atomic Bomb.* Center of Military History, United States Army, 1985.

J. Robert Oppenheimer Memorial Committee. *Behind Tall Fences: A Collection of Stories and Experiences about Los Alamos.* Los Alamos, NM: J. Robert Oppenheimer Memorial Committee,1994.

Jungk, Robert. *Brighter Than a Thousand Suns.* New York: Harcourt, Brace & World, 1958.

Kelly, Cynthia C. *A Guide to the Manhattan Project in New Mexico.* Washington, D.C.: Atomic Heritage Foundation, 2012.

Kelly, Cynthia C., editor. *The Manhattan Project: The Birth of the Atomic Bomb in the Words of Its Creators, Eyewitnesses, and Historians.* New York: Black Dog Press, 2007.

Kistiakowsky, George. *Trinity—A Reminiscence.* Bulletin of the Atomic Scientists, (June, 1980).

Knebel, Fletcher, and Charles W. Bailey III. *No High Ground.* New York: Harper & Brothers, 1960.

Kunetka, James. *Oppenheimer: The Years of Risk.* Englewood Cliffs, NJ: Prentice Hall, 1982.

Lamont, Lansing. *Day of Trinity.* New York: Atheneum, 1965.

Lang, Daniel. *Early Tales of the Atomic Age.* Garden City, NY: Doubleday & Co., 1948.

Laurence, William L. *Dawn Over Zero.* New York: Alfred A. Knopf, 1946.

Lawren, William. *The General and the Bomb: A Biography of General Leslie R. Groves, Director of the Manhattan Project.* New York: Dodd, Mead & Company, 1988.

LeMay, Curtis E., with MacKinlay Kantor. *Mission with LeMay.* New York: Doubleday, 1965.

Lewis, Richard S., and Jane Wilson, eds. *Alamogordo Plus Twenty-five Years.* New York: Viking Press, 1970.

Los Alamos Historical Society. *Behind Tall Fences: Stories and Experiences About Los Alamos At Its Beginnings.* Los Alamos, NM: Los Alamos Historical Society, 1996.

———. *When Los Alamos Was a Ranch School.* Santa Fe, NM: Sleeping Fox Enterprises, 1974.

Lyon, Fern, and Jacob Evans, editors. *Los Alamos: The First Forty Years.* Los Alamos, NM: Los Alamos Historical Society, 1984.

Maddox, Robert James, editor. *Hiroshima in History: The Myths of Revisionism.* Colombia, MO: University of Missouri Press, 2007.

———. *Weapons for Victory: The Hiroshima Decision Fifty Years Later.* Colombia, MO: University of Missouri Press, 1995.

Malik, John. *The Yields of the Hiroshima and Nagasaki Nuclear Explosions.* Los Alamos Report LA-8819. Los Alamos, NM: Los Alamos National Laboratory, 1985.

Malloy, Sean L. "'A Very Pleasant Way to Die': Radiation Effects and the Decision to Use the Atomic Bomb against Japan." *Diplomatic History* 36, no. 3 (April, 2012).

McPhee, John. *The Curve of Binding Energy.* New York: Farrar, Straus & Giroux, 1974.

Merlan, Thomas. *Life at Trinity Base Camp.* HRS Report Number 9831. White Sands Missile Range Archeological Research Report No. 01-07. Tularosa, NM: Human Systems Research, 2001.

———. *The Trinity Experiments.* HSR Report 9701. WSMR Archeological Report 97-15. Tularosa, New Mexico: Human Systems Research, Inc., 1997.

Michelmore, Peter. *The Swift Years: The Robert Oppenheimer Story.* New York: Dodd, Mead & Co., 1969.

Moss, Norman. *Men Who Play God: The Story of the Hydrogen Bomb.* New York: Harper & Row, 1969.

Nichols, K. D., *The Road to Trinity.* New York: William Morrow and Company, Inc., 1987.

Norris, Robert S. *Racing for the Bomb: General Leslie R. Groves, The Manhattan Project's Indispensible Man.* South Royalton, VT: Steerforth Press, 2002.

Pacific War Research Society. *The Day Man Lost: Hiroshima, 6 August 1945.* Palo Alto, CA: Kodansha International/USA, 1972.

Pettitt, Roland A. *Los Alamos Before the Dawn.* Los Alamos, NM: Pajarito Publications, 1972.

Rabi, Isidor, et al. *Oppenheimer.* New York: Charles Scribner's Sons, 1969.

Reed, Fred. Interview of Leslie R. Groves, n.d., RG200. NARA.

Rhodes, Richard. *The Making of the Atomic Bomb.* New York: Simon & Schuster, 1986.

Richards, Hugh T. *Through Los Alamos, 1945: Memoirs of a Physicist.* Madison, WI: Arlington Place Press, 1993.

Roensch, Eleanor (Jerry) Stone. *Life Within Limits.* Los Alamos, NM: Los Alamos Historical Society, 1993.

Rothman, Hal K. *On Rims & Ridges: The Los Alamos Area Since 1880.* Lincoln, NB: University of Nebraska Press, 1992.

Russ, Harlow W. *Project Alberta: The Preparation of Atomic Bombs for Use in World War II.* Los Alamos, NM: Exceptional Books, Ltd. 1990.

Savage, John, and Barbara Storms. "Reach to the Unknown: The Trinity Story, July 16, 1945." *Atom* 2, no. 8 (Los Alamos Scientific Laboratory, 1965).

Schweber, S. S. *In the Shadow of the Bomb: Oppenheimer, Bethe, and the Moral Responsibility of the Scientist.* Princeton: Princeton University Press, 2000.

Segre, Claudio G. *Atoms, Bombs & Eskimo Kisses: A Memoir of Father and Son.* New York: Viking, 1995.

Sherwin, Martin J. *A World Destroyed: The Atomic Bomb and the Grand Alliance.* New York: Alfred A. Knopf, 1975.

Smith, Alice Kimball, and Charles Weiner. *Robert Oppenheimer: Letters and Recollections.* Cambridge: Harvard University Press, 1980.

Smyth, Henry D. *Atomic Energy for Military Purposes.* Princeton, NJ: Princeton University Press, 1947.

Snyder, Sharon, Toni Michnovicz, and Los Alamos Historical Society. *Images of America: Los Alamos and the Pajarito Plateau.* Charleston, SC: Arcadia Publishing, 2011.

Stem, Phillip M. *The Oppenheimer Case: Security on Trial.* New York: Harper & Row, 1969.

Stimson, Henry L., and Bundy, McGeorge. *On Active Service in Peace and War.* New York: Harper & Brothers, 1948.

Streshinsky, Shirley, and Patricia Klaus. *An Atomic Love Story: The Extraordinary Women in Robert Oppenheimer's Life.* New York: Turner Publishing Company, 2013.

Swartley, Ron. *New Mexico's Atomic Tour.* Las Cruces, NM: Frontier Image Press, 1992.

Takaki, Ronald. *Hiroshima: Why America Dropped the Atomic Bomb.* New York: Back Bay Books, 1996.

Teller, Edward, with Judith Shoolery. *Memoirs: A Twentieth-Century Journey in Science and Politics.* Cambridge: Perseus Publishing, 2001.

Thomas, Gordon, and Max Morgan Witts. *Enola Gay.* New York: Stein & Day, 1977.

Ulam, Stan M. *Adventures of a Mathematician.* New York: Charles Scribner's Sons, 1976.

U.S. Atomic Energy Commission (USAEC). *[In the Matter of]. Robert Oppenheimer.* Washington, DC: Government Printing Office, 1954.

VanDemark, Brian. *Pandora's Keepers: Nine Men and the Atomic Bomb.* New York: Little Brown and Company, 2003.

Walker, Stephen. *Shockwave: Countdown to Hiroshima.* New York: HarperCollins, 2005.

Weart, Spencer R., and Gertrud Weiss Szilard. *Leo Szilard: His Version of the Facts.* Cambridge: MIT Press, 1978.

Westinghouse Electric Manufacturing Company. *The Book of Record of the Time Capsule of Cupaloy.* New York, 1938.

Williams, Robert Chadwell. *Klaus Fuchs, Atom Spy.* Cambridge: Harvard University Press, 1987.

Wilson, Jane, editor. *All In Our Time: The Reminiscences of Twelve Nuclear Pioneers.* Chicago: Bulletin of the Atomic Scientists, 1974.

Wilson, Jane S., and Charlotte Serber. *Standing By and Making Do: Women of Wartime Los Alamos.* Los Alamos, NM: Los Alamos Historical Society, 1988.

Wirth, John D., and Linda Harvey Aldrich. *Los Alamos: The Ranch School Years: 1917–1943.* Albuquerque: University of New Mexico Press. 2003.

Wohlberg, Margaret. *A Los Alamos Reader, 1200 A.D. to Today.* Los Alamos, NM: Los Alamos County Museum of History, 1976.

Works Progress Administration. *New Mexico: A Guide to the Colorful State.* 2nd ed. Albuquerque: University of New Mexico Press, 1945.

York, Herbert. *The Advisors: Oppenheimer, Teller and the Superbomb.* San Francisco: W. H. Freeman & Co., 1976.

INDEX

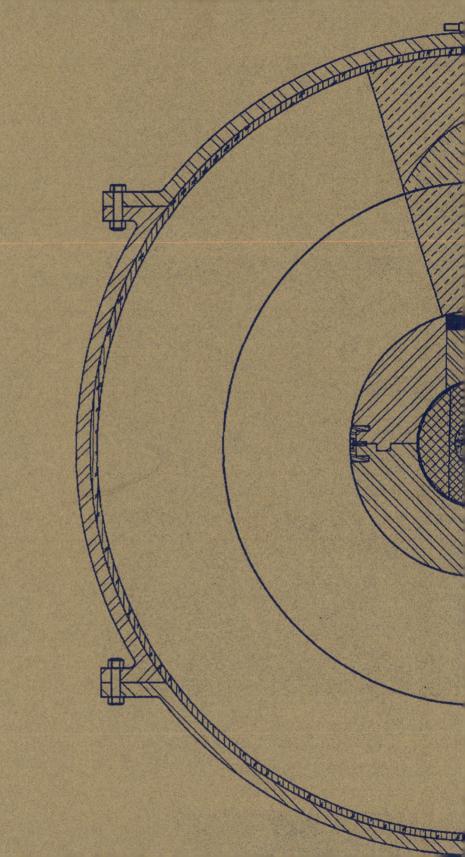